Theosophy

Theosophy

Alvin Boyd Kuhn

CONTENTS

Adultbrain Publishing is dedicated to breathing new life into timeless literary works by resurrecting old classics for the modern age. We meticulously curate and convert these masterpieces into high-quality digital and audio formats, making them accessible to a new generation of readers and listeners. Our commitment to preserving the essence of these works, while enhancing them with today's technology, allows us to offer immersive experiences that retain the authenticity of the original texts. Whether rediscovering a beloved classic or experiencing it for the first time, our editions invite readers to start using their Adultbrain today.

Published by Adultbrain Publishing.

ISBN: 978-1-998614-00-4

eISBN: 978-1-998614-01-1

Title: Theosophy: A Modern Revival of Ancient Wisdom

Start using your adultbrain today.

For more information, visit: www.adultbrain.ca

PREFACE

Since this work was designed to be one of a series of studies in American religions, the treatment of the subject was consciously limited to those aspects of Theosophy which are in some manner distinctively related to America. This restriction has been difficult to enforce for the reason that, though officially born here, Theosophy has never since its inception had its headquarters on this continent. The springs of the movement have emanated from foreign sources and influences. Its prime inspiration has come from ancient Oriental cultures.

America in this case has rather adopted an exotic cult than evolved it from the conditions of her native milieu. The main events in American Theosophic history have been mostly repercussions of events transpiring in English, Continental, or Indian Theosophy. It was thus virtually impossible to segregate American Theosophy from its connections with foreign leadership. But the attempt to do so has made it necessary to give meagre treatment to some of the major currents of world-wide Theosophic development. The book does not purport to be a complete history of Theosophy, but it is an attempt to present a unified picture of the movement in its larger aspects. No effort has been made to weigh the truth or falsity of Theosophic principles, but an effort has been made to understand their significance in relation to the historical situation and psychological disposition of those who have adopted it.

The author wises to express his obligation to several persons without whose assistance the enterprise would have been more onerous and less successful. His thanks are due in largest measure to Professor Roy F. Mitchell of New York University, and to Mrs. Mitchell, for placing at his disposal much of their time and of their wide knowledge of Theosophical material; to Mr. L. W. Rogers, President of the American Theosophical Society, Wheaton, Illinois, for cordial co-operation in the matter of the questionnaire, and to the many members of the Society who took pains to reply to the questions; to Mr. John Garrigues, of the United Lodge of Theosophists, New York, for valuable data out of his great store of Theosophic information, and to several of the ladies at the U.L.T. Reading Room for library assistance; to Professor Louis H. Gray, of Columbia University, for technical criticism in Sanskrit terminology; to Mr. Arthur E. Christy, of Columbia University, for data showing Emerson's indebtedness to Oriental philosophy; and to Professor Herbert W. Schneider, of Columbia University, for his painstaking criticism of the study throughout.

A. B. K.

New York City September, 1930

CHAPTER I THEOSOPHY

In the mind of the general public Theosophy is classed with Spiritualism, New Thought, Unity and Christian Science, as one of the modern cults. It needs but a slight acquaintance with the facts in the case to reveal that Theosophy is amenable to this classification only in the most superficial sense. Though the Theosophical Society is recent, theosophy, in the sense of an esoteric philosophic mystic system of religious thought, must be ranked as one of the most ancient traditions. It is not a mere cult, in the sense of being the expression of a quite specialized form of devotion, practice, or theory, propagated by a small group. It is a summation and synthesis of many cults of all times. It is as broad and universal a motif, let us say, as mysticism. It is one of the most permanent phases of religion, and as such it has welled up again and again in the life of mankind. It is that "wisdom of the divine" which has been in the world practically continuously since ancient times. The movement of today is but another periodical recurrence of a phenomenon which has marked the course of history from classical antiquity. Not always visible in outward organization-indeed never formally organized as Theosophy under that name until now-the thread of theosophic teaching and temperament can be traced in almost unbroken course from ancient times to the present. It has often been subterranean, inasmuch as esotericism and secrecy have been essential elements of its very constitution. The modern presentation of theosophy differs from all the past ones chiefly in that it has lifted the veil that cloaked its teachings in mystery, and offered alleged secrets freely to the world. Theosophists tell us that before the launching of the latest "drive" to promulgate Theosophy in the world, the councils of the Great White Brotherhood of Adepts, or Mahatmas, long debated whether the times were ripe for the free propagation of the secret Gnosis; whether the modern world, with its Western dominance and with the prevalence of materialistic standards, could appropriate the sacred knowledge without the risk of serious misuse of high spiritual forces, which might be diverted into selfish channels. We are told that in these councils it was the majority opinion that broadcasting the Ancient Wisdom over the Occidental areas would be a veritable casting of pearls before swine; yet two of the Mahatmas settled the question by undertaking to assume all karmic debts for the move, to take the responsibility for all possible disturbances and ill effects.

If we look at the matter through Theosophic eyes, we are led to believe that when in the fall of 1875 Madame Blavatsky, Col. H. S. Olcott, and Mr. W. Q. Judge took out the charter for the Theosophical Society in New York, the world was witnessing a really major event in human history. Not only did it signify that one more of the many recurrent waves of esoteric cultism was launched but that this time practically the whole body of occult lore, which had been so sedulously guarded in mystery schools, brotherhoods, secret societies, religious orders, and other varieties of organization, was finally to be given to the

world en pleine lumière! At last the lid of antiquity's treasure chest would be lifted and the contents exposed to public gaze. There might even be found therein the solution to the riddle of the Sphynx! The great Secret Doctrine was to be taught openly; Isis was to be unveiled!

To understand the periodical recurrence of the theosophic tendency in history it is necessary to note two cardinal features of the Theosophic theory of development. The first is that progress in religion, philosophy, science, or art is not a direct advance, but in advance in cyclical swirls. When you view progress in small sections, it may appear to be a development in a straight line; but if your gaze takes in the whole course of history, you will see the outline of a quite different method of progress. You will not see uninterrupted unfolding of human life, but advances and retreats, plunges and recessions.

Spring does not emerge from winter by a steady rise of temperature, but by successive rushes of heat, each carrying the season a bit ahead. Movement in nature is cyclical and periodic. History progresses through the rise and fall of nations. The true symbol of progress is the helix, motion round and round, but tending upward at each swirl. But we must have large perspectives if we are to see the gyrations of the helix.

The application of this interpretation of progress to philosophy and religion is this: the evolution of ideas apparently repeats itself at intervals time after time, a closed circuit of theories running through the same succession at many points in history. Scholars have discerned this fact in regard to the various types of government: monarchy working over into oligarchy, which shifts to democracy, out of which monarchy arises again. The round has also been observed in the domain of philosophy, where development starts with revelation and proceeds through rationalism to empiricism, and, in revulsion from that, swings back to authority or mystic revelation once more. Hegel's theory that progress was not in a straight line but in cycles formed by the manifestation of thesis, antithesis, and then synthesis, which in turn becomes the ground of a new thesis, is but a variation of this general theme.

Theosophists, then, regard their movement as but the renaissance of the esoteric and occult aspect of human thought in this particular swing of the spiral.

The second aspect of the occult theory of development is a method of interpretation which claims to furnish a key to the understanding of religious history. Briefly, the theory is that religions never evolve; they always degenerate. Contrary to the assumptions of comparative mythology, they do not originate in crude primitive feelings or ideas, and then transform themselves slowly into loftier and purer ones. They begin lofty and pure, and deteriorate into crasser forms. They come forth in the glow of spirituality and living power and later pass into empty forms and lifeless practices. From the might of the spirit they contract into the materialism of the letter. No religion can rise above its source, can surpass its founder; and the more exalted the founder and his message, the more certainly is degeneration to be looked for. There is always gradual change in the direction of obscuration and loss of primal vision, initial force. Religions tend constantly to wane, and need repeated revivals and reformations. Nowhere is it possible to discern anything remotely like steady growth in spiritual unfolding.

It is the occult theory that what we find when we search the many religions of the earth is but the fragments, the dissociated and distorted units of what were once profound and coherent systems. It is difficult to trace in the isolated remnants the contour of the original structure. But it is this completed system which the Theosophist seeks to reconstruct from the scattered remnants.

Religion, then, is a phase of human life which is alleged to operate on a principle exactly opposite to evolution, and theosophy believes this key makes it intelligible. Religions never claim to have evolved from human society; they claim to be gifts to humanity. They come to man with the seal of some divine authority and the stamp of supreme perfection. Not only are they born above the world, but they are brought to the world by the embodied divinity of a great Messenger, a Savior, a World-Teacher, a Prophet, a Sage, a Son of God. These bring their own credentials in the form of a divine life. Their words and works bespeak the glory that earth can not engender.

The two phases of theosophic explanation can now be linked into a unified principle. Religions come periodically; and they are given to men from high sources, by supermen. The theory of growth from crude beginnings to spirituality tacitly assumes that man is alone in the universe and left entirely to his own devices; that he must learn everything for himself from experience, which somehow enlarges his faculties and quickens them for higher conceptions. This view, says occultism, does unnatural violence to the fundamental economy of the universe, wrenching humanity out of its proper setting and relationship in an order of harmony and fitness. Humankind is made to be the sole manipulator of intelligence, the favored beneficiary of evolution, and as such is severed from its natural connection with the rest of the cosmic scheme. So small and poor a view does pitiable injustice to the wealth of the cosmic resources. Bruno, Copernicus, and modern science have taught us that man is not the darling of creation, nor the only child in the cosmic family, the pampered ward of the gods. Far from it; he is one among the order of beings, occupying his proper place in relation to vaster hierarchies than he has knowledge of, above and below him.1

What is the character of that relationship? It is, says the esoteric teaching, that of guardian and ward; of a young race in the tutelage of an older; of infant humanity being taught by more highly evolved beings, whose intelligence is to that of early man as an adept's to a tyro's. It is the relationship of children to parents or guardians. Throughout our history we have been the wards of an elder race, or at least of the elder brothers of our own race. The members of a former evolutionary school have turned back often, like the guardians in Plato's cave allegory, to instruct us in vital knowledge. The wisdom of the ages, the knowledge of the very Ancient of Days, has at times been handed down to us. The human family has produced some advanced Sages, Seers, Adepts, Christs, and these have cared for the less-advanced classes, and have from time to time given out a body of deeper wisdom than man's own. Theosophy claims that it is the traditional memory of these noble characters, their lives and messages, which has left the ancient field strewn with the legends of its Gods, Kings, Magi, Rishis, Avatars and its great semi-divine heroes. Such wisdom and knowledge as they could wisely and safely impart they have handed down, either coming themselves to earth from more ethereal realms, or commissioning competent representatives. And thus the world has periodically been given the boon of a new religion and a new stimulus from the earthly presence of a savior regarded as divine. And always the gospel contained milk for the babes and meat for grown men.

There was both an exoteric and an esoteric doctrine. The former was broadcast among the masses, and did its proper and salutary work for them; the latter, however, was imparted only to the fit and disciplined initiates in secret organizations. Much real truth was hidden behind the veil of allegory; myth and symbol were employed. This aggregate of precious knowledge, this innermost heart of the secret teaching of the gods to mankind, is, needless to say, the Ancient Wisdom-is Theosophy. Or at least Theosophy claims the key to

all this body of wisdom. It has always been in the world, but never publicly promulgated until now.

To trace the currents of esoteric influence in ancient religious literature would be the work of volumes. Theosophic or kindred doctrines are to be found in a large number of the world's sacred books or bibles. The lore of India, China, Persia, Babylon, Egypt, Greece, yields material for Theosophy.

Philosophy, not less than religion, bears the stamp of theosophical ideology. Traces of the occult doctrine permeate most of the thought systems of the past. All histories of philosophy in the western world begin, with or without brief apology to the venerable systems of the Orient, with Thales of Miletus and the early Greek thinkers of about the sixth century B.C. In the dim background stand Homer and Hesiod and Pindar and the myths of the Olympian pantheon. Contemporary religious faiths, too, such as the cult of Pythagoreanism,2 and the Orphic and Eleusinian Mysteries, influenced philosophical speculation.

It needs no extraordinary erudition to trace the stream of esoteric teaching through the field of Greek philosophy. What is really surprising is that the world of modern scholarship should have so long assumed that Greek speculation developed without reference to the wide-spread religious cult systems which transfused the thought of the near-Eastern nations. Esotericism was an ingrained characteristic of the Oriental mind and Greece could no more escape the contagion than could Egypt or Persia. The occultist endeavors to make the point that practically all of early Greek philosophy dealt with material presented by the Dionysiac and Orphic Mysteries and later by the Pythagorean revisions of these.3

Thales' fragments contain Theosophical ideas in his identification of the physis with the soul of the universe, and in his affirmation that "the materiality of physis is supersensible." Thales thought that this physis or natural world was "full of gods."4 Both these conceptions of the impersonal and the personal physis, the latter a reasoning substance approaching Nous, came out of the continuum of the group soul, as a vehicle of magic power.5 Man was believed to stand in a sympathetic relation to this nature or physis, and the deepening of his sympathetic attitude was supposed to give him nothing less than magical control over its elements.

Prominent among the Orphic tenets was that of reincarnation, possibly a transference to man of the annual rebirth in nature. Worship of heavenly bodies as aiding periodical harvests found a place here also.6 The conception of the wheel of Dike and Moira, the allotted flow and apportionment in time as well as place, of all things, nature and man together, was underlying in the ancient Greek mind. Persian occult ideas may have influenced the Orphic systems.7

Anaximander added to the scientific doctrines of Thales the idea of compensatory retribution for the transgression of Moira's bounds which suggests Karma. The sum of Heraclitus' teaching is the One Soul of the universe, in ever-running cycles of expression-"Fire8 lives the death of air, air lives the death of fire; earth lives the death of water, water lives the death of earth."9 And interwoven with it is a sort of justice which resembles karmic force.10

Dionysiac influence brought the theme of reincarnation prominently to the fore in metaphysical thinking.11
Socrates, in the Phaedo, speaks of "the ancient doctrine that souls pass out of this world to the other, and there exist, and then come back hither from the

dead, and are born again." In Hesiod's Works and Days there is the image of the Wheel of Life. In the mystical tradition there was prominent the wide-spread notion of a fall of higher forms of life into the human sphere of limitation and misery. The Orphics definitely taught that the soul of man fell from the stars into the prison of this earthly body, sinking from the upper regions of fire and light into the misty darkness of this dismal vale. The fall is ascribed to some original sin, which entailed expulsion from the purity and perfection of divine existence and had to be expiated by life on earth and by purgation in the nether world.

The philosophies of Parmenides, Empedocles, and Plato came directly out of the Pythagorean movement.13 Aristotle described Empedocles' poems as "Esoteric," and it is thought that Parmenides' poems were similarly so. Parmenides' theory that the earth is the plane of life outermost, most remotely descended from God, is re-echoed in theosophic schematism. Also his idea-"The downward fall of life from the heavenly fires is countered by an upward impulse which 'sends the soul back from the seen to the unseen'"-completes the Theosophic picture of outgoing and return. Parmenides "was really the 'associate' of a Pythagorean, Ameinias, son of Diochartas, a poor but noble man, to whom he afterwards built a shrine, as to a hero."14 "Strabo describes Parmenides and Zeno as Pythagoreans."15 Cornford's comment on the philosophy of Empedocles leaves little doubt as to its origin in the Mysteries. 16 Strife causes the fall, love brings the return.
Empedocles was a member of a Pythagorean society or school, for Diogenes tells us that he and Plato were expelled from the organization for having revealed the secret teachings.17

Of Pythagoras as a Theosophic type of philosopher there is no need to speak at any length. What is known of Pythagoreanism strongly resembles Theosophy.

As to Socrates, it is interesting to note that Cornford's argument "points to the conclusion that Socrates was more familiar with Pythagorean ideas than has commonly been supposed."18 Socrates gave utterance to many Pythagorean sentiments and he was associated with members of the Pythagorean community at Phlious, near Thebes.

R. D. Hicks comments on Plato's "imaginative sympathy with the whole mass of floating legend, myth and dogma, of a partly religious, partly ethical character, which found a wide, but not universal acceptance, at an early time in the Orphic and Pythagorean associations and brotherhoods."19

"The Platonic myths afford ample evidence that Plato was perfectly familiar with all the leading features of this strange creed. The divine origin of the soul, its fall from bliss and the society of the gods, its long pilgrimage of penance through hundreds of generations, its task of purification from earthly pollution, its reincarnation in successive bodies, its upward and downward progress, and the law of retribution for all offences . . ."20

There is evidence pointing to the fact that Plato was quite familiar with the Mystery teachings, if not actually an initiate.21 In the Phaedrus he says:

". . . being initiated into those Mysteries which it is lawful to call the most blessed of all Mysteries . . . we were freed from the molestation of evils which otherwise await us in a future period of time. Likewise in consequence of this divine initiation, we become spectators of entire, simple, immovable and blessed visions resident in the pure light."22

And his immersion in the prevalent esoteric attitude is hinted at in another passage:

"You say that, in my former discourse, I have not sufficiently explained to you the nature of the First. I purposely spoke enigmatically, for in case the tablet should have happened with any accident, either by land or sea, a person, without some previous knowledge of the subject, might not be able to understand its contents."23

Aristotle left the esoteric tradition, and went in the direction of naturalism and empiricism. Yet in him too there are many points of distinctly esoteric ideology. His distinction between the vegetative animal soul and the rational soul, the latter alone surviving while the former perished; his dualism of heavenly and terrestrial life; his belief that the heavenly bodies were great living beings among the hierarchies; and his theory that development is the passing of potentiality over into actualization, are all items of Theosophic belief.

Greek philosophy is said to have ended with Neo-Platonism-which is one of history's greatest waves of the esoteric tendency. It would be a long task to detail the theosophic ideas of the great Plotinus. He, Origen and Herrennius were pupils of Ammonius Saccas, whose teachings they promised never to reveal, as being occult. Plotinus' own teachings were given only to initiated circles of students.24 Proclus25 gives astonishing corroboration to a fragment of Theosophic doctrine in any excerpt quoted in Isis Unveiled:

"After death, the soul (the spirit) continueth to linger in the aerial (astral) form till it is entirely purified from all angry and voluptuous passions . . . then doth it put off by a second dying the aerial body as it did the earthly one. Whereupon the ancients say that there is a celestial body always joined with the soul, and which is immortal, luminous and star-like."26

The esotericist feels that the evidence, a meagre portion of which has been thus cursorily submitted, is highly indicative that beneath the surface of ancient pagan civilization there were undercurrents of sacred wisdom, esoteric traditions of high knowledge, descended from revered sources, and really cherished in secret.

Presumably the Christian religion itself drew many of its basic concepts directly or indirectly from esoteric sources. It was born amid the various cults and faiths that then occupied the field of the Alexandrian East and the Roman Empire, and it was unable to escape the influences emanating from these sources. Its immediate predecessors were the Mystery-Religions, the Jewish faith, and the syncretistic blend of these with Syrian Orientalism and Greek philosophy.

Judaism was itself deeply tinctured with Hellenistic and oriental influences. The Mystery cults were more or less esoteric; Judaism had received a highly allegorical formulation at the hands of Philo; the Hermetic Literature was similar to Theosophy; the Syrian faiths were saturated with the strain of "Chaldean" occultism; and Greek rationalism had yielded that final mysticism which culminated in Plotinus. Christianity was indebted to many of these sources and many scholars believe that it triumphed only because it was the most successful syncretism of many diverse elements. Numerous streams of esoteric doctrine contributed to Christianity; we can merely hint at the large body of evidence available on this point.

Christianity grew up in the milieu of the Mysteries, and those early Fathers who formulated the body of Christian doctrine did not step drastically outside the

traditions of the prevalent faiths. Their work was rather an incorporation of some new elements into the accepted systems of the time. In some cases, as in Alexandria, the two faiths were actually blended, for many Christians in the Egyptian city were at the same time connected with the Mystery cult of Serapis, as many in Greece and Judea were connected with that of Dionysus. But perhaps the most direct and prominent product of the two systems is to be seen in St.

Paul, about whose intimate relation to the Mysteries several volumes have been written. Much of his language so strikingly suggests his close contact with Mystery formulae that it is a moot question whether or not he was actually an Initiate.28 At all events many are of the opinion that he must have been powerfully influenced by the cult teachings and practices.29 He mentions some psychic experiences of his own, which are cited as savoring strongly of the character of the mystical exercises taught in the Mysteries.30

When in the third and fourth centuries the Church Fathers began the task of shaping a body of doctrine for the new movement, the same theosophic tendencies pressed upon them from every side. Clement and Origen brought many phases of theosophic doctrine to prominence, a fact which tended later to exclude their writings from the canon. And when Augustine drew up the dogmatic schematism of the new religion, he was tremendously swayed by the work of the Neo-Platonist Plotinus, who, along with Ammonius Saccas, Numenius, Porphyry, and Proclus, had been a member of one or several of the Mystery bodies.31

The presence of powerful currents of Neo-Platonic idealism in the early church is attested by the effects upon it of Manichaeism, Gnosticism and the Antioch heresy, which tendencies had to be exterminated before Christianity definitely took its course of orthodox development. Occult writers32 have indicated the forces at work in the formative period of the church's dogma which eradicated the theory of reincarnation and other aspects of esoteric knowledge from the orthodox canons. The point remains true, nevertheless, that Christianity took its rise in an atmosphere saturated with ideas resembling those of Theosophy.

Theosophy, the Gnosis, having been to a large extant rejected from Catholic theology, nevertheless did not disappear from history. It possessed an unquenchable vitality and made its way through more or less submerged channels down the centuries. Movements, sects, and individuals that embodied its cherished principles could be enumerated at great length. A list would include Paulicians, the Bogomiles, the Bulgars, the Paterenes, the Comacines, the Cathari; Albigensians, and pietists; Joachim of Floris, Roger Bacon, Robert Bradwardine, Raymond Lully; the Alchemists, the Fire Philosophers; Paracelsus,

B. Figulus; the Friends of God, led by Nicholas of Basle; L'Homme de Cuir, in Switzerland in the Engadine; the early Waldenses; the Bohemian tradition given in the Tarot; the great Aldus' Academy at Venice; the Rosicrucians and the Florentine Academy founded by Pletho. Some theosophists have attempted to find esoteric meanings in the literature of the Troubadours, and in such writings as The Romance of the Rose, the Holy Grail legends and the Arthurian Cycle, if read in an esoteric sense; Gower's Confessio Amantis, Spencer's Faërie Queen, the works of Dietrich of Berne, Wayland Smith, the Peredur Stories, and the Mabinogian compilations. German pietism expressed fundamentally Theosophic ideas through Eckhardt, Tauler, Suso, and Jacob Boehme. The names of such figures as Count Rakowczi, Cagliostro, Count St. Germain, and Francis Bacon have been linked with the secret orders. In fact there was hardly a period when the ghosts of occult wisdom did not hover in the background of European thought.

Sometimes its predominant manifestation was mystically religious; again it was cosmological and philosophical; never did it quite lose its attachment to the conceptions of science, which was at times reduced nearly to magic. And it is

upon the implications of this scientific interest that the occult theorist bases his claim that science, along with religion and philosophy, has sprung in the beginning from esoteric knowledge. Not overlooking the oldest scientific lore to be found in the sacred books of the East, our attention is called to the astronomical science of the "Chaldeans"; the similar knowledge among the Egyptians, such, for instance, as led them to construct the Pyramids on lines conformable to sidereal measurements and movements; the reputed knowledge of the precession of the equinoxes among the Persian Magi and the "Chaldeans"; the later work of the scientists among the Alexandrian savants, which had so important a bearing upon the direction of the nascent science in the minds of Copernicus, Galileo, Kepler, and Newton; the known achievements of Roger Bacon, Robert Grosseteste, Agrippa von Nettesheim, and Jerome Cardano in incipient empiricism. It has always been assumed that the strange mixture of true science and grotesque magic found, for instance, in the work of Roger Bacon, justifies the implication that the concern with magic operated as a hindrance to the development of science. It should not be forgotten that the stimulus to scientific discovery sprang from the presuppositions embodied in magical theory. It is now beyond dispute that the magnificent achievements of Copernicus, Kepler, and Galileo were actuated by their brooding over the significance of the Pythagorean theories of number and harmony. Both science and magic aim, each in its special modus, at the control of nature. Through the gateway of electricity, says theosophy, science has been admitted, part way at least, into the inner sanctum of nature's dynamic heart. Magic has sought an entry to the same citadel by another road.

The Theosophist, then, believes, on the strength of evidence only a fragment of which has been touched upon here, that esotericism has been weaving its web of influence, powerful even if subtle and unseen, throughout the religions, philosophies, and sciences of the world. It makes little difference what names have been attached from time to time to this esoteric tradition; and certainly no attempt is made here to prove an underlying unity or continuity in all this "wisdom literature." Suffice it to point out that in all ages there have been movements analogous to modern Theosophy, and that the modern cult regards itself as merely a regular revelation in the periodic resurgence of an ancient learning.

CHAPTER II THE AMERICAN BACKGROUND

An outline of the circumstances which may be said to constitute the background for the American development of Theosophy should begin with the mass of strange phenomena which took place, and were widely reported, in connection with the religious revivals from 1740 through the Civil War period. A veritable epidemic of what were known as the "barks" and the "jerks" swept over the land. They were most frequent in evangelical meetings, but also became common outside. The Kentucky revivals in the early years of the nineteenth century produced many odd phenomena, such as speaking in strange tongues, a condition of trance and swoon frequently attendant upon conversion, occasional illumination and ecstasy, resembling medieval mystic sainthood, and the apparently miraculous reformation of many criminals and drunkards. These phenomena impressed the general mind with the sense of a higher source of power that might be invoked in behalf of human interests.

During this period, too, several mathematical prodigies were publicly exhibited in the performance of quite unaccountable calculations, giving instantaneously the correct results of complicated manipulations of numbers.1 From about 1820, rumors were beginning to be heard of exceptional psychic powers possessed by the Hindus.

But a more notable stir was occasioned a little later when the country began to be flooded with reports of exhibitions of mesmerism and hypnotism. Couéism had not yet come, but the work of Mesmer, Janet, Charcot, Bernheim, and others in France had excited the amazement of the world by its revelations of an apparently supernormal segment of the human mind. "Healing by faith" had always been a wide-spread tradition; but when such people as Quimby and others added to the cult of healing the practice of mesmerism, and subjoined both to a set of metaphysical or spiritual formulae, the imaginative susceptibilities of the people were vigorously stimulated, and the ferment resulted in cults of "mind healing." Quimby was active with his public demonstrations throughout New England in the fifties and sixties.

The cult of Swedenborgianism, coming in chiefly from England, survived from the preceding century as a tremendous contribution to the feeling of mystic supernaturalism. Emanuel Swedenborg, who gave up his work as a noted mineralogist to take up the writing of his visions and prophecies, had profoundly impressed the religious world by the publication of his enormous works, the Arcana Coelestia, The Apocalypse Revealed, The Apocalypse Explained, and others, in which he claimed that his inner vision had been opened to a view of celestial verities. His descriptions of the heavenly spheres, and of the relation of the life of the Infinite to our finite existence, and his theory of the actual correspondence of every physical fact to some eternal truth, impressed the mystic sense of many people, who became his followers and organized his Church of the New Jerusalem. Though this following was never large in number, it was influential in the spread of a type of "arcane wisdom." In the first place, Swedenborg's statements that he had been granted direct glimpses of the angelic worlds carried a certain impressiveness in view of his detailed descriptions of what was there seen. He announced that the causes of all things are in the Divine Mind. The end of existence and creation is to bring man into conjunction with the higher spirit of the universe, so that he may become the image of his creator. The law of correspondence is the key to all the divine treasures of wisdom. He declared that he had witnessed the Last Judgment and that he was told of the second coming of the Lord. His teachings influenced among others Coleridge, Blake, Balzac, and, of course, Emerson and the James family. Though not so much of this influence was specifically Theosophic in character, it all served to bring much grist to the later Theosophical mill.

A certain identity of aims and characters between Theosophy and Swedenborgianism is revealed in the fact that "in December, 1783, a little company of sympathizers, with similar aims, met in London and founded the 'Theosophical Society,' among the members of which were John Flaxman, the sculptor, William Sharpe, the engraver, and F. H. Barthelemon, the composer."2 It was dissolved about 1788 when the Swedenborgian churches began to function. Many such religious organizations could well be called theosophical associations, as was the one founded by Brand in Cincinnati, Ohio, in 1825.

Another organization which dealt hardly less with heavenly revelations, and which must also be regarded as conducive to theosophical attitudes, was the "Children of the Light," the Friends, or Quakers. With a history antedating the nineteenth century by more than a hundred and fifty years, these people held a significant place in the religious life of America during the period we are delineating. Their intense emphasis upon the direct and spontaneous irradiation of the spirit of God into the human consciousness strikes a deep note of genuine mysticism. In fact, like Methodism, Quakerism was born in the midst of a series of spiritualistic occurrences. George Fox heard the heavenly voices and received inspirational messages directly from spiritual visitants. The report of his supernatural experiences, and of the miracles of healing which he was enabled to perform through spirit-given powers, caused hundreds of people to flock to his banner and gave the movement its primary impetus. His gospel was essentially one of spirit manifestation, and his whole ethical system grew out of his conception of the régime of personal life, conduct and mentality which was best designed to induce the visitations of spirit influence. The spiritistic and mystical experiences of the celebrated Madame Guyon, of France, enhanced the force of Fox's testimony. Not less inclined than the Friends to transcendental experiences were the Shakers, who had settled in eighteen communistic associations or colonies in the United States. They claimed to enjoy the power of apostolic healing, prophecy, glossolalia, and the singing of inspired songs. They were led by the spirit into deep and holy experiences, and claimed to be inspired by high spiritual intelligences with whom they were in hourly communion. One of their number, F. W. Evans, wrote to Robert Dale Owen, the Spiritualist, that the Shakers had predicted the advent of Spiritualism seven years previously, and that the Shaker order was the great medium between this world and the world of spirits. He asserted that

"Spiritualism originated among the Shakers of America; that there were hundreds of mediums in the eighteen Shaker communities, and that, in fact, nearly all the Shakers were mediums. Mediumistic manifestations are as common among us as gold in California."3 He maintained that there were three degrees of spiritual manifestation, the third of which is the "ministration of millennial truths to various nations, tribes, kindred and people in the spirit world who were hungering and thirsting after

righteousness."4 He further pronounced a panegyric upon Spiritualism, which is evidence that the Shakers were in sympathy with any phenomena which seemed to indicate a connection with the celestial planes:

"Spiritualism has banished scepticism and infidelity from the minds of thousands, comforted the mourner with angelic consolations, lifted up the unfortunate, the outcast, the inebriate, taking away the sting of death, which has kept mankind under perpetual bondage through fear-so that death is now, to its millions of believers,

The kind and gentle servant who unlocks,
With noiseless hand, life's flower-encircled door, To show us those we loved."5

Still another movement which had its origin in alleged supernaturalistic manifestations and helped to intensify a general belief in them, was the Church of the Latter Day Saints, or Mormons. In 1820, and again in 1823, Joseph Smith had a vision of an angel, who revealed to him the repository of certain records inscribed on plates of gold, containing the history of the aboriginal peoples of America. The ability to employ the mystic powers of Urim and Thummim, which are embodied in these records, constituted the special attribute of the seers of antiquity. The inscriptions on the gold plates were represented as the key to the understanding of ancient scriptures, and were said to be in a script known as Reformed Egyptian. The Book of Mormon claims to be an English translation of these plates of gold.

It is not necessary here to follow the history of Smith and his church, but it is interesting to point out the features of the case that touch either Spiritualism or Theosophy. We have already noted the origin of Smith's motivating idea in a direct message from the spirit world. We have also a curious resemblance to Theosophy in the fact that an alleged ancient document was brought to light as a book of authority, and that the material therein was asserted to furnish a key to the interpretation of the archaic scriptures of the world. Of the twelve articles of the Mormon creed, seven sections show a spirit not incongruous with the tendency of Theosophic sentiment. Article One professes belief in the Trinity; article Two asserts that men will be punished for their own sins, not for Adam's; Three refers to the salvation of all without exception; Seven sets forth belief in the gift of tongues, prophecy, revelations, visions, healing, etc.; Eight questions the Bible's accurate translation; Nine expresses the assurance that God will yet reveal many great and important things pertaining to his kingdom; and Eleven proclaims freedom of worship and the principle of toleration.

Orson Pratt, one of the leading publicists of the Mormon cult, said that where there is an end of manifestation of new phenomena, such as visions, revelations and inspiration, the people are lost in blindness. When prophecies fail, darkness hangs over the people. In a tract issued by Pratt it is stated that the Book of Mormon has been abundantly confirmed by miracles.

"Nearly every branch of the church has been blessed by miraculous signs and gifts of the Holy Ghost, by which they have been confirmed, and by which we know of a surety that this is the Church of Christ. They know that the blind see, the lame walk, the deaf hear, the dumb speak, that lepers are cleansed, that bones are set, that the cholera is rebuked, and that the most virulent diseases give way through faith in the name of Christ and the power of His gospel."6

About 1825, in a meeting at the home of Josiah Quincy in Boston, a philosophic- religious movement was launched which may seem to have had but meagre influence on the advent of Theosophy later in the century, but which in its motive and animating spirit was probably one of the cult's most immediate precursors. The Unitarian faith, courageously agitated from 1812 to 1814 by William E. Channing, Edward Everett, and Francis Parkman, flowered into a religious denomination in 1825 and thenceforth exercised, in a measure out of all proportion to its numerical strength, a powerful influence on American religious thought. Under Emerson and Parker a little later the principle of free expression of opinion was carried to such length that the formulation of an orthodox creed was next to impossible.

They questioned not only the Trinitarian doctrine, as pagan rather than Christian (the identical position taken by Madame Blavatsky in the volumes of Isis Unveiled), but the whole orthodox structure. The Bible was not to be regarded as God's infallible and inspired word, but a work of exalted human agencies. Christ was no heaven-born savior, but a worthy son of man. If he was man and anything more, his life is worthless to mere men. His life was a man's life, his gospel a man's gospel-otherwise inapplicable to us. Salvation is within every person. Death does not determine the state of the soul for all eternity; the soul passes on into spirit with all its earth-won character. In the life that is to be, as well as in the life that now is, the soul must reap what it sows. If there were a Unitarian creed, it might be summarized as follows: The fatherhood of God; the brotherhood of man; the leadership of Jesus; salvation by character; the progress of mankind onward and upward forever. All this, as far it goes, is strikingly harmonious with the Theosophic position.
That there was an evident community of interests between the two movements is indicated by the fact that Unitarianism, like Theosophy, sought Hindu connections, and strangely enough made a sympathetic entente with the Brahmo- Somaj Society, while Theosophy later affiliated with the Arya-Somaj.7
No examination of the American background of Theosophy can fail to take account of that movement which carried the minds of New England thinkers to a lofty pitch during the early half of the nineteenth century, Transcendentalism. It has generally been attributed to the impact of German Romanticism, transmitted by way of England through Carlyle, Coleridge, and Wordsworth. French influence was really more direct and dominating, but the powerful effect of Oriental religion and philosophy on Emerson, hitherto not considered seriously, should not be overlooked. "All of Emerson's notes on Oriental scriptures have been deleted from Bliss Perry's Heart of Emerson's Journals."8 No student conversant with the characteristic marks of Indian philosophy needs documentary corroboration of the fact that Emerson's thought was saturated with typically Eastern conceptions.
The evidence runs through nearly all his works like a design in a woven cloth. "Scores upon scores

of passages in his Journals and Essays show that he leaned often on the Vedas for inspiration, and paraphrased lines of the Puranas in his poems."9 But direct testimony from Emerson himself is not wanting. His Journals prove that his reading of the ancient Oriental classics was not sporadic, but more or less constant.10 He refers to some of them in the lists of each year's sources. In 1840 he tells how in the heated days he read nothing but the "Bible of the tropics, which I find I come back upon every three or four years. It is sublime as heat and night and the breathless ocean. It contains every religious sentiment. . . . It is no use to put away the book; if I trust myself in the woods or in a boat upon the pond, Nature makes a Brahmin of me presently."11 This was at the age of twenty-seven. In the Journal of 1845 he writes:

"The Indian teaching, through its cloud of legends, has yet a simple and grand religion, like a queenly countenance seen through a rich veil. It teaches to

speak the truth, love others as yourself, and to despise trifles. The East is grand-and makes Europe appear the land of trifles. Identity! Identity! Friend and foe are of one stuff . . . Cheerful and noble is the genius of this cosmogony."12

Lecturing before graduate classes at Harvard he later said: "Thought has subsisted for the most part on one root; the Norse mythology, the Vedas, Shakespeare have served the ages." In referring in one passage to the Bible he says:

"I have used in the above remarks the Bible for the ethical revelation considered generally, including, that is, the Vedas, the sacred writings of every nation, and not of the Hebrews alone."13

Elsewhere he says:

"Yes, the Zoroastrian, the Indian, the Persian scriptures are majestic and more to our daily purpose than this year's almanac or this day's newspaper. I owed-my friend and I owed-a magnificent day to the Bhagavat-Gita. It was the first of books; it was as if an empire spoke to us, nothing small or unworthy, but large, serene, consistent, the voice of an old intelligence which in another age and another climate had pondered and thus disposed of the same questions which exercise us. . . . Let us cherish the venerable oracle."14

The first stanza of Emerson's poem "Brahma, Song of the Soul," runs as follows: "If the red slayer thinks he slays,
Or if the slain thinks he is slain,
They know not well the subtle ways I keep, and pass and turn again."

Could the strange ideas and hardly less strange language of this verse have been drawn elsewhere than from the 19th verse of the Second Valli, of the Katha Upanishad,15 which reads?:

"If the slayer thinks I slay; if the slain thinks I am slain, then both of them do not know well. It (the soul) does not slay nor is it slain."

His poem "Hamatreya" comes next in importance as showing Hindu influence. In another poem, "Celestial Love," the wheel of birth and death is referred to:

"In a region where the wheel On which all beings ride, Visibly revolves."

Emerson argues for reincarnation in the Journal of 1845. "Traveling the path of life through thousands of births."

"By the long rotation of fidelity they meet again in worthy forms." Emerson's "oversoul" is synonymous with a Sanskrit term. He regarded matter as the negative manifestation of the Universal Spirit. Mind was the expression of the same Spirit in its positive power. Man, himself, is nothing but the universal spirit present in a material organism. Soul is "part and parcel of God." He says that "the soul in man is not an organ, but animates and exercises all organs; from within and from behind a light shines through us upon things, and makes us aware that we are nothing, that the light is all."16 This is Vedanta philosophy. In the Journal of 1866 he wrote:

"In the history of intellect, there is no more important fact than the Hindu theology, teaching that the beatitude or supreme good is to be attained through science: namely, by the perception of the real from the unreal, setting aside matter, and qualities or affections or emotions, and persons and actions, as mayas or illusions, and thus arriving at the conception of the One eternal Life and Cause, and a perpetual approach and assimilation to Him, thus escaping new births and transmigrations. . . . Truth is the principle and the moral of Hindu theology, Truth as against the Maya which deceives Gods and men; Truth, the principle, and Retirement and Self-denial the means of attaining it."17

Mr. Christy18 states that Emerson's concept of evolution must be thought of in terms of emanation; and a detailed examination of his concept of compensation reduces it to the doctrine of Karma.

The Journals are full of quotable passages upon one or another phase of Hinduism. And there are his other poems "Illusions" and "Maya," whose names bespeak Oriental presentations. But Mr. Christy thinks the following excerpt is Emerson's supreme tribute to Orientalism:

"There is no remedy for musty, self-conceited English life made up of fictitious hating ideas-like Orientalism. That astonishes and disconcerts English decorum. For once there is thunder he never heard, light he never saw, and power which trifles with time and space."19

It may seem ludicrous to suggest that Emerson was the chief forerunner of Madame Blavatsky, her John the Baptist. Yet seriously, without Emerson, Madame Blavatsky could hardly have launched her gospel when she did with equal hope of success. There is every justification for the assertion that Emerson's Orientalistic contribution to the general Transcendental trend of thought was preparatory to Theosophy. It must not be forgotten that his advocacy of Brahmanic ideas and doctrines came at a time when the expression of a laudatory opinion of the Asiatic religions called forth an opprobrium from evangelistic quarters hardly less than vicious in its bitterness. Theosophy could not hope to make headway until the virulent edge of that orthodox prejudice had been considerably blunted. It was Emerson's magnanimous eclecticism which administered the first and severest rebuke to that prejudice, and inaugurated that gradual mollification of sentiment toward the Orientals which made possible the welcome which Hindu Yogis and Swamis received toward the end of the century.

The exposition of Emerson's orientalism makes it unnecessary to trace the evidences of a similar influence running through the philosophical thinking of Thoreau and Walt Whitman. The robust cosmopolitanism of these two intellects lifted them out of the provincialisms of the current denominations into the realm of universal sympathies. We know that Thoreau became the recipient of forty-four volumes of the Hindu texts in 1854; but it is evident that he, like Emerson, had had contact with Brahmanical literature previous to that. His works are replete with references to Eastern ideas and beliefs. He could hardly have associated so closely with Emerson as he did and escaped the contagion of the latter's Oriental enthusiasm.

Mr. Horace L. Traubel, one of the three literary executors of Whitman, had in his possession the poet's own copy of the Bhagavad Gita. Perry and Binns, in their biographies of Whitman, give lists of the literature with which he was familiar; and many ancient authors are mentioned. Among them are Confucius, the Hindu poets, Persian poets, Zoroaster; portions of the Vedas and Puranas, Alger's Oriental Poetry and other Eastern sources. Dr. Richard M. Bucke, another

of the three literary executors, and a close friend and associate of "the good gray poet," was one of the prominent early Theosophists, and it is reasonable to presume that Whitman was familiar with Theosophic theory through the channel of this friendship. Whitman likewise gave form and body to another volume of sentiment which has contributed, no one can say how much, to the adoption of Theosophy. This was America's own native mysticism. It created an atmosphere in which the traditions of the supernatural grew robust and realistic.

Attention must now be directed to that wide-spread movement in America which has come to be known as New Thought. It came, as has been hinted at, out of the spiritualization, or one might say, doctrinization, of mesmerism. Observation of the surprising effects of hypnotic control, indicating the presence of a psychic energy in man susceptible to external or self-generated suggestion, led to the inference that a linking of spiritual affirmation with the unconscious dynamism would conduce to invariably beneficent results, that might be made permanent for character. If a jocular suggestion by the stage mesmerist could lead the subject into a ludicrous performance; if a suggestion of illness, of pain, of a headache, could produce the veritable symptoms; why could not a suggestion of adequate strength and authority lead to the actualization of health, of personality, of well-being, of spirituality? The task was merely to transform animal magnetism into spiritual suggestion. The aim was to indoctrinate the subconscious mind with a fixation of spiritual sufficiency and opulence, until the personality came to embody and manifest on the physical plane of life the character of the inner motivation. Seeing what an obsession of a fixed abnormal idea had done to the body and mind in many cases, New Thought tried to regenerate the life in a positive and salutary direction by the conscious implantation of a higher spiritual concept, until it, too, became obsessive, and wrought an effect on the outer life coördinate with its own nature. The process of hypnotic suggestion became a moral technique, with a potent religious formula, according to which spiritual truth functioned in place of personal magnetic force. Essentially it reduced itself to the business of self- hypnotization by a lofty conception. Thought itself was seen to possess mesmeric power. "As a man thinketh in his heart" became the slogan of New Thought, and the kindred Biblical adjuration-"Be ye transformed by the renewing of your

mind"-furnished the needed incentive to positive mental aggression. The world of today is familiar with the line of phrases which convey the basic ideology of the New Thought cults. One hears much of being in tune with the Infinite, of making the at-one-ment with the powers of life, of getting into harmony with the universe, of making contact with the reservoir of Eternal Supply, of getting en rapport with the Cosmic Consciousness, of keeping ourselves puny and stunted because we do not ask more determinedly from the Boundless.

Here is unmistakable evidence of a somewhat diluted Hinduism. Under the pioneering of P. P. Quimby, Horatio W. Dresser, and others, study clubs were formed and lecture courses given. Charles Brodie Patterson, W. J. Colville, James Lane Allen, C. D. Larson, Orison S. Marden, and a host of others, aided in the popularization of these ideas, until in the past few decades there has been witnessed an almost endless brood of ramifications from the parent conception, with associations of Spiritual Science, Divine Science, Cosmic Truth, Universal Light and Harmony carrying the message. So we have been called upon to witness the odd spectacle of what was essentially Hindu Yoga philosophy masquerading in the guise of commanding personality and forceful salesmanship! But grotesque as these developments have been, there is no doubting their importance in the Theosophical background. They have served to introduce the thought of the Orient to thousands, and have become stepping-stones to its deeper investigation.

A concomitant episode in the expansion of New Thought and Transcendentalism was the direct program of Hindu propaganda fathered by Hindu spokesmen themselves. When it became profitable, numerous Yogis, Swamis, "Adepts," and "Mahatmas" came to this country and lectured on the doctrines and principles of Orientalism to audiences of élite people with mystical susceptibilities. Some time in the seventies, Boston was galvanized into a veritable quiver of interest in Eastern doctrines by the eloquent P. C. Mazoomdar, author of The Oriental Christ, whose campaign left its deep impress. His work, in fact, formed one of the links between Unitarianism and Brahmanic thought, already noted. In 1893 Swami Vivekananda, chosen as a delegate to the World Congress of Religions at the Columbian Exposition at Chicago, and author of Yoga Philosophy, began preaching the Yoga principles of thought and discipline, and instituted in New York the Vedanta Society. Almost every year since his coming has brought public lectures and private instruction courses by native Hindus in the large American cities.

Concomitant with the evolution of New Thought came the sensational dissemination of Mrs. Eddy's Christian Science. Offspring of P. P. Quimby's mesmeric science, and erected by Mrs. Eddy's strange enthusiasm into a healing cult based on a reinterpretation of Christian doctrines-the allness of Spirit and the nothingness of matter-the organization has enjoyed a steady and pronounced growth and drawn into its pale thousands of Christian communicants who felt the need of a more dynamic or more fruitful gospel. The conception of the impotence of matter, as non-being, is as old as Greek and Hindu philosophy. Mrs. Eddy's contribution in the matter was her use of the philosophical idea as a psychological mantram for healing, and her adroitness in lining up the Christian scriptures to support the idea.

It would require a fairly discerning insight to mark out clearly the inter- connection of Christian Science and Theosophy. There is basically little similarity between the two schools, or little common ground on which they might meet. On the contrary there is much direct antagonism in their views and dogma. Nevertheless the Boston cult tended indirectly to bring some of its votaries along the path toward occultism. In the first place, like Unitarianism, it had induced thousands of sincere seekers for a new and liberal faith to sever the ties of their former servile attachment to an uninspiring orthodoxy. Secondly, Christian Science does yeoman service in "demonstrating" the spiritual view-point. Its emphasis on spirit, as opposed to material concepts of reality, is entirely favorable to the general theses of Theosophy. Thirdly, the intellectual limitations of the system develop the need of a larger philosophy, which Theosophy stands ready to supply. Christian Science, being primarily a Christian healing cult, with a body of ideas adequate to that function, often leads the intelligent and open-minded student in its ranks to become aware that it falls far short of offering a comprehensive philosophy of life. It has little or nothing to say about man's origin, his present rank in a universal order, or his destiny. It leaves the pivotal question of immortality in the same status as does conventional Christianity. Many Christian Science adherents have seen that Theosophy offers a fuller and more adequate cosmograph, and accordingly adopted it. Their experience in the Eddy system brought them to the outer court of the Occult Temple.[20]

Among major movements that paved the way for Theosophy, the one perhaps most directly conducive to it is Spiritualism, for the founder of the Theosophical Society began her career in the Spiritualistic ranks. On account of this close relationship it is necessary to outline the origin and spread of this strange movement more fully.

The weird behavior of two country girls, the one twelve and the other nine, in the hamlet of Hydesville, near Rochester, New York, in the spring of 1847, was like a spark to power for the release of religious fancy; for Margaret and Kate Fox were supposed to have picked up again the thread of communication between the world of human consciousness and the world of disembodied spirits, and thus to have given fresh reinforcement to man's assurance of immortality. From this bizarre beginning the movement spread rapidly to all parts of America, England, and France. In nearly every town in America groups were soon meeting, eager for manifestations and fervently invoking the denizens of the unseen worlds. Various methods and means were provided whereby the disembodied entities could communicate with dull mundane faculties. Many and varied were the types of response. Besides the simple "raps," there were tinklings of tiny aerial bells, flashings of light, tipping of tables, levitation of furniture and of human bodies, messages through the planchette, free voice messages, trumpet speaking, alphabet rapping, materialization of the hands and of complete forms, trance catalepsis and inspiration, automatic writing, slate writing, glossolalia, and many other variety of phenomena. Mediums, clairvoyants, inspirational speakers sprang forward plentifully; and each one became the focus of a group activity.

It is somewhat difficult for us to reconstruct the picture of this flare of interest and activity, the scope of this absorbing passion for spirit manifestation. It attests the eagerness of the human heart for tangible evidence of survival. With periodical ebb and flow it has persisted to the present day, when its vogue is hardly less general than at any former time. In the fifties and sixties the Spiritualistic agitation was in full flush, with many extraordinary occurrences accredited to its exponents.[21]

Spiritualism encountered opposition among the clergy and the materialistic scientists, yet it has hardly ever been wanting in adherents among the members of both groups. An acquaintance with its supporters would reveal a surprising list of high civil and government officials, attorneys, clergymen, physicians, professors, and scientists.[22]

One of the first Spiritualistic writers of this country was Robert Dale Owen, whose Footfalls on the Boundary of Another World and The Debatable Land were notable contributions. Two of the most eminent representatives of the movement in its earliest days were Prof. Robert Hare, an eminent scientist and the inventor of the oxyhydrogen blow-pipe, and Judge Edmonds, a leading jurist. Both these men had approached the subject at first in a skeptical spirit, with the intention of disclosing its unsound premises; but they were fair enough to study the evidence impartially, with the result that both were convinced of the genuineness of the phenomena. Both avowed their convictions courageously in public, and Judge Edmonds made extensive lecture tours of the country, the propaganda effect of which was great.23 Before the actual launching of the Theosophical Society in 1875 at least four prominent later Theosophists had played more or less important rôles in the drama of Spiritualism. Madame Blavatsky, as we shall see, had identified herself with its activities; Mr. J. R. Newton was a vigorous worker; and it was Col. Olcott himself who brought the manifestations taking place in 1873 at the Eddy farmhouse near Chittenden, Vermont, to public notice and who put forth one of the first large volumes covering these and other phenomena in 1874, People From the Other World. The fourth member was Mrs. Emma Hardinge Britten, who had served as a medium with the Bulwer-Lytton group of psychic investigators in England, and who added two books to Spiritualistic literature-Art Magic and Nineteenth Century Miracles. Col. Olcott, Madame Blavatsky, and Mrs. Britten made material contributions to several Spiritualistic magazines, especially The Spiritual Scientist, edited in Boston.

Meantime Spiritualistic investigation got under way and after the sixties a stream of reports, case histories, accounts of phenomena, and books from prominent advocates flooded the country. The Seybert Commission on Spiritualism, composed of leading officers and professors at the University of Pennsylvania, submitted its report in 1888. In the same year R. B. Davenport undertook to turn the world away from what he considered a delusion with his book Deathblow to Spiritualism: The True Story of the Fox Sisters; but he found that Spiritualism had a strange vitality that enabled it to survive many a "deathblow." As a result of studies in psychic phenomena in England came F. W. H. Myers' impressive work, The Human Personality and Its Survival of Bodily Death, in which the foundations for the theory of the subliminal or subconscious mind were laid.

But the work of the mediums themselves kept public feeling most keenly alert. A list of some of the most prominent ones includes Mrs. Hayden, Henry Slade, Pierre L. O. A. Keeler, the slate-writer, Robert Houdin (who bequeathed his name and exploits to the later Houdini), Ira and William Davenport, Anna Eva Fay, Charles Slade, Eusapia Paladino, Mrs. Leonara Piper. Robert Dale Owen, already mentioned as author, was a medium of no mean ability. In the same category was

J. M. Peebles, of California, whose books, Seers of the Ages and Who Are These Spiritualists? and whose public lecture tours, rendered him one of the most prominent of all the advocates of the cult. A career of inspirational public speaking was staged by Cora V. Richmond, who gave lectures on erudite themes with an uncommon flow of eloquence. W. J. Colville began where she ended, giving unprepared addresses on topics suggested by the audience.

The three most famous American mediums deserve somewhat more extended treatment. The first of the trio is Daniel Dunglas Home, who was a poor Scottish boy adopted in America. While a child, spiritual power manifested itself to him to his terror and annoyance. Raps came around him on the table or desk, on the chairs or walls. The furniture moved about and was attracted toward him. His aunt, with whom he lived was in consternation at these phenomena, and, deeming him possessed, sent for three clergymen to exorcise the spirit; when they did not succeed, she threw his Sunday suit and linen out the window and pushed him out-of-doors. He was thus cast on the world without friends, but the power that he possessed raised him friends and sent him forth from America to be the planter of Spiritualism all over Europe.24

The second of the triumvirate was Andrew Jackson Davis. His function seemed to be that of the seer and the scribe, rather than of the producer of material operations. He was born of poor parents, in 1826, in Orange Country, New York. He seems to have inherited a clairvoyant faculty. He received only five months' schooling in the village, it being "found impossible to teach him anything there."25 During his solitary hours in the fields he saw visions and heard voices. Removing to Poughkeepsie, he became the clairvoyant of a mesmeric lecturer, and in this capacity began to excite wonder by his revelations. This was before the Rochester knockings were heard. He diagnosed and healed diseases, and prescribed for scores who came to him, surprising both patients and physicians by his competence. Then he began to see "into the heart of things," to descry the essential nature of the world and the spiritual constitution of the universe. He could see the interior of bodies and the metals hidden in the earth. Adding his testimony to that of Fox and Swedenborg, he asserted that every animal represented some human quality, some vice or virtue. He gave Greek and Latin names of things, without having a knowledge of these languages. In a vision he beheld The Magic Staff on which he was urged to learn during life; on it was written his life's motto: "Under all circumstances keep an open mind." In 1845 he delivered one hundred and fifty-seven lectures in New York which

announced a new philosophy of the universe. They were published under the title, Nature's Divine Revelation, a book of eight hundred pages. Davis then became a voluminous writer.26

Thomas L. Harris, the third great representative, was much attracted by Davis' The Divine Revelations of Nature, but developed spiritistic powers along a somewhat different line, that of poetic inspiration. In his early exhibitions of this supernormal faculty he dictated who epics, containing occasionally excellent verse, under the alleged influence of Byron, Shelley, Keats and others. The interesting manner in which these poems-a whole volume of three or four hundred pages at a time-were created, is more amazing than their poetic merit. Mr. Brittan, an English publisher, tells us that Harris dictated and he wrote down The Lyric of the Golden Age, a poem of 381 pages, in ninety-four hours! The Lyric of the Morning Land and other pretentious works were produced in a similar manner.

"But," says William Howitt in his History of the Supernatural, "the progress of Harris into an inspirational oratory is still more surprising. He claims, by opening up his interior being, to receive influx of divine intuition in such abundance and power as to throw off under its influence the most astonishing strains of eloquence. This receptive and communicative power he attributes to an internal spiritual breathing corresponding to the outer natural breathing. As the body lungs imbibe air, so, he contends, the spiritual lungs inspire and respire the divine aura, refluent with the highest thought and purest sentiment, and that without any labor or trial of brain."27

Spiritualism is one of the most direct lines of approach to Theosophy, since an acceptance of the possibility of spiritistic phenomena is a prerequisite for the adoption of the larger scheme of occult truth. Spiritualism covers a portion of the ground embraced by the belief in reincarnation, and in so far constitutes an introduction to it. Theosophy is further, an endorsement of the primary position of the Spiritualists regarding the survival of the soul entity, and thus commends itself to their approbation. The Spiritualists have been considerably vexed by the question of reincarnation, and their ranks are split over the subject. Some of the message seem to endorse it, others evade it, and some negate the idea. What is significant at this point is that the Spiritualistic agitation prepared the way for Theosophic conceptions. A large percentage of the first membership came from the ranks of the Spiritualists.

But Spiritualism is but one facet of a human interest which has expressed itself in all ages, embracing the various forms of mysticism, occultism, esotericism, magic, healing, wonder-working, arcane science, and theurgy. The growing acquaintance with Yoga practice and Hindu philosophy in this country under the stimulus of many eloquent Eastern representatives has already been mentioned.

The demonstrations of mesmeric power lent much plausibility to Oriental pretensions to extraordinary genius for that sort of thing. More than might be supposed, there was prevalent in Europe and America alike a never-dying tradition of magical art, a survival of Medieval European beliefs in superhuman activities and powers both in man and nature. Among the rural and unschooled populations this tradition assumed the form of harmless superstitions. Among more learned peoples it issued in philosophic speculations dealing with the spiritual energies of nature, the hidden faculties of man, such as prophecy, tongues and ecstatic vision, and the extent and possibility of man's control over the external world through the manipulation of a subtle ether possessing magnetic quality. The heritage of Paracelsus, Robert Fludd, Thomas Vaughn and Roger Bacon, Agrippa von Nettesheim, the Florentine Platonists and their German, French, and English heirs still lingered. The Christian scriptures were

themselves replete with incidents of the supernatural, with necromancy, witchcraft, miracles, ghostwalking, spirit messages, symbolical dreams, and the whole armory of thaumaturgical exploits. The doctrine of Satan was itself calculated to enliven the imagination with ideas of demoniac possession, and was all the more credible by reason of the prevalence of insanity which was ascribed to spirit obsession. The early nineteenth century was must closer to the Middle Ages than our own time is, not only because education was less general, but also because a far larger proportion of the population was agrarian instead of metropolitan. Such cults were, however, by no means restricted to "backwoods" sections. They were astonishingly prevalent in the larger centers. More enlightened groups accepted a less crude form of the practices. Where knowledge ceases superstition may begin; and the problems of life that press upon us for solution and that are still beyond our grasp, lead the mind into every sort of rationalization or speculation.

Perhaps more people than acknowledge God in church pews believe in the existence of intelligences that play a part in life, whether in answer to prayer, in suggestive dreams, in occasional vision and apparitions, in messages through mediums, or in whatever guise; and out of such an unreflective theology arise many of the types of superstitious philosophy. To analyze this situation in its entirety would take us into extensive fields of folk-lore and involve every sort of old wives' tale imaginable. The chief point is that the varieties of chimney- corner legend and omnipresent superstition have had their origin in a larger primitive interpretation of the facts and forces of nature. They must be recognized as the modern progeny of ancient hylozoism and animism. In the childhood of our culture, as well as in the childhood of the race and of the individual, there is a close sympathy between man and nature which leads him to ascribe living quality to the external world. Countryside fables are doubtless the jejune remnant of what was once felt to be a vital magnetic relation between man's spirit and the spirit of the world. They are the distorted forms of some of the ancient rites for effecting magical intercourse between man and nature.

While it is not to be inferred that Theosophy itself was built on the material embodied in countryside credulity, it will be seen that the native inclination toward an animistic interpretation of phenomena was in a measure true to the deeper theses which the new cult presented. Madame Blavatsky herself says in Isis Unveiled that the spontaneous responsiveness of the peasant mind is likely to lead to a closer apprehension of the living spirit of Nature than can be attained by the sophistications of reason.

The major tendencies in the direction of Theosophy have now been enumerated. It remains only to mention the scattering of American students before 1875 whose researches were taking them into the realm where the fundamentals of Theosophy itself were to be found. We refer to the Rosicrucians, the Freemasons, the Kabalists, Hermeticists, Egyptologists, Assyriologists, students of the Mysteries, of the Christian origins, of the pagan cults, and the small but gradually increasing number of Comparative Religionists and Philologists.28 There were men of intelligence both in Europe and America, who had kept on the track of ancient and medieval esotericism, and the opening up of Sanskrit literature gave a decided impetus to a renaissance of research in those realms. The material that went into Frazer's Golden Bough, Ignatius Donnelley's Atlantis: the Antediluvian World, Hargrave Jennings' The Rosicrucians,and many other compendious works of the sort, was being collated out of the flotsam and jetsam of ancient survival and assembled into a picture beginning to assume definite outline and more than haphazard meaning. The great system of Neo- Platonism, the Gnostics, with Apollonius of Tyana, and Philo Judaeus were coming under inspection. The universality of religious myths and rites was being noted.

In short, the large body of ancient thought, so deeply imbued with the occult, was beginning to be scrutinized by the scholars of the nineteenth century.

It was into this situation that Madame Blavatsky came. Her office, she said, was that of a clavigera; she bore a key which would provide students with a principle of integration for the loose material which would enable them to piece together the scattered stones and glittering jewels picked up here and there into a structure of surpassing grandeur and priceless worth. She would show that the gems of literature, whose mystic profundity astonished and perplexed the savants, were but the fragments of a once-glorious spiritual Gnosis

CHAPTER III HELENA P. BLAVATSKY

HELENA P. BLAVATSKY: HER LIFE AND PSYCHIC CAREER
Who was Madame Blavatsky? Every new régime of belief or of social organization must be studied with a view to determining as far as possible how much of the movement is a contribution of the individuality of the founder and how much represents a traditional deposit. This inquiry is of first importance in a consideration of the Theosophical Society, because, more than in most systems, the personal endowment of its founder gave it its specific coloring, character and form. It should be said at this point that the career of Madame Blavatsky as outlined here does not purport to be a complete or authoritative biography. It was obviously impossible to undertake such an investigation of her life, as the difficulties of obscure research in three or four continents were practically prohibitive. We have been forced to base our study upon the body of biographical material that has been assembled around her name, emanating, first, from her relatives, secondly, from her followers and admirers, and thirdly, from her critics. Her life, up to the age of forty-two, narrowly escaped consignment to the realm of mythology, if not total oblivion, but was at least partially redeemed to the status of history by the exertions of Mr. A. P. Sinnett, who procured information from members of her own family in Russia. His book, Incidents in the Life of Madame Blavatsky, has been our chief source of information about her youth and early career. The Countess Wachtmeister's Reminiscences, Col. Olcott's Old Diary Leaves, V. Solovyoff's A Modern Priestess of Isis and William Kingsland's The Real Helena P. Blavatsky, together with Madame Blavatsky's own letters, especially those to Mr. And Mrs. A. P. Sinnett, are the main works relied upon to guide our story. If the eventful life of our subject is to be further redeemed from mystery and sheer tradition into which it already seems to be fading, a more thorough critical study of it should be undertaken, based upon authentic data collected from first-hand sources as far as this is possible.

It is to be understood, then, that the aim in this treatise is to present her career as it is told and believed by Theosophists, although it is admittedly already partly legendary. The precise extent it is to be regarded as mythological must be left to the individual reader, and to future study, to determine.

Helena Petrovna Blavatsky was born in the Ukrainian city of Ekaterinoslaw on the night between the 30th and 31st of July, 1831. Her father was Col. Peter Hahn, and her mother previous to her marriage, Helene Fadeef. The father was the son of Gen. Alexis Hahn von Rottenstern Hahn, from a noble family of Mecklenberg, Germany, settled in Russia. Her mother's parents were Privy Councillor Andrew Fadeef and the Princess Helene Dolgorouky. Madame Blavatsky's grandfather was a cousin of Countess Ida Hahn-Hahn, the authoress. Her own mother was known in the literary world between 1830 and 1840 under the nom de plume of Zenaïda R.-the first novel writer that had ever appeared in Russia, says the account. Though she died before her twenty-fifth year, she left some dozen novels of the romantic school, most of which have been translated into German. The theory of heredity would thus give us, apparently, abundant background for whatever literary propensities the daughter was later to display. On her mother's side she was a scion of the noble lineage of the Dolgorouky's, who could trace direct connections with Russia's founder, Rurik, and the Imperial line.

Madame Blavatsky came on to the Russian scene during a year fatal to the Slavic nation, as to all Europe, owing to the decimation of the population by the first visitation of the cholera. Her own birth was quickened by several deaths in the household. She was ushered into the world amid coffins and sorrowing. The infant was so sickly that a hurried baptism was resorted to in the effort to anticipate death. During the ceremony, which was signalized with elaborate Greek Catholic paraphernalia of lighted tapers, the child-aunt of the baby accidentally set fire to the long robes of the priest, who was severely burned. This incident was interpreted as a bad omen, and in the eyes of the townsfolk the infant was doomed to a life of trouble.

From the very date of her birth, a peculiar tradition operated to invest the life of the growing child with an odor of superstition and mystic awe. In Russia each household was supposed to be under the tutelary supervision of a Domovoy, or house goblin, whose guardianship was propitious, except on March 30th, when, for mysterious reasons, he became mischievous. But the tradition strangely excepted from this malevolent spell of the Domovoy those born on the night of July 30-31, a time closely associated in the annals of popular belief with witches and their doings. The child came early to learn why it was that, on every recurring March 30th, she was carried around the house, stables and cowpen and made personally to sprinkle the four corners with water, while the nurse repeated some mystic incantation. Her first conscious recognition of herself must thus have been tinged with a feeling that she was in some particular fashion set apart, that she was somehow the object of special care and attention from invisible powers.

The Dnieper aided in weaving a spell of enchantment about her infancy. No Cossack of Southern Ukraine ever crosses it without preparing himself for death. Along its banks, where the child strolled with her nurses, the Rusalky (undines, nymphs) haunted the willow trees and the rushes. She was told that she was impervious to their influences, and in this sense of superiority she alone dared to approach those sandy shores. She had heard the servants' tales of these nymphs. Filled with this realization of her favored standing with the Rusalky, she one day threatened a youngster who had roused her displeasure that she would have the nymphs tickle him to death, whereupon the lad ran wildly away and was found dead on the sands-whether from fright or from having stumbled into one of the treacherous sandpits which the swirling waters quickly turn into whirlpools.

Her mother died when Mlle. Hahn was still a child. She and her younger sister were taken to live with her father, in barracks with his regiment, and until the age of eleven, they were entertained, amused and spoiled as les enfants du régiment. After that they went to live at Saratow with their grandmother, where their grandfather was civil governor. The child was "alternately petted and punished, spoiled and hardened," and was difficult to manage. She was of uncertain health, "ever sick and dying," a sleep walker, and given to abnormal psychic peculiarities, ascribed by her orthodox nurses to possession by the devil; so that, as she afterwards said, "she was drenched with enough holy water to float a ship," and exorcised by priests. She was a born rebel against restraint, and went into ungovernable fits of passion, which left her violently

shaken; but at the opposite apogee of her disposition she was filled with impulses of the extremest kindliness and affection. Through life she had this dual temper. Those who knew her better nature tolerated the irascible element. She was lively, highly-gifted, full of humor, and of remarkable doing. She had a passionate curiosity for everything savoring of the weird, the uncanny, the mysterious; she was strangely attracted by the theme of death. Her imagination, wildly roaming, appeared to create about her a world of fairy or elfish creatures with whom she held converse in whispers by the hour. She defied all and everything. She had to be watched lest she escape from the house and mingle with ragged urchins. She preferred to listen to the tales of Madame Peigneur (her governess) than do her lessons. She would openly rebel against her text- books and run off to the woods or hide in the dusky corridors of the basement of the great house where her grandfather lived. In a secluded dark recess in the "Catacombs" she had erected a barrier of old broken chairs and tables, and there, up near the ceiling under an iron-barred window, she would secrete herself for hours, reading a book of popular legends known as Solomon's Wisdom. At times she bent to her books in a spasm of scholarly devotion to amend for mischief making. Her grandparents' enormous library was then the object of her constant interest. No less passionately would she drink in the wonders of narratives given in her presence. Every fairy-tale became a living event to her.

She would be found speaking to the stuffed animals and birds in the museum in the old house. She said the pigeons were cooing fairy-tales to her. She heard a voice in every natural object; nature was animate and, to her, articulate. She seemed to know the inner life and secrets of every species of insect, bird, and reptile found about the place. She would recreate their past and describe vividly their feelings. At this early date she detailed the events of the past incarnations of the stuffed animals in the museum.

Times without number the little girl was heard conversing with playmates of her own age, invisible to others. There was in particular a little hunchback boy, a favorite phantom companion of her solitude, for whose neglect by the servants and nurses she was often excited to resentment.

"But amidst the strange double life she thus led from her earliest recollections, she would sometimes have visions of a mature protector, whose imposing appearance dominated her imagination from a very early period. This protector was always the same, his features never changed; in after life she met him as a living man and knew him as though she had been brought up in his presence."[1]

In the neighborhood of the residence was an old man, a magician, whose doings filled the mind of the young seeress with wonder. The old man, a centenarian, learned to know the young girl and he used to say of her: "This little lady is quite different from all of you. There are great events lying in wait for her in the future. I feel sorry in thinking that I will not live to see my predictions of her verified; but they will all come to pass!"

Her whole career is dotted with miraculous escapes from danger and still more miraculous recoveries from wounds, sicknesses and fevers. One of the first appearances of a protective hand in her life came far back in her childhood. She had always entertained a marked curiosity about a curtained portrait in her grandfather's castle at Saratow. It was hung so high that it was far beyond her reach. Denied permission to see it, she awaited her opportunity to catch a glimpse of it by stealth; and when left alone on one occasion she dragged a table to the wall, set another table on that, and a chair on top, and managed to clamber up. On tiptoe she just contrived to pull back the curtain. The sight of

the picture was so startling that she made an involuntary movement backwards, lost her balance and toppled with her pyramid to the floor. In falling she lost consciousness; but when she came to her senses some moments afterwards, she was amazed to see the tables, chairs, and everything in proper order in the room.

The curtain was slipped back again on the rings, and no mark of the episode was left except the imprint of her small hand on the wall high up beside the picture.

At another time, when she was nearing the age of fourteen, her riding horse bolted and flung her, with her foot caught in the stirrup. As the animal plunged forward she expected to be dragged to death, but felt herself buoyed up by a strange force, and escaped without a scratch.

It was not many years more until the young girl's possession of gifts and extraordinary faculties, commonly classed as mediumistic, became an admitted fact among her relatives and close associates. She would answer questions locating lost property, or solving other perplexities of the household. She sometimes blurted out to visitors that they would die, or meet with misfortune or accident; and her prophecies usually came true.

In 1844 the father, Col. Hahn, took Helena for her first journey abroad. She went with him to Paris and London, but proved a troublesome charge.

Her youthful marriage deserves narration with some fulness, if only because it precipitated the lady out of her home and into that phase of her career which has been referred to as her period of preparation and apprenticeship. As her aunt, Madame Fadeef, describes her marriage:

"she cared not whether she should get married or not. She had been simply defied one day by her governess to find any man who would be her husband, in view of her temper and disposition. The governess, to emphasize the taunt, said that even the old man she had found so ugly and had laughed at so much calling him a 'plumeless raven,' that even he would decline her for his wife. That was enough; three days afterwards she made him propose, and then, frightened at what she had done, sought to escape from her joking acceptance of his offer. But it was too late. All she knew and understood was-when too late-that she was now forced to accept a master she cared nothing for, nay, that she hated; that she was tied to him by the law of the country, hand and foot. A 'great horror' crept upon her, as she explained it later; one desire, ardent, unceasing, irresistible, got hold of her entire being, led her on, so to say, by the hand, forcing her to act instinctively, as she would have done if, in the act of saving her life, she had been running away from a mortal danger. There had been a distinct attempt to impress her with the solemnity of marriage, with her future obligations and her duties to her husband and married life. A few hours later at the altar she heard the priest saying to her: 'Thou shalt honor and obey thy husband,' and at this hated word 'shalt' her young face-for she was hardly seventeen-was seen to flush angrily, then to become deadly pale. She was overheard to mutter in response through her set teeth-'Surely I shall not.'

"And surely she has not. Forthwith she determined to take the law and her future life into her own hands, and-she left her husband forever, without giving him an opportunity to ever even think of her as his wife.

"Thus Madame Blavatsky abandoned her country at seventeen and passed ten long years in strange and out-of-the-way places,--in Central Asia, India, South America, Africa and Eastern Europe."2

True, before taking this drastic step she acceded to her father's plea to do the conventional thing; and she let the old General take her, though even then not without attempts to escape, on what may by courtesy of language be called a honeymoon, which drawled out, amid bickerings, to a length of three months, and was terminated after a bitter quarrel by the bride's dash for freedom on horseback. Gen. Blavatsky by this time saw the impossibility of the situation and acceded to the inevitable.

Tracing the life of Madame Blavatsky from this event through her personally- conducted globe-roaming becomes difficult, owing to the meagreness of information. Her relatives and her later Theosophic associates have done their best to piece together the crazy-quilt design of her wanderings and attendant events of any significance. She herself kept no chronicle of her journeys, and it was only at long intervals, when she emerged out of the deserts or jungles of a country to visit its metropolis, or when she needed to write for money, that she sent letters back home. The family was at first alarmed by her defection from the fireside, but were constrained to acquiesce in the situation by their recognition of her immitigable distaste for her veteran husband. If no other tie kept her attached to the home circle, her need of funds obliged her to keep in touch with her father, who supplied her with money without betraying her confidences as to her successive destinations. He acceded to her plans because he had tried in vain to secure a Russian divorce; and he felt that a few years of travel for his daughter might best ease the family situation. Ten years elapsed before the fugitive saw her relatives again.

Her first emergence after her disappearance was in Egypt. She seems to have traveled there with a Countess K------, and at that time began to pick up some occult teaching of a poorer sort. She encountered an old Copt, a man with a great reputation as a magician. She proved an apt pupil, and the instructor became so much interested in her that when she revisited Egypt years later, the special attention he (then a retired ascetic) showed her, attracted the notice of the populace at Bulak.

After her appearance in Egypt she seems to have bobbed up in Paris, where she made the acquaintance of many literary people, and where a famous mesmerist, struck with her psychic gifts, was eager to put her to work as a sensitive. To escape his importunities she appears to have gone to London. There she stayed for a time with an old Russian lady, a Countess B., at Mivart's Hotel. She remained for some time after her friend's departure, but could not afterwards recall where she resided.

Occasionally in her travels she fell in with fellow Russians who were glad to accompany her and sometimes to befriend her. She indulged in a tour about Europe in 1850 with the Countess B., but was again in Paris when the New Year of 1851 was acclaimed. Her next move was actuated by a passionate interest in the North American Indians, which she had acquired from a perusal of Fenimore Cooper's Leatherstocking Tales. Her zeal in this pursuit took her to Canada in July of 1851. At Quebec her idealizations suffered a rude shock, when, being introduced to a party of Indians, both the noble Redskins and some articles of her property disappeared while she was trying to pry from the squaws a recital of the secret powers of their medicine men. Dropping the Indians, she turned her interest to the rising sect of the Mormons, being attracted doubtless by their possession of an alleged Hermetic document obtained through psychic revelation. But the destruction of the original Mormon city of Nauvoo, Missouri, by a mob, scattered the sect across the plains, and Madame Blavatsky thought the time propitious for exploring the traditions and arcana of Mexico. She came to New Orleans. Here the Voodoo practices of a settlement of Negroes from the West Indies engaged her

interest, and her reckless curiosity might have led her into dangerous contact with these magicians; but her protective power reappeared to warn her in a vision of the risk she was running, and she hastened on to new experiences.

Through Texas she reached Mexico, protected only by her own reckless daring and by the occasional intercession of some chance companion. She seems to have owed much in this way to an old Canadian, Père Jacques, who steered her safely through many perils. At Copau in Mexico she chanced to meet a Hindu, who styled himself a "chela" of the Masters (or adepts in Oriental occult science), and she resolved to seek that land of mystic enchantment and penetrate northward into the very lairs of the mystic Brotherhood. She wrote to an Englishman, whom she had met two years before in Germany, and who shared her interest, to join them in the West Indies. Upon his arrival the three pilgrims took boat for India. The party arrived at Bombay, via the Cape to Ceylon, near the end of 1852. Madame's own headstrong bent to enter Tibet via Nepal in search of her Mahatmas broke up the trio. She made the hazardous attempt to enter the Forbidden Land of the Lamas, but was prevented, she always believed, by the opposition of a British resident then in Nepal. Baffled, she returned to Southern India, thence to Java and Singapore and thence back to England.
But that country's embroilment in the Crimean War distressed her sense of patriotism, and about the end of the year 1853 she passed over again to America, going to New York, thence west to Chicago and on to the Far West across the Rockies with emigrant caravans. She halted a while at San Francisco. Her stay in America this time lengthened to nearly two years. She then once more made her way to India, via Japan and the Straits. She reached Calcutta in 1855.

In India, in 1856, she was joined at Lahore by a German gentleman who had been requested by Col. Hahn to find his errant daughter. With him and his two companions Madame Blavatsky traveled through Kashmir to Leli in Ladakh in company with a Tatar Shaman, who was instrumental in procuring for the party the favor of witnessing some magic rites performed at a Buddhist monastery. Her experiences there she afterwards described in Isis,3 and they are too long for recital here. One of the exploits of the old priest was the psychic vivification of the body of an infant who (not yet of walking age) arose and spoke eloquently of spiritual things and prophesied, while dominated by a magnetic current from the operator.4 The psychic feat performed by her Shaman guide was even more wonderful. Yielding to Madame's importunities at a time when she was herself in grave danger, he released himself from his body as he lay in a tent, and carried a message to a friend of the young woman residing in Wallachia, from whom he brought back an answer.5 Shortly after this incident, perceiving their danger, the Shaman, by mental telepathy apprised a friendly tribal ruler of their situation, and a band of twenty-five horsemen was sent to rescue the two travelers, finding them in a locality to which they had been directed by their chief, yet of which the two had had no possible earthly means of informing him.

Safely out of the Tibetan wilds-and she came out by roads and passes of which she had no previous knowledge-she was directed by her occult guardian to leave the country, shortly before the troubles which began in 1857. In 1858 she was once more in Europe.

By this time her name had accumulated some renown, and it was freely mentioned in connection with both the low and the high life of Vienna, Berlin, Warsaw, and Paris. Her alleged absence from these places at the times throws doubt on the accuracy of these reports. After spending some months in France and Germany upon her return from India, she finally ended her self-imposed exile and re-joined her own people in Russia, arriving at Pskoff, about 180 miles from St. Petersburg,

in the midst of a family wedding party on Christmas night. Her reason for going to Pskoff was that her sister Vera-then Madame Yahontoff-was at the time residing there with the family of her late husband, son of the General N. A. Yahontoff, Marechal de Noblesse of the place.

Soon afterwards, early in 1859, Madame Blavatsky and her sister went to reside with their father in a country house belonging to Madame Yahontoff. This was at Rougodevo, about 200 versts from St. Petersburg. About a year later, in the spring of 1860, both sisters left Rougodevo for the Caucasus on a visit to their grandparents, whom they had not seen for years. It was a three weeks' journey from Moscow to Tiflis, in coach with post horses. Madame Blavatsky remained in Tiflis less than two years, adding another year of roaming about in Imeretia, Georgia, and Mingrelia, exciting the superstitious sensibilities of the inhabitants of the Mingrelia region to an inordinate degree and gaining a reputation for witchcraft and sorcery. She was there taken down with a wasting fever, which an old army surgeon could make nothing of; but he had the good sense to send her off to Ti-flis to her friends. Recovering after a time, she left the Caucasus and went to Italy. Here, the legend goes, she, with some other European women, volunteered to serve with Garibaldi and was under severe fire in the battle of Mentana.6

The four years intervening between 1863 and 1867 seem to have been spent in European travel, though the records are barren of accurate detail. But the three from 1867 to 1870 were passed in the East,7 and were quite fruitful and eventful.

In 1870 she returned from the Orient, coming through the newly opened Suez Canal, spent a short time in Piraeus, and from there took passage for Spezzia on board a Greek vessel. On this voyage she was one of the very few saved from death in a terrible catastrophe, the vessel being blown to bits by an explosion of gunpowder and fireworks in the cargo. Rescued with only the clothes they wore, the survivors were looked after by the Greek government, which forwarded them to various destinations. Madame Blavatsky went to Alexandria and to Cairo, tarrying at the latter place until money reached her from Russia.

While awaiting the arrival of funds, the energetic woman determined to found a Société Spirite, for the investigation of mediums and manifestations according to the theories and philosophy of Allen Kardec. The latter was an outstanding advocate of Spiritualistic philosophy on the Continent. He had correlated the commonly reported spiritistic exploits to a more profound and involved theory of cosmic evolution and a higher spirituality in man. His work, Life and Destiny, written under the pseudonym of Leon Denis, unfolded a comprehensive system of spiritual truth identical in its main features with Theosophy itself. His interests were not primarily in spiritistic phenomena for themselves, but for what they revealed of the inner spiritual capacities and potentialities of our evolving Psyche.

It required but a few weeks to disgust Madame Blavatsky with her fruitless undertaking. Some French female spiritists, whom she had drafted for service as mediums, in lack of better, proved to be adventuresses following in the wake of

M. de Lesseps' army of engineers and workmen, and they concluded by stealing the Society's funds. She wrote home:

"To wind up the comedy with a drama, I got nearly shot by a madman-a Greek, who had been present at the only two public séances we held, and got possessed I suppose, by some vile spook."8

She terminated the affairs of her Société and went to Bulak, where she renewed her previous acquaintance with the old Copt. His unconcealed interest in his visitor aroused some slanderous talk about her. Disgusted with the growing gossip, she went home by way of Palestine, making a side voyage to Palmyra and other ruins, and meeting there some Russian friends. At the end of 1872 she returned without warning to her family, then at Odessa.

In 1873 she again abandoned her home, and Paris was her first objective. She stayed there with a cousin, Nicholas Hahn, for two months. While in Paris she was directed by her "spiritual overseers" to visit the United States, "where she would meet a man by the name of Olcott," with whom she was to undertake an important enterprise. Obedient to her orders she arrived at New York on July 7th, 1873.9 She was for a time practically without funds; actually, as Col.

Olcott avers, "in the most dismal want, having . . . to boil her coffee-dregs over and over again for lack of pence for buying a fresh supply; and to keep off starvation, at last had to work with her needle for a maker of cravats."10 During this interval she was lodged in a wretched tenement house in the East Side, and made cravats for a kindly old Jew, whose help at this time she never forgot.11 In her squalid quarters she was sought out by a veteran journalist, Miss Anna Ballard, in search of copy for a Russian story. She received, in late October, a legacy from the estate of her father, who had died early in that month. A draft of one thousand rubles was first sent her, and later the entire sum bequeathed to her. Then in affluence she moved to better quarters, first to Union Square, then to East 16th Street, then to Irving Place. But her money did not abide in her keeping long. In regard to the sources of her income after her patrimony had been flung generously to the winds, we are told, upon Col.

Olcott's pledged honor, that both his and her wants, after the organization of the Theosophical Society, were frequently provided for by the occult ministrations of the Masters. He claims that during the many years of their joint campaigns for Theosophy, especially in India, the treasure-chest at headquarters, after having been depleted, would be found supplied with funds from unknown sources. Shopping one day in New York with Colonel, she made purchases to the amount of about fifty dollars. He paid the bills. On returning home she thrust some banknotes into his hand, saying: "There are your fifty dollars." He is certain she had no money of her own, and no visitor had come in from whom she could have borrowed. Once during this period she created the duplicate of a thousand dollar note while it was held in the hand of the Hon.

John L. O'Sullivan, formerly Ambassador to Portugal; but it faded away during the two following days. Its serial number was identical with that of its prototype. The knowledge that financial help would come at need, however, did not dispose Madame Blavatsky to relax her effort toward her own sustenance.12 During this time, and for nearly all the remainder of her life, the Russian noblewoman spent large stretches of her time in writing occult, mystic, and scientific articles for Russian periodicals. This constituted her main source of income. Col. Olcott states that her Russian articles were so highly prized that "the conductor of the most important of their reviews actually besought her to write constantly for it, on terms as high as they gave Turgenev."13

A chronicle of her life during this epoch may not omit her second marriage, which proved ill-fated at the first. It came about as follows: A Mr. B., a Russian subject, learning of her psychic gifts through Col. Olcott, asked the Colonel to arrange for him a meeting with his countrywoman. He proceeded to fall into a profound state of admiration for Madame Blavatsky, which deepened though he was persistently rebuffed, and he finally threatened to take his life unless she would relent. He proclaimed his motives to be only protective, and expressly waived a husband's claims to the privileges of married life. In what appears to have been madness or some sort of desperation, she agreed finally, on these

terms, to be his wife. Even then it was specified that she retain her own name and be free from all restraint, for the sake of her work. A Unitarian clergyman married them in Philadelphia, and they lived for some few months in a house on Sansom Street. When taken to task by her friend Olcott, she explained that it was a misfortune to which she was doomed by an inexorable Karma; that it was a punishment to her for a streak of pride which was hindering her spiritual development; but that it would result in no harm to the young man. The husband forgot his earlier protestations of Platonic detachment, and became an importunate lover. Madame Blavatsky developed a dangerous illness at this time as a result of a fall upon an icy sidewalk in New York the previous winter, and her knee became so violently inflamed that a partial mortification of the leg set in. The physician declared that nothing but instant amputation could save her life; but she discarded his advice, called upon that source of help which had come to her in a number of exigencies, recovered immediately and left her husband's "bed and board." He, after some months of waiting, saw her obduracy and procured a divorce on the ground of desertion.14

During the latter part of her stay in New York she and Col. Olcott took an apartment of seven rooms at the corner of 47th Street and 8th Avenue, which came to be called "The Lamasery," in jocular reference to her Tibetan connections. "The Lamasery" became a social and intellectual center during her residence there. Col. Olcott says:

"... her mirthfulness, epigrammatic wit, brilliance of conversation, careless friendliness to those she liked ..., her fund of anecdote, and, chiefest attraction to most of her callers, her amazing psychical phenomena, made the 'Lamasery' the most attractive salon of the metropolis from 1876 to the close of 1878."15

Madame spent her day-hours in writing, her custom for years; and held open house for visitors in the evening. There was always discussion of one or another aspect of occult philosophy, in which she naturally took the commanding part.

She would pour out an endless flow of argument and supporting data, augmented at favorable times by a sudden exhibition of magical power. She seemed tireless in her psychic energy.

Several persons have left good word-pictures of her. Col. Olcott graphically describes her appearance upon the occasion of their first meeting in the old Eddy farmhouse, in Vermont, where they both came in '74 to study the "spooks." Col. Olcott had been on the scene for some time, as a representative of the New York Daily Graphic, when Madame Blavatsky arrived. He was struck by her general appearance, and he contrived to introduce himself to her through the medium of a gallant offer of a light for her cigarette.

"It was a massive Kalmuc face," he writes, "contrasting in its suggestion of power, culture and impressiveness, as strangely with the commonplace visages about the room, as her red garment did with the gray and white tones of the wall and the woodwork, and the dull costumes of the rest of the guests. All sorts of cranky people were continually coming and going at Eddy's, and it only struck me, on seeing this eccentric lady, that this was but one more of the sort.

Pausing on the doorstep I whispered to Kappes, 'Good Gracious! Look at that specimen, will you!'"16

In her autobiography the Princess Helene von Racowitza makes some interesting references to Madame Blavatsky, whom she knew intimately.

"I discovered in her the most remarkable being (for one hardly dare designate her with the simple name of woman). She gave me new life; . . . she brought new interest into my existence. Regarding her personal appearance, the head, which rose from the dark flowing garments, was immensely characteristic, although far more ugly than beautiful. A true Russian type, a short thick nose, prominent cheek bones, a small clever mobile mouth, with little fine teeth, brown and very curly hair, and almost like that of a negro's; a sallow complexion, but a pair of eyes the like of which I had never seen; pale blue, grey as water, but with a glance deep and penetrating, and as compelling as if it beheld the inner heart of things. Sometimes they held an expression as though fixed on something afar, high and immeasurably above all earthly things. She always wore long dark flowing garments and had ideally beautiful hands.

"But how shall I attempt to describe . . . her being, her power, her abilities and her character? She was a combination of the most heterogeneous qualities. By all she was considered as a sort of Cagliostro or St. Germain. She conversed with equal facility in Russian, English, French, German, Italian and certain dialects of Hindustani; yet she lacked all positive knowledge-even the most superficial European school training.

"In matters of social life she . . . joined an irresistible charm in conversation, that comprised chiefly an intense comprehension of everything noble and great, with the most original and often coarse humor, a mode of expression which was the comical despair of prudish Anglo-Saxons.

"Her contempt for and rebellion against all social conventions made her appear sometimes even coarser than was her wont, and she hated and fought conventional lying with real Don Quixotic courage. But whoever approached her in poverty or rags, hungry and needing comfort, could be sure to find in her a warm heart and an open hand. . . . No drop of wine, beer or fermented liquors ever passed her lips, and she had a most fanatical hatred of everything intoxicating. Her hospitality was genuinely Oriental. She placed everything she possessed at the disposal of her friends."17

Mr. J. Ranson Bridges, a none too kindly critic, who had considerable correspondence with her from 1888 till her death, says:

"Whatever may be the ultimate verdict upon the life and work of this woman, her place in history will be unique. There was a Titanic display of strength in everything she did. The storms that raged within her were cyclones. Those exposed to them often felt, with Solovyoff, that if there were holy and sage Mahatmas, they could not remain holy and sage and have anything to do with Helena Petrovna Blavatsky. Yet she could be as tender and sympathetic as any mother. Her mastery of some natures seemed complete. . . . To these disciples she was the greatest thaumaturgist known to the world since the time of Christ."18

In a moment of gayety she once dashed off the following description of herself:

"An old woman, whether 40, 50, 60 or 90 years old, it matters not; an old woman whose Kalmuco-Buddhisto-Tartaric features, even in youth, never made her appear pretty; a woman whose ungainly garb, uncouth manners, and masculine habits are enough to frighten any bustled and corseted fine lady of fashionable society out of her wits."19

For all her psychic insight, she seemed unable to protect herself against those who fawned upon her, cultivated her society, and then repaid her by desertion or

slander. She was open to any one who professed occult interest, and she readily took up with many such persons who later became bitter critics.

Much ado was made by delicate ladies in her day of her cigarette addiction. Her evident masculinity, her lack of many of the niceties which ladies commonly affect, her scorn of conventions, her failure to put on the airs of a woman of noble rank, her occasional coarse language, and her violence of temper over petty things, have led many people to infer that the message that she brought could not have been pure and lofty.

Theosophists put forward an explanation of her irascibility and nervous instability, in a theory which must sound exotic to the uninitiated. They state that when she studied in Tibet under her Masters, and was initiated into the mysteries of their occult knowledge, they extricated, by processes in which they are alleged to be adepts, one of her astral bodies and retained it so as to be able to maintain, through an etheric radio vibration, a constant line of communication with her in any part of the world. This left her in a state of unstable equilibrium nervously, and rendered her subject to a greater degree of irritation than would normally have been the case.

Madame Blavatsky's life story, covered now in its outward phases, is not complete without consideration of that remarkable series of psychic phenomena which give inner meaning to her career. In and of themselves they form a narrative of great interest, on a par with the legendary lives of many other saints. The story is a long one; a complete record of all her wonder-working, as told in the Theosophic accounts, would alone fill the space of this volume. A digest of this material must be made here, though a critical examination is, as said above, not attempted.

When, in 1858, she returned home from her first exile of ten years, Spiritualism was just looming on the horizon of Europe. Nothing seems to be mentioned in the several biographical sketches, of her coming in contact with the sweep of the Spiritualistic wave that was at full height in the United States during the early fifties, when she passed through that country. However the case may be, she returned home in 1858 with her occult powers already fully developed, and proceeded to make frequent display of them.

At Pskoff, with her sister's husband's family, the Yahontoff's, raps, knocks, and other sounds occurred incessantly; furniture moved without any contact; particles changed their weight; and either absent living folk or the dead were seen both by herself and her relatives many times. Wherever the young woman went "things" happened. Laughing at the continued recurrence of these mysterious activities, she averred to her sisters that she could make them cease or redouble their frequency and power, by the sheer force of her own will.20 The psychic demonstrations supposedly took place in entire independence of her coöperation, but she could, if she chose, interject her will and assume control. Her sister, Madame de Jelihowsky, remembers Helena's laughing when addressed as a medium, and assuring her friends that "she was no medium, but only a mediator between mortals and beings we know nothing about."21 The reports of her wonderful exploits following her arrival at Pskoff in 1858 threw that town into a swirl of excited gossip. There was a great deal of fashionable company at the Yahontoff home in those days. Madame's presence itself attracted many. Seldom did any of the numerous callers go away unsatisfied, for to their inquiries the raps gave answer, often long ones in different languages, some of which were not in Madame Blavatsky's repertoire. The willing "medium" was subjected to every kind of test, to which she submitted gracefully.

An instance of her power was her mystification of her own brother, Leonide de Hahn. A company was gathered in the drawing room, and Leonide was walking leisurely about, unconcerned with the stunts which his gifted sister was producing for the diversion of the visitors. He stopped behind the girl's chair just as some one was telling how magicians change the avoirdupois of objects. "And you mean to say that you can do it?" he asked his sister ironically. "Mediums can, and I have done it occasionally," was the reply. "But would you try?" some one asked. "I will try, but promise nothing." Hereupon one of the young men advanced and lifted a light chess table with great ease. Madame then told them to leave it alone and stand back. She was not near it herself. In the expectant silence that ensued she merely looked intently at the table. Then she invited the same young man who had just lifted it to do so again. He tried, with great assurance of his ability, but could not stir the table an inch. He grew red with the effort, but without avail. The brother, thinking that his sister had arranged the play with his friend as a little joke on him, now advanced. "May I also try?" he asked her. "Please do, my dear," she laughed. He seized the table and struggled; whereat his smile vanished. Try as he would, his effort was futile. Others tried it with the same result. After a while Helena urged Leonide to try it once more. He lifted it now with no effort.

A few months later, Madame Blavatsky, her father and sister, having left Pskoff and lodging at a hotel in St. Petersburg, were visited by two old friends of Col. Hahn, both now much interested in Spiritualism. After witnessing some of Helena's performances, the two guests expressed great surprise at the father's continued apathy toward his daughter's abilities. After some bantering they began to insist that he should at least consent to an experiment, before denying the importance of the phenomena. They suggested that he retire to an adjoining room, write a word on a slip of paper, conceal it and see if his daughter could persuade the raps to reveal it. The old gentleman consented, believing he could discredit the foolish nonsense, as he termed it, once for all. He retired, wrote the word and returned, venturing in his confidence the assertion that if this experiment were successful, he "would believe in the devil, undines, sorcerers, and witches, in the whole paraphernalia, in short, of old woman's superstitions; and you may prepare to offer me as an inmate of a lunatic asylum."22 He went on with his solitaire in a corner, while the friends took note of the raps now beginning. The younger sister was repeating the alphabet, the raps sounding at the desired letter; one of the visitors marked it down. Madame Blavatsky did nothing apparently. By this means one single word was got, but it seemed so grotesque and meaningless that a sense of failure filled the minds of the experimenters. Questioning whether that one word was the entire message, the raps sounded "Yes-yes-yes!" The younger girl then turned to her father and told them that they had got but one word. "Well what is it?" he demanded. "Zaïchik."23 It was a sight indeed to witness the change that came over the old man's face at hearing this one word. He became deadly pale. Adjusting his spectacles with a trembling hand, he stretched it out, saying, "Let me see it!

Hand it over. Is it really so?" He took the slips of paper and read in a very agitated voice "Zaïchik." Yes; Zaïchik; so it is. How very strange!" Taking out of his pocket the paper he had written on in the next room, he handed it in silence to his daughter and guests. On it they found he had written: "What was the name of my favorite horse which I rode during my first Turkish campaign?" And lower down, in parenthesis, the answer,--" Zaïchik."

The old Colonel, now assured there was more than child's play in his daughter's pretensions, rushed into the region of phenomena with great zeal. He did not matriculate at an asylum; instead he set Helena to work investigating his family tree. He was stimulated to this inquiry by having received the date of a certain event in his ancestral history of several hundred years before, which he verified by reference to old documents. Scores of historical events connected with his family were now given him; names unheard of, relationships unknown, positions held, marriages, deaths; and all were found on painstaking research to have been correct in every item! All this information was given rapidly and unhesitatingly. The investigation lasted for months.

In the spring of 1858 both sisters were living with their father in the country-house in a village belonging to Mme. Yahontoff. In consequence of a murder committed near their property, the Superintendent of the District Police passed through the villages and stopped at their house to make some inquiries. No one in the village knew who had committed the crime. During tea, as all were sitting around the table, the raps came, and there were the usual disturbances around the room. Col. Hahn suggested to the Superintendent that he had better try his daughter's invisible helpers for information. He laughed incredulously. He had heard of "spirits," he said, but was derisive of their ability to give information in "a real case." This scorn of her powers caused the young girl to desire to humble the arrogant officer. She turned fiercely upon him. "And suppose I prove to you the contrary?" she defiantly asked him. "Then," he answered, "I would resign my office and offer it to you, Madame, or, better still, I would strongly urge the authorities to place you at the head of the Secret

Police Department." "Now look here, Captain," she said indignantly. "I do not like meddling in such dirty business and helping you detectives. Yet, since you defy me, let my father say over the alphabet and you put down the letters and record what will be rapped out. My presence is not needed for this, and with your permission I shall even leave the room." She went out, with a book, to read. The inquiry in the next room produced the name of the murderer, the fact that he had crossed over into the next district and was then hiding in the hay in the loft of a peasant, Andrew Vlassof, in the village of Oreshkino. Further information was elicited to the effect that the murderer was an old soldier on leave; he was drunk and had quarreled with his victim. The murder was not premeditated; rather a misfortune than a crime. The Superintendent rushed precipitately out of the house and drove off to Oreshkino, more than 30 miles distant. A letter came by courier the following morning saying that everything given by the raps had proved absolutely correct. This incident produced a great uproar in the district and Madame's work was viewed in a more serious light. Her family, however, had some difficulty convincing the more distant authorities that they had no natural means of being familiar with the crime.

One evening while all sat in the dining room, loud chords of music were struck on the closed piano in the next room, visible to all through the open door. On another occasion Madame's tobacco pouch, her box of matches and her handkerchief came rushing to her through the air, upon a mere look from her. Many visitors to her apartment in later years witnessed this same procedure. Again, one evening, all lights were suddenly extinguished, an amazing noise was heard, and though a match was struck in a moment, all the heavy furniture was found overturned on the floor. The locked piano played a loud march. The manifestations taking place when the home circle was unmixed with visitors were usually of the most pronounced character.

Sometimes there were alleged communications from the spirits of historical personages, not the inevitable Napoleon and Cleopatra, but Socrates, Cicero and Martin Luther, and they ranged from great power and vigor of thought to almost flippant silliness. Some from the shade of the Russian poet Pushkin were quite beautiful.

While the family read aloud the Memoirs of Catherine Romanovna Dashkoff, they were interrupted many times by the alleged spirit of the authoress herself, interjecting remarks, making additions, offering explanations and refutations.

In the early part of 1859 the sister, Madame Jelihowsky, inherited a country village from the estate of her late husband at Rougodevo, and there the family, including Helena, went to reside for a period. No one in the party had ever known any of the previous occupants of the estate. Soon after settling down in the old mansion, Madame discerned the shades of half a dozen of the former inhabitants in one of the unoccupied wings and described them to her sister.
Seeking out several old servants, she found that every one of the wraiths could be identified and named by the aged domestics. The young woman's description of one man was that he had long finger nails, like a Chinaman's. The servant stated that one of the former residents had contracted a disease in Lithuania, which renders cutting of the nails a certain road to death through bleeding.

Sometimes the other members of the family would converse with the rapping forces without disturbing Helena at all. The forces played more strongly than every, it seemed, when Madame was asleep or sick. A physician once attending her illness was almost frightened away by the noises and moving furniture in the bedroom.

A terrible illness befell her near the end of the stay at Rougodevo. Years before, her relatives believed during her solitary travels over the steppes of Asia, she had received a wound. This wound reopened occasionally, and then she suffered intense agony, which lasted three or four days and then the wound would heal as suddenly as it had opened, and her illness would vanish. On one occasion a physician was called; but he proved of little use, because the prodigious phenomena which he witnessed left him almost powerless to act. Having examined the wound, the patient being prostrated and unconscious, he saw a large dark hand between his own and the wound he was about to dress. The wound was near the heart, and the hand moved back and forth between the neck and the waist. To make the apparition worse, there came in the room a terrific noise, from ceiling, floor, windows, and furniture, so that the poor man begged not to be left alone in the room with the patient.

In the spring of 1860 the two sisters left Rougodevo for a visit to their grandparents in the south of Russia, and during the long slow journey many incidents took place. At one station, where a surly, half-drunken station-master refused to lend them a fresh relay of horses, and there was no fit room for their accommodation over the night, Helena terrified him into sense and reason by whispering into his ear some strange secret of his, which he believed no one knew and which it was to his interest to keep hidden.

At Jadonsk, where a halt was made, they attended a church service, where the prelate, the famous and learned Isidore, who had known them in childhood, recognized them and invited them to visit him at the Metropolitan's house. He received them when they came with great kindliness; but hardly had they entered the drawing room than a terrible hubbub of noise and raps burst forth in every direction. Every piece of furniture strained and cracked, rocked and thumped.

The women were confused by this demoniacal demonstration in the presence of the amazed Churchman, though the culprit in the case was hardly able to repress her sense of humor. But the priest saw the embarrassment of his guests and understood the cause of it. He inquired which of the two women possessed such strange potencies. He was told. Then he asked permission to put to her invisible guide a mental question. She assented. His query, a serious one, received an instant reply, precise and to the point; and he was so struck with it all that he detained his visitors for over three hours. He continued his conversation

with the unseen presences and paid unstinted tribute to their seeming all- knowledge. His farewell words to his gifted guest were:

"As for you, let not your heart be troubled by the gift you are possessed of . . . for it was surely given to you for some purpose, and you could not be held responsible for it. Quite the reverse! For if you but use it with discrimination you will be enabled to do much good to your fellow-creatures."

Her occult powers grew at this period to their full development, and she seemed to have completed the subjection of every phase of manifestation to her own volitional control. Her fame throughout the Caucasus increased, breeding both hostility and admiration. She had risen above the necessity of resorting to the slow process of raps, and read people's states and gave them answers through her own clairvoyance. She seemed able, she said, to see a cloud around people in whose luminous substance their thoughts took visible form. The purely sporadic phenomena were dying away.

Her illness at the end of her stay in Mingrelia has already been noted. A psychic experience of unusual nature even for her, through which she passed during this severe sickness, seems to have marked a definite epoch in her occult development. She apparently acquired the ability from that time to step out of her physical body, investigate distant scenes or events, and bring back reports to her normal consciousness. Sometimes she felt herself as now one person, H. P. Blavatsky, and again some one else. Returning to her own personality she could remember herself as the other character, but while functioning as the other person she could not remember herself as Madame Blavatsky. She later wrote of these experiences: "I was in another far-off country, a totally different individuality from myself, and had no connection at all with my actual life."24 The sickness, prostrated her and appears to have brought a crisis in her inner life. She herself felt that she had barely escaped the fate that she afterwards spoke of as befalling so many mediums. She wrote in a letter to a relative:

"The last vestige of my psycho-physical weakness is gone, to return no more. I am cleansed and purified of that dreadful attraction to myself of stray spooks and ethereal affinities. I am free, free, thanks to Those whom I now bless at every hour of my life." (Her Guardians in Tibet.)25

Madame Jelihowsky writes too:

"After her extraordinary and protracted illness at Tiflis she seemed to defy and subject the manifestations entirely to her will. In short, it is the firm belief of all that there where a less strong nature would have been surely wrecked in the struggle, her indomitable will found somehow or other the means of subjecting the world of the invisibles-to the denizens of which she had ever refused the name of 'spirits' and souls-to her own control."26

As a sequel to this experience her conception of a great and definite mission in the world formulated itself before her vision. It is seen to provide the motive for her abortive enterprise in Cairo in 1871; it is again seen to be operative in her propagation of Theosophy in 1875. It will be considered more at length in the discussion of her connection with American Spiritualism.

By 1871 her power in certain phases had been greatly enhanced. She was able, merely by looking fixedly at objects, to set them in motion. In an illustrated paper of the time there was a story of her by a gentleman, who met her with some friends in a hotel at Alexandria. After dinner he engaged her in a long discussion. Before them stood a little tea tray, on which the waiter had placed

a bottle of liquor, some wine, a wine glass and a tumbler. As the gentleman raised the glass to his lips it broke to pieces in his hands. Madame Blavatsky laughed at the occurrence, remarking that she hated liquor and could hardly tolerate those who drank. He knew the glass was thick and strong, but, to draw her out, declared it must have been an accidental crumbling of a thin glass in his grasp. "What do you bet I do not do it again?" she flashed at him. He then half-filled another tumbler. In his own words:

"But no sooner had the glass touched my lips than I felt it shattered between my fingers, and my hand bled, wounded by a broken piece in my instinctive act of grasping the tumbler together when I felt myself losing hold of it."

"Entre les lèvres et la coupe, il y a quelquefois une grande distance," she observed, and left the room, laughing in his face "most outrageously."27

Another gentleman, a Russian, who encountered her in Egypt, sent the most enthusiastic letters to his friends about her wonders.

"She is a marvel, an unfathomable mystery. That which she produces is simply phenomenal; and without believing any more in spirits than I ever did, I am ready to believe in witchcraft. If it is after all but jugglery, then we have in Madame Blavatsky a woman who beats all the Boscos and Robert Houdin's of the country by her address. . . . Once I showed her a closed medallion containing a portrait of one person and the hair of another, an object which I had had in my possession but a few months, which was made at Moscow, and of which very few knew, and she told me without touching it: 'Oh! It is your godmother's portrait and your cousin's hair. Both are dead,' and she proceeded forthwith to describe them, as though she had both before her eyes. How could she know?"28

At Cairo she wrote her sister Vera that she had seen the astral forms of two of the family's domestics and chided her sister for not having written her about their death during her absence. She described the hospital in which one of them had passed away, and other circumstances connected with their history since she had last been in touch with them. It was only afterwards that she learned that when her letter from Egypt was received by Madame Jelihowsky, the latter was herself not aware of the death of the two servants. Upon inquiry she found every circumstance in relation to their late years and their death precisely as Helena had depicted it.

Upon Madame Blavatsky's arrival in America her open espousal of the cause of Theosophy was prefaced by much work done in and for the Spiritualistic movement. Col. Olcott has brought out the fact that the phenomena taking place at the Eddy farmhouse in Vermont in 1873 changed character quite decidedly the day she entered the household. Up to the time of her appearance on the scene the figures that had shown themselves were either Red Indians or Americans or Europeans related to some one present. But on the first evening of her stay spirits of other nationalities came up. A Georgian servant body from the Caucasus, a Mussulman merchant from Tiflis, a Russian peasant girl, and others, appeared.
Later a Kurdish cavalier and a devilish-looking Negro sorcerer from Africa joined the motley group.

From the Vermont homestead Madame Blavatsky went to New York, where Col. Olcott joined her shortly afterwards. Rappings and messages were much in evidence during this sojourn in the metropolis, the disembodied intelligence in the background purporting to be one "John King," a name familiar to all spiritists for many years before. The spirit finally declared itself to be the earth-haunting soul of Sir Henry Morgan, famous buccaneer, and so showed itself to the

sight of Col. Olcott during the séances with the Holmes mediums some months later in Philadelphia. From him as ostensible source came many messages both grave and gay.

All the while Madame Blavatsky posed as a Spiritualist and mingled in the Holmes séances in Philadelphia for the purpose of lending some of her own power to the rather feeble demonstrations effected by Mr. and Mrs. Holmes to bolster their reputation in the face of Robert Dale Owen's public denunciation of them as cheats. She says that on one occasion Mrs. Holmes was herself frightened at the real appearance of spirits summoned by herself.

One of the first indications Col. Olcott was to have of the interest of her distant sages in his own career was shown during the time that Madame Blavatsky was in Philadelphia. At her urgent invitation the Colonel determined quite suddenly to run over and spend a few days with her. On the evening of the same day on which he left his address at the Philadelphia Post Office the postman brought him several letters from widely distant places, all bearing the stamp of the sending station, but none that of the receiving station, New York. They were addressed to him at his New York office address, yet had come straight to him at Philadelphia without passing through the New York office. And nobody in New York knew his Philadelphia address. He took them himself from the postman's hand; so they could not have been tampered with by his occult friend. But the marvel did not end there. Upon opening them he found inside each something written in the same handwriting as that in letters he had received in New York from the Masters, the writing having been made either in the margins or on any other space left blank by the writers.

"These were the precursors of a whole series of those phenomenal surprises during the fortnight or so that I spent in Philadelphia. I had many, and no letter of the lot bore the New York stamp, though all were addressed to me at my office in that city."29

The series of vivid phenomena which took place during the Philadelphia visit may be listed briefly as follows:

1.-Col. Olcott purchased a note-book in which to record the rap messages. On taking it out of the store wrapper he found inside the first cover: "John King, Henry de Morgan, his book, 4th of the fourth month in A.D. 1875." And underneath this was a whole pictorial design of Rosicrucian symbols, the word Fate, the name Helen, the phrase "Way of Providence," a monogram, a pair of compasses, and various letters and signs. No one had touched it since its purchase at the stationary shop.

2.-Madame Blavatsky caused a photograph on the wall to disappear suddenly from its frame and give place to a sketch portrait of "John King" while a spectator was looking at it.

3.-Col. Olcott had bought a dozen unhemmed towels. As his companion was no seamstress, he bantered her to let an elemental do the hemstitching on the lot. She told him to put the towels, needle and thread inside a bookcase, which had glass doors curtained with green silk. He did so. After twenty minutes she announced that the job was finished. He found them actually, if crudely, hemmed. It was four P.M., and no other persons were in the room.

4.-Madame Blavatsky once suddenly disappeared from the Colonel's sight, could not be seen for a period, and then as suddenly reappeared. She could not explain to him how she did it.

5.-The increase overnight in the length of her hair, of about four to five inches, and its later recession to its normal length.

6.-The projection of a drawing of a man's head on the ceiling above the Colonel's head, where he had seen nothing a minute before.

7.-The precipitation by "John King," in answer to the Colonel's challenge to duplicate a letter he had in his pocket, of the said duplicate, correct in every word.

8.-The precipitation of a letter into the traveling bag of a Mr. B. while on the train, the letter not having been packed there originally.

9.-The same Mr. B. begged Madame Blavatsky to create for him a portrait of his deceased grandmother. She went to the window, put a blank piece of paper against the pane, and handed it to him in a moment with the portrait of a little old woman with many wrinkles and a large wart, which Mr. B. declared a perfect likeness of his ancestor.

10.-The actual production by an Italian artist, through "his control of the spirits of the air," during one evening of entirely clear sky, of a small shower of rain, sufficient to wet the sidewalks. Previously Madame Blavatsky had created a butterfly, following a similar production by the Italian visitor.

11.-The materialization by Madame Blavatsky of a heavy gold ring in the heart of a rose which had been "created" shortly before by Mrs. Thayer, a medium whom Col. Olcott was testing with a view to sending her to Russia for experimentation at a university there.

12.-The Colonel's own beard grew in one night from his chin down to his chest.30

After the return from Philadelphia psychic events continued with great frequency at the apartments in New York. In December of 1875, Madame Blavatsky, having invited a challenge to reproduce the portrait of the Chevalier Louis, reputed Adept author of Mrs. Emma Hardinge Britten's Art Magic, rubbed her hand over a sheet of paper and the desired photograph appeared on the under side. She had laid the bare sheet on the surface of the table. Col. Olcott had the opportunity nine years later of comparing this reproduction with the original photograph of the Chevalier Louis, and found the likeness perfect, yet the lines would not meet precisely when the one was superimposed on the other. It could not have been a lithographic reproduction.

Early in 1878, Mr. O'Sullivan asked Madame Blavatsky for one of a chaplet of large wooden beads which she was wearing. She placed one in a bowl and produced the bowlful of them.

For the same gentleman in plain sight of several people, she triplicated a beautiful handkerchief which he had admired.

To amuse the child of a caller, an English Spiritualist, one day she produced a large toy sheep mounted on wheels. Col. Olcott claimed it had not been there a moment before.

On Christmas eve of that year when she and the Colonel, went to his sister's apartment, Madame expressed regret that she had brought nothing for the youngsters. But saying, "Wait a minute," she took her bunch of keys from her

pocket, clutched three of them together in one hand, and a moment later showed the party a large iron whistle hanging on the ring instead of the three keys. Col. Olcott had to get three new keys from a locksmith.

Another time to placate a little girl Madame promised her "a nice present," and indicated to Col. Olcott that he should take it out of their luggage bag in the hall. He unlocked the already stuffed bag and immediately on top was a harmonica, or glass piano, about fifteen inches by four in size, with its cork mallet beside it. Colonel had himself packed the bag, having to use all his strength to close it, had reopened it on the train, and there was not a moment when his friend could have slipped an object of such size into it.

It was in New York at this epoch that she took Col. Olcott's large signet ring, rubbed it in her hands and presently handed him his original and another like it except that the new one was mounted with a dark green bloodstone, whereas the original was set with a red carnelian. That ring she wore till her death, and it has since been the valued possession of Mrs. Annie Besant.

Once, in Boston, Madame walked through the streets in a pelting rain and reached her lodgings without the trace of dampness or mud on her dress or shoes.

Similarly the Colonel found a handsome velvet-covered chair entirely dry, not even damp, after being left out all night in a driving rain.

One time when the two were talking about three members of the Colonel's family, a crash was heard in the next room. Rushing in he found that the photograph of one of the three had been turned face inward, the large water-color picture of another lay smashed on the floor, while the photograph of the third was unmolested.

Madame once made instantly a copy of a scurrilous letter received by the Colonel from a person who had done him an injustice. Again she duplicated a five-page letter from the eminent Spiritualist, W. Stainton Moses. There was not time for the receipt of the letter until its duplication for any one to have copied it.

The second sheets were copies, but not strictly duplicate, as the lines would not match when the two were placed together and held before the light.

At "The Lamasery" she produced an entire set of watercolors, which Mr. W. Q. Judge needed in making an Egyptian drawing. Next he needed some gold paint, whereupon she took a brass key, scraped it over the bottom of an empty saucer, and found the required paint instantly. The brass key was not consumed in the process, but was needed, she explained, to help aggregate the atomic material for the gold color.

When Olcott stated one evening that he would like to hear from one of the Adepts (in India) upon a certain subject, Madame told him to write his questions, seal them in an envelope, and place it where he could watch it. He did so, putting it behind the clock on the mantel, with one end projecting in plain view. The two went on talking for an hour, when she announced that the answer had come. He drew out his own envelope, the seal unbroken, found inside it his own letter, and inside that the Mahatma's answer in the script familiar to him, written on a sheet of green paper, such as he had not had in the house.

Through her agency the portrait of the Rev. W. Stainton Moses was precipitated on satin. It was a distinct likeness, and the head was rayed around with spiculae of light. It was surrounded with rolling clouds of vapor, his astral vehicle.

Olcott, Judge and a Dr. Marquette one evening asked her to produce the portrait of a particular Hindu Yogi on some stationery of the Lotus Club that the Colonel had brought home that same evening. She scraped some lead from a pencil on a half sheet of the paper, laid the other half-sheet over it, placed them between her hands, and showed the result. The likeness to the original could not be verified, but it was pronounced by Le Clear, the noted portrait painter, to be one "that no living artist within his knowledge could have produced."

Once Col. Olcott desired a picture of his Guru, or Hindu teacher, as yet unseen by him, and Madame essayed to have it painted through the hand of a French artist, M. Herisse. The artist's only instructions were that his subject was a Hindu. Madame concentrated, and he painted. The features, finished in an hour, were afterwards vouched for by Col. Olcott as being the likeness of his Guru, whom he met years later.

The Colonel testified to having seen Madame Blavatsky's astral form in a New York street while she was in Philadelphia; also that of a friend of his then in the South; again that of one of the Adepts, then in Asia, in an American railway train and on a steamboat. He stated that he took from the hand of another Mahatma at Jummu a telegram from H.P.B.31 who was in Madras, the messenger vanishing a moment later; and that he, H.P.B. and Damodar, a young Hindu devotee of hers, were greeted by one of these Teachers one evening in India. But the occurrence of this kind which he regarded as the most striking, affecting as it did his whole future career, happened at the close of one of his busy days, when his evening's toil with the composition of Isis was finished. He had retired to his own room and was reading, the room door locked. Suddenly he perceived a white radiance at his side and turning saw towering above him the great stature of an Oriental, clad in white garments and wearing a head-cloth of amber-striped fabric, hand-embroidered in yellow floss silk.

"Long raven hair hung from under his turban to the shoulders; his black beard, parted vertically on the chin in the Rajput fashion, was twisted up at the ends and carried over the ears; his eyes were alive with soul-fire; eyes which were at once benignant and piercing in glance; the eyes of a mentor and judge, but softened by the love of a father who gazes on a son needing counsel and guidance. He was so grand a man, so imbued with the majesty of moral strength, so luminously spiritual, so evidently above average humanity, that I felt abashed in his presence, and bowed my head and bent my knee as one does before a god or a god-like personage. A hand was laid lightly on my head, a sweet though strong voice bade me be seated, and when I raised my eyes the Presence was seated in the other chair beyond the table. He told me that he had come at the crisis when I needed him; that my actions had brought me to this point; that it lay with me alone whether he and I should meet often in this life as coworkers for the good of mankind; that a great work was to be done for humanity and I had the right to share in it if I wished; that a mysterious tie, not now to be explained to me, had drawn my colleague and myself together; a tie which could not be broken, however strained it might be at times."32

Then he arose and reading the Colonel's sudden but unexpressed wish that he might leave behind him some token of his visit, he untwisted the fehta from his head, laid it on the table, saluted benignantly and was gone.

Many a time, according to the Colonel's version, they were regaled with most exquisite music, or single bell sounds, coming from anywhere in the room and softly dying away.

Olcott tells of the deposit of one thousand dollars to his bank account by a person described by the bank clerk as a Hindu, while he (Olcott) was absent from the city for two months on business which he had undertaken at the behest of the Master through H.P.B. He had told her that his errand would cost him about five hundred dollars per month through his neglect of his business for the time.

In 1878 the Countess Paschkoff brought to light an adventure which she had had years before while traveling with Madame Blavatsky in the Libanus. The two women encountered each other in the desert and camped together one night near the river Orontes. Nearby stood a great monument on the border of the village. The Countess asked Madame to tell her the history of the monument.

At night the thaumaturgist built a fire, drew a circle about it and repeated several "spells." Soon balls of white flame appeared on the monument, then from a cloud of vapor emerged the spirit of the person to whom it had been dedicated. "Who are you?" asked the woman. "I am Hiero, one of the priests of the temple," said the voice of the spirit.

He then showed them the temple in the midst of a vast city. Then the image vanished and the priest with it.

To round out the story of her phenomena it is necessary to relate with the utmost brevity the incidents of the kind that transpired from the time of the departure from America to India at the end of 1878 until the latter days of her life. This narrative will include occurrences taking place in India, France, Germany, and England.

It was in India that the so-called Mahatma Letters were precipitated, upon which the basic structure of Theosophy is seen to rest. Mr. A. P. Sinnett, British journalist, editor of "The Pioneer," living in India, is the main authority for the events of the Indian period in Madame Blavatsky's life.

During the first visit of six weeks to Mr. Sinnett's home at Allahabad there were comparatively few incidents, apart from raps. A convincing exploit of her power was granted, however, for one evening while the party was sitting in the large hall of the house of the Maharajah of Vizianagaram at Benares, three or four large cut roses fell from the ceiling. The ceiling was bare and the room well lighted.

About the beginning of September 1880 she visited the Sinnetts at their home in Simla. Here some more striking incidents took place. During an evening walk with Mrs. Sinnett to a neighboring hilltop, Madame, in response to a suddenly- expressed wish of her companion, obtained for her a little note from one of the "Brothers." Madame had torn off a blank corner of a sheet of a letter received that day and held it in her hand for the Master's use. It disappeared. Then Mrs. Sinnett was asked where she would like the paper to reappear. She whimsically pointed up into a tree a little to one side. Clambering up into the branches she found the same little corner of pink paper sticking on a sharp twig, now containing a brief message and signed by some Tibetan characters.

A little later the most spectacular of the marvels said to have been performed by the "Messenger of the Great White Brotherhood" took place. A picnic party to the woods some miles distant was planned one morning and six persons prepared to set off. Lunches were packed for six, but a seventh person unexpectedly joined the group at the moment of departure. As the luncheon was unpacked for the noontide meal, there was a shortage of a coffee cup and saucer. Some one laughingly suggested that Madame should materialize an extra set. Madame Blavatsky held a moment's mental communication with one of her distant Brothers

and then indicated a particular spot, covered with grass, weeds, and shrubbery. A gentleman of the party, with a knife, undertook to dig at the spot. A little persistence brought him shortly to the rim of a white object, which proved to be a cup, and close to it was a saucer, both of the design matching the other six brought along from the Sinnett cupboard. The plant roots around the China pieces were manifestly undisturbed by recent digging such as would have been necessary if they had been "planted" in anticipation of their being needed. Moreover, when the party reached home and Mrs.

Sinnett counted their supply of cups and saucers of that design, the new ones were found to be additional to their previous stock. And none of that design could have been purchased in Simla.33

Before this same party had disbanded it was permitted to witness another feat of equal strangeness. The gentleman who had dug up the buried pottery was so impressed that he decided then and there to join the Theosophical Society. As Col. Olcott, President of the Society, was in the party, all that was needed was the usual parchment diploma. Madame Blavatsky agreed to ask the Master to produce such a document for them. In a moment all were told to search in the underbrush. It was soon found and used in the induction ceremony.

This eventful picnic brought forth still another wonder.

Every one of the water bottles brought along had been emptied when the need for more coffee arose. The water in a neighborhood stream was unfit. A servant, sent across the fields to obtain some at a brewery, stupidly returned without any. In the dilemma Madame Blavatsky took one of the empty bottles, placed it in one of the baskets, and in a moment took it out filled with good water.

Some days later the famous "brooch" incident occurred. The Sinnett party had gone up the hill to spend an evening with Mr. and Mrs. A. O. Hume, who were likewise much interested in the Blavatskian theories. Eleven persons were seated around the table and some one hinted at the possibility of a psychic exploit.

Madame appeared disinclined, but suddenly gave a sign that the Master was himself present. Then she asked Mrs. Hume if there was anything in particular that she wished to have. Mrs. Hume thought of an old brooch which her mother had given her long ago and which had been lost. Neither she nor Mr. Hume had thought of it for years. She described it, saying it contained a lock of hair. The party was told to search for it in the garden at a certain spot; and there it was found. Mrs. Hume testified that it was the lost brooch, or one indistinguishable from it.

According to the statements of Alice Gordon, a visitor at the Sinnett home, Madame Blavatsky rolled a cigarette, and projected it ethereally to the house of a Mrs. O'Meara in another part of Simla, in advance of Miss Gordon's going thither. To identify it she tore off a small corner of the wrapper jaggedly, and gave it to Miss Gordon. The latter found it at the other home and the corner piece matched.

Captain P. J. Maitland recites a "cigarette" incident which occurred in Mr. Sinnett's drawing room. Madame took two cigarette papers, with a pencil drew several parallel lines clear across the face of both, then tore off across these lines a piece of the end of each paper and handed the short end pieces to Captain Maitland; then she rolled cigarettes out of the two larger portions, moistened them on her tongue, and caused them to disappear from her hands. The Captain was told he would find one on the piano and the other on a bracket. He found them there, still moist along the "seam," and unrolling them found that the ragged edges of the torn sections and the pencil lines exactly matched.

Some days later came the "pillow incident." Mr. Sinnett had the impression that he had been in communication with the Master one night. During the course of an outing to a nearby hill the following day, Madame Blavatsky turned to him (he had not mentioned his experience to her) and asked him where he would like some evidence of the Master's visit to him to appear. Thinking to choose a most unlikely place, he thought of the inside of a cushion against which one of the ladies was leaning. Then he changed to another. Cutting the latter open, they found among the feathers, inside two cloth casings, a little note in the now familiar Mahatma script, in the writing on which were the phrases-"the difficulty you spoke of last night" and "corresponding through-pillows!" While he was reading this his wife discovered a brooch in the feathers. It was one which she had left at home.

Perhaps it was these cigarette feats which assured Madame Blavatsky that she now had sufficient power to dispatch a long letter to her Mahatma mentors. Mr.
Sinnett first suggested the idea to her, and her success in that first attempt was the beginning of one of the most eventful and unique correspondences in the world's history. It began his exchange of letters with the Master Koot Hoomi Lal Singh (abbreviated usually to K.H.), on which Theosophy so largely rests.

On several telegrams received by Mr. Sinnett were snatches of writing in K.H.'s hand speaking of events that transpired after the telegram had been sent.
Replies were received a number of times in less time than it would have taken Madame Blavatsky to write them (instantaneously in a few cases), yet they dealt in specific detail with the material in his own missives. More than once his unexpressed doubts and queries were treated. In many cases his own letter in a sealed envelope would remain in sight and within a very short interval (thirty seconds in one instance) be found to contain the distant Master's reply, folded inside his own sheets, with an appropriate answer,--the seal not even having been broken. Sometimes he would place his letter in plain view on the table, and shortly it would be gone. For a time when the Master K.H. was called away to other business, Mr. Sinnett continued to receive communications from the brother Adept, Master Morya, while Madame Blavatsky was hundreds of miles away. They continued in the distant absence of both H.P.B. and Col. Olcott. And not only were such letters received by Mr. Sinnett, and Mr. Hume, but by other persons as well. The list includes Damodar K. Mavalankar; Ramaswamy, an educated English- speaking native of Southern India in Government service; Dharbagiri Nath; Mohini Chatterji; and Bhavani Rao. Dr. Hübbe-Schleiden received a missive of the kind later on a railway train in Germany. Mr. Sinnett would frequently find the letters on the inside of his locked desk drawers or would see them drop upon his desk. Their production was attended with all manner of remarkable circumstances.

Then there was the notable episode of the transmission by the Master of a mental message to a Mr. Eglinton, a Spiritualist, on board a vessel, the Vega, far out at sea, and the instantaneous transmission of the letter's response, written on board ship, to some of his friends in India, the whole thing done in accordance with an arrangement made by letter to Mr. Sinnett by the Adept two days before. This incident has a certain importance from the fact that the Master had said in the preliminary letter that he would visit Mr. Eglinton on the ship on a certain night, impress him with the untenability of the general Spiritualistic hypothesis regarding communications, and if possible lead him to a change of mind on the point. Mr. Eglinton's reply recorded the visit of the Mahatma on the ship and admitted the desirability of a change to the Theosophic theory of the existence of the Brothers.

An interesting chapter of events in the sojourn of the two Theosophic leaders in India is that of the thousands of healings made by Col. Olcott, who states that he was given the power by the Overlords of his activities for a limited time with a special object in view. He is said to have cured some eight thousand Hindus of various ailments by a sort of "laying on of hands." Like Christ he felt "virtue" go out of his body until exhaustion ensued; and he stated that he was instructed to recharge his nervous depletion by sitting with his back against the base of a pine tree.

In 1885 Madame Blavatsky herself experienced the healing touch of her Masters when she was ordered to meet them in the flesh north of Darjeeling. Going north on this errand, she was in the utmost despondency and near the point of death. After two days spent with the Adepts she emerged with physical health and morale restored, her dynamic self once more.

The last sheaf of "miracles" takes us from India to France, Germany, Belgium, and England. In Paris, in 1884, her rooms were the resort of many people who came if haply they might get sight of a marvel, her thaumaturgic fame being now world-wide. A Prof. Thurmann reported that in his presence she filled the air of the room with musical sounds, from a variety of instruments. She demonstrated that darkness was not necessary for such manifestations.

Madame Jelihowsky is authority for the account of the appearance and disappearance of her sister's picture in a medallion containing only the small photograph of K.H.

A most baffling display of Madame's gifts took place in the reception room of the Paris Theosophical Society on the morning of June 11th, 1884. Madame Jelihowsky, Col. Olcott, W. Q. Judge, V. Solovyoff and two others were present and attested the bona fide nature of the incident in a public letter. In sight of all a servant took a letter from the postman and brought it directly to Madame Jelihowsky. It was addressed to a lady, a relative of Madame Blavatsky, who was then visiting her, and came from another relative in Russia. Madame Blavatsky, seeing that it was a family letter, remarked that she would like to know its contents. Her sister ventured the suggestion that she read it before it was opened. Helena held the letter against her forehead and proceeded to read aloud and then write down what she said were the contents. Then, to demonstrate her power further, she declared that she would underscore her own name, wherever it occurred within the letter, in red crayon, and would precipitate in red a double interlaced triangle, or "Solomon's Seal," beneath the signature. When the addressee opened the letter, not only was H.P.B.'s version of its contents correct to the word, but the underscoring of her name and the monogram in red were found, and oddly enough, the wavering in several of the straight lines in the triangle, as drawn first by Madame Blavatsky outside the letter, were precisely matched by the red triangle inside. Postmarks indicated it had actually come from Russia.34

While at Elberfeld, Germany, with her hospitable benefactress, Madame Gebhard, some of the usual manifestations were in evidence. Mr. Rudolph Gebhard, a son, recounts several of them. One was the receipt of a letter from one of the Masters, giving intelligence about an absent member of the household, found to be correct.

The Countess Constance Wachtmeister, who became Madame Blavatsky's guardian angel, domestically speaking, during the years of the composition of The Secret Doctrine in Germany and Belgium, has printed her account of a number of extraordinary occurrences of the period. She speaks of a succession of raps in H.P.B.'s sleeping room when there was special need of her

Guardians' care. She also tells of the thrice-relighted lamp at the sleeper's bedside, she herself

having twice extinguished it. She tells of her receiving a letter from the Master, inside the store-wrapper of a bar of soap which she had just purchased at a drug store.

It was under the Countess Wachtmeister's notice that there occurred the last of Madame Blavatsky's "miraculous" restorations to health. She had suffered for years from a dropsical or renal affection, which in those latter days had progressed to such an alarming stage that her highly competent physicians at one crisis were convinced that she could not survive a certain night. The great work she was writing was far from completed; the Countess was heart-broken to think that, after all, that heroic career was to be cut off just before the consummation of its labors for humanity; and she spent the night in grief and despair. Arising in the morning she found Madame at her desk, busy as before at her task. She had been revivified and restored during the night, and would not say how.

The Countess records the occasion of an intercession of the Masters in her own affairs, on behalf of their messenger. At her home in Sweden, while she was packing her trunks in preparation for a journey to some relatives in Italy, she clairaudiently heard a voice, which told her to place in her trunk a certain note-book of her containing notes on the Bohemian Tarot and the Kabala. It was not a printed volume but a collection of quotations from the above works in her own hand. Surprised, and not knowing the possible significance of the order, she nevertheless complied. Before reaching Italy she suddenly changed her plans, and postponed the trip to Italy and visited Madame Blavatsky in Belgium instead.

Upon arriving and shortly after greeting her beloved friend, she was startled to hear Madame say to her that her Master had informed her that her guest was bringing her a book dealing with the Tarot and the Kabala, of which she was to make use in the writing of The Secret Doctrine.

This must end, but does not by any means complete, the chronicle of "the Blavatsky phenomena." The list, long as it has become, is but a fragment of the whole. Without the narration of these phenomena an adequate impression of the personality and the legend back of them could not be given. Moreover they belong in any study of Theosophy, and their significance in relation to the principles of the cult is perhaps far other than casual or incidental. If her own display of such powers was made as a demonstration of what man is destined to become capable of achieving in his interior evolution, these things are to be regarded as an integral part of her message. They became, apparently in spite of herself, a part of her program and furnished a considerable impetus toward its advancement. Theosophy itself re-publishes the theory of man's inherent theurgic capacity. It can hardly be taken as an anomaly or as an irrelevant circumstance, then, that its founder should have been regarded as exemplifying the possession of that capacity in her own person.

CHAPTER IV FROM SPIRITUALISM TO THEOSOPHY

Nothing seems more certain than that Madame Blavatsky had no definite idea of what the finished product was to be when she gave the initial impulse to the movement. She knew the general direction in which it would have to move and also many objectives which it would have to seek. In her mind there had been assembled a body of material of a unique sort. She had spent many years of her novitiate in moving from continent to continent1 in search of data having to do with a widespread tradition as to the existence of a hidden knowledge and secret cultivation of man's higher psychic and spiritual capabilities. Supposedly the wielder of unusual abilities in this line, she was driven by the very character of her endowment to seek for the deeper science which pertained to the evolution of such gifts, and at the same time a philosophy of life in general which would explain their hidden significance. To establish, first, the reality of such phenomena, and then to construct a system that would furnish the possibility of understanding this mystifying segment of experience, was unquestionably the main drive of her mental interests in early middle life. Already well equipped to be the exponent of the higher psychological and theurgic science, she aimed to become its philosophic expounder.

But the philosophy Madame Blavatsky was to give forth could not be oriented with the science of the universe as then generally conceived. To make her message intelligible she was forced to reconstruct the whole picture of the cosmos. She had to frame a universe in which her doctrine would be seen to have relevance and into whose total order it would fall with perfect articulation. She felt sure that she had in her possession an array of vital facts, but she could not at once discern the total implication of those facts for the cosmos which explained them, and which in turn they tended to explain. We may feel certain that her ideas grow more systematic from stage to stage, whether indeed they were the product of her own unaided intellect, or whether she but transcribed the knowledge and wisdom of more learned living men, the Mahatmas, as the Theosophic legend has it.

Guided by the character of the situation in which she found herself, and also, it seems, by the advice of her Master, she chose to ride into her new venture upon the crest of the Spiritualist waves. America was chosen to be the hatching center of Theosophy because it was at the time the heart and center of the Spiritualist movement. It was felt that Theosophy would elicit a quick response from persons already imbued with spiritistic ideas. It cannot be disputed that Madame Blavatsky and Col. Olcott worked with the Spiritualists for a brief period and launched the Society from within the ranks of the cult. As a matter of fact it was the work of this pair of Theosophists that gave Spiritualism a fresh impetus in this country after a period of waning interest about 1874. Col. Olcott's letters in the Daily Graphic about the Eddy phenomena, and his book,

People From the Other World, did much to revive popular discussion, and his colleague's show of new manifestations was giving encouragement to Spiritualists. But the Russian noblewoman suddenly disappointed the expectations thus engendered by assigning a different interpretation and much lower value to the phenomena. Before this she and Col. Olcott not only lent moral support to a leading Spiritualist journal, The Spiritual Scientist, of Boston, edited by Mr. E. Gerry Brown, but contributed its leading editorials and even advanced it funds.

The motive behind their participation in a movement which they so soon abandoned has been misconstrued.

Spiritualists, and the public generally, assumed that of course their activity indicated that they subscribed to the usual tenets of the sect; that they accepted the phenomena for what they purported to be, i.e., actual communications in all cases from the spirits of former human beings. However true this estimate may have been as appertaining to Col. Olcott-and even to him it had a fast diminishing applicability after his meeting with H.P.B.-it was certainly not true of her. Madame Blavatsky shortly became the mark of Spiritualistic attack for the falsification of her original attitude toward the movement and her presumed betrayal of the cause.

Her ill-timed attempt to launch her Société Spirite at Cairo in 1871 foreshadowed her true spirit and motive in this activity. It is evident to the student of her life that she felt a contempt for the banal type of séance phenomena. She so expressed herself in writing from Cairo at the time. She felt that while these things were real and largely genuine, they were insignificant in the view that took in a larger field of psychic power. But the higher phenomena of that more important science were known to few, whereas she was constantly encountering interest in the other type. If she was to introduce a nobler psychism to the world, she seemed driven to resort to the method of picking up people who were absorbed in the lower modes of the spiritual science and leading them on into the higher. She would gather a nucleus of the best Spiritualists and go forward with them to the higher Spiritualism. To win their confidence in herself, it was necessary for her to start at their level, to make a gesture of friendliness toward their work and a show of interest in it.

Her own words may bring light to the situation:

"As it is I have only done my duty; first, toward Spiritualism, that I have defended as well as I could from the attacks of imposture under the too transparent mask of science; then towards two helpless slandered mediums [the Holmeses]. . . . But I am obliged to confess that I really do not believe in having done any good-to Spiritualism itself. . . . It is with a profound sadness in my heart that I acknowledge this fact, for I begin to think there is no help for it. For over fifteen years have I fought my battle for the blessed truth; have traveled and preached it-though I never was born for a lecturer-from the snow-covered tops of the Caucasian Mountains, as well as from the sandy valleys of the Nile. I have proved the truth of it practically and by persuasion. For the sake of Spiritualism2 I have left my home, an easy life amongst a civilized society, and have become a wanderer upon the face of the earth. I had already seen my hopes realized, beyond my most sanguine expectations, when my unlucky star brought me to America. Knowing this country to be the cradle of modern Spiritualism, I came over here from France with feelings not unlike those of a Mohammedan approaching the birthplace of his Prophet."3

After her death Col. Olcott found among her papers a memorandum in her hand entitled "Important Note." In it she wrote:

"Yes, I am sorry to say that I had to identify myself, during that shameful exposure of the Holmes mediums, with the Spiritualists. I had to save the situation, for I was sent from Paris to America on purpose to prove the phenomena and their reality, and show the fallacy of the spiritualistic theory of spirits. But how could I do it best? I did not want people at large to know that I could produce the same thing at will. I had received orders to the contrary, and yet I had to keep alive the reality, the genuineness and the possibility of such phenomena in the hearts of those who from Materialists had turned Spiritualists, but now, owing to the exposure of several mediums, fell back again and returned to their scepticism. . . . Did I do wrong? The world is not prepared yet to understand the philosophy of Occult Science; let them first assure themselves that there are beings in an invisible world, whether 'spirits' of the dead or elementals; and that there are hidden powers in man which are capable of making a god of him on earth."

"When I am dead and gone people will, perhaps, appreciate my disinterested motives. I have pledged my word to help people on to Truth while living and I will keep my word. Let them abuse and revile me; let some call me a medium and a Spiritualist, others an impostor. The day will come when posterity will learn to know me better."4

As long as it was a question of the actuality of the phenomena, she was alert in defence of Spiritualism. In the Daily Graphic of November. 13, 1874, she printed one of her very first newspaper contributions in America, replying to an attack of a Dr. George M. Beard, an electropathic physician of New York, on the validity of the Eddy phenomena. She went so far in this article as to wager five hundred dollars that he could not make good his boast that he could imitate the form-apparitions "with three dollars' worth of drapery." She refers to herself as a Spiritualist. In her first letter to Co. Olcott after leaving Vermont she wrote as follows:

"I speak to you as a true friend to yourself and as a Spiritualist anxious to save Spiritualism from a danger."5

A little later she even mentioned to her friend that the outburst of mediumistic phenomena had been caused by the Brotherhood of Adepts as an evolutionary agency. She could, of course, not believe the whole trend maleficent if it was in the slightest degree engineered by her trusted Confederates. She added later, however, that the Master soon realized the impracticability of using the Spiritualistic movement as a channel for the dissemination of the deeper occult science and instructed her to cease her advocacy of it.

Along with her reply and challenge to Beard in the Graphic there was printed an outline of her biography from notes furnished by herself. In it she says:

"In 1858 I returned to Paris and made the acquaintance of Daniel Home, the Spiritualist. . . . Home converted me to Spiritualism. . . . After this I went to Russia. I converted my father to Spiritualism."

Elsewhere she speaks of Spiritualism as "our belief" and "our cause." In an article in the Spiritual Scientist of March eighth she uses the phrases "the divine truth of our faith (Spiritualism) and the teachings of our invisible guardians (the spirits of the circles)."

Madame Blavatsky's apparently double-faced attitude toward Spiritualism is reflected in the posture of most Theosophists toward the same subject today. When Spiritualism, as a demonstration of the possibility and actuality of spiritistic phenomena, is attacked by materialists or unbelievers, they at once bristle in its defense; when it is a question of the reliability and value of the messages, or the dignity and wholesomeness of the séance procedure, they respond negatively.

It is the opinion of some Theosophic leaders, like Sinnett and Olcott, that Madame Blavatsky made a mistake in affiliating herself actively with Spiritualism, inasmuch as the early group of Spiritualistic members of her Theosophic Society, as soon as they were apprised of her true attitude, fell away, and the incipient movement was beset with much ill-feeling.

The controversy between the two schools is important, since Madame Blavatsky's dissent from Spiritualistic theory gave rise to her first attempts to formulate Theosophy. To justify her defection from the movement she was led to enunciate at least some of the major postulates and principles of her higher science.

Theosophy was born in this labor. It is necessary, therefore, to go into the issues involved in the perennial controversy.

To Spiritualists the phenomena which purported to be communications from the still-living spirits of former human beings with those on the earth plane, were assumed to be genuinely what they seemed. As such they were believed to be far the most significant data in man's religious life, as furnishing a practically irrefutable demonstration of the truth of the soul's immortality. They were regarded as the central fact in any attempt to formulate an adequate religious philosophy. Spiritualists therefore elevated this assumption to the place of supreme importance and made everything else secondary.

Not so Madame Blavatsky. To her the Spiritistic phenomena were but a meagre part of a larger whole. Furthermore-and this was her chief point of divergence,--she vigorously protested their being what Spiritualists asserted them to be. They were not at all genuine messages from genuine spirits of earth people-or were not so in the vast majority of cases. And besides, they were not any more "divine" or "spiritual" than ordinary human utterances, and were even in large part impish and elfin, when not downright demoniacal. They were mostly, she said, the mere "shells" or wraiths of the dead, animated not by their former souls but by sprightly roving nature-spirits or elementals, if nothing worse,-- such, for instance, as the lowest and most besotted type of human spirit that was held close to earth by fiendish sensuality or hate. There were plenty of these, she affirmed, in the lower astral plane watching for opportunities to vampirize negative human beings. The souls of average well-meaning or of saintly people are not within human reach in the séance. They have gone on into realms of higher purity, more etherealized being, and can not easily descend into the heavy atmosphere of the near-earth plane to give messages about that investment or that journey westward or that health condition that needs attention. At best it is only on rare and exceptional occasions that the real intelligence of a disembodied mortal comes "through." There are many types of living entities in various realms of nature, other than human souls. Certain of these rove the astral plane and take pleasure in playing upon gullible people who sit gravely in the dark. Most of the occurrences at circles are so much astral plane rubbish; and, besides, séance-mongering is dangerous to all concerned and eventually ruinous to the medium. If the mediums, she bantered, were really in the hands of benevolent "guides" and "controls," why do not the latter shield their protégés from the wrecked health and insanity so frequent among them? She

affirmed that she had never seen a medium who had not developed scrofula or a phthisical affection.6

Inevitably the Spiritualists were stunned by their one-time champion's sudden and amazed reversal of her position. A campaign of abuse and condemnation began in their ranks, echoes of which are still heard at times.

What Madame Blavatsky aimed to do was to teach that the phenomena of true Spiritualism bore not the faintest resemblance to those of table-tipping. True Spiritualism should envisage the phenomena of the divine spirit of man in their higher manifestations, the cultivation of which by the ancients and the East has given man his most sacred science and most vital knowledge. She wrote in a letter to her sister about 1875 that one of the purposes of her new Society was "to show certain fallacies of the Spiritualist. If we are anything we are Spiritualists, only not in the modern American fashion, but in that of the ancient Alexandria with its Theodidaktoi, Hypatias and Porphyries."7 In one of the letters of Mahatma K.H. to A. P. Sinnett the Master writes:

"It was H.P.B. who, acting under the orders of Atrya (one whom you do not know) was the first to explain in the 'Spiritualist' the difference between psyche and nous, nefesh and ruach-Soul and Spirit. She had to bring the whole arsenal of proofs with her quotations from Paul to Plato, from Plutarch and James before the Spiritualists admitted that the Theosophists were right."8

In 1879 she wrote in the magazine which she had just founded in India:

"We can never know how much of the mediumistic phenomena we must attribute to the disembodied until it is settled how much can be done by the embodied human soul, and to blind but active powers at work within those regions which are yet unexplored by science."9

In other words Spiritualism should be a culture of the spirits of the living, not a commerce with the souls of the dead. To live the life of the immortal spirit while here in the body is true Spiritualism. We can readily see that with such a purpose in mind she would not be long in discerning that the Spiritualistic enterprise could not be used to promulgate the type of spiritual philosophy that she had learned in the East.

When this conclusion had fully ripened in her mind, she began the undisguised formulation of her own independent teaching. Her new philosophy was in effect tantamount to an attack on Spiritualism, and that from a quarter from which Spiritualism was not prepared to repulse an assault. It came not from the old arch-enemy, materialistic scepticism, but from a source which admitted the authenticity of the phenomena.

Her first aim was to set forth the misconceptions under which the Spiritualists labored. She says:

"We believe that few of those physical phenomena which are genuine are caused by disembodied human spirits."10

Again she "ventures the prediction that unless Spiritualists set about the study of ancient philosophy so as to learn to discriminate between spirits and to guard themselves against the baser sort, twenty-five years will not elapse before they will have to fly to the Romish communion to escape these 'guides' and 'controls' that they have fondled so long. The signs of this catastrophe already exhibit themselves."11

Again she declares that

"it is not mediums, real, true and genuine mediums, that we would ever blame, but their patrons, the Spiritualists."12

In Isis Unveiled she rebukes Spiritualists for claiming that the Bible is full of phenomena just like those of modern mediums. She asserts that there were Spiritualistic phenomena in the Bible, but not mediumistic,--a distinction of great import to her. She declares that the ancients could tell the difference between mediums who harbored good spirits and those haunted by evil ones, and branded the latter type unclean, while reverencing the former. She positively asserts that "pure spirits will not and cannot show themselves objectively; those that do are not pure spirits, but elementary and impure. Woe to the medium that falls a prey to such!"13

Col. Olcott quotes her as writing:

"Spiritualism in the hands of an Adept becomes Magic, for he is learned in the art of blending together the laws of the universe without breaking any of them.

. . . In the hands of an inexperienced medium Spiritualism becomes unconscious sorcery, for . . . he opens, unknown to himself, a door of communication between the two worlds through which emerges the blind forces of nature lurking in the Astral Light, as well as good and bad spirits."14

In The Key to Theosophy15 written near the end of her life, she states what may be assumed to be the official Theosophic attitude on the subject:

"We assert that the spirits of the dead cannot return to earth-save in rare and exceptional cases-nor do they communicate with men except by entirely subjective means. That which does appear objectively is often the phantom of the ex- physical man. But in psychic and, so to say, 'spiritual' Spiritualism we do believe most decidedly."16

One of her most vigorous expressions upon this issue occurs toward the end of Isis.

According to Olcott the Hon. A. Aksakoff, eminent Russian Professor, states that "Prince A. Dolgorouki, the great authority on mesmerism, has written me that he has ascertained that spirits which play the most prominent part at séances are elementaries,--gnomes, etc. His clairvoyants have seen them and describe them thus."

"The totally insufficient theory of the constant agency of disembodied human spirits in the production of Spiritualistic phenomena has been the bane of the Cause. A thousand mortifying rebuffs have failed to open their reason or intuition to the truth. Ignoring the teachings of the past, they have discovered no substitute. We offer them philosophical deduction instead of unverifiable hypothesis, scientific analysis and demonstration instead of indiscriminating faith. Occult philosophy gives them the means of meeting the reasonable requirements of science, and frees them from the humiliating necessity to accept the oracular teachings of 'intelligences' which, as a rule, have less intelligence than a child at school. So based and so strengthened, modern phenomena would be in a position to command the attention and enforce the respect of those who carry with them public opinion. Without invoking such help Spiritualism must continue to vegetate, equally repulsed-not without cause-both

by science and theologians. In its modern aspect it is neither science, a religion nor a philosophy."17

In 1876, the writing of Isis was committing her to a stand which made further compromise with Spiritualism impossible. Her statement reveals what she would ostensibly have labored to do for that movement had it shown itself more plastic in her hands. She would have striven to buttress the phenomena with a more historical interpretation and a more respectable rationale.

In this context, however, the following passage from Isis is a bit difficult to understand. It seems to make a gesture of conciliation toward the Spiritualistic hypothesis after all. She says:

"We are far from believing that all the spirits that communicate at circles are of the classes called 'Elemental' and 'Elementary.' Many-especially among those who control the medium subjectively to speak, write and otherwise act in various ways-are human disembodied spirits. Whether the majority of such spirits are good or bad, largely depends on the private morality of the medium, much on the circle present, and a good deal on the intensity and object of their purpose. . . . But in any case, human spirits can never materialize themselves in propria persona."18

If this seems a recession from her consistent position elsewhere assumed, it must be remembered that she never, before or after, denied the possibility of the occasional descent of genuinely human spirits "in rare and exceptional cases."

Before 1875 she wrote to her sister that there was a law that sporadically, though periodically, the souls of the dead invade the realms of the living in an epidemic, and the intensity of the epidemic depends on the welcome they receive. She called it "the law of forced post-mortem assimilation." She elsewhere clarified this idea by the statement that our spirits here and now, being of kindred nature with the totality of spirit energy about us, unconsciously draw certain vibrations or currents from the life of the supermundane entities, whether we know it or not. Through this wireless circuit we sometimes drink in emanations, radiations, thought effluvia, so to speak, from the disembodied lives. The veil, she affirmed, between the two worlds is so thin that unsuspected messages are constantly passing across the divide, which is not spatial but only a discrepancy in receiving sets. And both she and the Master K.H. stated that during normal sleep we are en rapport with our loved ones as much as our hearts could desire. The reason we do not ordinarily know it is that the rate and wave length of that celestial communication can not be registered on the clumsy apparatus of our brains. It takes place through our astral or spiritual brains and can not arouse the coarser physical brain to synchronous vibration.

Her critique of the Spiritualistic thesis in general would be that something like ninety per cent of all ordinary "spirit" messages contain nothing to which the quality of spirituality, as we understand that term in its best significance, can in any measure be ascribed.

In rebuttal, Spiritualists point to many previsions, admonitory dreams, verified prophecies and other messages of great beauty and lofty spirituality, some of them leading to genuine reform of character, and they advance the claim, that genuine transference of intelligence from the spirit realms to earth is vastly more general than that fraction of experience which could be subsumed under her "rare and exceptional cases of "spirituality."

In one of the last works issued by Mr. Sinnett19 he deplores the unfortunate clash that has come between the two cults, points out that it is foolish and unfounded, and reminds both parties of the broad bases of agreement which are found in the two systems. He feels that there can be no insurmountable points of antagonism, inasmuch as Spiritualism, too, he asserts, is under the watch and ward of a member of the Great White Brotherhood, the Master known as Hilarion; and that it would be illogical to assume that members of that same spiritual Fraternity could foster movements among mankind that work at cross purposes with each other. But Mr. Sinnett does not give any authority for his statement as to Hilarion's regency over Spiritualism, and many Theosophists are inclined to doubt it. He feels that there is every good reason why Spiritualism should go forward with Theosophy in such a unity of purpose as would render their combined influence the most potent force in the world today against the menace of materialism. Whenever Spiritualists display an interest in the formulation of some scheme of life or cosmology in which their phenomena may find a meaningful allocation, they can hardly go in any other direction than straight into Theosophy. This is shown by their Articles of Faith, in which the idea of Karma, the divine nature of man, his spiritual constitution and other conceptions equally theosophic have found a place.

Perhaps Theosophists and Spiritualists alike may discern the bases of harmony between their opposing faiths in a singular passage from The Mahatma Letters, an utterance of the Master K.H.

"It is this [sweet blissful dream of devachanic Maya] during such a condition of complete Maya that the Souls or actual Egos of pure loving sensitivities, laboring under the same illusion, think their loved ones come down to them on earth, while it is their own Spirits that are raised towards those in the Devachan. Many of the subjective spiritual communications-most of them when the sensitives are pure-minded-are real; but it is most difficult for the uninitiated medium to fix in his mind the true and correct pictures of what he sees and hears. Some of the phenomena called psychography (though more rarely) are also real. The spirit of the sensitive getting idylized, so to say, by the aura of the Spirit in the Devachan, becomes for a few minutes that departed personality, and writes in the handwriting of the latter, in his language and in his thoughts, as they were during his life-time. The two spirits become blended in one; and, the preponderance of one over the other during such phenomena determines the preponderance of personality in the characteristics exhibited in such writings and 'trance-speaking.' What you call 'rapport' is in plain fact an identity of molecular vibration between the astral part of the incarnate medium and the astral part of the discarnate personality . . . there is rapport between medium and 'control' when their astral molecules move in accord. And the question whether the communication shall reflect more of the one personal idiosyncrasy or the other, is determined by the relative intensity of the two sets of vibrations in the compound wave of Akasha. The less identical the vibratory impulses the more mediumistic and less spiritual will be the message. So then measure your medium's moral state by that of the alleged 'controlling' Intelligence, and your tests of genuineness leave nothing to be desired."20

This plank in the Theosophic platform not having been laid down in 1875 to bridge the chasm between the two movements, Madame Blavatsky drew away from her Spiritualistic associates, and it became but a matter of time until some propitious circumstance should give to her divergent tendency a body and a name.

The break with Spiritualism and the launching of the Theosophical Society were practically contemporary. The actual formation of the new organization does not

on the surface appear to have been a deliberate act of Madame Blavatsky. While it would never have been organized without her presence and her influence, still she was not the prime mover in the steps which brought it into being. She seems merely to have gone along while others led. However her Society grew out of the stimulus that had gone forth from her.

It was Col. Henry Steele Olcott who assumed the rôle of outward leader in the young movement. He gave over (eventually) a lucrative profession as a corporation lawyer, an agricultural expert, and an official of the government, to expend all his energies in this enterprise. He had acquired the title of colonel during the Civil War in the Union army's manoeuvres in North Carolina. At the close of the war he had been chosen by the government to conduct some investigations into conditions relative to army contracts in the Quartermaster's Department and had discharged his duties with great efficiency, receiving the approbation of higher officials. He was regarded as an authority on agriculture and lectured before representative bodies on that subject. He had established a successful practice as a corporation counsel, numbering the Metropolitan Life Insurance Company among his clients. In addition to these activities he had done much reportorial work for the press, notably in connection with his Spiritualistic researches. His authorship of several works on the phenomena has already been mentioned. His career had achieved for him a record of high intelligence, great ability, and a character of probity and integrity.

It is the belief of Theosophists that he was expressly chosen by the Mahatmas to share with Madame Blavatsky the honor and the labor of spreading her message in the world. A passage from the Mahatma Letters puts this in clear light. The Master K.H. there says:

"So, casting about, we found in America the man to stand as leader-a man of great moral courage, unselfish, and having other good qualities. He was far from being the best, but-he was the best one available. . . . We sent her to America, brought them together-and the trial began. From the first both she and he were given to understand that the issue lay entirely with themselves."

In spite of difficulties, caused by the clash of temperaments and policies, this odd, "divinely-constituted" partnership held firmly together until the end.
Their relationship was one of a loyal camaraderie, both being actuated by an uncommon devotion to the same cause.

As early as May, 1875, the Colonel had suggested the formation of a "Miracle Club," to continue spiritistic investigation. His proposal was made in the interest of psychic research. It was not taken up. But Madame Blavatsky's sprightly evening chatter and her reported magical feats continued to draw groups of intelligent people to her rooms. Among those thus attracted was Mr. George H. Felt, who had made some careful studies in phases of Egyptology. He was asked to lecture on these subjects and on the 7th of September, 1875, a score of people had gathered in H.P.B.'s parlors to hear his address on "The Lost Canon of Proportion of the Egyptians." Dr. Seth Pancoast, a most erudite Kabbalist was present, and after the lecture he led the discussion to the subject of the occult powers of the ancient magicians. Mr. Felt said he had proven those powers and had with them evoked elemental creatures and "hundreds of shadowy forms." As the tense debate proceeded, acting on an impulse, Col.

Olcott wrote on a scrap of paper, which he passed over to Madame Blavatsky through the hands of Mr. W. Q. Judge, the following: "Would it not be a good thing to form a Society for this kind of study?" She read it and indicated assent.

Col. Olcott arose and "after briefly sketching the present condition of the Spiritualistic movement; the attitude of its antagonists, the Materialists; the irrepressible conflict between science and the religious sectaries; the philosophical character of the ancient theosophies and their sufficiency to reconcile all existing antagonisms; . . . he proposed to form a nucleus around which might gather all the enlightened and brave souls who are willing to work together for the collection and diffusion of knowledge. His plan was to organize a Society of Occultists and begin at once to collect a library; and to diffuse information concerning those secret laws of Nature which were so familiar to the Chaldeans and Egyptians, but are totally unknown to our modern world of science."21

It was a plain proposal to organize for occult research, for the extension of human knowledge of the esoteric sciences, and for a study of the psychic possibilities in man's nature. No religious or ethical or even philosophical interest can be detected in the first aims. The Brotherhood plank was a later development, and the philosophy was an outgrowth of the necessity of rationalizing the scientific data brought to light. The very nature of the movement committed it, of course, to an anti-materialistic view. Col. Olcott was still predominantly concerned to get demonstrative psychic displays. He was made Chairman, and Mr. Judge, Secretary.

It is interesting to note the personnel of this first gathering of Theosophists.

"The company included several persons of great learning and some of wide personal influence. The Managing Editors of two religious papers; the co-editors of two literary magazines; an Oxford LL.D.; a venerable Jewish scholar and traveler of repute; an editorial writer of one of the New York morning dailies; the President of the New York Society of Spiritualists; Mr. C. C. Massey an English barrister at law; Mrs. Emma Hardinge Britten and Dr. Britten; two New York lawyers besides Col. Olcott; a partner in a Philadelphia publishing house; a well-known physician; and . . . Madame Blavatsky herself."22

At a late hour the meeting adjourned until the following evening, when organization could be more fully effected. Those who were present at the Sept. 8th meeting, and who thus became the actual formers (Col. Olcott insists on the word instead of Founders, reserving that title to Madame Blavatsky and himself) of the Theosophical Society, were: Col. Olcott, H. P. Blavatsky, Chas. Sotheran, Dr. Chas. E. Simmons, H. D. Monachesi, C. C. Massey, of London, W. L. Alden, G.

H. Felt, D. E. deLara, Dr. W. Britten, Mrs. E. H. Britten, Henry J. Newton, John Storer Cobb, J. Hyslop. W. Q. Judge, H. M. Stevens. A By-Law Committee was named, other routine business attended to, a general discussion held and adjournment taken to Sept. 13th. Mr. Felt gave another lecture on Sept. 18th, after which several additional members were nominated, the name, "The Theosophical Society," proposed, and a committee on rooms chosen. Several October meetings were held in furtherance of the Society; and on the 17th of November, 1875, the movement reached the final stage of constitutional organization. Its President was Col. Henry Olcott; Vice-Presidents, Dr. Seth Pancoast and G. H. Felt; Corresponding Secretary, Madame H. P. Blavatsky; Recording Secretary, John S. Cobb; Treasurer, Henry J. Newton; Librarian, Chas. Sotheran; Councillors, Rev. H. Wiggin, R. P. Westbrook, LL. D., Mrs. E. H. Britten, C. E. Simmons, and Herbert D. Monachesi; Counsel to the Society, W. Q. Judge. Mr. John W. Lovell, the New York publisher, has the distinction of having paid the first five dollars (initiation fee) into the treasury, and is at the present writing the only surviving member of the founding group. At the November 17th meeting the President delivered his inaugural address. It was an amplification of his remarks made at the meeting of Sept. 7th, with some

prognostications of what the work of the Society was destined to mean in the changing conceptions of modern thought.

The infant Society did not at once proceed to grow and expand. The chief reason for this was that Mr. Felt, whose theories had been the immediate object of strongest interest, and who was expected to be the leader and teacher in their quest of the secrets of ancient magic, for some unaccountable reason failed them utterly. His promised lectures were never scheduled, his demonstrations of spirit-evocation never shown. This disappointment weighed heavily upon some of the members. Mrs. Britten, Mr. Newton, and the other Spiritualists in the group, finding that Madame Blavatsky was not disposed to investigate mediums in the conventional fashion, or in any way to make the Society an adjunct of the Spiritualistic movement, suffered another disappointment and became inactive or openly withdrew. Mr. Judge and Col. Olcott were busy with their professional labors, and Madame Blavatsky had plunged into the writing of Isis Unveiled. The Society fell into the state of "innocuous desuetude," and was domiciled solely in the hearts of three persons, Olcott, Judge, and Madame Blavatsky. However dead it might be to all outward appearance, it still lived in the deep convictions of this trio. True, an occasional new recruit was admitted, two names in particular being worthy of remark. On April 5th, 1878, Col. Olcott received the signed application for membership from a young inventor, one Thomas Alva Edison, and near the same time General Abner W. Doubleday, veteran Major-General in the Union Army, united with the Society. Edison had been attracted by the objects of the Society, largely because of certain experiences he had had in connection with the genesis of some of his ideas for inventions. They had seemed to come to him from an inner intelligence independent of his voluntary thought control. Also he had experimented to determine the possibility of moving physical objects by exertion of the will. He was doubtless in close sympathy with the purposes of the Society, but the main currents of his mechanical interests drew him away from active coöperation with it. As for Major-General Doubleday, Theosophy gave articulate voice to theories as to life, death, and human destiny which he had long cherished without a formal label. He stated that it was the Theosophic idea of Karma which had maintained his courage throughout the ordeals of the Civil War and he testified that his understanding of this doctrine nerved him to pass with entire fearlessness through those crises in which he was exposed to fire.23 When Theosophy was brought to his notice he cast in his lot with the movement and was a devoted student and worker while he lived. When the two Founders left America at the end of 1878 for India, Col.

Olcott constituted General Doubleday the President of the American body.24

Concerning Mr. W. Q. Judge, there is only to be said that he was a young barrister at the time, practicing in New York and making his home in Brooklyn, where until about 1928 a brother, John Judge, survived him. He was a man of upright character and had always manifested a quick interest in such matters as Theosophy brought to his attention. It is reported among Theosophists that Madame Blavatsky immediately saw in him a pupil upon whose entire sympathy with her own deeper aims and understanding of her esoteric situation she could rely implicitly. He is believed always to have stood closer to her in a spiritual sense than Col. Olcott; in fact it is hinted that there was a secret understanding between them as to the inner motivations behind the Society. Later developments in the history of the movement seem to give weight to this theory.

Mr. Judge and General Doubleday were the captains of the frail Theosophic craft in America during something like four years, from 1878 to 1882, following the sailing of the two Founders for India. If little activity was displayed by the Society during this period, it was not in any measure the fault of those left in charge. They were not lacking in zeal for the cause. It is to be attributed

chiefly to a state of suspended animation in which it was left by the departure of the official heads. This condition itself was brought about by the long protracted delay in carrying out a measure which in 1878 Col. Olcott had designed to adopt for the future expansion of the Society. Madame Blavatsky's work in Isis had disclosed the fact that there was an almost complete sympathy of aims in certain respects between the new Society and the Masonic Fraternity; that the latter had been the recipient and custodian down the ages of much of the ancient esoteric tradition which it was the purpose of Theosophy to revive. The idea of converting the Theosophical Society into a Masonic body with ritual and degrees had been under contemplation for some time, and overtures toward that end had been made to persons in the Masonic order. In fact the plan had been so favorably regarded that on his departure Col. Olcott left Mr. Judge and General Doubleday under instructions to hold all other activities in abeyance until he should prepare a form of ritual that would properly express the Society's spiritual motif and aims. It happened, however, that on reaching India both his and his colleague's time was so occupied with other work and other interests that for three years they never could give attention to the matter of the ritual. By that time they found the Society beginning to grow so rapidly without the support they had intended for it in the union with an old and respected secret order, that the project was abandoned. But it was this tentative plan that was responsible for the apparent lifelessness of the American organization during those years. A number of times the two American leaders telegraphed Olcott in India to hasten the ritual and hinted that its

non-appearance forced them to keep the Society here embalmed in an aggravated condition of status quo. When the scheme was definitely abandoned, straightforward Theosophic propaganda was initiated and a period of healthy expansion began.

It is of interest in this connection to note that on March 8, 1876, on Madame Blavatsky's own motion, it was "resolved, that the Society adopt one or more signs of recognition, to be used among the Fellows of the Society or for admissions to the meetings." This might indicate her steady allegiance to the principle of esotericism. The practice fell into disuse after a time. Yet it was this idea of secrecy always lurking in the background of her mind that eventually led to the formation of a graded hierarchy in the Theosophical Society when the Esoteric School was formally organized.

Another development that Col. Olcott says "I should prefer to omit altogether if I could" from the early history of the Society was the affiliation of the organization with a movement then being inaugurated in India toward the resuscitation of pure Vedic religion. This proceeded further than the contemplated union with Masonry, and it led to the necessity of a more succinct pronouncement of their creed by Col. Olcott and Madame Blavatsky.

Naturally Madame Blavatsky's accounts of the existence of the great secret Brotherhood of Adepts in North India and her glorification of "Aryavarta" as the home of the purest occult knowledge, had served to engender a sort of nostalgia in the hearts of the two Founders for "Mother India." It seemed quite plausible that, once the aims of the Theosophical Society were broadcast in Hindustan, its friendly attitude toward the ancient religions of that country would act as an open sesame to a quick response on the part of thousands of native Hindus. It was not illogical to believe that the young Theosophical Society would advance shortly to a position of great influence among the Orientals, whose psychology, ideals, and religious conceptions it had undertaken to exalt, particularly in the eyes of the Western nations. India thus came to be looked upon as the land of promise, and the "return home," as Madame Blavatsky termed it, became more and more a consummation devoutly to be wished. With Isis completed and published

the call to India rang ever louder, and finally in November, 1878, came the Master's orders to make ready. It was not until the 18th of December that the ship bearing the two pilgrims passed out of the Narrows.

There had seemed to be no way opened for them to make an effective start in India, no appropriate channel of introduction to their work there, until 1878. Then Col. Olcott chanced to learn of a movement recently launched in India, whose aims and ideals, he was given to believe, were identical with those of his own Society. It was the Arya Samaj, founded by one Swami Dhyanand, who was reputed to be a member of the same occult Brotherhood as that to which their own Masters, K.H. and M., belonged. This latter allegation was enough to win the immediate interest of the two devotees in its mission, and through intermediaries Col. Olcott was put in touch with the Swami, to whom he made overtures to join forces. The Arya Samaj was represented to the Colonel as world-wide in its eclecticism, devoted to a revival of the ancient purity of Vedantism and pledged to a conception of God as an eternal impersonal principle which, under whatever name, all people alike worshipped. An official linking of the two bodies was formally made in May, 1878, and the title of the Theosophical Society was amended to "The Theosophical Society of the Arya Samaj." But before long the Colonel received a translation of the rules and doctrines of the Arya Samaj, which gave him a great shock. Swami Dhyanand's views had either radically changed or had originally been misrepresented. His cult was found to be drastically sectarian-merely a new sect of Hinduism-and quite narrow in certain lines. Even then the Colonel endeavored to bridge the gap, drawing up a new definition of the aims of his Society in such an open fashion that the way was left clear for any Theosophists to associate with the Samaj if they should so desire. It was not until several years after the arrival in India that final disruption of all connection between the two Societies was made, the Founders having received what Col. Olcott calls "much evil treatment" from the learned Swami.

When the first discovery of the real character of the Arya Samaj was made in 1878, it was deemed necessary to issue a circular defining the Theosophical Society in more explicit terms than had yet been done. Olcott does not quote from this circular of his own, but gives the language of the circular issued by the British Theosophical Society, then just organized, as embodying the essentials of his own statement. This enables us to discern how far the originally vague Theosophical ideals had come on their way to explicit enunciation.

1.   The British Theosophical Society is founded for the purpose of discovering the nature and powers of the human soul and spirit by investigation and experiment.

2.   The object of the Society is to increase the amount of human health, goodness, knowledge, wisdom, and happiness.

3.   The Fellows pledge themselves to endeavor, to the best of their powers, to live a life of temperance, purity, and brotherly love. They believe in a Great First Intelligent Cause, and in the Divine Sonship of the spirit of man, and hence in the immortality of that spirit, and in the universal brotherhood of the human race.

4.   The Society is in connection and sympathy with the Arya Samaj of Aryavarta, one object of which Society is to elevate, by a true spiritual education, mankind out of degenerate, idolatrous and impure forms of worship wherever prevalent.25

In his own circular, Olcott, with the concurrence of H.P.B., made the first official statement of the threefold hierarchical constitution of the Theosophical Society. This grouping naturally arose out of the basic facts in the situation itself. There were, first, at the summit of the movement, the Brothers or Adepts; then there were persons, like H.P.B., Olcott himself and Judge, with perhaps a few others, who were classified in the category of "chelas" or accepted pupils of the Masters; then there were just plain members of the Society, having no personal link as yet with the great Teachers. A knowledge of this graduation is essential to an understanding of much in the later history of the Society.

In the same circular the President said:

"The objects of the Society are various. It influences its Fellows to acquire an intimate knowledge of natural law, especially its occult manifestations."

Then follow some sentences penned by Madame Blavatsky:

"As the highest development, physically and spiritually, on earth of the creative cause, man should aim to solve the mystery of his being. He is the procreator of his species, physically, and having inherited the nature of the unknown but palpable cause of his own creation, must possess in his inner psychical self this creative power in lesser degree. He should, therefore, study to develop his latent powers, and inform himself respecting the laws of magnetism, electricity and all other forms of force, whether of the seen or unseen universes."

The President proceeds:

"The Society teaches and expects its Fellows to personally exemplify the highest morality and religious aspirations; to oppose the materialism of science and every form of dogmatic theology . . .; to make known, among Western nations, the long-suppressed facts about Oriental religious philoso-phies, their ethics, chronology, esotericism, symbolism . . . ; to disseminate a knowledge of the sub-lime teachings of the pure esoteric system of the archaic period which are mirrored in the oldest Vedas and in the philosophy of Gautauma Buddha, Zoroaster, and Confucius; finally and chiefly, to aid in the institution of a Brotherhood of Humanity, wherein all good and pure men of every race shall recognize each other as the equal effects (upon this planet) of one Uncreate, Universal, Infinite and Everlasting Cause."26

He sums up the central ideas as being:

1. The study of occult science.
2. The formation of a nucleus of universal brotherhood.
3. The revival of Oriental literature and philosophy.

And these three became later substantially the permanent platform of the Society. In their final and present form they stand:

1. To form a nucleus of the Universal Brotherhood of Humanity without distinction of race, creed, sex, caste, or color.

2. To encourage the study of Comparative Religion, Philosophy, and Science.

3. To investigate the unexplained laws of nature and the powers latent in man.

The inclusion of a moral program to accompany occult research and comparative religion was seen to be necessary. Madame Blavatsky's disapprobation of Spiritualism had as its prime motivation that movement's lack of any moral bases for psychic progress. Therefore the ethical implications which she saw as fundamental in any true occult system were embodied in the Theosophic platform in the Universal Brotherhood plank. Brotherhood, a somewhat vague general term, was made the only creedal or ethical requirement for fellowship in the Society. At that it is, as a moral obligation, a matter of the individual's own interpretation, and it is the Society's only link with the ethical side of religion. Not even the member's clear violation of accepted or prevalent social codes can disqualify him from good standing. The Society refuses to be a judge of what constitutes morality or its breach, leaving that determination to the member himself. At the same time through its literature it declares that no progress into genuine spirituality is possible "without clean hands and a pure heart." It ad-heres to the principle that morality without freedom is not morality. Thus the movement which began with an impulse to investigate the occult powers of ancient magicians, was moulded by cir-cumstances into a moral discipline, which placed little store in magic feats.

CHAPTER V ISIS UNVEILED

ISIS UNVEILED
One morning in the summer of 1875 Madame Blavatsky showed her colleague some sheets of manuscript which she had written. She explained: "I wrote this last night 'by order,' but what the deuce it is to be I don't know. Perhaps it is for a newspaper article, perhaps for a book, perhaps for nothing: anyhow I did as I was ordered."

She put it away in a drawer and nothing more was said about it for some months. In September of that year she went to Syracuse on a visit to Prof. and Mrs.
Hiram Corson, of Cornell University, and while there she began to expand the few original pages. She wrote back to Olcott in New York that "she was writing about things she had never studied and making quotations from books she had never read in all her life; that, to test her accuracy Prof. Corson had compared her quotations with classical works in the University Library and had found her to be right."1

She had never undertaken any extensive literary production in her life and her unfamiliarity with English at this time was a real handicap. When she returned to the city Olcott took two suites of rooms at 433 West 34th Street, and there she set to work to expound the rudiments of her great science. From 1875 to 1877 she worked with unremitting energy, sitting from morning until night at her desk. In the evenings, after his day's professional labors, Olcott came to her help, aiding her with the English and with the systematic arrangement of the heterogeneous mass of material that poured forth. Later Dr. Alexander Wilder, the Neo-Platonic scholar, helped her with the spelling of the hundreds of classical philological terms she employed. But Madame Blavatsky wrote the book, Isis Unveiled.

After the first flush of its popularity it has been forgotten, outside of Theosophic circles. Even among Theosophists, or at any rate in the largest organic group of the Theosophical Society, the book is hardly better known than in the world at large. During the last twenty-five years there has been a tendency in the Society to read expositions of Madame Blavatsky's ponderous volumes rather than the original presentation; neophytes in the organization have been urged to pass up these books as being too recondite and abstruse. It has even been hinted that many things are better understood now than when the Founder wrote, and that certain crudities of dogma and inadequacies of presentation can be avoided by perusing the commentary literature. As a result of this policy the percentage of Theosophic students who know exactly what Madame Blavatsky wrote over fifty years ago is quite small. Thousands of members of the Theosophical Society have grown old in the cult's activities and have never read the volumes that launched the cult ideas.

Isis must not, however, be regarded as a text-book on Theosophy. The Secret Doctrine, issued ten years later, has a better claim to that title. Isis makes no formulation, certainly not a systematic one, of the creed of occultism. It is far from being an elucidation or exegesis of the basic principles of what is now known as Theosophy. Isis makes no attempt to organize the whole field of human and divine knowledge, as does The Secret Doctrine. It merely points to the evidence for the existence of that knowledge, and only dimly suggests the outlines of the cosmic scheme in which it must be made to fit. It is in a sense a panoramic survey of the world literature out of which she essayed in part to draw the system of Theosophy. If Theosophy is to be found in Isis, it is there in seminal form, not in organic expression. Perhaps it were better to say that the book prepared the soil for the planting of Madame Blavatsky's later teaching. Her impelling thought was to reveal the traces, in ancient and medieval history and literature, of a secret science whose principles had been lost to view. She aimed to show that the most vital science mankind had ever controlled had sunk further below general recognition now than in any former times. She would relight the lamp of that archaic wisdom, which would illuminate the darkness of modern scientific pride.

Her work, then, was to make a restatement of the occult doctrine with its ancient attestations. This was a gigantic task. It meant little short of a thorough search in the entire field of ancient religion, philosophy, and science, with an eye to the discernment of the mystery tradition, teachings, and practices wherever manifested; and then the collation, correlation, and systematic presentation of this multifarious material in something like a structural unity. The many legends of mystic power, the hundreds of myths and fables, were to be traced to ancient rites, whose far-off symbolism threw light on their significance. It would be not merely an encyclopedia of the whole mythical life of the race, but a digest and codification, so to speak, of the entire mass into a system breathing intelligible meaning and common sense. Her task, in a word, was to redeem the whole ancient world from the modern stigma of superstition, crude ignorance, and childish imagination.

In view of the immensity of her undertaking we are forced to wonder whence came the self-assurance that led her to believe she could successfully achieve it.
She was sadly deficient in formal education; her opportunities for scholarship and research had been limited; her command of the English language was imperfect. Yet her actual accomplishment pointed to her possession of capital and resources the existence of which has furnished the ground for much of the mystery now enshrouding her life. There seems to be an obvious discrepancy between her qualifications and her product, to account for which diverse theories have been adduced.

Just how, when and where Madame Blavatsky gained her acquaintance with practically the entire field of ancient religions, philosophies, and science, is a query which probably can never be satisfactorily answered. The history of many portions of her life before 1873 is unrecorded. We do not know when or where she studied ancient literature. Books from which she quoted were not within her reach when she wrote Isis. Can her knowledge be attributed to a phenomenal memory? Olcott does say:

"She constantly drew upon a memory stored with a wealth of recollections of personal perils and adventures and of knowledge of occult science, not merely unparalleled, but not even approached by any other person who had ever appeared in America, so far as I have heard."2

Throughout the two volumes of Isis there are frequent allusions to or actual passages from ancient writings, a list of which includes the following: The Codex Nazareus; the Zohar, the great Kabbalistic work of the Jews; Chaldean3 Oracles; Chaldean Book of Numbers; Psellus' Works; Zoroastrian Oracles; Magical and Philosophical Precepts of Zoroaster; Egyptian Book of the Dead; Books of Hermes; Quiché Cosmogony; Book of Jasher; Kabala of the Tanaim; Sepher Jezira; Book of Wisdom of Schlomah (Solomon); Secret Treatise on Mukta and Badha; The Stangyour of the Tibetans; Desatir (pseudo-Persian4); Orphic Hymns; Sepher Toldos Jeshu (Hebrew MSS. of great antiquity); Laws of Manu; Book of Keys (Hermetic Work); Gospel of Nicodemus; The Shepherd of Hermas; (Spurious) Gospel of the Infancy; Gospel of St. Thomas; Book of Enoch; The History of Baarlam and Josaphat; Book of Evocations(of the Pagodas); Golden Verses of Pythagoras; various Kabbalas; Tarot of the Bohemians.

In the realm of more widely-known literature, she uses material from Plato and to a minor extent, Aristotle; quotes the early Greek philosophers, Thales, Heraclitus, Parmenides, Empedocles, Democritus; is conversant with the Neo- Platonist representatives, Ammonius Saccas, Plotinus, Porphyry, Iamblichus and Proclus; shows familiarity with Plutarch, Philo, Apollonius of Tyana, the Gnostics, Basilides, Bardesanes, Marcion, and Valentinus. She had examined the Church Fathers, from Augustine to Justin Martyr, and was especially familiar with Irenaeus, Tertullian and Eusebius, whom she charged with having wrecked the true ancient wisdom. Beside this array she draws on the enormous Vedic, Brahmanic, Vedantic, and Buddhistic literatures; likewise the Chinese, Persian, Babylonian, "Chaldean," Syrian, and Egyptian. Nor does she neglect the ancient American contributions, such as the Popul Vuh. Her acquaintance also with the vast literature of occult magic and philosophy of the Middle Ages seems hardly less inclusive. She levies upon Averroës, Maimonides, Paracelsus, Van Helmont, Robert Fludd, Eugenius Philalethes, Cornelius Agrippa von Nettesheim, Roger Bacon, Bruno, Pletho, Mirandolo, Henry More and many a lesser-known expounder of mysticism and magic art. She quotes incessantly from scores of compendious modern works.

Because of this show of prodigious learning some students later alleged that Isis was not the work of Madame Blavatsky, but of Dr. Alexander Wilder; others declared that Col. Olcott had written it.5

There are three main sources of testimony bearing on the composition of the books: (1) Statements of her immediate associates and co-workers in the writing;
(2) Her own version; (3) The evidence of critics who have traced the sources of her materials.

First, there is the testimony of her colleague, Olcott, who for two years collaborated almost daily with her in the work. He says:

"Whence, then, did H.P.B. draw the materials which comprise Isis and which cannot be traced to accessible literary sources of quotation? From the Astral Light, and by her soul-senses, from her Teachers-the 'Brothers,' 'Adepts,' 'Sages,' 'Masters,' as they have been variously called. How do I know it? By working two years with her on Isis and many more years on other literary work."6

He goes on:

"To watch her at work was a rare and never-to-be-forgotten experience. We sat at opposite sides of one big table usually, and I could see her every movement. Her pen would be flying over the page; when she would suddenly stop, look out into space with the vacant eye of the clairvoyant seer, shorten her vision as though

to look at something held invisibly in the air before her, and begin copying on the paper what she saw. The quotation finished, her eyes would resume their natural expression, and she would go on writing until again stopped by a similar interruption."7

Still more remarkable is the following:

"Most perfect of all were the manuscripts which were written for her while she was sleeping. The beginning of the chapter on the civilization of ancient Egypt (Vol. I., Chapter XIV) is an illustration. We had stopped work the evening before at about 2 A.M. as usual, both too tired to stop for our usual smoke and chat before parting; she almost fell asleep in her chair, while I was bidding her goodnight; so I hurried off to my bed room. The next morning, when I came down after my breakfast, she showed me a pile of at least thirty or forty pages of beautifully written H.P.B. manuscript, which, she said, she had had written for her by------, a Master . . . It was perfect in every respect and went to the printers without revision."8

It is the theory of Olcott that the mind of H.P.B. was receptive to the impressions of three or four intelligent entities-other persons living or dead- who overshadowed her mentally, and wrote through her brain. These personages seemed to cast their sentences upon an imperceptible screen in her mind. They sometimes talked to Olcott as themselves, not as Madame Blavatsky. Their intermittent tenancy of her mind he takes as accounting for the higgledy- piggledy manner in which the book was constructed. Each had his favorite themes and the Colonel learned what kind of material to expect when one gave place to another. There was in particular, in addition to several of the Oriental "Sages," a collaborator in the person of an old Platonist-"the pure soul of one of the wisest philosophers of modern times, one who was an ornament to our race, a glory to his country." He was so engrossed in his favorite earthly pursuits of philosophy that he projected his mind into the work of Madame Blavatsky and gave her abundant aid.

"He did not materialize and sit with us, nor obsess H.P.B. medium-fashion, he would simply talk with her-psychically, by the hour together, dictating copy, telling her what references to hunt up; answering my questions about details, instructing me as to principles; and, in fact, playing the part of a third person in our literary symposium. He gave me his portrait once-a rough sketch in colored crayons on flimsy paper . . . from first to last his relation to us both was that of a mild, kind, extremely learned teacher and elder friend."9

The medieval occultist Paracelsus manifested his presence for a brief time one evening.10 At another time Madame produced two volumes necessary to verify questions which Olcott doubted.

"I went and found the two volumes wanted, which, to my knowledge, had not been in the house until that very moment. I compared the texts with H.P.B.'s quotation, showed her that I was right in my suspicions as to the error, made the proof correction, and then . . . returned the two volumes to the place on the étagère from which I had taken them. I resumed my seat and work, and when, after while, I looked again in that direction, the books had disappeared."11

As Olcott states, when one or another of these unseen monitors was in evidence, the work went on in fine fashion. But, he notes, when Madame was left entirely to her own devices, she floundered in more or less helpless ineptitude. She would write haltingly, scratch it over, make a fresh start, work herself into a fret and get nowhere.

Olcott's testimony, as that of Dr. Wilder, Mr. Judge, Dr. Corson, the Countess Wachtmeister, the two Keightleys, Mr. Fawcett and all the others who at one time or another were in a position to observe Madame Blavatsky at work, must be accepted as sincere. But if anybody could be supposed to know unmistakably what was happening in her mind, that person would be the subject herself. What has she to say? She states decisively that she was not the author, only the writer of her books. In one of her home letters she says, speaking of Isis:

"since neither ideas nor teachings are mine."

In another letter to Madame Jelihowsky she writes:

"Well, Vera, whether you believe me or not, something miraculous is happening to me. You cannot imagine in what a charmed world of pictures and vision I live. I am writing Isis; not writing, rather copying out and drawing that which She personally shows to me. Upon my word, sometimes it seems to me that the ancient goddess of Beauty in person leads me through all the countries of past centuries which I have to describe. I sit with my eyes open and to all appearances see and hear everything real and actual around me, and yet at the same time I see and hear that which I write. I feel short of breath; I am afraid to make the slightest movement for fear the spell might be broken. Slowly century after century, image after image, float out of the distance and pass before me as if in a magic panorama; and meanwhile I put them together in my mind, fitting in epochs and dates, and know for sure that there can be no mistake. Races and nations, countries and cities, which have long disappeared in the darkness of the prehistoric past, emerge and then vanish, giving place to others; and then I am told the consecutive dates. Hoary antiquity makes way for historical periods; myths are explained to me with events and people who have really existed, and every event which is at all remarkable, every newly-turned page of this many- colored book of life, impresses itself on my brain with photographic exactitude. My own reckonings and calculations appear to me later on as separate colored pieces of different shapes in the game which is called casse-tête (puzzles). I gather them together and try to match them one after the other, and at the end there always comes out a geometrical whole. . . . Most assuredly it is not I who do it all, but my Ego, the highest principle that lives in me. And even this with the help of my Guru and teacher who helps me in everything. If I happen to forget something I have just to address him, and another of the same kind in my thought as what I have forgotten rises once more before my eyes-sometimes whole tables of numbers passing before me, long inventories of events. They remember everything. They know everything. Without them, from whence could I gather my knowledge? I certainly refuse point blank to attribute it to my own knowledge or memory, for I could never arrive alone at either such premises or conclusions. I tell you seriously I am helped. And he who helps me is my Guru."12

In another letter to the same sister Helena assures her relative about her mental condition:

"Do not be afraid that I am off my head; all I can say is that someone positively inspires me. . . . More than this; someone enters me. It is not I who talk and write; it is something within me; my higher and luminous Self; that thinks and writes for me. Do not ask me, my friend, what I experience, because I could not explain it to you clearly. I do not know myself! The one thing I know is that now, when I am about to reach old age, I have become a sort of storehouse of somebody else's knowledge. . . . Someone comes and envelops me as a misty cloud and all at once pushes me out of myself, and then I am not 'I' any more-Helena P. Blavatsky-but somebody else. Someone strong and powerful, born in

a totally different region of the world; and as to myself it is almost as if I were asleep, or lying by not quite conscious-not in my own body, but close by, held only by a thread which ties me to it. However at times I see and hear everything quite clearly; I am perfectly conscious of what my body is saying and doing-or at least its new possessor. I can understand and remember it all so well that afterwards I can repeat it, and even write down his words.   At
such a time I see awe and fear on the faces of Olcott and others, and follow with interest the way in which he half-pityingly regards them out of my own eyes, and teaches them with my physical tongue. Yet not with my mind, but his own, which enwraps my brain like a cloud. . . . Ah, but I really cannot explain everything!"13

Again writing to her relatives, she states:

"When I wrote Isis I wrote it so easily that it was certainly no labor but a real pleasure. Why should I be praised for it? Whenever I am told to write I sit down and obey, and then I can write easily upon almost anything-metaphysics, psychology, philosophy, ancient religions, zoölogy, natural sciences or what not. I never put myself the question: 'Can I write on this subject?'   or,
'Am I equal to the task?' but I simply sit down and write. Why? Because someone who knows all dictates to me. My Master and occasionally others whom I knew on my travels years ago. . . . I tell you candidly, that whenever I write upon a subject I know little or nothing of, I address myself to them, and one of them inspires me, i.e., he allows me to simply copy what I write from manuscripts, and even printed matter, that pass before my eyes, in the air, during which process I have never been unconscious one single instant."14

To her aunt she wrote:

"At such times it is no more I who write, but my inner Ego, my 'luminous Self,' who thinks and writes for me. Only see . . . you who know me. When was I ever so learned as to write such things? Whence was all this knowledge?"

Whatever the actual authorship of the two volumes may have been, their publication stirred such wide-spread interest that the first editions were swept up at once, and Bouton, the publisher, was taken off guard, there being some delay before succeeding editions of the bulky tomes could be issued.
Professional reviewers were not so generous; but the press critics were frankly intrigued into something like praise.15

Years after the publication of Isis, Mr. Emmette Coleman, a former Theosophist and contributor to current magazines, stated that he spent three years upon a critical and exhaustive examination of the sources used by Madame Blavatsky in her various works. He attempted to discredit the whole Theosophic movement by casting doubt upon the genuineness of her knowledge. He accused her of outright plagiarism and went to great pains to collect and present his evidence. In 1893 he published his data. We quote the following passage from his statement:

"In Isis Unveiled, published in 1877, I discovered some 2,000 passages copied from other books without proper credit. By careful analysis I found that in compiling Isis about 100 books were used. About 1,400 books are quoted from and referred to in this work; but, from the 100 books which its author possessed, she copied everything in Isis taken from and relating to the other 1,300. There are in Isis about 2,100 quotations from and references to books that were copied, at second-hand, from books other than the originals; and of this number only about 140 are credited to the books from which Madame Blavatsky copied them at second-hand. The others are quoted in such a manner as to lead the reader to

think that Madame Blavatsky had read and utilized the original works, and had quoted from them at first-hand,--the truth being that these originals had evidently never been read by Madame Blavatsky. By this means many readers of Isis . . . have been misled into thinking Madame Blavatsky an enormous reader, possessed of vast erudition; while the fact is her reading was very limited, and her ignorance was profound in all branches of knowledge."16

Coleman went on to assert that "not a line of the quotations" made by H.P.B. ostensibly from the Kabala, from the old-time mystics at the time of Paracelsus, from the classical authors, Homer, Livy, Ovid, Virgil, Pliny, and others, from the Church Fathers, from the Neo-Platonists, was taken from the originals, but all from second-hand usage. He charged her with having picked all these passages out of modern books scattered throughout which she found the material from a wide range of ancient authorship. The reader of Isis will readily find her many references to modern authors. Coleman mentioned a half dozen standard works that she used; it is well worth while glancing at a fuller list. She had read, or was more or less familiar with: King's Gnostics; Jennings' Rosicrucians; Dunlop's Sod, and Spirit History of Man; Moor's Hindu Pantheon; Ennemoser's History of Magic; Howitt's History of the Supernatural; Salverte's Philosophy of Magic; Barrett's Magus; Col. H. Yule's The Book of Ser Marco Polo; Inman's Pagan and Modern Christian Symbolism and Ancient Faiths and Modern; the anonymous The Unseen Universe and Supernatural Religion; Bunsen's Egypt's Place in Universal History; Lundy's Monumental Christianity; Horst's Zauber-Bibliothek; Cardinal Wiseman's Lectures on Science and Religion; Draper's The Conflict of Science with Religion; Dupuis' Origin of All the Cults; Bailly's Ancient and Modern Astronomy; Gibbon's Decline and Fall of the Roman Empire; Des Mousseaux's Roman Catholic writings on Magic, Mesmerism, Spiritualism; Eliphas Levi's works; Jacolliot's twenty-seven volumes on Oriental systems; Max Müller's, Huxley's, Tyndall's, and Spencer's works.

It is hardly to be doubted that Madame Blavatsky culled many of her ancient gems from these works, and she probably felt that it was a matter of minor importance how she came by them. What she was bent on saying was that the ancients had said these things and that they were confirmatory of her general theses. Yet Coleman's findings must not be disregarded. His work brought into clearer light the meagreness of her resources and her lack of scholarly preparation for so pretentious a study.

We have adduced the several hypotheses that have been advanced to account for the writing of Isis Unveiled. It must be left for the reader to arrive at what conclusion he can on the basis of the material presented. We pass on to an examination of the contents.

A hint as to the aim of the work, is given in the sub-title: A Master-key to the Mysteries of Ancient and Modern Science and Theology. She says:

"The work now submitted to the public judgment is the fruit of a somewhat intimate acquaintance with Eastern Adepts and study of their science. It is a work on magico-spiritual philosophy and occult science. It is an attempt to aid the student to detect the vital principles which underlie the philosophical systems of old."17

She affirms it to be her aim "to show that the pretended authorities of the West must go to the Brahmans and Lamaists of the far Orient and respectfully ask them to impart the alphabet of true science."18

Isis, then, is a glorification of the ancient Orientals. Their knowledge was so profound that we are incredulous when told about it. If we have "harnessed the forces of Nature to do our work," they had subjugated the world to their will. They knew things we have not yet dreamed of. She states:

"It is rather a brief summary of the religions, philosophies and universal traditions in the spirit of those secret doctrines of which none,--thanks to prejudice and bigotry-have reached Christendom in so unmutilated a form as to secure it a fair judgment. Since the days of the unlucky Mediaeval philosophers, the last to write upon these secret doctrines of which they were the depositaries, few men have dared to brave persecution and prejudice by placing their knowledge on record. And these few have never, as a rule, written for the public, but only for those of their own and succeeding times who possessed the key to their jargon. The multitude, not understanding them or their doctrines, have been accustomed to regard them en masse as either charlatans or dreamers.
Hence the unmerited contempt into which the study of the noblest of sciences- that of the spiritual man-has gradually fallen."19

She plans to restore this lost and fairest of the sciences. Materialism is menacing man's higher spiritual unfoldment.

"To prevent the crushing of these spiritual aspirations, the blighting of these hopes, and the deadening of that intuition which teaches us of a God and a hereafter, we must show our false theologies in their naked deformity and distinguish between divine religion and human dogmas. Our voice is raised for spiritual freedom and our plea made for the enfranchisement from all tyranny, whether of Science or Theology."20

She here sets forth her attitude toward orthodox religionism as well as toward materialistic science. She intimates that since the days of the true esoteric wisdom, mankind has been thrown back and forth between the systems of an unenlightening theology and an equally erroneous science, both stultifying in their influence on spiritual aspiration, both blighting the delicate culture of beauty and joyousness.

"It was while most anxious to solve these perplexing problems [Who, where, what is God? What is the spirit in man?] that we came into contact with certain men, endowed with such mysterious powers and such profound knowledge that we may truly designate them as the Sages of the Orient.

To their instruction we lent a ready ear. They showed us that by combining science with religion, the existence of God and the immortality of man's spirit may be demonstrated like a problem of Euclid."

She adds:

"Such knowledge is priceless; and it has been hidden only from those who overlooked it, derided it or denied its existence."21

The soul within escapes their view, and the Divine Mother has no message for them. To become conversant with the powers of the soul we must develop the higher faculties of intuition and spiritual vision.22

She says that there were colleges in the days of old for the teaching of prophecy and occultism in general. Samuel and Elisha were heads of such academies, she affirms. The study of magic or wisdom included every branch of science, the metaphysical as well as the physical, psychology and physiology, in their common and occult phases; and the study of alchemy was universal, for it

was both a physical and a spiritual science. The ancients studied nature under its double aspect and the claim is that they discovered secrets which the modern physicist, who studies but the dead forms of things, can not unlock. There are regions of nature which will never yield their mysteries to the scientist armed only with mechanical apparatus. The ancients studied the outer forms of nature, but in relation to the inner life. Hence they saw more than we and were better able to read meaning in what they saw. They regarded everything in nature as the materialization of spirit. Thus they were able to find an adequate ground for the harmonization of science and religion. They saw spirit begetting force, and force matter; spirit and matter were but the two aspects of the one essence. Matter is nothing other than the crystallization of spirit on the outer periphery of its emanative range. The ancients worshipped, not nature, but the power behind nature.

Madame Blavatsky contrasts this fulness of the ancient wisdom with the barrenness of modern knowledge. She characterizes the eighteenth century as a "barren period," during which "the malignant fever of scepticism" has spread through the thought of the age and transmitted "unbelief as an hereditary disease on the nineteenth." She challenges science to explain some of the commonest phenomena of nature; why, for instance, the moon affects insane people, why the crises of certain diseases correspond to lunar changes, why certain flowers alternately open and close their petals as clouds flit across the face of the moon. She says that science has not yet learned to look outside this ball of dirt for hidden influences which are affecting us day by day. The ancients, she declares, postulated reciprocal relations between the planetary bodies as perfect as those between the organs of the body and the corpuscles of the blood. There is not a plant or mineral which has disclosed the last of its properties to the scientist. She declares that theurgical magic is the last expression of occult psychological science; and denies the "Academicians" "the right of expressing their opinion on a subject which they have never investigated." "Their incompetence to determine the value of magic and Spiritualism is as demonstrable as that of the Fiji Islander to evaluate the labors of Faraday or Agassiz." There was no missing link in the ancient knowledge, no hiatus to be filled "with volumes of materialistic speculation made necessary by the absurd attempt to solve an equation with but one set of quantities." She runs on:

"Our 'ignorant' ancestors traced the law of evolution throughout the whole universe. As by gradual progression from the star-cloudlet to the development of the physical body of man, the rule holds good, so from the universal ether to the incarnate human spirit, they traced one uninterrupted series of entities.

These evolutions were from the world of spirit into the world of gross matter; and through that back again to the source of all things. The 'descent of species' was to them a descent from the spirit, primal source of all, to the 'degradation of matter.' In this complete chain of unfoldings the elementary, spiritual beings had as distinct a place, midway between the extremes, as Darwin's missing link between the ape and man."23

Modern knowledge posits only evolution; the old science held that evolution was neither conceivable nor understandable without a previous involution.

The existence of myriads of orders of beings not human in a realm of nature to which our senses do not normally give us access, and of which science knows nothing at all, is posited in her arcane systems. She catches at Milton's lines to bolster this theory:

"Millions of spiritual creatures walk this earth,

Unseen both when we sleep and when we wake."

She says that if the spiritual faculties of the soul are sharpened by intense enthusiasm and purified from earthly desire, man may learn to see some of these denizens of the illimitable air.

The physical world was fashioned on the model of divine ideas, which, like the unseen lines of force radiated by the magnet, to throw the iron-filings into determinate shape, give form and nature to the physical manifestation. If man's essential nature partakes of this universal life, then it, too, must partake of all the attributes of the demiurgic power. As the Creator, breaking up the chaotic mass of dead inactive matter, shaped it into form, so man, if he knew his powers, could to a degree do the same.

To redeem the ancient world from modern scorn Madame Blavatsky had to vindicate magic-with all its incubus of disrepute and ridicule-and lift its practitioners to a lofty place in the ranks of true science. She had to demonstrate that genuine magic was a veritable fact, an undeniable part of the history of man; and not only true, but the highest evidence of man's kinship with nature, the topmost manifestation of his power, the royal science among all sciences! To her view the dearth of magic in modern philosophies was at once the cause and the effect of their barrenness. If they are to be vitalized again, magic must be revived. "That magic is indeed possible is the moral of this book."24

And along with magic she had to champion its aboriginal bed-fellows, astrology, alchemy, healing, mesmerism, trance subjection, and the whole brood of "pseudo- science."

"It is an insult to human nature to brand magic and the occult sciences with the name of imposture. To believe that for so many thousands of years one half of mankind practiced deception and fraud on the other half is equivalent to saying that the human race is composed only of knaves and incurable idiots. Where is the country in which magic was not practiced? At what age was it wholly forgotten?"25

She explains magic as based on a reciprocal sympathy between celestial and terrestrial natures. It is based on the mysterious affinities existing between organic and inorganic bodies, between the visible and the invisible powers of the universe. "That which science calls gravitation the ancient and the medieval hermeticists called magnetism, attraction, affinity." She continues:

"A thorough familiarity with the occult faculties of everything existing in Nature, visible as well as invisible; their mutual relations, attractions and repulsions; the cause of these traced to the spiritual principle which pervades and animates all things; the ability to furnish the best conditions for this principle to manifest itself, in other words a profound and exhaustive knowledge of natural law- this was and is the basis of magic."26

Out of man's kinship with nature, his identity of constitution with it, she argues to his magical powers:

"As God creates, so man can create. Given a certain intensity of will, and the shapes created by the mind become subjective. Hallucinations they are called, although to their creator they are real as any visible object is to any one else. Given a more intense and intelligent concentration of this will, and the forms become concrete, visible, objective; the man has learned the secret of secrets; he is a Magician."27

She makes it clear that this power is built on the conscious control of the substrate of the material universe. She states that the key to all magic is the formula: "Every insignificant atom is moved by spirit." Magic is thus conditioned upon the postulation of an omnipresent vital ether, electro- spiritual in composition, to which man has an affinity by virtue of his being identical in essence with it. Over it he can learn to exercise a voluntary control by the exploitation of his own psycho-dynamic faculties. If he can lay his hand on the elemental substance of the universe, if he can radiate from his ganglionic batteries currents of force equivalent to gamma rays, of course he can step into the cosmic scene with something of a magician's powers. That such an ether exists she states in a hundred places. She calls it the elementary substance, the Astral Light, the Alkahest, the Akasha. It is the universal principle of all life, the vehicle or battery of cosmic energy. She says Newton knew of it and called it "the soul of the world," the "divine sensorium." It is the Book of Life; the memory of God,--since it never gives up an impression.
Human memory is but a looking into pictures on this ether. Clairvoyants and psychometers but draw upon its resources through synchronous vibrations.

"According to the Kabalistic doctrine the future exits in the astral light in embryo as the present existed in embryo in the past . . . and our memories are but the glimpses that we catch of the reflections of this past in the currents of the astral light, as the psychometer catches them from the astral emanations of the object held by him."28

Madame Blavatsky goes so far as to link the control of these properties with the tiny pulsations of the magnetic currents emanating from our brains, under the impelling power of will. Thus she attempts to unite magic with the most subtle conceptions of our own advanced physics and chemistry. She thus weds the most arrant of superstitions with the most respected of sciences.

The magnetic nature of gravitation is set forth in more than one passage. She wrote:

"The ethereal spiritual fire, the soul and the spirit of the all-pervading mysterious ether; the despair and puzzle of the materialists, who will some day find out that that which causes the numberless forces to manifest themselves in eternal correlation is but a divine electricity, or rather galvanism, and that the sun is one of the myriad magnets disseminated through space. . . . There is no gravitation in the Newtonian sense, but only magnetic attraction and repulsion; and it is only by their magnetism that the planets of the solar system have their motions regulated in their respective orbits by the still more powerful magnetism of the sun; not by their weight or gravitation.   The passage of light through this (cosmic ether) must produce enormous friction. Friction generates electricity and it is this electricity and its correlative magnetism which forms those tremendous forces of nature. . . . It is not at all to the sun that we are indebted for light and heat; light is a creation sui generis, which springs into existence at the instant when the deity willed." She "laughs at the current theory of the incandescence of the sun and its gaseous substance. . . . The sun, planets, stars and nebulae are all magnets. . . .

There is but One Magnet in the universe and from it proceeds the magnetization of everything existing."29

It is this same universal ether and its inherent magnetic dynamism that sets the field for astrology, as a cosmic science. Of this she says that astrology is a science as infallible as astronomy itself, provided its interpreters are as infallible as the mathematicians. She carries the law of the instantaneous interrelation of everything in the cosmos to such an extent that, quoting Eliphas Levi, "even so small a thing as the birth of one child upon our insignificant planet has its effect upon the universe, as the whole universe has its reflective influence upon him." The bodies of the entire universe are bound together by attractions which hold them in equilibrium, and these magnetic influences are the bases of astrology.

With so much cosmic power at his behest, man has done wonders; and we are asked to accept the truth of an amazing series of the most phenomenal occurrences ever seriously given forth. They range over so varied a field that any attempt at classification is impossible. Of physical phenomena she says that the ancients could make marble statues sweat, and even speak and leap! They had gold lamps which burned in tombs continuously for seven hundred to one thousand years without refueling! One hundred and seventy-three authorities are said to have testified to the existence of such lamps. Even "Aladdin's magical lamp has also certain claims to reality." There was an asbestos oil whose properties, when it was rubbed on the skin, made the body impervious to the action of fire. Witnesses are quoted as stating that they observed natives in Africa who permitted themselves to be fired at point blank with a revolver, having first precipitated around them an impervious layer of astral or akashic substance. Cardinal de Rohan's testimony is adduced to the effect that he had seen Cagliostro make gold and diamonds. The power of the evil eye is enlarged upon and instances recounted of persons hypnotizing, "charming," or even killing birds and animals with a look. She avers that she herself had seen Eastern Adepts turn water into blood. Observers are quoted who reported a rope-climbing feat in China and Batavia, in which the human climbers disappeared overhead, their members fell in portions on the ground, and shortly thereafter reunited to form the original living bodies! Stories are narrated of fakirs disemboweling and re-embowling themselves. She herself saw whirling dancers at Petrovsk in 1865, who cut themselves in frenzy and evoked by the magical powers of blood the spirits of the dead, with whom they then danced. Twice she was nearly bitten by poisonous snakes, but was saved by a word of control from a Shaman or conjurer. The close affinity between man and nature is illustrated by the statement that in one case a tree died following the death of its human twin. Speaking of magical trees, she several times tells of the great tree Kumboum, of Tibet, over whose leaves and bark nature had imprinted ten thousand spiritual maxims. The magical significance of birthmarks is brought out, with remarkable instances.

She dwells at length on the inability of medical men to tell definitely whether the human body is dead or not, and cites a dozen gruesome tales of reawakening in the grave. This takes her into vampirism, which she establishes on the basis of numerous cases taken mostly from Russian folklore. It is stated that the Hindu pantheon claimed 330,000,000 types of spirits. Moses was familiar with electricity; the Egyptians had a high order of music and chess over five thousand years ago; and anaesthesia was known to the ancients. Perpetual motion, the Elixer of Life, the Fountain of Youth and the Philosopher's Stone are declared to be real. She adduces in every case a formidable show of testimony other than her own. And back of it all is her persistent assertion that purity of life and thought is a requisite for high magical performance.

"A man free from worldly incentives and sensuality may cure in such a way the most 'incurable' diseases, and his vision may become clear and prophetic."30

"The magic power is never possessed by those addicted to vicious indulgences."31

Phenomena come, she feels, rather easily; spiritual life is harder won and worthier.

"With expectancy, supplemented by faith, one can cure himself of almost any morbific condition. The tomb of a saint; a holy relic; a talisman; a bit of paper or a garment that has been handled by a supposed healer; a nostrum, a penance; a ceremonial; a laying on of hands; or a few words impressively pronounced-will do. It is a question of temperament, imagination, self-cure."32

"While phenomena of a physical nature may have their value as a means of arousing the interest of materialists, and confirming, if not wholly, at least inferentially, our belief in the survival of our souls, it is questionable whether, under their present aspect, the modern phenomena are not doing more harm than good."33

Theosophists themselves often quarrel with Isis because it seems to overstress bizarre phenomena. They should see that Volume I of the book aims to show the traces of magic in ancient science, in order to offset the Spiritualist claims to new discoveries, and to attract attention to the more philosophic ideas underlying classic magic. Volume II labors to reveal the presence of a vast occultism behind the religions and theologies of the world. Again the contention is that the ancient priests knew more than the modern expositor, that they kept more concealed than the present-day theologian has revealed. Modern theology has lost its savor of early truth and power, as modern technology no longer possesses the "lost arts." Paganism was to be vindicated as against ecclesiastical orthodoxies.

She believed that her instruction under the Lamas or Adepts in Tibet had given her this key, and that therefore the whole vast territory of ancient religion lay unfruitful for modern understanding until she should come forward and put the key to the lock. The "key" makes her in a sense the exponent and depository of "the essential veracities of all the religions and philosophies that are or ever were."

"Myth was the favorite and universal method of teaching in archaic times."34

We can not be oblivious of the use made by Plato of myths in his theoretical constructions. "Fairy tales do not exclusively belong to nurseries; all mankind-except those few who in all ages have comprehended their hidden meaning, and tried to open the eyes of the superstitious-have listened to such tales in one shape or other, and, after transforming them into sacred symbols, called the product Religion."35

"There are a few myths in any religious system but have an historical as well as a scientific foundation. Myths, as Pococke ably expresses it, 'are now found to be fables just in proportion as we misunderstand them; truths, in proportion as they were once understood.'"36

The esotericism of the teachings of Christ and the Buddha is manifest to anyone who can reason, she declares. Neither can be supposed to have given out all that a divine being would know.

"It is a poor compliment paid the Supreme, this forcing upon him four gospels, in which, contradictory as they often are, there is not a single narrative, sentence or peculiar expression, whose parallel may not be found in some older doctrine of philosophy. Surely the Almighty-were it but to spare future generations their present perplexity-might have brought down with Him, at His first and only incarnation on earth, something original-something that would

trace a distinct line of demarcation between Himself and the score or so of incarnate Pagan gods, who had been born of virgins, had all been saviors, and were either killed or were otherwise sacrificed for humanity."37

She says that not she but the Christian Fathers and their successors in the church have put their divine Son of God in the position of a poor religious plagiarist!

Ancient secret wisdom was seldom written down at all; it was taught orally, and imparted as a priceless tradition by one set of students to their qualified successors. Those receiving it regarded themselves as its custodians and they accepted their stewardship conscientiously.

To understand the reason for esotericism in science and religion in earlier times, Madame Blavatsky urges us to recall that freedom of speech invited persecution.

"The Rosicrucian, Hermetic and Theosophical Western writers, producing their books in epochs of religious ignorance and cruel bigotry, wrote, so to say, with the headman's axe suspended over their necks, or the executioner's fagots laid under their chairs, and hid their divine knowledge under quaint symbols and misleading metaphors."38

To give lesser people what they could not appropriate, to stir complacent conservatism with that threat of disturbing old established habitudes which higher knowledge always brings, was unsafe in a world still actuated by codes of arbitrary physical power. High knowledge had to be esoteric until the progress of general enlightenment brought the masses to a point where the worst that could happen to the originator of revolutionary ideas would be the reputation of an idiot, instead of the doom of a Bruno or a Joan. Madame Blavatsky was willing to be regarded as an idiot, but her Masters could not send her forth until

autos-da-fé had gone out of vogue.

We have seen in an earlier chapter that the Mystery Religions of the Eastern Mediterranean world harbored an esotericism that presumably influenced the formulation of later systems, notably Judaism and Christianity. In recent decades more attention has been given to the claims of these old secret societies. St. Paul's affiliation with them is claimed by Theosophists, and his obvious indebtedness to them is acknowledged by some students of early Christianity. It is impossible for Madame Blavatsky to understand the Church's indifference to its origins, and she arrays startling columns of evidence to show that this neglect may be fatal. The Mystery Schools, she proclaims, were not shallow cults, but the guardians of a deep lore already venerable.

"The Mysteries are as old as the world, and one well versed in the esoteric mythologies of various nations, can trace them back to the days of the Ante- Vedic period in India."39

She does not soften her animosity against those influences and agencies that she charges with culpability for smothering out the Gnosis. The culprit in the case is Christianity.

"For over fifteen centuries, thanks to the blindly-brutal persecution of those great vandals of early Christian history, Constantine and Justinian, ancient wisdom slowly degenerated until it gradually sank into the deepest mire of monkish superstition and ignorance. The Pythagorean 'knowledge of things that are'; the profound erudition of the Gnostics; the world- and time-honored

teachings of the great philosophers; all were rejected as doctrines of Antichrist and Paganism and committed to the flames. With the last seven Wise Men of the Orient, the remnant group of Neo-Platonists, Hermias, Priscianus, Diogenes, Eulalius, Damaskius, Simplicius and Isodorus, who fled from the fanatical persecutions of Justinian to Persia, the reign of wisdom closed. The books of Thoth . . . containing within their sacred pages the spiritual and physical history of the creation and progress of our world, were left to mould in oblivion and contempt for ages. They found no interpreters in Christian Europe; the Philalethians, or wise 'lovers of truth' were no more; they were replaced by the light-fleers, the tonsured and hooded monks of Papal Rome, who dread truth, in whatever shape and from whatever quarter it appears, if it but clashes in the least with their dogmas."40

She speaks of the

"Jesuitical and crafty spirit which prompted the Christian Church of the late third century to combat the expiring Neo-Platonic and Eclectic Schools. The Church was afraid of the Aristotelian dialectic and wished to conceal the true meaning of the word daemon, Rasit, asdt (emanations); for if the truth of the emanations were rightly understood, the whole structure of the new religion would have crumbled along with the Mysteries."41

This motive is stressed again when she says that the Fathers had borrowed so much from Paganism that they had to obliterate the traces of their appropriations or be recognized by all as merely Neo-Platonists! She is keen to point out the value of the riches thus thrown away or blindly overlooked, and to show how Christianity has been placed at the mercy of hostile disrupting forces because of its want of a true Gnosis. She avers that atheists and materialists now gnaw at the heart of Christianity because it is helpless, lacking the esoteric knowledge of the spiritual constitution of the universe, to combat or placate them. Gnosticism taught man that he could attain the fulness of the stature of his innate divinity; Christianity substituted a weakling's reliance upon a higher power.

Had Christianity held onto the Gnosis and Kabbalism, it would not have had to graft itself onto Judaism and thus tie itself down to many of the developments of a merely tribal religion. Had it not accepted the Jehovah of Moses, she says, it would not have been forced to look upon the Gnostic ideas as heresies, and the world would now have had a religion richly based on pure Platonic philosophy and "surely something would then have been gained." Rome itself, Christianized, paid a heavy penalty for spurning the wisdom of old:

"In burning the works of the theurgists; in proscribing those who affected their study; in affixing the stigma of demonolatry to magic in general; Rome has left her exoteric worship and Bible to be helplessly riddled by every free-thinker, her sexual emblems to be identified with coarseness, and her priests to unwittingly turn magicians and sorcerers in their exorcisms. Thus retribution, by the exquisite adjustment of divine law, is made to overtake this scheme of cruelty, injustice and bigotry, through her own suicidal acts."42

Yet Christianity drew heavily from paganism. It erected almost no novel formulations. Christian canonical books are hardly more than plagiarisms of older literatures, she affirms, compiled, deleted, revised, and twisted. She believed that the first chapters of Genesis were based on the "Chaldean" Kabbala and an old Brahmanical book of prophecies (really later than Genesis). The doctrine of the Trinity as purely Platonic, she says. It was Irenaeus who identified Jesus with the "mask of the Logos or Second Person of the Trinity." The doctrine of the Atonement came from the Gnostics. The Eucharist was common before Christ's time. Some Neo-Platonist, not John, is alleged to have written the Fourth Gospel. The Sermon on the Mount is an echo of the essential principles of monastic Buddhism.

Jesus is torn away from allegiance to the Jewish system and stands neither as its product nor its Messiah. Wresting him away from Judaism, and likewise from the emanational Trinity, both of which rôles were thrust upon him gratuitously by the Christian Fathers, she declares him to have been a Nazarene, i.e., a member of the mystic cult of Essenes of Nazars, which perpetuated Oriental systems of the Gnosis on the shores of the Jordan.

"One Nazarene sect is known to have existed some 150 years B.C. and to have lived on the banks of the Jordan, and on the eastern shore of the Dead Sea, according to Pliny and Josephus. But in King's 'Gnostics' we find quoted another statement by Josephus from verse 13 which says that the Essenes had been established on the shores of the Dead Sea 'for thousands of ages' before Pliny's time."43

Jesus, one of this cult, had become adept in the occult philosophies of Egypt and Israel, and endeavored to make of the two a synthesis, drawing at times on more ancient knowledge from the old Hindu doctrines. He was simply a devout occultist and taught among the people what they could receive of the esoteric knowledge, reserving his deeper teachings for his fellows in the Essene monasteries. He had learned in the East and in Egypt the high science of theurgy, casting out of demons, and control of nature's finer forces, and he used these powers upon occasion. He posed as no Messiah or Incarnation of the Logos, but preached the message of the anointing (Christos) of the human spirit by its baptismal union with the higher principles of our divine nature.44

In short, Madame Blavatsky leaves to Christianity little but the very precarious distinction of having "copied all its rites, dogmas and ceremonies from paganism" save two that can be claimed as original inventions-the doctrine of eternal damnation (with the fiction of the Devil) "and the one custom, that of the anathema."

"The Bible of the Christian Church is the latest receptacle of this scheme of disfigured allegories which have been erected into an edifice of superstition, such as never entered into the conceptions of those from whom the Church obtained her knowledge. The abstract fictions of antiquity, which for ages had filled the popular fancy with but flickering shadows and uncertain images, have in Christianity assumed the shapes of real personages and become historical facts. Allegory metamorphosed, becomes sacred history, and Pagan myth is taught to the people as a revealed narrative of God's intercourse with His chosen people."45

The final proposition which Isis labors to establish is that the one source of all the wisdom of the past is India. Pythagoreanism, she says, is identical with Buddhistic teachings. "The laws of Manu are the doctrines of Plato, Philo, Zoroaster, Pythagoras and the Kabala." She quotes Jacolliot, the French writer:

"This philosophy, the traces of which we find among the Magians, the Chaldeans, the Egyptians, the Hebrew Kabalists, and the Christians, is none other than that of the Hindu Brahmans, the sectarians of the pitris, or the spirits of the invisible worlds which surround us."46

She, with the key in her hand, sees the solution of the problem of comparative religion as an easy one.

"While we see the few translators of the Kabala, the Nazarene Codex and other abstruse works, hopelessly floundering amid the interminable pantheon of names, unable to agree as to a system in which to classify them, for the one hypothesis contradicts and overturns the other, we can but wonder at all this trouble, which could be so easily overcome. But even now, when the translation and even the perusal of the ancient Sanskrit has become so easy as a point of comparison, they would never think it possible that every philosophy-whether Semitic, Hamitic or Turanian, as they call it, has its key in the Hindu sacred works.
Still, facts are there and facts are not easily destroyed."47

"What has been contemptuously termed Paganism was ancient Wisdom replete with Deity. . . . Pre-Vedic Brahmanism and Buddhism are the double source from which all religions spring; Nirvana is the ocean to which all tend."48

She says there are many parallelisms between references to Buddha and to Christ. Many points of identity also exist between Lamaico-Buddhistic and Roman Catholic ceremonies. The idea here hinted at is the underlying thesis of the whole Theosophic position. Successive members of the great Oriental Brotherhood have been incarnated at intervals in the history of mankind, each giving out portions of the one central doctrine, which therefore must have a common base. The puzzling identities found in the study ofComparative Religion thus find an explanation in the identity of their authorship.
Mrs. Annie Besant later elaborated this view in the early pages of her work, Esoteric Christianity.

She contrasts it with the commonly accepted explanation of religious origins of the academicians of our day. Summing up this position she writes:

"The Comparative Mythologists contend that the common origin is a common ignorance, and that the loftiest religious doctrines are simply refined expressions of the crude and barbarous guesses of savages, of primitive men, regarding themselves and their surroundings. Animism, fetishism, nature-worship- these are the constituents of the primitive mud out of which has grown the splendid lily of religion. A Krishna, a Buddha, a Lao-Tze, a Jesus, are the highly civilized, but lineal descendants of the whirling medicine-men of the savage. God is a composite photograph of the innumerable gods who are the personifications of the forces of nature. It is all summed up in the phrase: Religions are branches from a common trunk-human ignorance.

"The Comparative Religionists consider, on the other hand, that all religions originated from the teachings of Divine Men, who gave out to the different nations, from time to time, such parts of the verities of religion as the people are capable of receiving, teaching ever the same morality, inculcating the use of similar means, employing the same significant symbols. The savage religions- animism and the rest-are degenerations, the results of decadence, distorted and dwarfed descendants of true religious beliefs. Sun-worship and pure forms of nature worship were, in their day, noble religions, highly allegorical, but full of profound truth and knowledge. The great Teachers . . . form an enduring Brotherhood of men, who have risen beyond humanity, who appear at certain periods to enlighten the world, and who are the spiritual guardians of the human race. This view may be summed up in the phrase: Religions are branches from a common trunk-Divine Wisdom."49

This is the view of religions which Madame Blavatsky presented in Isis. Religions, it would say, never rise; they only degenerate. Theosophic writers50 are at pains to point out that once a pure high religious impulse is given by a Master-Teacher, it tends before long to gather about it the incrustations of the

human materializing tendency, under which the spiritual truths are obscured and finally lost amid the crudities of literalism. Then after the world has blundered on through a period of darkness the time grows ripe for a new revelation, and another member of the Spiritual Fraternity comes into terrestrial life. Madame Blavatsky says:

"The very corner-stone of their (Brahmans' and Buddhists') religious systems is periodical incarnations of the Deity. Whenever humanity is about merging into materialism and moral degradation, a Supreme Being incarnates himself in his creature selected for the purpose, . . . Christna saying to Arjuna (in the Bhagavad Gita): 'As often as virtue declines in the world, I make myself manifest to save it.'"51

Madame Blavatsky stated that she was in contact with several of these supermen, who sent her forth as their messenger to impart, in new form, the old knowledge.

CHAPTER VI THE MAHATMAS AND THEIR LETTERS

The Masters whom Theosophy presents to us are simply high-ranking students in life's school of experience. They are members of our own evolutionary group, not visitants from the celestial spheres. They are supermen only in that they have attained knowledge of the laws of life and mastery over its forces with which we are still struggling. They are also termed by Theosophists the "just men made perfect," the finished products of our terrene experience, those more earnest souls of our own race who have pressed forward to attain the fulness of the stature of Christ, the prize of the high calling of God in Christhood. They are not Gods come down to earth, but earthly mortals risen to the status of Christs. They ask from us no reverence, no worship; they demand no allegiance but that which it is expected we shall render to the principles of Truth and Fact, and to the nobility of life. They are our "Elder Brothers," not distant deities; and will even make their presence known to us and grant us the privilege of coöperating with them when we have shown ourselves capable of working unselfishly for mankind. They are not our Masters in the sense of holding lordship over us; they are the "Masters of Wisdom and Compassion." Moved by an infinite sympathy with the whole human race they have renounced their right to go forward to more splendid conquests in the evolutionary field, and have remained in touch with man in order to throw the weight of their personal force on the side of progress.

But the rank of the Mahatmas must not be underrated because they still fall under the category of human beings. They have accumulated vast stores of knowledge about the life of man and the universe; about the meaning and purpose of evolution; the methods of progress; the rationale of the expansion of the powers latent in the Ego; the choice and attainment of ends and values in life; and the achievement of beauty and grandeur in individual development. Upon all these questions which affect the life and happiness of mortals they possess competent knowledge which they are willing to impart to qualified students. They have by virtue of their own force of character mastered every human problem, perfected their growth in beauty, gained control over all the natural forces of life. They stand at the culmination of all human endeavor. They have lifted mortality up to immortality, have carried humanity aloft to divinity. Through the mediatorship of the Christos, or spiritual principle in them, they have reconciled the carnal nature of man, his animal soul, with the essential divinity of his higher Self. And they, if they have been lifted up, stand patiently eager to draw all men unto them.

Madame Blavatsky's exploitation of the Adepts (or their exploitation of her) is a startling event in the modern religious drama. It was a unique procedure and took the world by surprise. To be sure, India and Tibet, even China, were familiar with the idea of supermen. India had its Buddhas, Boddhisatvas, and Rishis. But what not even India was prepared to view without suspicion was that

several of the hierarchical Brotherhood should carry on a clandestine intercourse with a nondescript group, made up of a Russian, an American, and several Englishmen, and issue to them fragments of the ancient lore for broadcasting to the incredulous West, which would mock it, scorn it, and trample it underfoot.

It was only justified, according to Madame Blavatsky, by certain considerations which influenced the final decision of the Great White Brotherhood Council.

Majority opinion was against the move; but the minority urged that two reasons rendered it advisable. The guillotine and the fagot pile had been eliminated from the historical forms of martyrdom; and, secondly, the esotericism of the doctrines was, in a manner, an automatic safety device. The teachings would appeal to those who were "ready" for them; their meaning would soar over the heads of those for whom they were not suited.

The matter was decided affirmatively, we are informed, by the assumption of full karmic responsibility for the launching of the crusade by the two Adepts, Morya and Koot Hoomi Lal Singh. The latter, in the early portion of his present incarnation, had been a student at an English University and felt that he had found sufficient reliability on the part of intelligent Europeans to make them worthy to receive the great knowledge. Morya, we are told, had taken on Madame Blavatsky as his personal attaché, pupil or chela. She had earned in former situations the right to the high commission of carrying the old truth to the world at large in the last quarter of the nineteenth century.

It is hinted that Madame Blavatsky had formed a close link with the Master Morya in former births, when she was known to him as a great personage. It is also said that she was herself kept from full admission to the Brotherhood only by some special "Karma" which needed to be "worked out" in a comparatively humble station and personality during this life. She said the Masters knew what she was accountable for, though it was not the charlatanism the world at large charged her with. We are led to assume that the Master Morya exercised a guardianship over her in early life, and later, that he occasionally manifested himself to her, giving her suggestions and encouragement. One or two of these encounters with her Master are recorded. She met him in his physical body in London in 1851. In one of her old note-books, which her aunt Madame Fadeef sent to her in Würzburg in 1885, there is a memorandum of her meeting with Morya in London. The entry is as follows:

"Nuit mémorable. Certaine nuit par un clair de lune que se couchait à-Ramsgate--12 août, 1851,--lorsque je rencontrai le Maître de mes rêves."

Hints are thrown out as to other meetings on her travels, and we are told that she studied ancient philosophy and science under the Master's direct tutelage in Tibet covering periods aggregating at least seven years of her life. The testimony of Col. Olcott is no less precise. He says:

"I had ocular proof that at least some of those who worked with us were living men, from having seen them in the flesh in India, after having seen them in the astral body in America and in Europe; from having touched and talked with them. Instead of telling me that they were spirits, they told me they were as much alive as myself, and that each of them had his own peculiarities and capabilities, in short, his complete individuality. They told me that what they had attained to I should one day myself acquire, how soon would depend entirely on myself; and that I might not anticipate anything whatever from favor, but, like them, must gain every step, every inch, of progress by my own exertions."1

The fact that the Masters were living human beings made their revelations of cosmic and spiritual truth, say the Theosophists, more valuable than alleged revelations from hypothetical Gods in other systems of belief. That their knowledge is, in a manner of speaking, human instead of heavenly or "divine" should give it greater validity for us. The Mahatmas were, it is said, in direct contact with the next higher grades of intelligent beings standing above them in the hierarchical order, so that their teachings have the double worth of high human and supernal authority. This, occultists believe, affords the most trustworthy type of revelation.

It was not until the two Theosophic Founders had reached India, in whose northernmost vastnesses the members of the Great White Brotherhood were said to maintain their earthly residence, that continuous evidence of their reality and their leadership was vouchsafed. The Theosophic case for Adept revelation rests upon a long-continued correspondence between persons (Mr. A. P. Sinnett, mainly, Mr. A. O. Hume, Damodar and others in minor degree) of good intelligence, but claiming no mystical or psychical illumination, and the two Mahatmas, K.H. and

M. Sinnett, Editor of The Pioneer, at Simla in northern India, was an English journalist of distinction and ability. Although he had manifested no special temperamental disposition toward the mystical or occult, he was the particular recipient of the attention and favors of the Mahatmas over a space of three or four years, beginning about 1879. It was at his own home in Simla, later at Allahabad, that most of the letters were received, addressed to him personally. Most, if not all, were in answer to the queries which he was permitted, if not invited, to ask his respected teachers.

Mr. Sinnett's book, The Occult World, was the first direct statement to the West of the existence of the Masters and their activity as sponsors for the Theosophical Society. He undertook the onerous task of vindicating, as far as argument and the phenomenal material in his hands could, the title of these supermen to the possession of surpassing knowledge and sublime wisdom. His work supplemented that of Madame Blavatsky in Isis, yet it went beyond the latter in asserting the connection of the Theosophical Society with an alleged association of perfected individuals. It put the Theosophical Society squarely on record as an organization, not merely for the purpose of eclectic research, but standing for the promulgation of a body of basic truths of an esoteric sort and arrogating to itself a position of unique eminence in a spiritual world order.

In the Introduction to The Occult World Mr. Sinnett elaborates his apologetic for the general theory of Mahatmic existence and knowledge. Fundamental for his argument is, of course, the theory of reincarnational continuity of development which would enable individual humans, through long experience, to attain degrees of learning far in advance of the majority of the race. But his "proofs" of both the existence and the superior knowledge of these exceptional beings are offered in the book itself, in which his experience with them, and the material of some of their letters to him, are presented. His introductory dissertation is a justification of the Mahatmic policy of maintaining their priceless knowledge in futile obscurity within the narrow confines of their exclusive Brotherhood. He then attempts to rectify our scornful point of view as regards esotericism. Of the superlative wisdom of the Masters he posits his own direct knowledge. The Brothers are to him empirically real. But the logical justification of their attitude of seclusion and aloofness, or worse, of their selfish appropriation of knowledge which it must be assumed would be of immense social value if disseminated, is the point upon which he chiefly labors.

"There is a school of philosophy," he says, "still in existence of which modern culture has lost sight . . . modern metaphysics, and to a large extent modern

physical science, have been groping for centuries blindly after knowledge which occult philosophy has enjoyed in full measure all the while. Owing to a train of fortunate circumstances I have come to know that this is the case; I have come into contact with persons who are heirs of a greater knowledge concerning the mysteries of Nature and humanity than modern culture has yet evolved. . . . Modern science has accomplished grand results by the open method of investigation, and is very impatient of the theory that persons who have attained to real knowledge, either in science or metaphysics, could have been content to hide their light under a bushel. . . . But there is no need to construct hypotheses in the matter. The facts are accessible if they are sought for in the right way."2

Spiritual science is foremost with the Adepts; physical science being of secondary importance. The main strength of occultism has been devoted to the science of metaphysical energy and to the development of faculties in man, not instruments outside him, which will yield him actual experimental knowledge of the subtle powers in nature. It aims to gain actual and exact knowledge of spiritual things which, under all other systems, remain the subject of speculation or blind religious faith.

Summing up the extraordinary powers which Adeptship gives its practitioners, he says they are chiefly the ability to dissociate consciousness from the body, to put it instantaneously in rapport with other minds anywhere on the earth, and to exert magical control over the sublimated energies of matter. Occultism postulates a basic differentiation between the principles of mind, soul, and spirit, and gives a formal technique for their interrelated development. It has evolved a practique, also, based on the spiritual constitution of matter, which, it alleges, vastly facilitates human growth. The skilled occultist is able to shift his consciousness from one to another plane of manifestation. In short, his control over the vibrational energies of the Akasha makes him veritably lord of all the physical creation.

The members of the Brotherhood remain in more or less complete seclusion among the Himalayas because, as they have said, they find contact with the coarse heavy currents of ordinary human emotionalism-violent feeling, material grasping, and base ambitions-painful to their sensitive organization. This great fraternity is at once the least and most exclusive body in the world; it is composed of the world's very elect, yet any human being is eligible. He must have demonstrated his possession of the required qualifications, which are so high that the average mortal must figure on aeons of education before he can knock at the portals of their spiritual society. The road thither is beset with many real perils, which no one can safely pass till he has proven his mastery over his own nature and that of the world.

"The ultimate development of the adept requires amongst other things a life of absolute physical purity, and the candidate must, from the beginning, give practical evidence of his willingness to adopt this. He must . . . for all the years of his probation, be perfectly chaste, perfectly abstemious, and indifferent to physical luxury of every sort. This regimen does not involve any fantastic discipline or obtrusive asceticism, nor withdrawal from the world. There would be nothing to prevent a gentleman in ordinary society from being in some of the preliminary stages of training without anybody about him being the wiser. For true occultism, the sublime achievement of the real adept, is not attained through the loathsome asceticism of the ordinary Indian fakeer, the yogi of the woods and wilds, whose dirt accumulates with his sanctity-of the fanatic who fastens iron hooks into his flesh or holds up an arm till it withers."3

How did the Mahatmas impart their teaching? Mr. Sinnett was the channel of transmission, and to him the two Masters sent a long series of letters on philosophical and other subjects, they themselves remaining in the background. The Mahatma Letters themselves, as originally received by Mr. Sinnett, were not published until 1925.4 Sinnett, early in his acquaintance with the Masters, asked K.H. for the privilege of a personal interview with him. The Master declined. His messages came in the form of long letters which dropped into his possession by facile means that would render the Post Office authorities of any nation both envious and sceptical. The correspondence began when Madame Blavatsky suggested that Mr. Sinnett write certain questions which were on his mind in a letter addressed to K.H., saying she would dispatch it to him, several hundred miles distant, by the exercise of her magnetic powers. She would accompany it with the request for a reply. The idea in Mr. Sinnett's mind was one which he thought, could the Adept actually carry it out, would demonstrate at one stroke the central theses of occultism and practically revolutionize the whole trend of human thinking. His suggestion to K.H. in that first letter was that the Mahatma should use his superior power to reproduce in far-off India, on the same morning on which it issued from the press, a full copy of the London Times. Madame Blavatsky disintegrated the missive and wafted its particles to the hermit in the mountains. The answer came in two days. The test of the London newspaper, he wrote, was inadmissible precisely because "it would close the mouths of the sceptics." The world is unprepared for so convincing a demonstration of supernormal powers, he argued, because, on the one hand the event would throw the principles and formulae of science into chaos, and on the other, it would demolish the structure of the concepts of natural law by the restoration of the belief in "miracle." The result would thus be disastrous for both science and faith. Incompetent as the thesis of mechanistic naturalism is to provide mortals with the ground of understanding of the deeper phenomena of life and mind, it does less harm on the whole than would a return to arrant superstition such as must follow in the wake of the wonder Sinnett had proposed. The Master asked his correspondent if the modern world had really thrown off the shackles of ignorant prejudice and religious bigotry to a sufficient extent to enable it to withstand the shock that such an occurrence would bring to its fixed ideas. If this one test were furnished, he went on, Western incredulity would in a moment ask for others and still others; shrewd ingenuity would devise ever more bizarre performances; and since not all the millions of sceptics could be given ocular demonstrations, the net outcome of the whole procedure would be confusion and unhappiness. The mass of humanity must feel its way slowly toward these high powers, and the premature exhibition of future capacity would but overwhelm the mind and unsettle the poise of people everywhere.

Mr. Sinnett replied, venturing to believe "that the European mind was less hopelessly intractable than Koot Hoomi had represented it." The Master's second letter continued his protestations:

"The Mysteries never were, never can be, put within reach of the general public, not, at least, until the longed-for day when our religious philosophy becomes universal. At no time have more than a scarcely appreciable minority of men possessed Nature's secret, though multitudes have witnessed the practical evidences of the possibility of their possession."

Letters followed on both sides, Mr. Sinnett taking advantage of many opportunities afforded by varying circumstances in each case to fortify his assurance that Madame Blavatsky herself was not inditing the replies in the name of the Adept. Frequently replies came, containing specific reference to detailed matters in his missives, when she had not been out of his sight during the interim between the despatch and the return. The letters came and went as well

when she was hundreds of miles away. The answers would often be found in his locked desk drawer, sometimes inside his own letter, the seal of which had not been broken. On occasion the Mahatma's reply dropped from the open air upon his desk while he was watching.

Madame Blavatsky and the Master both explained the method by which the letters were written. Theoretically, they were not written at all, but "precipitated." Among the Adept's occult or "magical" powers is that of impressing upon the surface of some material, as paper, the images which he holds vividly before his mind. He may thus impress or imprint a photograph, a scene, or a word, or sentence, upon parchment. He uses materials, of course, paper, ink or pencil graphite. But in his ability to disintegrate atomic combinations of matter, he can seize upon the material present, or even at a distance, and "precipitate" or reintegrate it, in conformity with the lines of his strong thought-energies. He can thus image a sentence, word for word, in his mind, and then pour the current of atomic material into the given form of the letters, upon the plane of the paper. The idiosyncrasies of his own chirography would be carried through the mental process. K.H., we are told, always used blue ink or blue pencil, while the epistles from M. always came in red. Specimens of the two handwritings are given in the frontispiece of the Mahatma Letters. The art of occult precipitation appears still more marvelous when we are told by Madame Blavatsky that the Adept did not attend to the actual precipitation himself but delegated it to one of his distant chelas, who caught his Master's thought-forms in the Astral Light and set them down by the chemical process which he had been taught to employ. The Master thus needed only to think vividly the words of his sentences, so as to impress them upon the mind of his pupil, and the latter did the rest. This was explained by H.P.B. in an article, Lodges of Magic, in Lucifer, Oct., 1888, while she was being accused of issuing false messages from the Master.

"For it is hardly one out of one hundred 'Occult' letters that is ever written by the hand of the Masters in whose names and on whose behalf they are sent, as the Masters have neither need nor leisure to write them; and that when a Master says: 'I wrote that letter,' it means only that every word in it was dictated by him and impressed under his direct supervision. Generally they make their chela . . . write (or precipitate) them. It depends entirely upon the chela's state of development how accurately the ideas may be transmitted and the writing model imitated. Thus the non-adept recipient is left in the dilemma of uncertainty whether if one letter is false, all may not be."

For example, when a Mr. Henry Kiddle, an American lecturer on Spiritualism, accused the writer of the Mahatma Letters of having plagiarized whole passages from his lecture delivered at Mt. Pleasant, New York, in 1880, a year prior to the publication of The Occult World, the Master K.H. explained in a letter to Mr. Sinnett that the apparent forgery of words and ideas came about through a bit of carelessness on his part in the precipitation of his ideas through a chela. While dictating the letter to the latter, he had caught himself "listening in" on Mr. Kiddle's address being delivered at the moment in America; and as a consequence the chela took down portions of the actual lecture as reflected from the mind of K.H.

Mr. Sinnett used the opportunity thus given him to draw from the Mahatma an outline of a portion of the esoteric philosophy and science which was presumed to be in his custody. The Master exhibited readiness to comply with Mr.
Sinnett's requests for information upon all vital and important matters.

Koot Hoomi tells Sinnett first that the world must prepare itself for the manifestation of phenomenal elements in constantly augmenting volume and force. The age of miracles, he says, is not past; it really never was. Plato was right in asserting that ideas ruled the world; and as the human mind increases its receptivity to larger ideas, the world will advance, revolutions will spring from the spreading ferment, creeds and powers will crumble before their onward march.

The duty set before intelligent people is to sweep away as much as possible of the dross left by our pious forefathers to make ready for the apotheosis of human life. The great new ideas

"touch man's true position in the universe, in relation to his previous and future births; his origin and ultimate destiny; the relation of the mortal to the immortal; of the temporary to the eternal; of the finite to the infinite; ideas larger, grander, more comprehensive, recognizing the universal reign of Immutable Law, unchanging and unchangeable in regard to which there is only an Eternal Now, while to uninitiated mortals time is past or future as related to their finite existence on this material speck of dirt. This is what we study and what many have solved."5
Many old idols must be dethroned, chief of all being that of an anthropomorphized Deity, with its train of debasing superstitions.

"And now," says K.H., "after making due allowance for evils that are natural and that cannot be avoided . . . I will point out the greatest, the chief cause of nearly two thirds of the evils that pursue humanity ever since that cause became a power. It is religion, under whatever form and in whatever nation. It is the sacerdotal caste, the priesthood and the churches; it is in those illusions that man looks upon as sacred that he has to search out the source of that multitude of evils which is the great curse of humanity and that almost overwhelms mankind. Ignorance created gods and cunning took advantage of the opportunity.
Look at India and look at Christendom and Islam, at Judaism and Fetichism. It is priestly imposture that rendered these Gods so terrible to man; it is religion that makes of him the selfish bigot, the fanatic that hates all mankind outside his own sect without rendering him any better or more moral for it. It is belief in God and Gods that makes two-thirds of humanity the slaves of a handful of those

who deceive them under the false pretence of saving them.   Remember
the sum of human misery will never be diminished unto that day when the better portion of humanity destroys in the name of Truth, Morality and universal Charity the altars of their false Gods."6
He goes on to clarify and delimit his position:

"Neither our philosophy nor ourselves believe in a God, least of all in one whose pronoun necessitates a capital G. Our philosophy falls under the definition of Hobbes. It is preëminently the science of effects by their causes and of causes by their effects, and since it is also the science of things deduced from first principle, as Bacon defines it, before we admit any such principle we must know it, and have no right to admit even its possibility. . .
. Therefore we deny God both as philosophers and as Buddhists. We know there are planetary and other spiritual lives, and we know there is in our system no such thing as God, either personal or impersonal. Parabrahm is not a God, but absolute immutable law, and Ishwar is the effect of Avidya (ignorance) and Maya (illusion), ignorance based on the great delusion. The word 'God' was invented to designate the unknown cause of those effects which man has ever admired or dreaded without understanding them, and since we claim-and that we are able to

prove what we claim-i.e., the knowledge of that cause and causes, we are in a position to maintain there is no God or Gods behind them."7

The causes assigned to phenomena by the Mahatmas, he says, are natural, sensible, supernatural, unintelligible, and unknown. The God of the theologians is simply an imaginary power, that has never yet manifested itself to human perception. The cause posited by the Adept is that power whose activities we behold in every phenomenon in the universe. They are pantheists, never agnostics. The Deity they envisage is everywhere present, as well in matter as elsewhere.

"In other words we believe in Matter alone, in matter as visible nature and matter in its invisibility as the invisible omnipresent omnipotent Proteus with its unceasing motion which is its life, and which nature draws from herself, since she is the great whole outside of which nothing can exist. The
existence of matter, then, is a fact; the existence of motion is another fact, their self-existence and eternity or indestructibility is a third fact. And the idea of pure Spirit as a Being or an Existence-give it whatever name you will-is a chimera, a gigantic absurdity."8

Furthermore, says K.H., your conceptions of an all-wise Cosmic Mind or Being runs afoul of sound logic on another count. You claim, he says, that the life and being of this God pervades and animates all the universe. But even your own science predicates of the cosmic material ether that it, too, already permeates all the ranges of being in nature. You are thus putting two distinct pervading essences in the universe. You are postulating two primordial substances, two basic elemental essences, where but one can be. Why posit an imaginary substrate when you already have a concrete one? Find your God in the material you are sure is there; do not forge a fiction and put it outside of real existence to account for that existence. Why constitute a false God when you have a real Universe?

There is an illimitable Force in the universe, but even this Force is not God, since man may learn to bend it to his will. It is simply the visible and objective expression of the absolute substance in its invisible and subjective form.

From this strict and inexorable materialism K.H. seems to relent a moment when he says to Mr. Hume:

"I do not protest at all, as you seem to think, against your theism, or a belief in abstract ideal of some kind, but I cannot help asking you, how do you or can you know that your God is all-wise, omnipotent and love-ful, when everything in nature, physical and moral, proves such a being, if he does exist, to be quite the reverse of all you say of him? Strange delusion and one which seems to overpower your very intellect!"9

The intricate problem, then, of how the blind and unintelligent forces of matter in motion do breed and have bred "highly intelligent beings like ourselves" "is covered by the eternal progression of cycles, and the process of evolution ever perfecting its work as it goes along." Intelligence lies somehow in the womb of matter, and evolution brings it to birth. Matter and spirit, we must constantly be reminded, are but the two polar aspects of the One Substance.

The great philosophical problem of whether reality is monistic or pluralistic finds clear statement and elucidation in the Letters. It can be gathered from all the argument of K.H. that primordial nature is a monism, but that when the hidden energy, or sheer potentiality, of the unit principle deploys into action,

or what the occultists speak of as manifestation, it splits, first into a duality, or polarization, and then into an infinity of modifications arising from varying intensities of vibration and modes of combination. Through the spectacles of time and space we see life as multiple; could we be freed from the limitations of our sensorium, however, we could see life whole, as a single essence. Non-polarized force is, in any terms of our apperceptive nature, an impossibility and a nonentity; pure spirit is a sheer abstraction. Spirit must be changed into matter, to be seen.

It is a silly philosophy which would exalt spirit and debase matter, as many ascetic or idealistic religious systems have done. Matter is the garment of spirit, and needs but to be beautified and refined. Spirit is helpless without it. "Bereaved of Prakriti, Purusha (Spirit) is unable to manifest itself, hence ceases to exist-becomes nihil."10 Likewise Spirit is necessary to the faintest stir of life in matter.

"Without Spirit or Force even that which Science styles as 'not-living' matter, the so-called mineral ingredients which feed plants, could never have been called into form."11

Form will vanish the moment spirit is withdrawn from it.

"Matter, force and motion are the trinity of physical objective nature, as the trinitarian unity of spirit-matter is that of the spiritual or subjective nature. Motion is eternal because spirit is eternal. But no modes of motion can ever be conceived unless they are in conjunction with matter."12

"Unconscious and non-existing when separated, they become consciousness and life when brought together,"13

says K.H. in reference to the two poles of being. If the spirit or force were to fail, the electron would cease to swirl about the proton, the atom would collapse, the worlds would vanish. The world is an illusion in the same way that the solid appearance of the revolving spokes of a wheel is an illusion. Stop the swirl, and the universe not only collapses-it goes out of manifestation.

A novel and startling corollary of the teaching that the forces of nature are "blind unconscious" laws, is seen in the query of K.H. to Mr. Hume, whether it had ever occurred to him that "universal, like finite human mind, might have two attributes or a dual power-one, the voluntary and conscious, and the other the involuntary and unconscious, or the mechanical power. To reconcile the difficulty of many theistic and anti-theistic propositions, both these powers are a philosophical necessity. . . . Take the human mind in connection with the body. Man has two distinct physical brains; the cerebrum . . . the source of the voluntary nerves; and the cerebellum-the fountain of the involuntary nerves which are the agents of the unconscious or mechanical powers of the mind to act through. And weak and uncertain as may be the control of man over his involuntary, such as the blood circulation, the throbbings of the heart and respiration, especially during sleep-yet how far more powerful, how much more potential appears man as master and ruler over the blind molecular motion . . . than that which you will call God shows over the immutable laws of nature.
Contrary in that to the finite, the 'infinite mind' . . . exhibits but the functions of its cerebellum."14

That Master admits that he is arguing the case for such a duality of cosmic mental function only on the basis of the theory that the macrocosm is the

prototype of the microcosm, and that the high planetary spirits themselves have no more concrete evidence of the operation of a "cosmic cerebrum" than we have.

The Master has taken many pages to detail to Mr. Sinnett the information relative to the evolution of the worlds from the nebular mist, and the outline of the whole cosmogonic scheme. As this will be dealt with more fully in our review of The Secret Doctrine, it need only be glanced at here to give coherence to the material in the Letters. Force or spirit descends into matter and creates or organizes the universes. Its immersion in the mineral kingdom marks the lowest or grossest point of its descent, and from there it begins to return to spirit, carrying matter up with it to self-consciousness. Impulsions of life energy emanate from "the heart of the universe" and go quivering through the various worlds, vivifying them and bringing to each in turn its fitting grade of living organisms. Thus came the races of men on our Earth, which is now harboring its Fifth great family, the Aryan.

What is of great interest in the scheme of Theosophy is that

"At the beginning of each Round, when humanity reappears under quite different conditions than those afforded by the birth of each new race and its sub-races, a 'Planetary' has to mix with these primitive men, and to refresh their memories and reveal to them the truths they knew during the preceding Round. Hence the confused traditions about Jehovahs, Ormazds, Osirises, Brahms and the tutti quanti. But that happens only for the benefit of the First Race. It is the duty of the latter to choose the fit recipients among its sons, who are 'set apart'- to use a Biblical phrase-as the vessels to contain the whole stock of knowledge to be divided among the future races and generations until the close of that Round. . . . Every race has its Adepts; and with every new race we are allowed to give them as much of our knowledge as the men of that race deserve. The last seventh race will have its Buddha, as every one of its predecessors had."15

And then Koot Hoomi undertakes to meet the inevitable query: What comes out of the immense machinery of the cycles and globes and rounds?

"What emerges at the end of all things is not only 'pure and impersonal spirit,' but the collected 'personal' remembrances" . . .16 The individual, imperishable, will enjoy the fruits of its collective lives.

If the Mahatma's attempt to solve the eternal riddle of the "good" of earthly life is not so complete and satisfactory as might have been wished, we at least gather from this interesting passage that its ultimate meaning can be ascertained only by our personal experience with every changing form and aspect of life itself. We must taste of all the modes of existence. This inflicts upon us the "cycle of necessity," the imperative obligation to tread the weary wheel of life on all the globes. We will know the "good" of it all only by living through it. There is no vindication for ethics, for religion, for philosophy, for teleology and optimism, save in life and experience itself. Reason, dialectic, can do nothing for us if life does not first furnish us the material content of the good. All we can do is look to life with the confident expectation that its processes will justify our wishes. We must in the end stand on faith. If life prove not ultimately sweet to the tasting, no rationalization will make it so.

We are assured, however, that the unit of personal consciousness built up in the process of cosmic evolution is never annihilated, but expands until it becomes inclusive of the highest. It enjoys the fruitage of its dull incubations in the

lower worlds in its ever-enhancing capacities for a life "whose glory and splendor have no limits."

But, says K.H. immortality is quite a relative matter. Man, being a compound creature, is not entirely immortal. You know, he reminds us, that the physical body has no immortality. Neither the etheric double nor the kama rupa (astral body), nor yet the lower manasic (mental) principle survive disintegration. Only the Ego in the causal body holds its conscious existence between lives on earth. Even the planetary spirits, high as they are in the scale of being, suffer breaks in their conscious life,-- the periods of pralaya. In the true sense of the term only the one life has absolute immortality, for it is the only existence which has neither beginning nor end, nor any break in its continuity. All lower aspects and embodiments have immortality, but with periodic recessions into inanition.

The problem of evil received treatment at K.H.'s hands, and is summarized in the statement that "Evil has no existence per se and is but the absence of good and exists but for him who is made its victim. It proceeds from two causes, and no more than good is it an independent cause in nature. Nature is destitute of goodness or malice; she follows only immutable laws, when she either gives life and joy or sends suffering and death and destroys what she has created. Nature has an antidote for every poison and her laws a reward for every suffering. The butterfly devoured by a bird becomes that bird, and the little bird killed by an animal goes into a higher form. It is the blind law of necessity and the eternal fitness of things, and hence cannot be called evil in Nature. The real evil proceeds from human intelligence and its origin rests entirely with reasoning man who dissociates himself from Nature. Humanity then alone is the true source of evil. Evil is the exaggeration of good, the progeny of human selfishness and greediness. Think profoundly and you will find that save death-which is no evil but a necessary law, and accidents which will always find their reward in a future life-the origin of every evil, whether small or great, is in human action, in man whose intelligence makes him the one free agent in Nature. It is not Nature that creates diseases, but man. . . . Food, sexual relations, drink, are all natural necessities of life; yet excess in them brings on disease, misery, suffering, mental and physical. . . . Become a glutton, a debauchee, a tyrant, and you become the originator of diseases, of human suffering and misery. Therefore it is neither Nature nor an imaginary Deity that has to be blamed, but human nature made vile by selfishness."[17]

It will be of interest to hear what K.H. says about "heaven." "It (Devachan)[18] is an idealed paradise in each case, of the

Ego's own making, and by him filled with the scenery, crowded with the incidents and thronged with the people he would expect to find in such a sphere of compassionate bliss."[19]

Man makes his own heaven or hell, and is in it while he is making it. It is subjective; only, Theosophy postulates a certain (refined and sublimated) objectivity to the forms of our subjectivity. Man does in heaven only what he does on earth-forms a conception and then hypostatizes or reifies it. Only, in the case of nirvanic states, the reification is instantaneously externalized. On earth it is a slower formation. The "Summerland" of the Spiritualists is but the objectification of the Ego's buoyant dreams, when freed from the heavy limitations of the earth body.

"In Devachan the dreams of the objective life become the realities of the subjective."[20]

This means that the ideal creations, the highest aspirations of man on earth, become the substance of his actual consciousness in heaven. They are the only elements of his normal human mind that are pitched at a vibration rate high enough to impress the matter or stuff of his permanent body, and hence they alone cause a repercussion or response in his pure subjective consciousness when the lower bodies are lost. On this theory the day dreams and the ideal longings of the human soul become the most vital and substantial, and abiding, activities of his psychic life.

The only memories of the earth life that intrude into this picture of heavenly bliss are those connected with the feelings of love and hate.

"Love and hatred are the only immortal feelings, the only survivors from the wreck of the Yedamma or phenomenal world."[21]

All other feelings function at too low a rate to register on the ethereal body of the Devachanee, and are lost.

"Out of the resurrected past nothing remains but what the Ego has felt spiritually-that was evolved by and through, and lived over by his spiritual faculties-be it love or hatred."[22]

Suicides, says K.H., must undergo a peculiar discipline following their premature death. Since they have arbitrarily interrupted a cycle of nature before its normal completion, the operation of law requires that they hang suspended, so to speak, in a condition of near-earthly existence until what would have been their natural life-term has expired.

"The suicides who, foolishly hoping to escape life, found themselves still alive, have suffering enough in store for them from that very life. Their punishment is in the intensity of the latter."[23]

Their distress consists, it seems, in remaining within the purview of their earthly life without being able to express its impulses. They are often tempted to enjoy life again by proxy, i.e., through mediums or by efforts at a sort of vampiristic obsession. Victims of death by accident have a happier fate. They are more quickly released from earth's lure to partake of the lethal existence in the higher Devachan.

All those souls who do not slip down into the eighth sphere-Avichi-through a "pull" of the animal nature which proved too strong for their spiritual fibre to resist, go on to the Devachan-to Heaven. To the Theosophist heaven is not "that bourne from which no traveler e'er returns," nor is access to it a matter of even rare exception. Millions of persons in earth life have had glimpses through its portals, in sleep, trance, catalepsis, anaesthesia, hypnosis, or in the open-eyed mystic's vision. It is a realm of sweet surcease from pain and sorrow, of happiness without alloy. But it is far from being the same place, or from providing identically the same experience, for every soul. Each one's heaven is determined by the capacities for spiritual enjoyment developed on earth. Only the spiritual senses survive.

To enrich heaven one must have laid up spiritual treasure on earth. Furthermore, the life there is not without break. The released Ego does not loll away an

eternal existence there, but after due rest returns to earth. Nor is his enjoyment of the Devachan the same in each sojourn there. He bites deeper into the bliss of heaven each time he takes his flight from body. The constant enrichment of his experience in the upper spheres provides a never-ending novelty.

To Mr. Sinnett's assertion that a mental condition of happiness empty of sensational, emotional, and lower mental (manasic) content would be an intolerable monotony K.H. replies by asking him if he felt any sense of monotony during that one moment in his life when he experienced the utmost fulness of conscious being. Devachan is like that, he assured the complainant, only much more so. As our climatic moments in this life seem by their ineffable opulence to swallow up the weary sense of the time-drag, so the ecstatic consciousness of the heaven state is purged of all sense of ennui or successive movement. To put it succinctly, there is no sense of time in which to grow weary.

"No; there are no clocks, no timepieces in Devachan, . . . though the whole Cosmos is a gigantic chronometer in one sense . . . I may also remind you in this connection that time is something created entirely by ourselves; that while one short second of intense agony may appear, even on earth, as an eternity to one man, to another, more fortunate, hours, days and sometimes whole years may seem to flit like one brief moment. . . . But finite similes are unfit to express the abstract and the infinite; nor can the objective ever mirror the subjective. . . . To realize the bliss in Devachan, or the woes in Avitchi, you have to assimilate them-as we do. . . . Space and time may be, as Kant has it, not the product but the regulators of the sensations, but only so far as our sensations on earth are concerned, not those in Devachan. . . Space and time cease to act as 'the frame of our experience' 'over there.'"24

The land of distinctions is transcended and the here and there merge into the everywhere, as the everywhere into the here and there, and the now and then into the now.

Koot Hoomi is sure that the materialistic attitudes of the Occidental mind have played havoc with the subtle spirituality embodied in Eastern religions, in the effort at translation and interpretation.

"Oh, ye Max Müllers and Monier Williamses, what have ye done with our philosophy?"25

You can not take the higher spiritual degrees by mere study of books. Progress here has to do largely with the development of latent powers and faculties, the cultivation of which is attended with some dangers. In this juncture it avails the student far more to be able to call upon the personal help of a kindly guardian who is truly a Master of the hidden forces of life, than to depend upon his own efforts, however consecrated. Each grade in the hierarchy of evolved beings stands ready to tutor the members of the class below.

"The want of such a 'guide, philosopher and friend' can never be supplied, try as you may. All you can do is to prepare the intellect: the impulse toward 'soul-culture must be furnished by the individual. Thrice fortunate they who can break through the vicious circle of modern influence and come above the vapors!

… Unless regularly initiated and trained-concerning the spiritual insight of things and the supposed revelations made unto man in all ages from Socrates down to Swedenborg … no self-tutored seer or clairvoyant ever saw or heard quite correctly."26

The Master Morya has a word to say to Sinnett about "the hankering of occult students after phenomena" of a psychic nature. It is a maya27 against which, he says, they have always been warned. It grows with gratification; the Spiritualists, he says, are thaumaturgic addicts. It adds no force to metaphysical truth that his own and K.H.'s letters drop into Sinnett's lap or come under his pillow. If the philosophy is wrong a "wonder" will not set it right. Spiritual knowledge, made effective for growth, is the desideratum.

Trance mediumship, he reiterates, is itself both undesirable and unfruitful. No mind should submit itself passively to another. "We do not require a passive mind, but on the contrary are seeking for those most active." Nothing can give the student insight save the unfolding of his own inner powers. Much of the Adept's writing to Sinnett has to do with the conditions of probation and "chelaship" in the master science of soul-culture. He says there are certain rigid laws the fulfilment of which is absolutely essential to the disciple's secure advancement. They have to do with self-mastery, meditation, purity of life, fixity of purpose. These laws, which at first seem to the neophyte to bar his path, will be seen, as he persists in obedience to them, to be the road to all he can ask. But no one can break them without becoming their victim. Too eager expectation on the part of the aspirant is dangerous. It disturbs the balance of forces.

"Each warmer and quicker throb of the heart wears so much life away. The passions, the affections, are not to be indulged in by him who seeks to know; for they wear out the earthly body with their own secret power; and he who would gain his aim must be cold."28

A hint as to the occult desirability of vegetarianism is dropped in the sentence:

"Never will the Spiritualists find reliable trustworthy mediums and Seers (not even to a degree) so long as the latter and their 'circle' will saturate themselves with animal blood and the millions of infusoria of the fermented fluids."29

Arcane knowledge has always been presented in forms such that only the most determined aspirants could grasp the meanings. K.H. interjects that Sir Isaac Newton understood the principles of occult philosophy but "withheld his knowledge very prudently for his own reputation." The "scientific" attitude of mind is declared to be unpropitious for the attainment of clear insight into truth, and the pretensions of modern scientists that they comprehend "the limits of the natural" receive some of the Master's irony. "Oh, century of conceit and mental obscuration!" he jeers.

"All is secret for them as yet in nature. Of man-they know but the skeleton and the form . . . their school science is a hotbed of doubts and conjectures."30

Furthermore, "to give more knowledge to a man than he is fitted to receive is a dangerous experiment." In his ignorance or his passion he may make a use of it fatal both to himself and those about him. The Adepts, it appears also, have their own reasons for not wishing to impart knowledge more rapidly than the pupil can assimilate it. The misuse of knowledge by the pupil always reacts upon the initiator; the Teacher becomes responsible in a measure for the results. The Master would only hinder and complicate his own progress by indiscreet generosity to his chela.

As one means of lightening this responsibility the chela is required, when accepted, to take a vow of secrecy covering every order he may receive and the specific information imparted. The Master knows whether the vow is ever broken, without a question being put.

The prime qualification for the favor of receiving the great knowledge is rectitude of motive. Wisdom must be sought only for its serviceability to Brotherhood and progress, not even as an end in itself:

"The quality of wisdom ever was and will be yet for a long time-to the very close of the fifth race-denied to him who seeks the wealth of the mind for its own sake, and for its own enjoyment and result, without the secondary purpose of turning it to account in the attainment of material benefits."31

The applicant for chelaship is tested-unknown to himself-in subtle ways before he is accepted, and often afterwards, too. It is not a system of secret espionage, but a method of drawing out the inner nature of the neophytes, so that they may become self-conquerors.

K.H. reminds Sinnett that the efforts of theosophic adherents to restore or propagate esoteric doctrines have ever been met by the determined opposition of the vested ecclesiastical interests, which have not scrupled to resort to forgery of documents, alleged confessions of fraud, or other villainous subterfuge, to crush out the "heresy."

"Some of you Theosophists are now wounded only in your 'honor' or your purses, but those who held the lamp in previous generations paid the penalty of their lives for their knowledge."32

He points out, too, the distressful state into which certain over-eager aspirants have brought themselves by "snatching at forbidden power before their moral nature is developed to the point of fitness for its exercise." He says: "it would be a sorry day for mankind" if any sharper or deadlier powers-such as those the high Adepts are privileged to wield-were put in the hands of those unaccustomed to use them, or morally untrustworthy.

K.H. volunteers to explain the occult significance of the interlaced black and white triangles in the circle which forms part of the monogram on the seal of the Theosophical Society. The Jewish Kabbalists viewed the insignia as Solomon's Seal. It is "a geometrical synthesis of the whole occult doctrine."

"The two interlaced triangles . . . contain the 'squaring of the circle,' the 'philosophical stone,' the great problems of Life and Death, and-the Mystery of Evil."33

The upward-pointing triangle is Wisdom concealed, and the downward-pointing one is Wisdom revealed-in the phenomenal world.

"The circle indicates the bounding, circumscribing quality of the All, the Universal Principle which expands . . . to embrace all things."

The three sides represent the three gunas, or finite attributes. The double triangles likewise symbolize the Great Passive and the Great Active principles, the male and female, Purusha (Spirit) and Prakriti (Matter).34 The one triangle points upward to Spirit, the other downward to Matter, and their interlacing represents the conjunction of Spirit and Matter in the manifested universe. The

six points of the two triangles, with the central point, yield the significant Seven, the symbol of Universal Being.

Manifestation of the Absolute Life creates universes, and starts evolutionary processes; but, says K.H. to Sinnett,

"neither you nor any other man across the threshold has had or ever will have the 'complete theory' of Evolution taught him; or get it unless he guesses it for himself. . . . Some-have come very near to it. But there is always . . . just enough error . . . to prove the eternal law that only the unshackled Spirit shall see the things of the Spirit without a veil."35

Pride of intellect grows enormously more dangerous the farther one goes toward the higher realms; and after that is overcome spiritual pride raises its head. An average mortal finds his share of sin and misery rather equally distributed over his life; but a chela has it concentrated all within one period of probation. One who essays the higher peaks of knowledge must overcome a heavier drag of moral gravitation than one who is content to walk the plain.

From a purely political standpoint it is interesting to note that in 1883 K.H. had taken hold of a project to launch in India a journal to be named "The Phoenix," which, with Mr. Sinnett as editor, was to function as an agent for the cultivation of native Hindu patriotism, of which the Master saw a sore need in India's critical situation at that time. Native princes were looked to for financial support, as well as Theosophists, and propaganda for the venture had already been set in motion. But K.H. declares that his closer inspection of the situation and his discovery of the wretched political indifference of his countrymen made the enterprise dubious, financially and spiritually. He then ordered Sinnett to drop it entirely, as he saw certain failure ahead.

The Mahatma Letters, in the latter portion, go deeply into the affairs of the London Lodge, T. S., which Mr. Sinnett had founded on his return to England, and they even advise as to the "slate" of officers to stand for election. There was a factional grouping in the Lodge at the time, the Kingsford-Maitland party standing for Christian esotericism as against the paramount influence of the Tibetan Masters, whose existence was regarded by them as at least hypothetical; and the Sinnett wing adhering closely to H.P.B. and her Adepts. Mrs. Anna B. Kingsford had had a series of communications in her own right from high teachers, which K.H. himself stated were in accord with his own doctrine. These were published in a volume, The Perfect Way. The Master counsels harmony between the two parties, preaching, with Heraclitus, that harmony is the equilibrium established by the tension of two opposing forces.

Much or most of the substance of the later Letters is personal, touching Sinnett's relations with persons of prominence in the Theosophical movement. The Adepts make no claim to omniscience- they themselves are in turn disciples of higher and grander beings whom they speak of as the Dhyan Chohans,36 and whom they rank next to the "planetaries"-but they assert their ability to look from any distance into the secret minds of Sinnett's associates as well as into his own. They gave him the benefit of this spiritual "shadowing" to guide him in the Society's affairs.

Many complimentary things are said to Mr. Sinnett for his encouragement; but he is not spared personal criticism of the sharpest sort. He is told that his attitude of Western pride stands in the way of his true spiritual progress.
While his admirable qualities have won him the distinction of being used as a

literary aid to the Mahatmas, still he is pronounced far from eligible for chelaship.

Much of the material in the Letters, being of a quite personal and intimate nature, was, to be sure, never intended for publication; in fact, was again and again forbidden publication. But the Sinnett estate was persuaded, in 1925, to give out the Letters for the good they might be expected to do in refutation of the many bizarre divergencies which Neo-Theosophy was making from the original teachings. Their publication came at the conclusion of the half-century period of the existence of the Theosophical Society and was supposed to terminate an old and begin a new cycle with some exceptional significance such as Theosophists attribute to times and tides in the flow of things.

To most Theosophists the existence of the Masters and the contents of their teaching form the very corner-stone of their systematic faith. And ultimately they point to the wisdom and spirituality displayed in the Letters themselves as being sufficient vindication of that faith.

CHAPTER VII STORM, WRECK, AND REBUILDING

Reverting from philosophy to history we must now give some account of what happened in India from the date the two Founders left America late in 1878.

India welcomed Theosophy with considerable warmth. Col. Olcott toured about, founding Lodges rapidly, and Madame Blavatsky bent herself to the more esoteric work of corresponding with her Masters and of establishing her official mouthpiece, The Theosophist. Though Isis Unveiled had been put forth in America, Theosophy was first really propagated in India.

The early history of the Society in India need not concern us here, save as it had repercussions in the United States. But it is necessary to touch upon the conspicuous events that transpired there in 1884-85, for they shook the Theosophic movement to its foundations and for a time threatened to end it. We refer to the official Reports issued in those two years by the Society for Psychical Research in England upon the genuineness of the Theosophic phenomena.1

The S.P.R., having been founded shortly before 1884 by prominent men interested in the growing reports of spiritistic and psychic phenomena (the early membership included at least three Theosophists, Prof. F. W. H. Myers, Mr. W. Stainton Moses and Mr. C. C. Massey), manifested a pronounced interest in the recently-published and widely-read works of Mr. Sinnett, The Occult World and Esoteric Buddhism. Madame Blavatsky's Isis Unveiled and the works and experiments of Prof. William Crookes had done much to foster this new study.

Accordingly when Col. Olcott and Mohini M. Chatterji, a devoted follower of H.P.B., were in Europe in 1884, the S.P.R. requested the three to sit for friendly questioning concerning Madame Blavatsky's reported marvels. She was herself interrogated at this time. This procedure led to the publication "for private and confidential use" of the First Report of the Committee in the fall of 1884. In sum the Report expressed decided incredulity as to the genuine nature of the phenomena. Ascribing fraud only to Madame Blavatsky, it says:

"Now the evidence in our opinion renders it impossible to avoid one or other of two alternative conclusions: Either that some of the phenomena recorded are genuine, or that other persons than Madame Blavatsky, of good standing in society, and with characters to lose, have taken part in deliberate imposture."

The conclusion was:

"On the whole, however, (though with some serious reserves) it seems undeniable that there is a prima facie case for some part at least of the claim made, which
. . . cannot, with consistency, be ignored."

Later in the same year the S.P.R. sent one of its members, Mr. Richard Hodgson, a young University graduate, to India to conduct further investigation of the phenomena reported to have taken place at the Headquarters of the Theosophical Society, at Madras. He was given untrammeled access to the premises and

permitted to examine in person members of the household who had witnessed some of the events in question.

H.P.B.'s nemesis in these ill-started proceedings was one Madame Coulomb. In 1871, when Madame Blavatsky had been brought to Cairo, along with other survivors of their wrecked vessel, the French woman, a claimant to the possession of mediumistic powers, became interested in H.P.B.'s psychic abilities and rendered her some assistance. When, in 1879, the Founders arrived in India, Madame Coulomb in her turn resorted to her Russian friend for aid, and H.P.B. made her the housekeeper, and her husband the general utility man, of the little Theosophic colony. They proved to be ungrateful, meddlesome, and unscrupulous, became jealous and discontented, and when left in charge of Madame Blavatsky's own rooms in the building during her absence on the journey to Europe in 1884, they fell into bickering and open conflict with Mr. Lane-Fox, Dr. Franz Hartmann and others of the personnel over questions of authority and small matters of household management. Both they and the Theosophists took up the matters of dispute by letter with H.P.B. and Col. Olcott in Europe, and the two leaders urged conciliation and peace on both sides. But finally the ill- repressed resentment of Madame Coulomb broke out into secret machinations with the Christian missionaries to expose Madame Blavatsky as a fraud. Madame Coulomb placed in the hands of the missionaries letters allegedly written to her by her former friend, in which evidence of the latter's connivance with her French protégé to perpetrate deception in phenomena was revealed. Just before exploding this bombshell the Coulombs had become unendurable, and had finally been compelled to leave the premises.

Madame Coulomb bartered her incriminating material to the missionaries for a considerable sum of money, and the purchasers spread the alleged exposure before the public in their organ, the Christian College Magazine.2 Madame Blavatsky, in Europe, made brief replies in the London Times and the Pall Mall Gazette, stating that the Coulomb letters were forgeries. She wished to bring recrimination proceedings against her accusers to vindicate herself and the Society. Friends dissuaded her, or deserted her, and nothing was done. But the Founders prepared to hasten back to India. Col. Olcott seems to have taken a vacillating course, and the resolution adopted at a Convention held in India upon their return expressed the opinion of the delegates that Madame Blavatsky should take no legal action.

She resigned her office as Corresponding Secretary, but later was requested to resume her old place.

Mr. Hodgson submitted his report, which was published near the end of 1885.3 He had not witnessed any phenomena nor examined any. He questioned witnesses to several of the wonders a full year after the latter had taken place. He rendered an entirely ex parte judgment in that he acted as judge, accuser, and jury and gave no hearing to the defense. He ignored a mass of testimony of the witnesses to the phenomena, and accepted the words of the Coulombs whose conduct had already put them under suspicion.4 The merits of the entire case have been carefully gone into by William Kingsland in his The Real H. P. Blavatsky, and by the anonymous authors of The Theosophical Movement. The matter of most decisive weight in Mr. Hodgson's unfavorable judgment was the secret panel in H.P.B.'s "shrine" or cabinet built in the wall of her room, and a sliding door exhibited by the Coulombs to the investigators, and described as having been used by Madame Blavatsky for the insertion of alleged Mahatma letters from the next room by one of the Coulomb accomplices. The Theosophists resident at Headquarters charged that the secret window had been built in, at the instigation of the missionaries, by M. Coulomb during H.P.B.'s absence. He alone had the keys to

Madame's apartment, and one of the points of his quarrel with the house members was the possession of the keys. He refused to give them up, alleging that Madame Blavatsky had placed him in exclusive charge of her rooms during her absence.

The charges of course threw doubt upon the existence of the Masters, the genuineness of their purported letters and the whole Mahatmic foundation of Theosophy.

A great point at issue was the comparison of H.P.B.'s handwriting with that of the Mahatma Letters. Two experts, Mr. F. G. Netherclift and Mr. Sims, first testified they were not identical, but later reversed their testimony. Mr. F. W. H. Myers confessed there was entire similarity between the handwriting of the Mahatma Letters and a letter received by Madame Blavatsky's aunt, Madame Fadeef, back in 1870 at Odessa, Russia, from the hand of a Hindu personage who then vanished from before her eyes. (Madame Blavatsky was at some other quarter of the globe at the time.) A distinguished German handwriting expert later declared there was no similarity between H.P.B.'s chirography and those of the Master M. and K.H.

It remained for Mr. Hodgson to assign an adequate motive for Madame Blavatsky's colossal career of deception, and here he confesses difficulty. He finally concludes that her motive was patriotism for her native land: she was a Russian spy! Mr. Solovyoff, in his A Modern Priestess of Isis, gives some substance to this charge. It is conceivable that Madame Blavatsky could have felt sentimental interest in the Russianizing, rather than the Anglicizing, of India; yet it appears preposterous to think that she would have endured the privations and hardships to which she was subjected in her devotion to Theosophy merely to cloak a subterranean machination for Russian dominance in India. She was an American citizen, having been naturalized before she left the United States.

Mr. Hodgson declared Madame Blavatsky to be "one of the most accomplished, ingenious and interesting impostors in history." In a letter to Sinnett, June 21, 1885, she records her reciprocal opinion of Mr. Hodgson. She writes:

"They very nearly succeeded [in killing both her and the Theosophical Society]. At any rate they have succeeded in fooling Hume and the S.P.R. Poor Myers! and still more, poor Hodgson! How terribly they will be laughed at some day!"

The attack of the S.P.R. upon Theosophy and its leaders fell with great force upon the followers of the movement everywhere and only a few remained loyal through the storm.

Among the faithful in America was Mr. W. Q. Judge. It remained for him to effect a reorganization of the forces in the United States in 1885, when the S.P.R. attack was raging abroad. In the previous year he had gone to France, had met H.P.B., continued on to India and back to America. In 1885 he reorganized the sparse membership into the Aryan Lodge. In 1886 he started the publication of The Path, long the American organ for his expression of Theosophy. Active study and propaganda followed quickly thereupon and the number of branches soon tripled. Col. Olcott had appointed an American Board of Control. This body met at Cincinnati in 1886 and organized "The American Section of the Theosophical Society." In April, 1887, the branches held their first Convention, and adopted constitution and by-laws. Mr. Judge became General Secretary. The organization was a copy of that of the Federal Government, though allegiance was subscribed to the General Council in India. In 1888 the second Convention was held, with Mr. Archibald Keightley present as a representative from England. Theosophical organization was at last in full swing in America.

Brief mention may be made at this point of a somewhat divergent movement within the ranks of Theosophy itself about 1886. A Mr. W. T. Brown, of Glasgow, had had close fellowship with the Theosophists at Adyar, Madras, from 1884 to 1886. He then came to this country and associated himself with Mrs. Josephine W. Cables, who had been a Christian Spiritualist, but who had as early as 1882 organized the Rochester Theosophical Society. This was the first Theosophical Lodge established in America after the original founding in New York in 1875. But Mrs. Cables tried to represent Theosophy as a mixture of Christianity, Spiritualism, Mysticism, personal ideas on diet and occultism in general. She founded The Occult World, a magazine which Prof. Elliott Coues, then President of the American Board of Control, tried to make the official organ of Theosophy in America. But Mr. Judge's Path was in the field, and Mrs. Cables and Mr. Brown gave expression to some jealousy of the rival publication, alleging that the Theosophical Society was not a unique instrument for the spreading of occult knowledge, but that Christ was to be accepted as the final guide and authority. They referred to the Theosophic teaching as "husks," while Christ had fed the world the real kernel. To this H.P.B. replied through The Path for December, 1886, and cast the blame for their losing touch with her Masters on Mrs. Cables and Mr. Brown themselves.5 Mrs. Cables turned her Rochester Theosophical Society into the "Rochester Brotherhood" and her magazine into an exponent of Mystical Spiritualism. Mr. Brown returned to the fold of orthodox Christianity. Prof. Coues was destined to contribute a sensational chapter to Theosophic history before he broke with the movement forever.6

A close study of the record will reveal that it was during these years that the germ of a hierarchical division in the Theosophical organization developed. In the theory of the existence and evolutionary attainments of the Masters themselves was enfolded the conception of a graded approach to their elevated status. As the Theosophical Society came to be understood as only an appanage of the Masters in their service of humanity, its inner intent was soon seen to be that of affording a means of access to these high beings. It was recognized as an organization whose supreme headship was vested in the Mahatmas and whose corporate membership formed a lower degree of spiritual discipleship. This hierarchical grading naturally fell into three degrees, predicated on the thesis that the Adepts accept pupils for personal tutelage. There were first, the Masters, then their accepted pupils or chelas, and lastly just plain Theosophists or members of the Society. The third class might or might not be led to aspire to chelaship, on the terms of a serious pledge to consecrate all life's efforts to spiritual mastery. These three divisions came to be called the First, Second and Third Sections of the Theosophical Society. It is the theory advanced in the Theosophic Movement that H.P.B. represented the First Section, Mr. Judge the Second and Col. Olcott the Third. The Russian noble-woman was regarded as the only bona fide or authoritative link of communication with the First Section (though the Masters might at any time grant the favor of their special interest to others, as they did to Mr. Sinnett); Judge was held to be an accepted chela, in the high confidence of Madame Blavatsky and her mentors, their reliable agent to head the order of lay chelaship; Col. Olcott was the active and visible head of the Theosophical Society, the accepted instrument of the Masters in the work of building up that organization which was to present the ancient doctrine of their existence to the world and mark out anew the path of approach to them. H.P.B. and Judge worked behind the scenes, while Olcott stood in the gaze of the world. To them belonged the task of bringing out the teaching and keeping it properly related to its sources; to him fell the executive labor of providing ways and means to serve it to a sceptical public.

The functions of the former two were esoteric; those of Olcott exoteric. It was understood that the Colonel was not advanced beyond the position of a lay or

probationary chela. He himself seems to have accepted this ranking as deserved, and generously admitted that

"to transform a worldly man such as I was in 1874--a man of clubs, drinking parties, mistresses, a man absorbed in all sorts of worldly, public, and private undertakings and speculations-into that purest, wisest, noblest, and most spiritual of human beings-a 'Brother,' was a wonder demanding next to miraculous efficacy. . . . No one knows until he really tries it, how awful a task it is to subdue all his evil passions and animal instincts and develop his higher nature."[7]

The Theosophical Movement ascribes most of the trials and tribulations of Theosophy to the Colonel's indifferent success, at times, in the "awful task." Years later, Olcott says:

"She was the teacher, I the pupil; she the misunderstood and insulted messenger of the Great Ones, I the practical brain to plan, the right hand to work out the practical details."[8]

Out of this situation eventuated the formation of the Esoteric Section of the Theosophical Society. So many members were reaching out after the chelaship that Judge wrote to H.P.B. in 1887 for advice as to what to offer them. She replied, telling him to go ahead in America and she would soon do something herself. She then began the publication of Lucifer, in which the qualifications, dangers, obstacles, and status of chelaship were set forth in article after article.

Judge went to London; and there, at the request of Madame Blavatsky drew the plans and wrote the rules for the guidance of the new body. Col. Olcott looked on with some perturbation while his spiritual superiors stepped lightly over his authority to inaugurate the higher enterprise. In October, 1888, the first public statement relative to the Esoteric Section appeared. It announced the purpose of the formation of the Esoteric Section to be:

"To promote the esoteric interests of the Theosophical Society by the deeper study of esoteric philosophy."

All authority was vested in Madame Blavatsky and official connection with the Theosophical Society itself was disclaimed.

A further hint as to the impelling motive back of the new branch of activity was given by H.P.B. in the letter she addressed to the Convention of the American Section meeting in April, 1889. She says:

"Therefore it is that the ethics of Theosophy are even more necessary to mankind than the specific aspects of the psychic facts of nature and man ..."

She made a plea for solidarity in the fellowship of the Theosophical Society, to form a nucleus of true Brotherhood.

Unity had to be achieved to withstand exterior onslaught, as well as interior discord. An attack upon one must be equally met by all. The first object of the Society is Universal Brotherhood. She asked in the finale:

"How many of you have helped humanity to carry its smallest burden, that you should all regard yourselves as Theosophists? Oh, men of the West, who would play at being the Saviors of mankind before they can spare the life of a mosquito whose sting threatens them! Would ye be partakers of Divine Wisdom or true Theosophists? Then do as the gods when incarnated do. Feel yourselves the

vehicles of the whole humanity, mankind as part of yourselves, and act accordingly ..."

She then sent out a formal letter, marked strictly private and confidential, to all applicants for entry into the new school. It contained an introductory statement, the "Rules of the Esoteric Section (Probationary) of the Theosophical Society" and the "Pledge of Probationers in the Esoteric Section." The latter was as follows:

"I pledge myself to support, before the world, the Theosophical Movement, its leaders and its members; and in particular to obey, without cavil or delay, the orders of the Head of the Section, in all that concerns my relation with the Theosophical Movement."

It can be seen that such a pledge carried the possibility of far-reaching consequences and might be difficult to fulfil under certain precarious conditions. Much controversy in the Society from 1906 onwards hinges about this pledge.

Madame Blavatsky went on to say:

"It is through an Esoteric Section alone ... that the great exoteric Society may be redeemed and made to realize that in union and harmony alone lie its strength and power. The object of the Section, then, is to help the future growth of the Theosophical Society as a whole in the true direction, by promoting brotherly union at least among a choice minority."

The Book of Rules provided that the work to be pursued was not practical occultism, but mutual help in the Theosophic life; it outlined measures for suppressing gossip, slander, cant, hypocrisy, and injustice; for limiting the claims of occult interests and psychic inclinations; it inculcated the widest charity, tolerance, and mutual helpfulness as the prime condition of all true progress. Said the Rule:

"The first test of true apprenticeship is devotion to the interest of another." It concludes: "It is not the individual or determined purpose of attaining oneself Nirvana, which is, after all, only an exalted and glorious selfishness, but the self- sacrificing pursuit of the best means to lead our

neighbor on the right path . .
."

Conditions for membership in the Esoteric Section were three: (1) one must be a Fellow of the Theosophical Society; (2) the pledge must be signed; (3) the applicant must be approved by the Head of the Section. And warning was issued that, while no duties would be required in the Order that would interfere with one's family or professional obligations, "it is certain that every member of the Esoteric Section will have to give up more than one personal habit . . . and adopt some few ascetic rules." The habits referred to were alcoholism and meat- eating, mainly, and the ascetic rules were those regulating meditation, sleep, diet, kindly speech, altruistic thought, etc.

The establishment of the Esoteric Section was one of the moves undertaken to rebuild the structure of Theosophy which had been so badly shattered by the
S.P.R. attack and its consequences. But while this was going forward, largely under the direction of Judge, Madame Blavatsky had already begun to devote her

tireless energies to the accomplishment of another great work of reconstruction. Its inception bore a logical relation to the promulgation of the Esoteric branch. If students were to be taken deeper into the essentials of the occult life, there was need of a fuller statement of the scheme of the world's racial and cosmogonic history, so that the task of personal and social development might be seen and understood in its most intimate rapport with the larger streams of life. The arcane knowledge had to be further unveiled.

The combined attack of the Coulombs, the Christian missionaries and the English Psychic Research Society on Madame Blavatsky in 1885 was indeed a fiery-furnace test. She had vigorously, in Isis and elsewhere, attacked orthodoxy and conservative interests in religion and science. She was now to feel the full force of the blow which society, through the representatives of these vested interests, was impelled to strike back at her, and it was greater than she had anticipated. It nearly ended her career. Not that she was one to cringe and wince under attack. Far from it. She wanted to bring suit against her calumniators. She burned under a sense of injustice. She even contemplated the possibility of startling a crowded court room with a display of her suspected phenomena. But the trial would have necessitated dragging her beloved Masters into the mire of low human emotions, and this she could not do. Instead, the storm within her soul had to wear itself out by degrees. It nearly cost her life itself; but she was saved, as has been maintained, by the intervention of her Master's power. She wished to die, feeling that her life work was irreparably defeated. At this juncture she was summoned, as we gather from her letters to the Sinnetts, to a quiet nook north of Darjeeling, met the Mahatmas in person, and returned after a few days to her friends, "fixed" once more. Whatever the "inside" facts in the case, she went north broken in body and spirit, and two days later emerged from her retirement apparently well, and with a new zest for life, ready to battle again for her "Cause."

Not long thereafter came the journey from India, which she was never to see again, back to Europe, where she spent more peaceful days of work among devoted friends, the Gebhards at Würzburg, Germany, the Countess Wachtmeister, the Keightleys, and many more in Belgium, France, and England. She said the secret of her new lease on life at this time was that the Master had indicated to her that he wished her to perform one more service in the interests of Theosophy before she relinquished the body. Her task was not finished. Isis was little more than a clearing away of old rubbish and the announcement that a great secret science lay buried amid the ruins of ancient cities. The Mahatma Letters gave but a fragmentary outline of the great Teaching, enough to stimulate inquiry in the proper direction. But the magnum opus, the fundamentals of the Secret Doctrine, had not yet been produced. The "Secret Doctrine" was still secret. Restored to comparative health, and given certain reassurances of support from her Masters, her courage we renewed. One finds the motive of vindication running strong in her mind at this time; all thought of defence, of retaliation given up, she would disprove all the charges of knavery, deception and disingenuousness of every stripe by a master-work before whose brilliance all suggestion of petty human motives would vanish. She writes in a letter to Sinnett:

"As for [the charges of] philosophy and doctrine invented, the Secret Doctrine shall show. Now I am here alone, with the Countess [Wachtmeister] for witness. I have no books, no one to help me. And I tell you that the Secret Doctrine will be twenty times as learned, philosophical and better than Isis, which will be killed by it. Now there are hundreds of things which I am permitted to say and explain. I will show what a Russian spy can do, an alleged forger-plagiarist, etc. The whole doctrine is shown to be the mother stone, the foundation of all

the religions including Christianity, and on the strength of exoteric published Hindu books, with their symbols explained esoterically. The extreme lucidity of 'Esoteric Buddhism' [Mr. Sinnett's book expounding the summarized teaching of the Mahatma Letters] will also be shown, and its doctrines proven correct, mathematically, geometrically, logically and scientifically. Hodgson is very clever, but he is not clever enough for truth, and it shall triumph, after which I can die peacefully."[9]

The work was intended in its first conception to be an "expansion of Isis." It was soon seen, however, that the fuller clarification of the hints in the earlier work would necessitate the practically complete unveiling of the whole occult knowledge. So Isis was forgotten, and the new production made to stand on its own feet.

The hint in her letter just quoted that she would do the actual writing of the new volumes practically without the aid of reference or source books is to be taken to mean, doubtless, that the very manner of her production of the work would constitute the final irrefutable proof of the existence and powers of the Mahatmas. The composition as well as the contents of the book was to be phenomenal. She says in a letter to Madame Jelihowsky, her sister, written at this time that "it is the phenomena of Isis all over again." Yet there were some variations. In a Sinnett letter she writes:
"There's a new development and scenery every morning. I live two lives again! Master finds that it is too difficult for me to be looking consciously into the astral light for my Secret Doctrine, and so, it is now about a fortnight, I am made to see all I have to as though in my dream. I see large and long rolls of paper on which things are written, and I recollect them. Thus all the Patriarchs from Adam to Noah were given me to see, parallel with the Rishis; and in the middle between them the meaning of these symbols or personifications. I was ordered to . . . make a rapid sketch of what was known historically and in literature, in classics and in profane and sacred histories-during the five hundred years that followed it; of magic, the existence of a universal Secret Doctrine known to the philoso-

phers and Initiates of every country, and even to several of the Church Fathers such as Clement of Alexandria, Origen and others, who had been initiated themselves. Also to describe the Mysteries and some rites; and I can assure you that the most extraordinary things are given out now, the whole story of the Crucifixion, etc., being shown to be based on a rite as old as the world-the Crucifixion of the Lathe of the Candidate-trials, going down to Hell, etc., all Aryan . . . I have facts for twenty volumes like Isis; it is the language, the cleverness for compiling them, that I lack."10

Writing to her niece, Madame Vera Johnston, she said:

"You are very green if you think that I actually know and understand all the things I write. How many times am I to repeat to you and your mother that the things I write are dictated to me; that sometimes I see manuscripts, numbers and words before my eyes of which I never knew anything?"11

In a letter to Judge in America, March 24, 1886, H.P.B. says:

"Such facts, such facts, Judge, as Masters are giving out, will rejoice your old heart. . . . The thing is becoming enormous, a wealth of facts."

Madame Johnston quotes Franz Hartmann, who accompanied Madame Blavatsky on her trip from Madras to Europe in April, 1885, when she was so ill that she had to be hoisted aboard, as saying that

"while on board the S.S. 'Tibre' and on the open sea, she very frequently received in some occult manner many pages of manuscript referring to the Secret Doctrine, the material of which she was collecting at the time. Miss Mary Flynn was with us, and knows more about it than I; because I did not take much interest in those matters, as the receiving of 'occult correspondence' had become almost an everyday occurrence with us."12

The person who had most continuous and prolonged opportunity to witness whatever display of extraordinary assistance was afforded the compiler of The Secret Doctrine was the Countess Constance Wachtmeister, already mentioned as being the companion and guardian of Madame Blavatsky during must of the period of the composition at Würzburg, Ostend, and in London. In her Reminiscences of H. P. Blavatsky, and The Secret Doctrine she writes in detail of the many facts coming under her observation which pointed to exterior help in the work. She wrote:

"The Secret Doctrine will be indeed a great and grand work. I have had the privilege of watching its progress, of reading the manuscripts, and witnessing the occult way in which she derived her information."

The Countess states that on two or three occasions she saw on H.P.B.'s desk in the morning numbers of sheets of manuscript in the familiar handwriting of the Masters. She writes that at times a piece of paper was found on the desk in the morning with unfamiliar characters traced in red ink. It was an outline of the author's work for the day,--the "red and blue spook-like messages." Questioned how it was precipitated, H.P.B. stated that elementals were used for the purpose, but that they had nothing to do with the intelligence of the message, only with the mechanics of the feat. More significant, perhaps, than these details is the question of the origin of the many quotations and references, as in Isis, from old works, or from books not in her possession. The testimony on this score is more voluminous and challenging than in the case of Isis. 13

Madame Blavatsky was practically without reference books and was too ill to leave the house to visit libraries. She worked from morning until night at her desk. Dr. Hübbe-Schleiden, her German convert, says she had scarcely half-a- dozen books. Her niece writes:

"Later on when we three went to Ostend [in the very midst of the work], it was I who put aunt's things and books in order, so I can testify that the first month or two in Ostend she decidedly had no other books but a few French novels, bought at railway stations and read whilst traveling, and several odd numbers of some Russian newspapers and magazines. So there was absolutely nothing where her numerous quotations could have come from."14

Two young Englishmen, Dr. Bertram Keightley and his nephew Archibald, worked with Madame Blavatsky on the arrangement of her material. It fell to them eventually to edit the work for her. They contribute their testimony as to what took place of a phenomenal sort. Says Bertram:

"Of phenomena in connection with The Secret Doctrine I have very little indeed to say. Quotations, with full references, from books which were never in the house-quotations verified after hours of search, sometimes at the British Museum, for a rare book-of such I saw and verified not a few."15

The nephew speaks to the same effect. As a matter of fact, during the writing of the latter portions of the book in London, Madame Blavatsky kept two or three young men, students from the University of Dublin, busily engaged in the daily search for quotations, which she said would be found in books of which she gave not only the titles, but the exact location of the passages. These men have repeatedly borne testimony to the facts in this connection. They were Mr. E. Douglass Fawcett, Mr. S. L. McGregor Mathers, Mr. Edgar Saltus, and one or two more.16

There were frequent and notable visitors in the evenings, when the day's writing was put aside. Mr. Archibald Keightley tells that:

"Mr. J. G. Romanes, a Fellow of the Royal Society, comes in to discuss the evolutionary theory set forth in her Secret Doctrine. Mr. W. T. Stead, Editor of the Pall Mall Gazette, who is a great admirer of The Secret Doctrine, finds much in it that seems to invite further elucidation. Lord Crawford, Earl of Crawford and Balcarres, another F.R.S.-who is deeply interested in occultism and cosmography, and who was a pupil of Lord Lytton and studied with him in Egypt- comes to speak of his special subject of concern. Mr. Sidney Whitman, widely known for his scathing criticism upon English cant, has ideas to express and thoughts to interchange upon the ethics of Theosophy; and so they come."17

Untiringly through 1885, 1886 and 1887, in Germany with the Gebhards, then in Belgium and finally in London, she labored to get the voluminous material in form. Unable on account of her dropsical condition to take exercise, she was again and again threatened with complete breakdown by the accumulation of toxins in her system. A young physician of London, Dr. Bennett, who attended her at times, pronounced her condition most grave, on one occasion declaring it impossible for her to survive the night. In our third chapter we have seen Countess Wachtmeister's account of her surprising recovery. The Countess alleges that Madame destroyed many pages of manuscript already written, in obedience to orders from the Master. There was left, however, enough material for some sixteen hundred close-printed pages which now make up the two volumes commonly accepted as her genuine product. To an examination of the contents of this pretentious work we now invite the reader.

CHAPTER VIII THE SECRET DOCTRINE

The Secret Doctrine sets forth what purports to be the root knowledge out of which all religion, philosophy, and science have grown. The sub-title-"The Synthesis of Science, Religion, and Philosophy" reveals the daring aim and scope of the undertaking. It is an effort to present and align certain fundamental principles in such a way as to render possible a synthesis of all knowledge.

The first volume deals with cosmogenesis, the second with anthropogenesis. A third, to deal with the lives of the great occultists down the ages, was in form for the press, as testified to by the Keightleys, who typed the manuscript, and by Alice L. Cleather and others, but never came to the public. A fourth was projected and almost entirely written, but likewise went to oblivion instead of to the printer. A third volume, issued five years after H.P.B.'s death under the editorship of Mrs. Annie Besant, is made up of some other writings of Madame Blavatsky, dealing in part with the Esoteric Section, but is not regarded by close students as having been the original third volume.

The whole book professes to be a commentary on The Stanzas of Dzyan,1 which H.P.B. alleged to be a fragment of Tibetan sacred writings of two types, one cosmological, the other ethical and devotional. The Secret Doctrine elucidates the former section of the Stanzas, and her later work, The Voice of the Silence, the latter. The Stanzas of Dzyan are of great antiquity, she claimed, drawn from the Mani Koumboum,2 or sacred script of the Dzungarians,3 in the north of Tibet. She is not sure of their origin, but says she was permitted to memorize them during her residence in the Forbidden Land. They show a close parallel with the Prajna Paramita Sutras of Hindu sacred lore.

There are of course charges that she invented the Stanzas herself or plagiarized them from some source. Max Müller is reported to have said that in this matter she was either a remarkable forger or that she has made the most valuable gift to archeological research in the Orient. She says herself in the Preface:

"These truths are in no sense put forward as a revelation; nor does the author claim the position of a revealer of mystic lore, now made public for the first time in the world's history. For what is contained in this work is to be found scattered throughout thousands of volumes embodying the scriptures of the great Asiatic and early European religions, hidden under glyph and symbol, and hitherto left unnoticed because of this veil. What is now attempted is to gather the oldest tenets together and to make of them one harmonious and unbroken whole. The sole advantage which the writer has over her predecessors, is that she need not resort to personal speculation and theories. For this work is a partial statement of what she herself has been taught by more advanced students, supplemented in a few details only, by the results of her own study and observation."4

Near the end of her Introductory she printed in large type, quoting Montaigne:

"I have here made only a nosegay of culled flowers, and have brought nothing of my own but the string that ties them."

Then she adds:

"Pull the 'string' to pieces, if you will. As for the nosegay of facts-you will never be able to make away with these. You can only ignore them and no more."

In the Introductory she presents once more the thesis of esotericism as the method used throughout former history for the preservation and propagation of the precious deposit of the Ancient Wisdom. She affirms that under the sandswept plains of Tibet, under many a desert of the Orient, cities lie buried in whose secret recesses are stored away the priceless books that the despoiling hands of the bigot would have tossed into the flames. Books which held the key to thousands of others yet extant, she alleges, unaccountably disappeared from view-but are not lost. There was a "primeval revelation," granted to the fathers of the human race, and it still exists. Furthermore, it will reappear. But unless one possesses the key, he will never unlock it, and the profane world will search for it in vain. The Golden Legend traces its symbolic pattern mysteriously through the warp and woof of the oldest literatures, but only the initiated will see it. A strange prophecy is dropped as she passes on.

"The rejection of these teachings may be expected and must be accepted beforehand. No one styling himself a 'scholar,' in whatever department of exact science, will be permitted to regard these teachings seriously. They will be derided and rejected a priori in this century; but only in this one. For in the twentieth century of our era scholars will begin to recognize that the Secret Doctrine has neither been invented nor exaggerated, but on the contrary, simply outlined; and finally that its teachings antedate the Vedas."5

Her book is not the Secret Doctrine in its entirety, but a select number of fragments of its fundamental tenets. But it will be centuries before much more is given out. The keys to the Zodiacal Mysteries "must be turned seven times before the whole system is divulged." One turn of the key was given in Isis.

Several turns more are given in The Secret Doctrine.

"The Secret Doctrine is not a treatise, or a series of vague theories, but contains all that can be given out to the world in this century."6

She is to deal with the entire field of life, in all its manifestations, cosmic, universal, planetary, earthly, and human. Omnipresent eternal life is assumed as given, without beginning or end, yet periodical in its regular manifestations.

It is always in being for Itself, yet for us it comes into and goes out of existence with periodical rhythm. Its one absolute attribute, which is itself, is eternal causeless motion, called the "Great Breath." Life eternal exhales and inhales, and this action produces the universes and withdraws them. It is in regular and harmonious succession either passive or active. These conditions are the "Days" and "Nights" of Brahm, when, so to say, universal life is either awake or asleep. This characteristic of the One Life stamps everything everywhere with the mark of an analogous process. No work of Life is free from this law. It is the immutable law of the All and of every part of the All. It is the universal law of Karma, and makes reincarnation the method of life expression everywhere. Life swings eternally back and forth between periods of activity and rest. Upon inaugurating an active period after a "Night" of rest, life begins to expand, and continues until it fills all space with cosmical

creation; in turn, at the end of this activity, it contracts and withdraws all the energy within itself. The Secret Doctrine is an account of the activities of the One Life from the beginning of one of these periods of reawakening to its end, treating the cosmic processes generally, and the earth and human processes specifically. It is the cryptic story of how the universe is created, whence it em-anates, what Powers fashion it, whither it goes and what it means.

The period of universal rest is known in esoteric circles as "Pralaya,"7 the active period as a "Man-vantara."8 A description of the Totality of Things is nothing but an account of the Life Force alter-nating, shuttle-like, between these two conditions.

The universe comes out of the Great Being and disappears into it. Life repeats in any form it takes the metaphor of this process. It vacillates forever between the opposite poles of Unity and Infinity, noumenon and phenomenon, absoluteness and relativity, homogeneity and heterogeneity, reality and appearance, the unconditional and the conditioned, the dimensionless and the dimensioned, the eternal and the temporal. What Life is when not manifest to us is as indescribable, as unthink-able as is space. The Absolute-God-is just this Space. Space is neither a "limitless void" nor a "condi-tioned fulness," but both. It appears void to finite minds, yet is the absolute container of all that is. Where the universe goes when it dissolves-and still remains in being-is where anything else goes when it dissolves,--into solution. Not in a purely mechanical sense, yet that too. It goes from infinite particularity back into the one genus, from form back to formlessness, from differentiation back to homogeneity. Matter goes to bits, finer, finer, till it is held in solution in the infinite sea of pure Non-Being. It goes from actuality to latency.

Occultism is the study of the worlds in their latent state; material science is the study of the same worlds in their actual or manifest condition. Or, to use Aristotelian terms, since no attributes can be predicated of pure potentiality, matter is privation. Matter is sheer possibility, with no capacity but to be acted upon, shaped, formed, impregnated. Nothing can be affirmed of it save that it is, and even then it is not as matter, but the pure essence, germ, or root of matter. It is just the Absolute, i.e., freed from all marks of differentiation. Since nothing can be asserted of it, it is pure negation, non-being. Absolute being, paradoxically, ultimately equals non-being. Being has so far retreated from actuality that it ends in sheer Be-ness. The eternal "dance of life" is a rhythmic movement of the All from Be-ness to Being, through the path of Becoming. This brings us to the famous three funda-mentals of the Secret Doctrine, the three basic principles of the Sacred Science. They are:

1. The Omnipresent, Eternal, Boundless and Immutable Principle, on which all speculation is impossible-beyond the range and reach of thought-the One Absolute Reality, Infinite Cause, the Unknowable, the Unmoved Mover and Rootless Root of all-pure Be-ness-Sat. It is symbolized in esotericism under two aspects, Absolute Space and Absolute Motion; the latter representing uncon-ditioned Consciousness. The impersonal reality of the cosmos is the pure noumenon of thought. Parabrahm (Be-ness) is out of all relation to conditioned existence. In Sanskrit, parabrahman means "the Supreme Spirit of Brahma." Whenever the life of Parabrahm deploys into manifestation, it as-

sumes a dual aspect, giving rise to the "pairs of opposites," or the polarities of the conditioned universe. The One Life splits into Spirit-Matter, Subject-Object. The contrast and tension of these two aspects are essential to hold the universes in manifestation. Without cosmic substance cosmic ideation would not manifest as individual self- consciousness, since only through matter can there be effected a focus of this

undifferentiated intelligence to form a conscious being. Similarly cosmic matter apart from cosmic ideation, would remain an empty abstraction.

Madame Blavatsky here introduces the conception of a force whose function it is to effect the linkage between spirit and matter. This is an energy named Fohat (supposedly a Tibetan term), which becomes at once the solution of all mind-body problems. It is the "bridge" by which the "Ideas" existing in the Divine Intelligence are impressed on cosmic substance as the "Laws of Nature." It is the Force which prescribes form to matter, and gives mode to its activity. It is the agent of the formative intelligences, the various sons of the various trinities, for casting the creations into forms of "logical structure."

2.   The periodical activity already noted, which makes Space the "playground of numberless universes incessantly manifesting and disappearing," the rhythmic pulse which causes "the appearance and disappearance of worlds like a regular tidal ebb and flow." This second fundamental affirms that absolute law of periodicity, of flux and reflux, which physical science has noted and recorded in all departments of nature, and which the old science termed the Law of Karma. It has been treated briefly above, and a later chapter will trace its operations in nature more fully.

3.   The identity and fundamental unity of all individual Souls with the universal Over-Soul, the microcosm with the macrocosm. The history of the individual or personalized Soul is thus of necessity a miniature or copy of the larger life of the universe, a pilgrimage through the worlds of matter and sense, under the cyclic karmic law,--"cycles of necessity" and incarnation. In fact individual self-consciousness is only acquirable by the Spirit, in its separated though still divine aspect-the Soul-by an independent conscious existence that brings it in contact with every elementary form of the phenomenal world. This demands of it a "descent into matter" to its lowest and most inert forms, and a re- ascent through every rising grade until immaterial conditions are once more attained. The road downward and upward is marked by seven steps, grades or planes of cosmic formation, on each of which man acquires a nature and faculties consonant with the type of structure of the atom there encountered. On the downward arc (or Involution, a process unknown to modern science which deals only with Evolution), Life undergoes at each step an increased degree of differentiation; and the naming of the various potentialities emerging into potencies, gives us the dualities, the trinities, the tetractys, and the numberless hierarchies of the ancient Greeks and Orientals. The Gods, the Mothers-Fathers-Sons, Spirits, Logoi, Elohim, Demiurges, Jehovahs, Pitris, Aeons, are but names of the Intelligent Forces that are first emanated from the impregnated womb of time. The first emanated principles are sexless, but sex is introduced (in symbolic form) as soon as the dual polarization of Spirit-Matter takes place. The whole story of the Cosmogenesis (Volume I) is a recital of the scheme according to which the primal unity of unmanifest Being breaks up into differentiation and multiformity and so fills space with conscious evolving beings.

Thus the three fundamentals express respectively the Be-ness, the Becoming, and the Being of the everlasting That, which is Life.

The First Stanza describes the state of the Absolute during Pralaya, the "Night of Brahm," when nothing is in existence, but everything only is. Such a description can obviously be only a grouping of symbolisms. The only fit symbol of the Absolute is darkness, "brooding over the face of the deep" (Space). It is the night of Life, and all Nature sleeps. The worlds were not. The only description is privative. Time was not; mind was not; "the seven ways to bliss,"

or the evolutionary paths, were not; the "causes of misery," of the worlds of illusion, were not; even the hierarchies who would direct the "new wheel," were not. The first differentiation of the That, viz., Spirit, had not been made. ("That" is a reminiscence of the phrase tat tvam asi "that [i.e., the All] thou art," found in the Indian Upanishads.) Matter was not; but only its formless essence.

Nature had thus slept for "seven eternities," however they may have been registered in a timeless consciousness; for time was not, since there was no differentiation, hence no succession. Mind was not, having no organ to function through. All was noumenon. The Great Breath, on whose out-going energy worlds sprang into existence, had not yet gone forth. The universe was a blank; metaphysics had not begun to generate physics; the universe held in solution had not yet begun to precipitate into crystallization. All life was hidden in the formless embrace of the protyle, or primal substance. Darkness is the "Father of Lights," but the Son had not yet been born. When day dawns, Father (Spirit) and Mother (Substance) unite to beget their Son, who will then cleave the Cimmerian darkness and issue forth to flood all space.

Stanza II continues the description of the sleeping universe, pointing, however, to the signs of reawakening. "The hour had not yet struck; the ray had not yet flashed into the germ; the mother-lotus had not yet swollen." From the darkness soon would issue the streak of dawn, splitting open by its light and warmth the shell of each atom of virgin matter, and letting issue thence the Seven Creators, who will fashion the universe. In the Mundane Egg the germ of life was deposited from the preceding Manvantaras, and the Divine Energy, brooding over it for aeons, caused it to hatch out its brood of new worlds. In immaterial form within the germ dwelt the archetypal ideas, the (Platonic) memories of former experiences, which will determine the form of the new structures as the Divine Architects of the worlds. All things on earth are but patterns of things in the heavens; spiritual ideas crystallized into concretion on the plane of manifestation-"sermons in stones." The lotus is the symbol of esoteric teaching because its seed contains a miniature of the future plant, and because, like man, it lives in three worlds, the mud (material), the water (typifying the emotional), and the air (spiritual).

Creation starts with incubation. The Cosmic Egg must be fertilized ere it can be hatched. A ray, or first emanation, from the Darkness opens the womb of the Mother (Primal Substance), and it then emanates as three, Father-Mother-Son, which, with the energy of Fohat makes the quaternary. Thus occultism explains all the mysteries of the trinity and the Immaculate Conception. The first dogma of Occultism is universal unity under three aspects. The Son was born from virgin (i.e., unproductive, unfertilized) matter (Root Substance, the Mother), when the latter was fecundated by the Father (Spirit).

The archetypal ideas do not imply a Divine Ideator, nor the Divine Thought a Divine Thinker. The Universe is Thought itself, reflected in a manifested material. But the Universe is the product, or "Son," which during the prologue of the drama of the creation lies buried in the Divine Thought. The latter has "not yet penetrated unto the Divine Bosom."

Stanza III rings with the concluding vibrations of the seventh eternity as they thrill through boundless space, sounding the cock-crow of a new Manvantaric daybreak. The Mother (Substance) swells, expanding from within. The vibration sweeps along, impregnating the quiescent germs of life in the whole expanse.

Darkness gives out light; light drops into virgin matter, opening every bud. Divine Intelligence impregnates chaos. The germs float together into the World-

Egg, the ancient symbol of Nature fructified. The aggravation of units of matter under the impulse of dynamic spirit is symbolized by the term "curdling." Pure Spirit curdles pure matter into the incipient granules of hyle, or substance.

The serpent symbol is prominent in the early cosmology, typifying at different times the eternity, infinitude, regeneration and rejuvenation of the universe, and also wisdom. The familiar serpent with its tail in its mouth was a symbol not only of eternity and infinitude, but of the globular form of all bodies shaped out of the fire mist. In general the "fiery serpent" represented the movement of Divine Wisdom over the face of the waters, or primary elements.

The text of the whole doctrine of the early stages, in fact, of the entire creative process, is the statement "that there is but One Universal Element, infinite, unborn and undying, and that all the rest-as the world of phenomena- are but so many various differentiated aspects and transformations of that One, from Cosmical down to micro-cosmical effects, from superhuman down to human and sub-human beings, the totality in short of objective existence."9

Naturally but one tiny segment of all that activity is cognizable by man, whose perceptive powers are limited to a small range of vibratory sensitivity. Only that part of nature which comes within hail of his sense equipment, only the expressions of life which take physical form, are known (directly) to him. Were it not, says Theosophy, for the fact that superhuman beings, whose cognitive powers have been vastly extended beyond ordinary human capacity, have imparted to those qualified to receive it information relative to the upper worlds and the inner realities of nature, we would know nothing of cosmology.

"In order to obtain clear perception of it, one has first of all to admit the postulate of a universally diffused, omnipresent, eternal Deity in Nature; secondly, to have fathomed the meaning of electricity in its true essence; and thirdly, to credit man with being a septenary symbol, on the terrestrial plane, of the One Great Unit, (the Logos), which is itself the seven-vowelled sign, the Breath, crystallized into the Word."10

Madame Blavatsky starts with the Absolute, the All-That-Is, not even the One, but the No-Number.

In Stanza IV we see this primordial essence awakening to activity. It emanates or engenders the One, the homogeneous substrate of all. It in turn projects or splits itself into the Two, Father-Mother, and these, interacting, produce the "Sons" or Rays, who by their word of power, the "Army of the Voice" (the laws of nature), build the worlds of the universe. These sons are always seven in number, and their created works are thus given a seven-fold constitution.

Christians know them as the Seven Logoi, or the Seven Archangels. These carry the differentiation of the one cosmic substrate to its furthest extent in the production of the ninety-two or more elements of our globe, which their forces weld into an infinity of combinations to compose our structural earth. All the physical forces we know, light, heat, cold, fire, water, gas, earth, ether, are the progeny of the great universal agent, Fohat, which we know under its form of electricity. Electricity is the universal agent employed by the Sons of God to create and uphold our world.

In bold outline this is the whole story. But Madame Blavatsky supplies a wealth of detail and a richness of illustration that go far to clarify the various phases of the process and the diversified agents coöperating in it.

When the One has created the Two-Spirit and Matter-the allegory goes on to say, the interaction of these Two "spin a web whose upper end is fastened to Spirit and the lower one to Matter." This web is the universe, ranging in constituent elements from coarse matter up to vibrant Spirit. Yet Spirit and Matter are but two phases of one and the same Prime Element.

Cosmic Fire, Fohat, Divine Electricity, energizes the universe. But to the natural concept of electricity the occult science adds the property of intelligence. Cerebration is attended by electrical phenomena, it is said.

Humanity is a materialized and as yet imperfect expression of the seven hierarchical Devas, or the seven conscious intelligent powers in nature. The planetary deities, or the planets as living beings, are fundamental in the Theosophic view, as to the Aristotelian and ancient Greek view generally. Mankind is but repeating the history of precedent life units, which have risen to celestial heights and magnitudes.

The forms of created life are all determined by the geometrical forms in the minds of the Intelligences. "Nature geometrizes universally in all her manifestations." There is an inherent law by which nature coördinates or correlates all her geometrical forms, and her compound elements; and in it there is no room for chance. The worlds are all subject to Rulers or Regents, and the apparent deviations from precise natural programs are due to voluntary actions on the part of those great Beings who, like ourselves, are in the cycle of experience and evolution. The Solar Logoi can err in their spheres as we in ours. Some of the exceptional oddities in nature are the effects of their efforts to experiment and learn.

The "Lipika" ("scribes") "write" the eternal records of nature on the imperishable scroll of the Akashic ether. They are the "amanuenses of the Eternal Ideation," who copy the archetypal ideas and imprint them on the material substance. They write the Book of Eternal Life and exercise an influence on the science of horoscopy.

Stanza V elaborates in more detail the creative process, controlled by the various "sevens," the "Breaths" (prana, basic category in Indian philosophy) and the "Sons." The Doctrine teaches that to become a fully conscious divine "god," the spiritual primeval Intelligence must pass through the human stage. And "human" in this usage is not limited to the humanity of our globe, but applies also to the numberless other mortal incarnations of varying types on other planets. A human state is one in which Intelligence is embodied in a condition of material organization in which there is established an equilibrium between matter and spirit,--and this state is reached in the middle point of the Fourth Round on each chain of globes, or when spirit is most deeply enmeshed in matter, and is ready to begin its emergence. The hierarchical entities must have won for themselves the right of divinity through self-experience, as we are doing. "The 'Breath' or first emanation becomes a stone, the stone a plant, the plant an animal, the animal a man, the man a spirit and the spirit a god." All the great planetary gods were once men, and we men shall in the future take our places in the skies as Lords of planets, Regents of galaxies and wielders of fire-mist! As our human wills (the divine elements in us) are now masters over small potencies, so our expanded Intelligences will direct vast elemental energies, and worlds will arise under the impulsion of our thought. There is room in space for us all. The "flaming fire" (electricity) shall be our minister, to flash at our bidding. The "fiery wind" is the incandescent cosmic dust which follows the impulsion of the will as iron filings follow a magnet. Yet this cosmic dust is "mind-stuff," has the potentiality of self-consciousness in it, and is, like the

Monad of Leibnitz, a universe in itself and for itself. "It is an atom and an angel." Fohat is the universal fiery agent of Divine Will, and the electricity we know is one aspect, not by any means the highest, of it. In a higher state Fohat is the "objectivized thought of the gods," the Word made flesh. In another aspect he is the Universal Life Force, solar energy. He is said to take "three and seven strides through the seven regions above and the seven below," which is taken to mean the successive waves of vital force impregnating the seven levels of nature. "God is a living Fire,"-the Christians are fire-worshippers, too, says Madame Blavatsky. God is the One Flame. It burns within every material thing. The ultimate essence of each constituent part of the compounds of nature is unitary, whether in the spiritual, the intellectual or the physical world.

In order that the One may become the many, there must be a principium individuationis, and this is provided by the qualities of matter. A spark of Divine Fire, so to speak, is wrapped in a vesture of matter, which circumscribes the energies of spirit with a "Ring Pass-Not." Each embodied Monad or Spiritual Ego looks out through its sense windows to perceive another Ego; but perceives only the material garment of that Ego. The process of evolution will make this garment thinner, so that the inner splendor of the Self can be seen luminously through it.

The fiery energy of the great planetary beings, our author says, will never "run down," as it is constantly being fed by intra-cosmic fuel, a theory which Prof. Millikan has made familiar in recent days.

Stanza VI carries out the further stages of differentiation of the life principle in its first or virgin forms. Man's physical body is but one of seven constituents of his being, and a planet likewise presents only its outer garment, its physical vehicle, to our view. The stars, as beings, are septenary, having astral, mental, and spiritual bodies in addition to their physical globes. It is affirmed that this septiform constitution of man, which makes him an analogue of the great cosmic beings and of the cosmos itself, is to be taken as the true significance of the Biblical phrase "man, the image and likeness of God." The more real or more spiritual essences of the being of both man and stars are not visible to sense. The life impulse animating man contacts the material world only in and through his physical body; the same thing is true of the chain of globes. Both man and the planet have one physical body on the material plane, two on the vital etheric plane, two on the mental plane, and two on the upper plane of spirit. The latter two are beyond the powers of human ken, and to us are material only in the sense that they are not entirely devoid of differentiation. They are still vestures of spirit, not spirit itself. But they are the first garments of "pure" spirit. A life wave, in man or planet, comes forth from spirit, enters one after the other the bodies of increasing material density, until it has descended to a perfect equilibrium between matter and spirit, in the gross physical or fourth body; and then begins its ascent through three other vehicles of increasingly tenuous organization. And it runs seven times round each cycle of bodies and dwells for milliards of years in each of the seven kingdoms of nature, the mineral, vegetable, animal, and human, and three sub-mineral kingdoms of an elementary character, not known to science. The waves of life pass successively from one globe to another, lifting one into active existence as another goes "dead." They traverse the seven globes of a chain like a great spiral serpent, revolving like a barber's pole, every turn of the axis carrying a kingdom of nature one stride higher. For instance, hitting Globe A of the chain the impulsion builds up the mineral kingdom there; as this first wave swings onward to Globe B (where it builds the mineral kingdom for it) the second impulsion hits Globe A and lifts the mineral kingdom erected by the previous wave into the vegetable evolution. As the first wave leaps over from

Globe B to Globe C, to start mineral life there, the second wave has brought the vegetable kingdom to Globe B, and the animal kingdom on Globe A. The fourth outgoing of force will introduce the mineral world on Globe D, the vegetable on Globe C, the animal on Globe B, and the human on Globe A. After the human come the superhuman or spiritual evolutions. The detailed explanation of the entire cycle of birth, growth, life, and death of solar systems is of such complexity that it is the work of years for the Theosophic student to grasp it with any clearness. It is immensely involved, so that charts and graphs are generally resorted to. The student is referred to standard Theosophic works for the minutiae of this subject. We can but note here the principles of the system and some of their implications.

The earth, as the one visible representative of its six invisible principles, has to live through seven Rounds. The first three take it through the process of materialization; the fourth fully crystallizes it, hardens it; the last three take it gradually out of physical, back to ethereal and finally spiritual form. The Fourth Globe of each chain is thus always the nadir of the process of involution, and the Fourth Round is always the time in which this process is consummated. The earth is now a little past the nethermost point of material existence, as we have passed the middle of the Fourth Round. We have finished the descending arc and have begun our return to Deity, both the globe and the human family on it. Exiles from God, prodigal sons in a far country, we have set out on our homeward journey.

Man came on our globe at the beginning of the Fourth Round in the present series of life cycles and races, following the evolution of the mineral, vegetable, and animal kingdoms thereon. Every life cycle on our earth brings into being seven Root Races. The First Root Race were the progeny of "celestial men," or the Lunar Pitris,11 of which again there are seven hierarchies.

Human Egos continue to come into the stream of our evolution on earth up to the Fourth Round. But at this point the door into the human kingdom closes. Those Monads who have not reached the human kingdom by this time will find themselves so far behind that they will have to wait over, in a state of suspended vitality, until the next wave bears them onward. But for their loss of opportunity on this chain they will be rewarded by becoming men on a higher chain altogether.

The hosts of Monads are divided into three classes: Lunar Pitris, present Men, and the laggards. The first class are advanced Egos who reached "Manhood" in the First Round. The laggards are those who come in last, and are still in an undeveloped state.

The Moon is the parent of our Earth-and this in spite of the fact that it is our satellite. It is older, and its spirit has passed from its now lifeless body into our planet. In brief, the Earth is the new body or reincarnation of the Moon,--or more correctly, of that great Spirit which tenanted the Moon aeons ago. Madame Blavatsky uses the apt illustration of a mother circling around her child's cradle, to vindicate the anomaly of a parent body in a satellitic relation to its offspring.

There exists in nature a triple evolutionary scheme, or three separate schemes of evolution, which proceed contemporaneously in our system and are inextricably interblended at every point. These are the Monadic, the intellectual, and the physical. Here again analogy steps in to clarify thought. As man is a Monad, or spark of the Infinite Essence, which is evolving in connection both with a principle of mind and a physical body, so nature is a combination of three

streams of development. The higher part must find its way to growth through connection with the lower and the lowest. But each of these three evolutions has its own laws, and the interconnection of them all in man makes him the complex being he is. Every speck of matter strives to reach its model in man; and every man aspires to be a self-conscious Monad.

Out of this assertion of a threefold nature in man grows one of the unique conceptions of Theosophy: that Man, a divine spiritual Monad, is in this evolution dwelling in and controlling (if he has learned how to prevent it controlling him) the body of an animal. And the body is the animal's, not man's, in the strict sense. The body has its own type of consciousness, primal urgings, its own independent soul, but no intellect or spiritual nature. Through its association with us in the same house it is supposed to develop in a way it could never do unaided, first a mind and later the inkling of spirituality. But every organism has its principle, and the soul of the animal is capable of attending to those functions which pertain to the life of the body. Hence, the commonplace functions of our bodies are regulated by a cerebration which is so far from being directly our own that we are at any rate totally unconscious of it. This amounts to saying that our subconscious, or the operations of our sympathetic, as distinguished from our cerebral, nervous system, is the "soul" of our animal mate. The hope of the animal lies in his fairly ready susceptibility to training, so that he is able quickly to take up by an automatism whatever "we" do habitually.

Theosophy affirms that man has to control, not his own lower nature, but a lower order of being whose body he is tenanting.

Theosophists point to the development of a child as corroborative of this theory. Before mind develops, the child is an animal simply. Later comes intellect, and after more time comes spirituality. Man is not simple; he is a congeries of individuals in association. As the individual's unfoldment in his own life is a recapitulation of the growth of humanity as a unit, it follows the same order of evolution. The great Creative Lords did not implant the principle of mind in our order until, in the

Fourth Race, appropriate bodies had been built up. We are only now beginning to evolve spiritual faculty.

The so-called Fall "was the fall of Spirit into generation, not the fall of mortal man." Madame Blavatsky undertakes to show that on this point of theology, as on that of the Virgin Birth, Christian doctrine is childishly literal-minded. It has taken a fact of cosmology, which like all others in ancient thought had been symbolized in various forms, and rendered it in a literal historical sense. The "Falls" are but phases of the universal "descent into matter," which appears under several aspects, one being the general outgoing of spirit into the material worlds, another the "fall of the angels" and a third the "fall of man." The taint of sexuality associated with certain conceptions of man's fall is a reference to the fact that when the spiritual Monads who descended to earth to inhabit the bodies of a lower race (the animals spoken of above), they were of necessity forced into sexual procreation, whereas they had propagated by powers of the intellectualized will in their previous high estate.

Then in regard to the Satans, the Serpents, the Dragons, the Devils, the Demons, the Demiurges, the Adversaries, Madame Blavatsky delves deep into ancient lore to prove that, when read properly in their esoteric meaning, all the old legends of the Evil Ones, the Powers of Darkness, refer to no essentially evil beings, great or small, but to the Divine Wisdom of the Sons of Light (all light emanates from darkness) who impregnate the universe with the principle of intelligence. Adam's eating of the fruit of the forbidden tree gave him

knowledge of good and evil. This can mean only that beings of a "pure" spiritual nature represented symbolically by resident life in Eden or Paradise, sought, through incarnation in physical bodies in a material world, the opportunity to bring the latent intelligence in their divine nature to actualization in self- conscious knowledge. Dragons are always found guarding a tree-the tree of knowledge.

"When the Church, therefore, curses Satan, it curses the cosmic reflection of God; it anathematizes God made manifest in matter or in the objective; it maledicts God, or the ever-incomprehensible Wisdom, revealing itself as Light and Shadow, good and evil in nature in the only manner comprehensible to the limited intellect of man."12

"Satan, once he ceases to be viewed in the superstitious dogmatic unphilosophical spirit of the Churches, grows into the grandiose image of one who made of terrestrial a divine Man; who gave him . . . the law of the Spirit and Life and made him free from the sin of ignorance, hence of death."13

All references to Satan stood for an aspect of nature that was evil only as the negative pole of electricity is evil, i.e., as it stands in opposition to the positive, a necessary and benignant phase of activity. "Deus est Demon inversus."

The globes, or their constituent matter, go through seven fundamental transformations in their life history: (1), the homogeneous; (2), the aëriform and radiant (gaseous); (3), curd-like (nebulous); (4), atomic, ethereal (beginning of differentiation); (5), germinal, fiery; (6), vapory (the future Earth); (7), cold, depending on the sun for life.

When the worlds are populated and the Monads have entered the human chain, certain great beings who have risen to knowledge on other chains supervise the instruction of the oncoming races, keeping closely in touch with the spiritual condition of the unenlightened masses. Either they themselves descend into the world or they send forth lesser teachers to keep alive the seed of spiritual wisdom. Kapila, Hermes, Enoch, Orpheus, Krishna were a few of their emissaries. They voluntarily forego their own higher evolution, at least temporarily, "to form the nursery for future human adepts," during the rest of our cycle.

Stanza VII goes into the numerology of the primal and later hierarchies, and gives the inner cosmological significance of the numbers. Two, of course, symbolizes the polarization of original essence into the duality of Spirit- Matter. Three refers to the triune constitution of the Divine Men, or Planetary Beings, who manifest the union of the three highest principles, Atma-Buddhi- Manas,14 in one organism. Man on his plane reflects this trinitarian union. The quaternaries represent the cardinal points which square the circle of infinity and typify manifestation. Four sometimes also stands for the basic states of elementary essence, or the four perceptible planes of material existence, earth, water, air, and ether. Five is the symbol of man in his present stage of evolutionary development, as he stands in the fifth lap of his progression round the spiral, and has consequently developed five of his ultimate seven capacities. This accounts for his having five senses, five fingers and toes. The pentacle or five-pointed star is often his symbol. The six-pointed star refers to the six forces or powers of nature, all synthesized by the seventh or central point in the star. Seven is, of course, the number of life in its final form of organization on the material plane. This is because the Logoi created man in their own septenary image. Man is really, in his totality, a sevenfold being, or a being made up of the union of seven distinct constituent parts. His threefold

nature is a truth for his present status only. He is sevenfold potentially, threefold actually. This means that of his seven principles only the lower three have been brought from latency to activity, as he is engaged in awakening to full function his fourth or Buddhic principle. At the far-off summit of his life in the seventh Round he will have all his seven principles in full flower, and will be the divine man he was before-only now conscious of his divinity. At the end of each Round,

"when the seventh globe is reached the nature of everything that is evolving returns to the condition it was in at its starting point--plus, every time, a new and superior degree in the states of consciousness."15

The theory of an inner permanent unit of life, repeatedly touching the outer material worlds in order to gain experience, is symbolized in Theosophy by the Sutratma ("thread-soul"), or string of pearls. The permanent life principle is the thread running through all, and the successive generations in matter are the beads strung along it.

To understand these postulations, we must envisage man as dwelling only partially in the physical embodiment, and having segments of his constitution in the invisible worlds. In the latter lies the ground-plan of his earth life, shaped by his previous life histories. The present physical life will contribute its quota of influence to modify that ground-plan when it becomes in turn the determinant of his succeeding incarnation.

The Sabbath, according to Madame Blavatsky, has an occult significance undreamed of by our theologians. It means the rest of Nirvana, and refers to the seventh or final Round of each emanation through the planes of nature. But the Sabbath should be as long as the days of activity.

A passage in a footnote says that the introductory chapters of Genesis were never meant to represent even a remote allegory of the creation of our earth.
They

"embrace a metaphysical conception of some indefinite period in the eternity, when successive attempts were being made by the law of evolution at the formation of universes. The idea is plainly stated in the Zohar."16

Had its purpose been to give the true genesis, the narrative would have followed the outline laid down in The Secret Doctrine. The creation in which Adam Kadmon ("Primal Man") has a part, did not take place on our earth, but in the depths of primordial matter.

The theory is adduced that each Round of the emanational wave of life engenders one of the four elements, of which the Greeks spoke so much. The First Round developed one element, "one-dimensional space," fiery energy. The Second Round brought forth the second element, air. Matter in the Second Round was two- dimensional. The Third Round brought water, and the Fourth produced earth in its hard encrusted state. The Fifth will beget ether, the gross body of the immaterial Akasha.17 The senses of man in that distant day will be refined to the point at which responsiveness to ethereal vibrations will be general. Our range of cognition will be thus vastly enhanced, for whole realms of nature's life now closed to us because of our low pitch of faculty, will then be opened up. Phenomena manifesting the permeability of matter will be to our higher senses then a daily commonplace. We will have X-ray vision, so that we shall be able "to see into the heart of things."

If man's nature is sevenfold, so is his evolution. The seven principles in him are enumerated as "the Spiritual or Divine; the psychic or semi-divine; the intellectual; the passional; the instinctual or cognitional; the semi-corporeal; and the purely material or physical. All these evolve and progress cyclically, passing from one into another . . . one in their ultimate essence, seven in their aspects."

An important point is made by the expounder of Occultism as to the way in which we should think of all spirits in the supersensible and the sub-sensible worlds. Those superior to us have all been men, whether in this or former evolutions on other globes or in other Manvantaras; and those below us, the elementaries, nature spirits, will be men in the future. If a spirit has intelligence he must have got it in the human stage, where alone that principle is developed. Spirits are not to be regarded as exotic products of nature, beings of a

17 "The fourth dimension of space" enters the discussion at this point. The phrase should be, says the writer, "the fourth dimension of matter in space," since obviously space has no dimensions. The dimensions, or characteristics of matter are those determinations which the five senses of man give to it. Matter has extension, color, motion (molecular), taste, and smell; and it is the development of the next sense in man-normal clairvoyance-that will give matter its sixth characteristic, which she calls permeability. Extension-which covers all concepts of dimension in our world-is limited to three directions. Only when man's perceptive faculties unfold will there be a real fourth dimension, a foreign universe, creatures of a type unrelated to ourselves. They are either our lower or our higher brothers.

"The whole order of nature evinces a progressive march toward a higher life. There is design in the action of the seemingly blindest forces. The whole process of evolution with its endless adaptations, is a proof of this."18

All nature is animated and controlled by lofty Intelligences, who could not be supposed to act with less of conscious design than ourselves. Design is exhibited everywhere in the universe, in proportion to the degree of intelligence evolved. There is no blind chance in the cosmos, but only varying grades of intelligence. The laws of nature are inviolable, but individual beings of every grade of intelligence move and act amid those laws, learning gradually to bring their actions into harmony with them. The deus implicitus within each of us-in every atom-must become the deus explicitus, and the difficulties and risks of the process are commensurate with its glorious rewards.

Some of these Intelligences are veritable genii who preside over our lives. They are our good or evil demons. Hermes says

"they imprint their likeness on our souls, they are present in our nerves, our marrow, our veins and our very brain substance. At the moment when each of us receives life and being he is taken in charge by the genii (Elementals) who preside over births. . . . The genii have then the control of mundane things and our bodies serve them as instruments."19

Part II of Book One begins with an analysis of the evolution of Symbolism. No traditional folk lore, according to Madame Blavatsky, has ever been pure fiction; it represented a natural form of primitive language. Ideography was a stage of growth in the art of human communication. Symbolism was no mere intellectual device of idealistic algebra, but a natural idiom of thought. Mythology was a primitive pictographic mode of conveying truths. An ideograph could be understood "in any language."

A later development of this art brought the mystery language, or particular set of symbols to represent the esoteric truths. The cross, the lamb, the bull, the hawk, the serpent, the dragon, the sword, the circle, the square, the triangle, and many other signs were adopted for special significances. There are seven keys, however, to the mystery tongue, and some of them, as well as the knowledge of how to turn them, have been lost. Only in Tibet, it is maintained, is the code still intact. No religion was ever more than a chapter or two of the entire volume of archaic mysteries. No system except Eastern Occultism was ever in possession of the full secret, with its seven keys.

There is a chapter on the Mundane Egg, which in all theologies is taken to represent the prototype of life hidden in the lotus symbol. Here we find a special sacredness attributed to the letter M, as symbolizing water, i.e., waves, or the great deep, the sea of prime substance. And such sacred names as Maitreya, Makara, Messiah, Metis, Mithras, Monad, Maya, Mother, Minerva, Mary, Miriam and others are said to carry the hidden significance of the letter. The Moon and its place in symbolism is the subject of a chapter. All the lunar goddesses had a dual aspect, the one divine, the other infernal. All were the virgin mothers of an immaculately born Son,--the sun. Here, as nearly everywhere else, Christian dogmas and terms are traced to an origin in pagan ideas. The Satan myth is again taken up in a separate chapter, where it is said that the only diabolical thing about it are its perversions under Christian handling.

The Sevens are given more thorough elucidation in another chapter. There were seven creations, or rather creation had seven stages. The first was that of the Divine Mind, Universal Soul, Infinite Intellect; the second was the first differentiation of indiscrete Substance; the third was the stage of organic evolution. These three steps were sub-mineral, and had yet brought nothing visible to being. The fourth brought the minerals; the fifth brought animals, in germ form; the sixth produced sub-human divinities, and the seventh crowned the work with man. Man is thus the end and apex of the evolutionary effort. Man completes all forms in himself. But esoterically there is a primary creation and a secondary creation, and each is sevenfold. The first created Spirit, the second Matter.

Madame Blavatsky traces the working of the septenates in nature through many forms not commonly thought of. Many normal and abnormal processes have one or more weeks (seven days) as their period, such as the gestation of animals, the duration of fevers, etc. "The eggs of the pigeon are hatched in two weeks; those of the fowl in three; those of the duck in four; those of the goose in five; and those of the ostrich in seven." We are familiar with the incidence of seven in many aspects of physics, in color, in sound, the spectrum; in chemistry, in the law of atomic weights; in physiology; in nature. Madame Blavatsky cites a long list of the occurrence of the mystic number in the ceremonials, cosmologies, architecture, and theologies of all nations.

Scientific authorities are adduced by the author to corroborate her contention that the material universe is ordered on a system which has seven as its constitutional groundplan.

"The birth, growth, maturity, vital functions . . . change, diseases, decay, and death, of insects, reptiles, fishes, birds, mammals and even of man, are more or less controlled by a law of completion in weeks," or seven day periods.20

From the seven colors of the rainbow to the seven-year climacterics in man's life and his allotted seven decades on earth, all the living universe seems to

run in sevens and reflects the sevenfold nature of the precosmic patterns of things.

Volume II concerns the planetary history of our earth, the inception of human life on it, and the evolution of the latter through the previous races up to now. Humanity is assigned an age on the globe of infinitely greater length than the science of her day was willing to concede, which even outstretches the ampler figures set down by contemporary science.

We must start with the earth's place in the solar cosmos. As will be recalled, our planet is the one physically perceptible (to ordinary human vision) globe of a chain of seven (the six others being of rarefied impalpable materials), this chain being itself but one of seven, each of which has a physical representative revolving about our sun. These physical globes are subject to the cyclic law which brings to them successive waves of vivification and sterility, and this law operates as well with all the productions of life on the globe as with the globe itself.

The story of man then becomes that of a succession of great world races preceding the present one, with the various continents inhabited by each, and the form, the condition and the progress of mankind in each manifestation.
Evolution is postulated as the working modus, but it is evolution in cycles, not in a straight line.

The very beginning of life on our planet occurred with the first impact upon it of the initial life wave in the First Round. But this first wave brought life only in the form and to the degree of mineral organizations. When that life impetus passed on to the next globe in the septenary chain to integrate mineral structure there, the second wave struck the earth and carried evolution forward from the mineral to the vegetable stage. The third crest carried life on into the animal kingdom; and the Fourth Round then became the epoch of the entry of man on the scene. The advent of man on the physical or fourth globe of every planetary chain is coincident with the Fourth Round, because the middle of that round is the central point-three and one-half-in a seven series, and man's life represents the perfect balance between spirit and matter. This point would be reached at the exact half-way mark, where the impulsion of life energy would have spent itself in the outward or downward direction (from spirit to matter), and the energies in play would begin to gather force for the rebound or return of spirit, bearing matter with it to "its home on high." The middle of the Fourth Round, therefore, would find a perfect balance established between the spiritual and the physical; and that point would be located in the middle of the fourth sub-race of the fourth root-race of human life on the earth. As we are now in the fifth sub-race (the Anglo-Saxon) of the fifth root-race (the Aryan), we are by some millions of years past the turning point of our cosmical destiny.

On the reascending arc spirit slowly reasserts itself at the expense of the physical. At the close of the seventh Round at the end of the Manvantara, the Monad will find itself again free from matter, as it was in the beginning, but with the rich treasure of experience stowed safely away in indestructible consciousness, to become in turn the germ of growth in the next Manvantara. On the descending arc the pressure is centrifugal for spirit, centripetal for matter; the ascending path will see these conditions reversed. Downward, the spirit was being nailed on the cross of matter and buried; upward, it is the gradual resurrection of spirit and the transfiguration of matter. Our fifth race is struggling to liberate itself from the inhibitions of matter; the sixth will take us far from flesh and material inertia. The cycle of spirituality will begin, when all humans are Adepts.21 Henceforward spirit will emerge victorious

as it has the whole weight of cosmic "gravity" on its side. This is the cosmic meaning of Easter.

The account in Genesis of the appearance of man is not far awry, but must be read esoterically, and in several different senses. It is in no sense the record of the Primary Creation, which brought the heavenly hierarchies into purely noumenal existence; it is that of the Secondary Creation, in which the Divine Builders bring cosmical systems into material form. The accounts given in the Puranas and the older literature are of pre-cosmic creation; the one given in Genesis is only of the cosmic or phenomenal creation. The former deal with a spiritual genesis, the latter only with a material genesis.

Man was the first of mammalian creatures to arrive in the Fourth Round. He came in the first race of the Round, several hundred million years ago. But he was not then the kind of being he is now. He was not then compounded of three elements, body, mind, and spirit. His body was being organized by the slow accretion of material around a purely ethereal or astral matrix or shell, provided for the purpose by the Lunar Pitris, in successive sojourns in the mineral, vegetable, and animal realms, during the three preceding Rounds. These Lunar progenitors started his mundane existence by furnishing first the nucleating shell and the earthly house made ready for occupancy finally by the living Monad, the indestructible spark of the Eternal Fire. The latter is the true being, Man himself. But at this early time he was, comparatively speaking, in the condition of formless spiritual essence. He had not yet come to live in a physical body, but was hovering over the scene, awaiting the preparation of that body by the forces guiding material evolution. He was temporarily clothed in ethereal forms, which became more densely material as he descended toward the plane of embodiment. He, a Divine Spirit, descended to meet the material form, which rose to become his fit vehicle. The two can not be conjoined, however,-- the gap between crass materiality and sheer spirit being too great-without the intermediating offices of a principle that can stand between them and eventually unify them. This principle is Manas or Mind. As Fohat in the cosmos links spirit with matter, so Manas in the microcosmic man brings a Divine Monad into relation with a physical form. The complete conjunction of all three of these principles in one organism was not effected by nature until the middle of the Third Root- Race. Then only can the life of man properly be said to have begun. That date was eighteen million years ago. Men then first became "gods," responsible for good and evil, divine beings struggling with the conditions of terrestrial life, undergoing further tutelage in the school of experience under the teachers, Nature and Evolution. They were the Kumaras, "princes," "virgin youths"-beings dwelling on the planes of spiritual passivity, who yet yearned for the taste of concrete life, and whose further evolution made necessary their descent into material condition on earth. They were the rebels (against inane quiescence), spirits longing for activity, the angels who "fell" down to earth (not to hell), but only to rise with man to a state higher than their former angelhood. They stepped down into their earthly encasement in the Fourth Round. Their prospective physical bodies were not ready till then.

Humanity had run the course of two races before having developed a physical body comparable to the ones we are familiar with. What and where were these two races? The first is given no specific name, but it inhabited the "Imperishable Sacred Land," about which there is little information. It was a continent that lay in a quarter of the globe where the climate was suited to the forms of life then prevalent. At the end of its long history it was sunk by great cataclysms beneath the ocean. Men in this race were boneless, their bodies plastic; in fact "organisms without organs."

In due time the second great continent appeared, to be the home of the Second Race, the Hyperboreans. This, we are told, lay around the present region of the North Pole. But the climate then was equable and even tropical, owing to the position of the earth's axis, which was then at a quite decided angle of divergence from the present inclination. The author claims that the axis had twice shifted radically; that Greenland once had a torrid climate and luxuriant vegetation. Spitzbergen and Nova Zembla are mentioned as remnants of the Hyperborean Land.

The Third Race was the Lemurian, and it occupied a vast continent extending south from the Gobi Desert and filling the area of the Indian Ocean, west to Madagascar and east to New Zealand. Madame Blavatsky gives its boundaries with considerable explicitness. Australia is one of its remnants and the much- discussed Easter Island another. Some of the Australian aborigines, some races in China, and some islanders, are lingering descendants of the Lemurians. It was destroyed mainly by fire, and eventually submerged.

As it sank its successor arose in the Atlantic Ocean and became the seat of Fourth Race civilization. This is the fabled Atlantis, to which Plato and the ancient writers have alluded, the existence of which Madame Blavatsky says was a general tradition among the early nations.22 The Azores, Cape Verde, Canary Islands and Teneriffe are the highest peaks of the alleged Atlantean Land. The Fourth Race flourished there some 850,000 years ago, though the last portion, the island of Poseidonis, north of the Sahara region, carried the surviving remnant of the race to a watery doom only eleven thousand years ago. This final cataclysm became the basis of the world-wide deluge myth. The later Lemurians and the Atlanteans were men like the present humanity, fully compounded of mind, body, and spirit or soul. They had reached in some lines (the mechanical and the psycho-spiritual) a development far higher than our own, wielding psychic forces with which we are not generally familiar and having, beside airships, a more ready method of tapping electric and super-electric forces. In the early centuries of the race's history its members were gigantic in stature, and Madame Blavatsky uses this assertion to explain the historical riddle of the erection of the Druidical temples, the pyramids, and other colossal forms of their architecture.23

It must be understood that the races overlapped in temporal history, the former ones being progenitors of their successors. Nature never makes sudden leaps over unbridged gaps. Her progressions are gradual. Many circum-Mediterranean nations were descendants of the Atlanteans, and a few degenerate Lemurian stocks yet linger on. Nor were their several continents annihilated at one stroke. Portions of the old lands remained long after the new ones had risen from the waters.

This permitted migrations and the continuity of propagation. The races were in no sense special creations, but attained distinct differentiations through the modifying influences of time and environment. The Atlanteans permitted their ego-centric development to outstrip their spiritual progress, fell into dangerous practices of sorcery and magic, and through the operation of karmic law their civilization had to be blotted out, so that a more normal evolution of the Egos involved could be initiated under new conditions in succeeding races.

The Fifth Race, our present Aryan stock, took its rise in northern Asia, spread south and west, and ran the course that is known to history. The Anglo-Saxon is the fifth sub-race of the seven that will complete the life of this Root-Race. The beginnings of the sixth sub-race are taking form in America, we are told.

Mentality is the special characteristic of human development which our fifth sub-race is emphasizing. Each race, so to say, sounds in its life one note in a scale of seven.

This in outline is the story of the five races and their continental homes. Two other great races are yet to appear, before the cosmic life impulses complete their expenditure of energy in this Fourth Round. At the termination of that period the present humanity will have reached the end of its allotted cycle of evolution and the life impulse will withdraw from our globe. The latter will lose its living denizens and its own life and will be left in a condition of deadness or pralaya, to await the return of the wave on its fifth swing round the chain of spheres.

Back in the first race the "propagation of the species" was, strictly speaking, creation, not generation. The phrase, "fall into generation," applicable to the Asuras (demons) or Kumaras who descended into earthly bodies for physical experience, has been wrongly linked with "the fall of the angels." It was the procedure which ensued at that stage of evolution, occurring in the middle of the Third Race period, when spiritual methods of propagation were superseded by sexual ones. Until then the attraction of the sexes was not the incentive, or the condition precedent, to breeding, for there were no sexes. Man was male- female, hermaphroditic. Before that he was asexual, and earlier still he was sexless. Coition was by no means the only method employed by nature to carry life forward. There were several other methods prior to this, and there will be others succeeding it in the long course of growth. To the men of the First Race sex union was impossible since they did not possess physical bodies. Their bodies were astral shells. They were wraiths, umbrae, only ethereal counterparts of dense bodies. In matter of such tenuity, subject largely to the forces of will, procreation amounted to a renewal of old tissue rather than the upbuilding of a new body exterior to the old. Reproduction was thus a re-creation, a constant or periodical rejuvenation. The Stanzas state that the humanity of that First Race never died. Its members simply renewed their life, revivified their organisms, from age to age. The serpent was used as a sacred symbol for many reasons, and one of them is that it periodically casts off an old exterior garment and emerges a new creature from within. This process is somewhat analogous to what took place with the First Race men. Each individual at stated periods, by the exercise of some potency of the creative will described as abstract meditation, extruded from his form a new version of itself. Such bodies could not be affected by climate or temperature. The First Race men were known as the Mind-Born.

Among the Second Race, the Hyperboreans, reproduction was still spiritual, but of a form designated asexual. The early part of the race were the "fathers of the Sweat-Born," the latter part were the Sweat-Born themselves. These terms, taken from Sanskrit literature, will have no meaning for the materialist. Yet she declares that analogues are not wanting in nature. The process comes closest to what is known in biology as "budding". The astral form clothing the spiritual Monad, at the season of reproduction,

"extrudes a miniature of itself from the surrounding aura. This germ grows and feeds on the aura till it becomes fully developed, when it gradually separates from its parent, carrying with it its own sphere of aura; just as we see living cells reproducing their like by growth and subsequent division into two."24

The process of reproduction had seven stages in each race, and this was one of them. Each covered aeons of time.

The later Second and early Third Race men were oviparous and hermaphroditic. Man in this race became androgyne. But there were two stages of androgynous development. In the first stage, in the late Second and early Third Races,

reproduction took place by a modification of the budding process. The first exudations of spores had separated from the parent and then grown to the size of the latter, becoming a reproduction of the old. Later the ejected spores developed to such a form that instead of being but miniature copies of the parents, they became an embryo or egg of the latter. This egg was formed within the organism, later extruded, and after a period it burst its shell, releasing the young offspring. But it was not fully androgyne, for the reason that it required no fertilization by a specialized male aspect or organ of the parent.

It was a process midway between the Self-Born and the Sex-Born.

Later on this process had become so modified by gradual evolution that the embryonic egg produced by one portion of the parent organism remained inert and unproductive until fructified by the positively polarized elements segregated in another portion of the procreator's body. Thus was developed the method of fertilization of the ovum by the male organs, when both were contained within the same organism.

It seems that the Third Race was marked by three distinct divisions, consisting of three orders of men differently procreated. "The first two were produced by an oviparous method presumably unknown to modern Natural History." The infants of the two earlier forms were entirely sexless, "shapeless even for all one knows, but those of the later races were born androgynous."

"It is in the Third Race that the separation of the sexes occurred. From being previously asexual, Humanity became distinctly hermaphroditic or bisexual; and finally the man-bearing eggs began to give birth, . . . first to beings in which one sex predominated over the other, and finally to distinct men and women.

Enos, the son of Seth, represents the first true men-and-women humanity. Adam represents the pure spiritual or androgyne races, who then separating into man and woman, becomes Jah-Heva in one form or race, and Cain and Abel (male and female) in its other form, the double-sexed Jehovah. Seth represents the later Third Race."25

Thus man, at one time more spiritual than physical, started by creating through the inner powers of his mind, and again in the distant future he will be destined to create by spiritual will,--Kriyasakti.26 Creation, we are told, "is but the result of will acting on phenomenal matter." There are yet many mysteries in sex which humanity will bring to light as it unfolds its knowledge of the spiritual control of nature.

Madame Blavatsky weaves into her story the Promethean myth, the war of the Titans against Zeus being interpreted to mean the rebellion of the Asuras and Kumaras against the inertia and passivity of an unfruitful spiritual state, and their consequent drive for physical incarnation. This myth was the Greek version of "the war in heaven" and the succeeding "fall of the angels." The author ridicules the idea that mankind lacked fire in its common form before Prometheus brought it from heaven. The "fire" he brought as a divine gift was "the opening of man's spiritual perceptions." In the Greek allegory Zeus represents the hosts of the primal progenitors, the Pitris, or "Fathers" who created man senseless and without mind, who provided the first element of his nature, the chhaya or astral shell about which as a nucleus his material form was to be aggregated, this combination later to receive the gift of mind and later still that of divine monadic individuality or spirit. These Pitris represented the lower host, who were masters of all the purely blind cosmic and "titanic forces"; Prometheus typified the higher host, or the devas possessing the higher intellectual and spiritual fire. Prometheus, then, added to mindless man his endowment of intellect and spiritual wisdom. But once united with the lower being to render

it the service of raising it to eventual Godhead, the divine Titan fell under the partial dominance of the fleshly nature, and suffered the humiliation of having to procreate by sexual union. This procreation was not unnatural, not immoral, not a sin and shame intrinsically; but it was a comparative degradation for beings who formerly created by free spiritual will. The vulture torture of the legend is only the constant preying of the carnal nature upon the higher man.

"This drama of the struggle of Prometheus with the Olympian tyrant, sensual Zeus, one sees enacted daily within our actual mankind; the lower passions chain the higher aspirations to the rock of matter, to generate in many cases the vulture of sorrow, pain and repentance.

"The divine Titan is moved by altruism, but the mortal man by selfishness and egoism in every instance."27

The gift of Prometheus thus became "the chief cause, if not the sole origin of evil," since it joined in an unstable equilibrium in one organism the free will and spiritual purity of the angel hosts with the heavy surgings of the bestial nature; linked divine aspiration with sensual appetence. Theosophists view this situation as the ground of man's whole moral struggle.

The Promethean gift, the sacrifice of the devas for the apotheosis of humanity, was received 18,000,000 years ago.

It is significant that it came at the epoch of the separation of the sexes. This fact would appear to indicate that the independent privilege of procreation, involving the free action of two organisms, could not well be vouchsafed to man until he was possessed of the power of discriminative wisdom. This middle period of the Third Race thus marks the definite beginning of human life on the globe, as the principle of manas (Sanskrit man, to think) was essential to constitute the complete thinking entity.

These Titans or Kumaras were themselves of seven grades of development, and as they took birth in different racial and national groups, their varying natures at once gave differentiation to the human divisions. Madame Blavatsky uses this situation to explain the origin of racial differences.

It will be noted that Madame Blavatsky's account of human racial progression explains how the first life came onto the earth. Her postulations enable her to declare that life came hither not from the outside, from another planet, but emerged from the inner or ethereal vestures of its physical embodiment. Life does not come from a place, but from a state or condition. Life and its materials are everywhere; but the two need to pass from a static to an active relation to each other, and wherever certain processes of interaction between the two take place, there living things appear. They emerge from behind the veil of invisibility. Their localization on earth or elsewhere is simply a matter of some fundamental principle of differentiation. A great cosmical process analogous to a change of temperature will bring a cloud before our eyes where none was before. Life, says Madame Blavatsky, comes here in ethereal forms, from ethereal realms, and takes on physical semblance after it is here. All life evolved by concretion out of the fire-mist. The pathway of life is not from the Moon, Mars, Venus, or Mercury to the Earth, but from the metaphysical to the physical.

Esoteric ethnology extends the periodic law to world geography in keeping with the moral evolution of the races.

"Our globe is subject to seven periodical entire changes which go pari passu with the races. For the Secret Doctrine teaches that during this Round there must be seven terrestrial pralayas, three occasioned by the change in the inclination of the earth's axis. It is a law which acts at its appropriate time and not at all blindly, as science may think, but in strict accordance and harmony with karmic law. In occultism this inexorable law is referred to as "the Great Adjuster."28

There have already been four such axial disturbances; when the old continents- save the first one-were sucked in the oceans. The face of the globe was completely changed each time; the survival of the fittest races and nations was secured through timely help; and the unfit ones-the failures-were disposed of by being swept off the earth.

"If the observer is gifted with the faintest intuition, he will find how the weal and woe of nations is intimately connected with the beginning and close of this sidereal cycle of 25,868 years."29

In each case the continent destroyed met its fate in consequence of racial degeneration or degradation. This was notably the lot of Atlantis, the Fourth Race home. As Lemuria succumbed to fire and Atlantis to water, the Aryan Race may expect that fiery agencies (doubtless subterranean convulsions of the earth's crust) will prove its undoing.

CHAPTER IX. EVOLUTION, REBIRTH, AND KARMA

The spiral sweep of Madame Blavatsky's grandiose cosmology carries with it an elaborate rationale of human life. Life is a continuum, says Theosophy, and reincarnation is its evolutionary method, Karma its determinant.

Theosophists feel that in fostering the renaissance in modern Western thought of the idea of rebirth they are presenting a conception of evolution which makes Darwinism but an incident in a larger process. It becomes but a corollary of a more general truth. Darwinism, according to Theosophy, conceives of the evolution of a species or class through the successive advances of a line of individuals, who live and die in the effort to carry some new development forward for their successors. For themselves, they reap no reward-save the precarious satisfaction, while living, of having fought the good fight and kept the line intact.

But reincarnation makes evolution significant for the only thing that does evolve-the individual. The race does not evolve, as it is nothing but a mental figment, and has no permanent organic individuality. It does not exist apart from its individual constituents. The latter are the real and, for Theosophy, permanent existences, and hence, if evolution is to have solid relevance, it must appertain to the continuing life of the conscious units or Monads. It is a conclusion that can be deduced from empirical observation that growth at any stage leads to conditions out of which continued growth springs in the future. In short, the effect of growth, and its significance, is-just more growth.1 The entire program of universal activity is just the procedure of endless growth. with halts and rests at relay stations, but with no termini. The meaning of present growth only comes to light in the products of later growth. But it is a matter of infinite importance whether the growth accruing from the individual's exertions in his life span are effects for him or for another. It is not growth-if one struggle only to die. How can race history have significance if the history of the individuals in it has none? Under Madame Blavatsky's thesis the evolutionary reward of effort will go to the rightful party.

Theosophists base their endorsement of the reincarnation theory upon a number of dialectical considerations.

First there is the "argument from justice." Briefly, this holds that the concept of justice as applicable to mundane affairs can not be upheld on the basis of the data furnished by a one-life existence of human beings, and that if justice is to be predicated of the mundane situation, reincarnation is dialectically a necessary postulate to render the concept tenable. Looking at the world we see conditions that force us to admit the presence of inequalities which, on the theory of but one life spent here, must be interpreted as inequities or iniquities. If the single life here is the entirety of mortal existence, then

the cosmos is socially unjust. The concept of justice must go, if, with but one chance for happiness, two persons are placed by forces beyond their control in conditions so flagrantly at variance. The vaunted Love and Justice that are alleged to rule at the heart of Nature become a travesty of even human fair play. No meanest man could wreak such a havoc of injustice in the world; no tyrant could so pitilessly outrage the fitness of things.

But, one may ask the Theosophists, how is it that obvious inequities can become reconstrued as equities, how can cosmic wrongs be turned to cosmic righteousness, merely by admitting additional existences? A wrong today is not made right simply because more days are to follow. Because, the reincarnationist replies, that event which when seen in its isolated setting in the one day's activities, takes on the appearance of injustice, when viewed in its relation to former days' doings is discerned to be a sequential event, proper in its time and nature, and fulfilling the requirements of justice in an enlarged scope of reactions. By mounting the hill of this evolutionary hypothesis, one becomes able to locate the grounds of justice over a wider area, to discover them, perhaps, entirely outside the bounds of the one-only life that was observable from the lowlands. The causes of all that one life unfolds for us can not in most cases be found in the occurrences of that life. The assumption that events in life come raw and uncolored ethically is only tenable if we are willing to regard many occurrences as unrelated and uncaused. Holding the theorem that every event in the world's history is a link in a chain of cause and effect, and that no occurrence stands alone as an absolute cause or final effect, modern moral theory (postulating but one life) arbitrarily breaks this continuum in illogical fashion in its assumption that the fortunes of a single life are not exactly the resultants of antecedents adequate to account for them. The vague and uncertain "laws of heredity" are dragged in to adjust the uneven balance of accounts. But they are found incompetent. Nothing can be found in Shakespeare's parents, or in Mozart's, or in Lincoln's to explain the flowering of power and genius in their progeny, or again the sterility of their descendants. Did this man sin or his parents, that he was born blind? Did Mozart learn to play the organ or his parents, that he could render a sonata on the pipe organ at four?

Biological science stands in perplexity before the problems thus presented, and ethical science stands equally baffled by anomalous situations where right and wrong are apparently unaccountable. Theosophy says the difficulty here is that modern theory is trying to understand Chapter XV of the Book of Life without knowing that fourteen chapters have preceded it. The acts and the predicament of an individual today are inexplicable because he has had a long past, which is not known, but which, were it known, would enable us to say: nature is just after all; he has earned his present lot. What the reincarnation program offers is the identification of causation and justice. Things are justly caused. The modern eye can not see this because it has refused to view things in their true perspective, and instead sees them as partial, isolated, and out of their context; yet justice reaches its fulfilment in the individual

"Today or after many days."2

One life does not give Nature time to arrange her trial, hear the evidence, and render a verdict. The law of compensation must for the most part await the slow grinding of the mills of God, until its adjustments can be nicely achieved. When we give up the exaggerated mediaeval view of man's importance, and cease to limit to a few thousand years the time allotted the divine plan to work out our salvation, we may be open to the persuasion that to crowd the whole procedure of the law of compensation, with its millions of entangled situations, into the span of a human life, is as egregious an absurdity as that of trying to cram into the Biblical six thousand years the entire evolution of mankind, on a

planet which has been fitted for habitation for millions of years. Theosophy affirms that man's life will never be properly interpreted until the whole long course of its unfoldment on the globe is envisaged. The individual is the cumulative product of a long experience, the fruits of which have passed into his subjective life and character, whence, though invisible, they will function as the causes of action. His relation to the past is the most substantial part of his constitution. His present can be explained only in the light of his past, and if our gaze is foreshortened to the scant confines of a single incarnation, the materials for understanding will be wanting.

The protagonist of rebirth attacks the one-life theory also with the argument that it defeats the attempt of the mind to read "meaning" into the terms of the life experience. To be sure, he admits, nobody perhaps can tell just what this consists of, or in what particular aspect of experience it is to be found.3 Ultimate "meaning" of world events is doubtless another of those abstract finalities which we reach only by a process of infinite regress to sheer negation, like ultimate being and ultimate reality, or ultimate substance. But it is permissible to employ the term for the purposes of the argument in its commonly accepted sense of the later outcome, result or eventuation of a set of conditions at any time prevalent, in accordance with the design of some directing intelligence. In this general sense the term is more or less equivalent to effect or consequence, now hidden but eventually revealed. The present or past comes to meaning in the future. The reincarnationist, of course, casts his "meanings" in the stream of an assumed teleological evolution-process.

But if "meaning" is thus assumed to be discoverable within the constant flow of things, the difficulty arises that it proves to be an ever-receding entity like a shadow. When we try to stabilize or grasp it, it has moved forward out of reach. The Theosophist's solution is, of course, that the ultimate and stable meaning of things in a temporal sequence is to be found only in that higher level of consciousness in which past, present, and future are gathered up in one eternal Now. The meaning of events in their three-dimensional aspects of time, space, and causality must be located in a four-dimensional world of consciousness, where the extended life history of the series appears as a unit. As all directions merge into one in the center of a circle, or at the pole of the earth, so all relations merge into a fixity of character in the center of consciousness. Down (or out) here, says the Theosophist, we are in a realm of relativity; we can not look for absolute meaning. All significance is relative, to the past, as cause, to the future, as effect. No event can have meaning if lifted out of the continuum and viewed by itself alone. An occurrence is the product of its precedents and the cause of its consequents. A single life, therefore, has meaning, only when scanned as one of a series. It is admittedly but a fragment of the life of the race; Theosophy adds that it is but a fragment of the life of the individual.

By this line of reasoning the occultist arrives at his grand conclusion: it is meaningless, first from man's viewpoint, for him to live but one physical life on Earth or any planet; it would be equally meaningless, from the viewpoint of a Cosmic Mind (if the laws of logic, the connotations of "meaning," are laws of all mind) to have man live but one such life. For a Deity to send us down here but once would be without logic or sense-as senseless as for a parent to send the child to school for one day only, or one term. Thus Theosophic argument sees the one-life theory reduced to absurdity.

The race's one sure verdict about this life is that it wants completeness and self-sufficiency. To what larger experience is it then related? And if related in some way to a hidden history of infinite reach and significance, where is the

logic of the relation which brings us out of that infinite sea of other being for only one brief dip into the life of matter? Certain metaphysical schools of thought would answer that we go on progressing infinitely in the ethereal worlds. That very affirmation, says the occultist, makes the one life here infinitely illogical: on what imaginable basis can one mundane life be necessarily related to an infinite spiritual existence? Even were it whole, successful, and well-rounded, it would stand as but one moment somehow postulated as determining eternity. But suppose that one dies in infancy, or has every effort to live well thwarted?--the necessary inclusion of one physical life in a totality of indefinite being is empirically shown as invalid. To get a logical picture, in the Theosophist's view, you must trace a long series of short life-lines at intervals along your line of infinite being, and only then does the possibility arise of discerning logical structure, interrelation, and the "meanings" hidden in successive stages of growth.

Occultism points to another irrationality in the mundane situation if one life is predicated. It says briefly that we are only beginning to learn wisdom and the art of life, when we are torn away from the arena where those fruits of our experience can best be exploited. What irrationality possesses Nature that she exerts a tremendous effort to evolve in us gifts, faculties, and knowledge only to throw her mechanism away when she is just about to get us in shape for some good? Nature is thus convicted of being a prodigious spendthrift-unless she has a means of conserving the fruits of our present experience and putting them into practice in a later cycle. Unless we live again to profit by what we have learned, Nature is seen to create values only to destroy them. The only logical alternative is to believe that we reincarnate to carry on with the values and the capacities we have developed in our former turns at the earthly chores. Then Nature does not waste her products, but uses them as tools for further operations.

Again, Theosophy declares that philosophy in the West will find no place in which to deposit value unless it accepts the rebirth idea. Philosophy-the attempt to locate reality and permanent value-has been baffled in its effort because the organism in which it has presumed to find the value of evolution localized persists in dying under its eye. It has nowhere to place value except in the race, the components of which are constantly vanishing. Value can not be located in any structure which will continue to hold it. The race is a fiction, at any rate, and if the individual can not hold his gains, Nature can not be said to have achieved any progress that will be permanent. If the individual can not reap what he has sown, there is chaos in the counsels of evolution. If experience is to head up somewhere so as to become capital, Theosophy says it must do so in the individual. The very reason, affirms the esotericist, that the Greeks, that all races, "lost their nerve," lost their zest for earth life and turned away from it to an hypothecated heaven as a compensation for its unbearable hardships, was that in the face of death, at the relentless approach of what appeared to spell the doom of all one's efforts and one's loves, they were not fortified with the saving knowledge that the good done in this life was "made safe for permanency."

The Theosophist's case for reincarnation may be concluded with a quotation from L. Adams Beck,[4] popular publicist of Orientalism, as follows:

"Therefore the logic of the Orient has seen as necessary the return of man to the area of experience . . . and if the truth of that law be denied, I have never heard from either priest or prophet any explanation of the mysteries or the apparent injustices of life. Seen by its light they are set at once in luminous clarity. That the earliest Christianity was itself imbued with belief

in this fundamental law there can be no doubt, though it was soon overlaid with the easier, less individually responsible and more primitive teaching of interference by angry or placated Deity, and of the general supernatural order of things which commends itself to more primitive man and places his interests in the hands of intercessors or priests. It is much simpler as well as more comfortable to believe that intercession can obliterate a life's transgressions affecting millions of men or events, and a moment's penance fix an eternal destiny. So the Western churches set aside the great stream of philosophy and shut their eyes to its implications."

Here, alleges the Theosophist, was the real loss of nerve on the part of the human race. And it was the Christian theology that caused it. The Christian doctrine of the forgiveness of sins is regarded by the Orientals as a cheap and tawdry device of a cowardly spirit. The readoption of the rebirth hypothesis, avers the Theosophist, would yield for humanity the immense boon of a restored faith in the universal law of causality. Because our concept of inviolable law in every realm of life has been shattered, or left to stand unsupported by cosmic fact, we have reaped the natural harvest of a lawless age. The idea of salvation has taught us that law can be shirked, evaded, bought off.

The second great argument for reincarnation is "the argument from cyclic law." This is a deduction from a known process of nature, and not the postulate of a procedure in nature. Nature's activity is said to be but the play of the one Energy, manifesting to our eyes in countless modifications of the same general laws. There are not many laws in nature, but one law, taking on a variety of modes in adaptation to varying conditions and instruments. In a certain deep sense, then, all natural processes are analogous, the occultist tells us. Life knows but the one Law and all its manifestations typify it. On this generalization the Theosophists have justified their employment of the law of analogy, which figures so extensively in the cosmology and methodology of the cult. The principle is stated in Theosophic terminology in the phrase, "As above so below." As in the macrocosm so in the microcosm. As in heaven (ideally), so on earth (physically). As in the universe at large, so in man, its image.

Conceiving this principle as substantiated by empirical observation of the universe itself, the Theosophist proceeds to look at nature, and there observes in her mechanics a certain modus. She works by methods which suggest the terms periodic, cyclic, rhythmic. In the fields of natural science such processes are to be noted with considerable frequency. Chemistry, physics, music, biology, astronomy, and physiology yield instances. It was the thought of many an ancient philosophy that life runs in ever-revolving cycles. It has been affirmed that rhythmic pulsation is nature's invariable law. All life processes exhibit some form or other of the wave-motion principle. Inorganic nature shows it no less than organic. The atom itself displays an orbital swing; the stars gyrate in cycles. All force flows out in the form of a rhythmic or periodic beat in the pulse of energy. Vibration appears to be the very essence of such things as light, color, sound, music, electricity, magnetism, heat, pressure, radio wave, X, N, alpha, beta, gamma, and the cosmic rays. Next the process of plant life, with startling clearness, reveal the same orderly periodicity of function. The pulse, the breathing, alternation of work and rest, of expenditure and repair, of intermittent fevers, are some of the more pronounced and observable evidences of this law, in the realm of the bodily mechanism. Life appears to be vibrational.

The Theosophist, too, points to each day as a miniature cycle, representative of the larger cycle of a life. It exemplifies the endless succession of active life and (comparative or partial) death for the human personality, in which respect the latter is seen as reflecting the nature of the Absolute Being, Brahm. Each

day, furthermore, is to a degree an actual reincarnation; for the soul returns not to the same body, but to one vastly changed in cell structure and component elements throughout. The same soul takes up its life in a renewed body each day! Why, then, argues Theosophy, should the idea of reincarnation seem so bizarre and objectionable to the mind, when it is the recognized daily law of our being?

Outside the life of man, in the life of nature, the same procedure is revealed on an even larger scale. The life, the soul, of the vegetable kingdom (and of even large portions of the animal kingdom) reincarnates each springtime. The life energies of the plant world come to being in new forms. When these end their cycle, life withdraws into immaterial status for the winter. But it sleeps only to wake again. There is no commoner fact than reincarnation, the Theosophist reminds us; it is all about us and within us. And so we are asked: Does nature omit human life in its universal law of rhythmic progression? If so, it is the only place in the entire life of the cosmos, where periodical repetition of process is not found.

If it be objected that this is mere reasoning from analogy, the occultist rejoins that it is more: it is the application of a law seen to be applicable everywhere else in the universe to a particular portion of the universe. It is again, as in the argument from justice, the postulation of law for an area of experience to which we-in the West-do not believe or know that the law applies. The Oriental covers all life with his blanket of law; we segregate a portion of life from the rest and make it lawless. He says that history is rhythmic, racial life is rhythmic, planetary life is rhythmic, solar life is rhythmic and that even the life of God, Brahm, the Absolute, is rhythmic. Is the life of man then the only thing not rhythmic? A single life from this point of view seems to be a weird anomaly.

If one asks the Theosophist,--How does the individual survive and carry forward his values?--he advances an elaborate scheme based on knowledge allegedly obtained from the Supermen.

The peregrinations of the individual unit of consciousness through the worlds is but a minor detail in a vastly larger mechanism. Theosophy elaborates Platonic psychology by teaching that we have at least three principles lower than the spiritual one which survives. At any rate the outer part of us is but a temporary construction; the inner or subjective part of us is in truth the real "we." The body and several etheric or semi-material "souls" are but the temples, for a period, of the immortal spirit. If we may use St. Paul's language again, when the "natural body" disintegrates, we still have a "spiritual body" in which our unit of spirit functions and retains its identity. The Theosophist calls this underlying vehicle his "causal body," because in it are gathered up the effects of the causes he has generated in his various earth lives. That more ethereal vesture is the principle or part of the principle, that links the individual Ego to the permanent home of the human entity.

Man in his real inner nature is a unit portion of (originally) undifferentiated cosmic Being. He is a fragment of God, but plunged now in conditions described as material, for the purpose, as often stated, of lifting the blank spiritual consciousness of the Monad to acute spiritual self-consciousness. He must have traversed the whole vast gamut of the systems to make his experience complete. For the purposes of this varied experience he must clothe himself in garments of the matter composing the plane of life on which he finds himself; and as matter subsists in varying grades of density, as solid, liquid, gaseous, etheric, he must be provided with a garment of each type of material. This makes him a multiple being. Each garment of matter becomes his instrument of contact with

the life of that plane. He thus expresses himself in a different capacity on each plane. In the world in which he now is he has his permanent body, the causal, and three temporary vestures through which he reacts to the vibrations of sensation (through his physical body), emotion (through his astral or kamic body), and thought (through his mental body). The Ego, the lord of the body, can project his attention, or his focus of force, into any one of the three. He is the animating principle of all. He himself dwells aloft and surveys the results of his contact with the three worlds below. These contacts constitute his experience. No touch of experience is ever lost or forgotten. It is the postulate of Theosophy that on the substrate ether of nature there is an indelible record of every impression. Each one has inscribed his own history ineradicably on the Astral Light or Akasha. The causal body, like the brain in the nervous system, receives the inner and ultimate impress of each stimulus from the outer world and records it there in perpetuity. So equipped, both for time and for eternity, man makes his début upon the earth level again and again, and takes back into himself each time a harvest of experience. But what becomes of him after physical death? He lives on in his causal body on its own plane- Devachan, the "heaven world"-after having dropped first his physical body, then his astral and finally his lower mental. It is the soul's time for rest, for assimilation, for renewal. The soul is not omniscient in its own right, except potentially. Its experiences in the lower worlds are calculated to unfold its latent powers. Normally the spirit of man, on these sublimated levels of the immaterial world, does not have full cognizance of its every act while in the lower realms. Our sojourn on earth is in a manner an exile from our true home.

The difference in vibration rate between the two levels of life makes it impossible either for the fragment of the soul in flesh to remember its former high condition, except in flashes, or for the higher Ego in the supernal regions to know what its lower counterpart is doing. However there are moments when a line of communication is established. During earth life the lower fragment is occasionally elevated to a momentary rapport with its higher Self, and in that instant receives a whole volume of helpful instruction, advice, or inspiration. These are the experiences that change the whole view and alter a life. On the other hand the higher principle at least twice during the sojourn of its lower self in the causal body is put in touch with its earthly life. Just after the conclusion of each earth period, and again just before the commencement of the next, the soul is granted a view of its total history, retrospective in the first case and prospective in the second. The first of these experiences may occur while the soul is still in the body just before death, or, most commonly, in the finer sheaths just after it.5 It is an elevation of normal consciousness to a high pitch and covers a complete survey of the whole past life, with emphasis on the inner moral value of its acts.6 The Ego, in the light of this panoramic retrospect, is put in position to reflect over its past, note its progress, evaluate its record in relation to total evolutionary requirements, and is thus enabled to fix permanently the gain made, the faculty sharpened, the insight deepened, the poise established, and the capacity developed.

In similar fashion, just preceding its outgoing upon another mundane adventure the Ego, aided by higher and more resourceful beings known as the Lords of Karma, is shown in a summary manner the situation in which he stands in relation to cosmic evolution, the stage he has reached, the next succeeding problems to be met, the ground to be covered, and the possibilities of a variety of careers open to him in his next dip into concrete experience. In view of the most important considerations involved in this manifold situation, the Ego himself makes the choice of his next environment and personality! It is the man himself who prearranges the main outlines of his coming life on earth, and the great Lords of Karma aid him to carry his chosen plan into execution. We ourselves preside over our next-life destiny. But we make that choice, not at random, but

in strictly logical relation to the total retrospective view. Being shown in a moment of vivid lucidity what we have next to learn, we make our selection of ways and means to meet the immediate requirements of the situation. Our choice is not entirely free, for we must choose with reference to past obligations and karmic encumbrances, which must be liquidated. The soul with vision opened in the world of causes, sees oftentimes that salvation, progress, lies in no other course. The lower entity would not so choose, to be sure, but the higher Ego sees better what is good for its lower self to undergo. An outwardly untoward condition may provide the requisite setting for the working out of some particular moral advance. So he chooses his own parents, the race, nation or locale of his next life, the type of physical personality he will animate, the specific phases of character he will seek to build up. It is likely that he will aim to concentrate his experience upon the development of some one virtue which he has sadly lacked hitherto, and will choose a situation with a view to its influence in that direction. He must acquire all the virtues one after another.

His choice once made, the veil of Lethe is again drawn over his vision, the two elements of his being are again drawn apart into their separate spheres, and the lower man descends into the world of matter for another trial at life. But he is now oblivious of the fact that it was his own wish to be thrown into the habitat where he finds himself. He may either wonder at the fortunate fate that has befallen him, or rebel against a seeming injustice. He seeks happiness in diverse ways, but is seldom satisfied with what he gets. What he is sure to get, however, in whatever direction he may seek, is experience. And this is the one thing that evolution is concerned about. Growth, not happiness (except incidentally), is the goal of his life. Under the illusion that happiness may be found in this condition or in that, he will plunge into all sorts of experiences, which will prove educative.

There is much detail in connection with the methods used by nature to effect the transition of the soul into and out of the successive bodies. At death the Ego drops first the physical vehicle, which goes back to its mineral components. For a brief time thereafter it has for its outermost and densest sheath the etheric double, pictures of which have been caught in photography, and the material of which is the ectoplasm of the Spiritualists. All the finer bodies, be it understood, interpenetrate the physical and each other in turn, as solid, liquid, gas, and ether might be put into the same earthly vessel. The dropping of the outermost leaves the others intact and capable of freer activity. The occasional appearance of the etheric double, which while it lasts, has an affinity for the physical body, gives us the basis for ghost stories. It is not usually discernible by normal vision, but can be seen by sensitives. After a few weeks at most this body likewise disintegrates, and the astral body is then the peripheral envelope. It keeps the Ego within the realm of emotional vibrations, and in this world the experiences which the Ego shared of this sort must be digested. The consciousness of the Ego must tarry on this plane until the strength of his desire and passional nature wears itself out, and he is purged of gross feeling. After months or a few years the astral in turn disintegrates. This leaves but one of the "onion-peels" to be thrown off before the soul is released finally from the interests and tendencies that held it on earth. This is the lower manas, or lower mental body, whose material responds to the energies of thought. As the physical body is absent, the forces going into concrete thought expend themselves, so to say, in thin air, until this body of "mind-stuff" eventually dissolves, like the others. The soul is then housed only in its spirit body, in which it abides until, after a long rest, it feels again the urge for additional physical experience.

The nature of the soul's life in the body of spirit is practically beyond the resources of human description. We can only conceive of it by making the effort to picture the play of immaterial vibrational energies apart from a mechanism. Its manifestations in terms of our cognitions are those of unimaginable bliss, buoyancy, elation, and vividness. It is the heaven world which all mystical religions have striven to depict. The tradition of its glories has served as the basic fact in all religions of post-modern compensation. Theosophy names it Deva-Chan, the home of the Devas. During the soul's residence there it bathes itself in the currents of finer energy, which serve to renew its vitality, somewhat depleted by its last contacts with the coarser vibrations of earth life. (The analogy with the nightly recuperation from the day's fatigues is obvious here.) The Theosophists and the Orientals have fixed the length of this interim roughly at 1,500 years, but analogy with human life would indicate a shorter duration. It is said, however, that the rest periods shorten as evolution proceeds, until finally an advanced Ego requires but a few years between incarnations. The less experienced souls require more rest.

However long or short, the soul's sleep, or life in the ethereal realms, comes to an end and the craving for another day's activities asserts itself. It is given the preliminary vision already spoken of, and then it begins its "descent" from a world of subtle to a world of coarse vibrations. A vibratory energy has the power to organize matter of appropriate constitution. The ideal forces of the Ego, emanating from the higher planes, contact in turn each lower plane, throw the matter of each plane into organization along the lines of magnetic radiation marked out by the subtle energies in play, and thus construct bodies shaped by their own inner nature. In this way the Ego builds up successively a lower mental, an astral, an etheric, and a new physical body. Taking possession of the last is a gradual process, which begins in reality about the age of seven and is not completed, we are told, until the later stages of youth. Before seven the infant body is said to be in control of an elemental entity or animal soul, a being quite distinct from the Ego himself. The Ego hovering over it, must make a gradual adaptation of its new home to its own nature, and the process is sometimes not easy. Sometimes the Ego realizes after a time of observation and trial that the young body is not capable of being properly used for a life period, and re-nounces its attempt to ensoul it. The body then languishes and is carried off by death.

With all its new vehicles gathered around it, the soul begins to function in the earth life once more. Its equipment is now complete for registering every type of contact, physical, emotional, and mental, and this activity constitutes its life. The new bodies are built on the model of the inner character, which as we have seen, has been preserved in germinal form within the depths of the spiritual organization, in a fashion analogous to the vegetable seed. All the bodies are thus the tell-tale indices of the inner nature. Our character comes to expressive form in our garments of flesh, feeling, and thought. The results of former practice, training, discipline, skill come to light as inherent ability, natural brilliancy, precocity, genius. We think these are the gifts of the child's parents. But the parents only furnish a fine body in which a fine soul may fitly incarnate. By the law of affinity a fine soul would not be drawn to a coarse body. Such a combination would also infringe the law of justice.

Naturally the question as to why we do not remember our former lives arises here. Theosophy explains, firstly, that many people have remembered their former lives, and, secondly, that the reason most of us do not is that the Ego, which does remember, can not easily impress its memories upon the new personality. At each rebirth the soul finds itself in a totally new body of flesh, and the old life must express itself through a new nervous mechanism, with a new brain. The

lower personality does not have any memory of its former experiences, because they were strictly not its experiences. Those experiences were registered on another brain which is now mouldered away, and only the digest, the moral quintessence of those activities has been preserved, and even they have accrued to the higher Ego, not to the personality. As it is the purpose of our long evolution to effect the union between the lower and the higher personalities, we shall eventually come to the time when the Ego will be able to bring its accumulated memory of all its past through to the brain of the man on earth.

The occult psychologist asserts that by hypnotic methods one can be made to catch glimpses of his past life or lives through the subconscious mind. Likewise Oriental Yoga claims that without hypnotism, resolute mental control will enable the consciousness to penetrate into this past field. Theosophists allege that their practiced clairvoyants can at will direct their vision upon a person's former lives, and many records of these investigations have been published.

Indissolubly connected with the idea of reincarnation is the doctrine of Karma. If reincarnation is the method by which the individual reaps what he has sown, Karma is the principle back of the method. Reincarnation is the technique of justice in the universe, and hence Karma is the ¢rc" or deterministic principle. It is the law of necessity that determines the play of forces in evolution; it is in plain terms the law of cause and effect, of the equivalence of action and reaction. The word in Sanskrit etymology means "action." Acts bind the actor to consequences. Actions produce movements in the currents of evolutionary forces. The law which guides these forces into their inevitable courses and eventuations, is the law of Karma. It is the law of equilibrium and balance, the law of compensation. Nature abhors a moral vacuum (which the Theosophist alleges exists in want of the rebirth hypothesis) as she does a physical one, and Karma is the pressure which she brings to bear about and upon a moral deficiency to remove it.

A widespread idea has grown up among non-Theosophists that Karma means retributive punishment. This is essentially a misconception, though a certain measure of the law's operation may take a form roughly resembling that which punishment might take. But nature does not say to the culprit, "You have done wrong; now take that!" She says to him, "You have done wrong; now see what it has brought you." She does not hit back, even to redeem; she attaches consequences to acts.

There is much misunderstanding upon this point, even among Theosophists. It is a common expression among them, when some one is mentioned as having met with mishap, that it is the working out of his evil Karma. This may be crudely correct, yet it is more likely to be a misinterpretation of the doctrine. The educative value of experience may at times point to the future, and not always to the past. We live to learn, and we learn in order to move on to more expanded life. We can not be eternally paying off old scores. A strenuous ordeal may be the beginning of a new education, not the graduation from an old one. The Ego must be confronted with new problems and come into its heritage of evolved capacity through the solution of new difficulties. Much misconstrued "bad Karma" is simply our embroilment in new problems for our advanced lessons in the ars maius vivendi. It is thus difficult to dogmatize about the significance of karmic disabilities or predicaments. Strictly, in a sense, both past and future references are indicated in any experience. Karma links us all to the chain of cause and effect through the entire time process.

Not only are the causes set up by the individual persons bound to work out to fruition, but there is also what is called collective Karma. Wherever bodies or

groups of people act together, as in a senate, a tribe, or a mob, their collective action must bear its fruit like any other action. Karma engendered aggregately must, of course, be carried aggregately. A nation or a race may be guilty of wrong on a colossal scale; reincarnation must reassemble these groups in order that the totality of responsible persons may pay the debt. A senate declares war: millions are killed; that senate, acting well or ill, must be brought within the sweep of the reaction later on. So there is community Karma, tribal Karma, national, racial, and other types of collective Karma. An organization such as the Church, the Government, even conventional social mentality, has its Karma, and not only the individual members of these groups, but more especially the single heads of them, must bear in themselves the brunt of nature's subsequent reactions.7

We are now ready to ask what the goal of all this long evolutionary training of the individual or groups may be. What is the purpose and in what will it eventuate? Or will the law of spiral growth carry us round and round eternally? That the question is one of primary importance is indicated by the fact that the answers commonly advanced for it have given determinate shape to most of the Oriental religions. The point at issue has been the central theme of the great religious faiths, and a dominant consideration in their ethical systems.

The answer accepted by Theosophy is-Nirvana. In much Oriental thought mortal life is endured only because it leads to Nirvana. The Buddhist philosophies of escape contemplate the bliss of Nirvana as the eventual house of refuge from these existences in the conditions of time, relativity, and imperfection.

But the Oriental does not seek annihilation. The West has discovered, or is discovering, that the interpretations forced upon the term Nirvana by its early scholars and Orientalists have missed the point quite decidedly. Opinion has wavered for a long time but inclines now to believe that the concept behind the term does not connote total extinction of conscious being. Oldenburg contended that it meant "a state beyond the conception or reason," and that satisfies most Orientals. Theosophy has, with practical unanimity, taken the position that it implies in no sense an annihilation of being, but that it does quite definitely involve the extinction of the personality of man. The personality, Theosophy claims, is only a temporary shadow of the man anyway, and its eventual dispersion and annihilation is highly desirable as liberating the true Self from hampering obstruction in the exercise of his full capacities for life. This lower counterpart or representative of the inner Self is what the Buddhists and Theosophists declare is destined for annihilation, partly at the end of each life, completely at the end of the cycle. But the eradication of his personality permits him a grander, freer life than ever before. Many schools of Hindu thought regard Nirvana as a life of bliss. This is a postulate of Theosophy likewise. Nirvana, then, instead of being the extinction of consciousness, is the elevation of consciousness to a state of ineffable splendor and ecstasy.

Feeling, thought, sensation are lost in the beatific vision

CHAPTER X ESOTERIC WISDOM AND PHYSICAL SCIENCE

It is interesting to scan Theosophic doctrine with an eye to noting its relation to the discoveries of modern science. We might begin by comparing it with the Darwinian conception of evolution. Madame Blavatsky puts the Theosophic view of the evolution of man in four propositions in The Secret Doctrine:

1. Man is a product of animal evolution on our planet only with reference to his physical body. The Deva evolution in other worlds was the source of his independent spirit and his intellect, his will and his divine nature.

2. Man preceded the mammalian animals on earth, instead of being evolved from them.

3. Man is not at all a descendant from any ape-like ancestor in an advancing line of evolution; on the contrary, the monkey is the descendent of (early) man.

4. Man has never been other than man, though not always as now.

Darwinian evolution and materialistic science envisage the development of matter into organic form, and out of that the unfolding of subjective ideation or psychic life-consciousness, reason, intuition-as products of the two elements, matter and motion or energy. Occultism views this process as predicable only of the building of the physical forms. Instead of regarding the body as having evolved the faculties of reason and intelligence, the secret teaching speaks of a spiritual evolution as going on concomitantly, and in attachment with, a physical one. The conscious intelligence in man is not the evolved expression of the psychic life of his organism. There is such a cell psychism in the body, and its totality is the subconscious mind, but it is in no sense the thinking, willing soul of the man. There are many "missing links" between organic instinct and conscious rationality. Evolution in its higher aspects can not be accounted for if we limit the agencies at work to the blind forces of matter and motion acting under the mechanical influences of environment. "Nature unaided fails." The purely mechanical or semi-intelligent energies are able to carry the growing organisms of any kingdom from the lower to the higher forms of life in that kingdom, but without the aid of the superior intelligences of the kingdom just above them they are never able to leap over the gap-the difference in the atomic structure-which separates them from the next realm of higher vibratory existence. Plants bring minerals over the gap to cell organization; animals introduce plant cells to some degree of sensation experience; man tutors the higher animals right up to the door of rudimentary intelligence. In similar relationship the Deva evolution, completed in the Venus chain, is linked with animal man to bridge the gap for him into the kingdom of spiritual intelligence.

In line with this thesis Madame Blavatsky asserts that the principles of wisdom and spiritual aspiration never were evolved out of the material constitution of man's bodily life. They were super-added to his organism from the celestial worlds. They could not have come up to him from earth; they descended upon him from the skies. Each succeeding wave of outpouring life from the Logos carries evolution a step higher, and the law of the interrelation of all life is that each higher grade reaches back to help its lower neighbor ahead, the while it reaches out to grasp the hand of its superiors. This must be taken as accounting for the fact that all the religious Saviors have been depicted as Mediators coming down from a heavenly or celestial realm. Man's divine nature is the beautified angelic product of a former cycle of growth, and his true Self is itself the Deva that had consummated its salvation elsewhere. The fragment of divinity that constitutes our innermost Selfhood had itself been refined and purged in the fiery furnace of earlier experiences. Between man's purely physical development and the evolution of his spiritual nature "there exists an abyss which will not easily be crossed by any man in the full possession of his intellectual faculties. Physical evolution, as modern Science teaches it, is a subject for open controversy; spiritual and moral development on the same lines is the insane dream of a crass materialism."1

To trace the origin of human morals back to the social instincts of the ant and the bee, and to affirm that our divine consciousness, our soul, intellect, and aspirations have worked their way up from the lower capacities of the simple cell-soul of the "gelatinous Bathybius," hopelessly condemns modern thought to imbecility and renders its efforts to understand our growth futile. Instead of blind forces Madame Blavatsky posits not only a germinal design, but Designers.

"They are neither omnipotent nor omniscient in the absolute sense of the term. They are simply Builders, or Masons, working under the impulse given them by the
. . . Master-Mason, the One Life and Law."2

Nature works not blindly, but through her own highly perfected agents, the Logoi, the Creators.

The second proposition-that man preceded the mammalian orders-runs counter to Darwinian hypothesis. The Secret Doctrine affirms that the mammalia were the products of early man. Man had gone first over the evolutionary ground of the stone, the plant, and the animal realms. But these stones, plants, animals were the astral prototypes, the filmy presentments, of those of the Fourth Round, and even those at the beginning of the Fourth Round were the spectral shadows of the present forms. No forms of life had as yet become physical. Around these ethereal shells, then, in the succeeding Round, which brought them closer to the physical scene, were aggregated the bodily forms which brought them into objective existence. The cast-off shells of man's former embodiments became the moulds of lower species. Before astral man descended into physical begetting, he had, it will be remembered, the power of Kriyasakti, by which he could procreate his replica by "the will, by sight, by touch, and by Yoga." So before the separation into sexes, "all this vital energy, scattered far and wide from him, was used by Nature for the production of the first mammalian-animal forms."3

All lower types, struggling toward man as their "divine" goal, are helped by receiving the effluvia from man's own life as animating principles and constructive models.

The third proposition follows: that man is not the descendant of any line of animal evolution, hence certainly not of the apes. The truth is, the monkey is the descendant of man. The case is stated as follows:

"Behold, then, in the modern denizens of the great forests of Sumatra, the degraded and dwarfed examples-'blurred copies,' as Mr. Huxley has it-of ourselves, as we (the majority of mankind) were in the earliest sub-races of the Fourth Root-Race. . . . The ape we know is not the product of natural evolution, but an accident, a cross-breed between an animal being, or form, and man."4

The apes are millions of years later than the speaking human being. They are entities compelled by their Karma to incarnate in the animal forms which resulted from the bestiality of the latest Third and earliest Fourth Race men. The numberless traditions about Satyrs are not fables, but represent an extinct race of animal-men. The animal Eves were their foremothers and the early human Adams their forefathers. All this means, as we are told, that the late Lemurian or Third Race men cohabited with huge female animals. This occurred when these early forebears of ours had not yet been endowed with the Manasic principle, or Mind. Their animal appetencies being fully active, with no check of mind or discernment of good and evil upon their acts, they thus committed the "Sin of the Mindless" in begetting hybrid monsters, half man, half animal. This is the occult explanation of the blending of both animal and human characteristics in the one creature. Later on in the Fourth or Atlantean Race, the men of that epoch, who were now endowed with Mind and should have known better, committed the same crime with the descendants of the Lemuro-animal conjunctions, and thus established the breeds of monkeys of the present era. But these semi-intelligent creatures will reach the human stage in the next cycle.

Madame Blavatsky endeavors to show that in animal evolution we see anything but an unbroken steady drift toward perfection of form. Evidence of one continuous line of unfoldment is totally wanting. There are many diverse lines, and furthermore, some of them apparently are retrograding.

Then the argument based on the study of the human embryo is pressed vigorously. Occultism accepts the evidence that the human foetus recapitulates quickly all the previous stages of racial evolution. Based on that fact there should be found a stage of foetal growth in which ape characteristics predominate. But there is no monkey stage of the foetus in evidence.

The fourth proposition-that man has never been less than man, though to be sure he has been different-is the outcome of the basic statement that he is, in his inner nature, a being who had already perfected his evolution. Theosophy claims that a thousand oddities and disparities manifest in our present life are elucidated by the assumption that we are high beings functioning at a level far beneath our proper dignity-for the sake of lifting up a host of animal souls to their next station. We have never been less than divine; it is our animal lower self that presents the aspects of fallibility and depravity.

But in relation to all these theories as to man's constitution, the question always arises: What is the authority for all this secret knowledge? Theosophy stands firmly on the affirmation that the only basis of authority in the revelation of any religion is long training in actual experience with life.

Knowledge can be engendered only by living experience. There is no road to knowledge other than that of learning. Theosophic knowledge comes from our Elders in the school of life. They alone have been through enough of earthly experience to have acquired a master knowledge of its laws. Hence it is the

position of Theosophy that no religion can claim more empirical authority than the esoteric ancient wisdom.

Madame Blavatsky declared that occultism had no quarrel with so-called exact science "where the conclusions of the latter are grounded on a substratum of unassailable fact." It is only when its exponents attempt to "wrench the formation of Cosmos and its living Forces from Spirit, and attribute all to blind matter, that the Occultists claim the right to dispute their theories." She declares that Science is limited to the investigation of one single aspect of human life, that which falls within the range of sense objectivity and rational inference. There are other aspects of that life and of nature,--the metaphysical, the supersensual, for the cognition of which science has no instrumentalities. Science is devoting its energies to a study of the forces of life as they come to expression in the phenomenal or sense domain. Hence it is constantly viewing nothing but the residuary effects of the activity of such forces. These are but the shadow of reality, says Madame Blavatsky. Science is thus dealing only with appearances, hints, adumbrations, and effects of life, and this is all it ever can deal with so long as it shuts its eyes to the postulates of occultism. Science clings to the plane of effects; occultism rises to the plane of causes. Science studies the expressions of life; esotericism looks at life itself, the real force behind the phenomenon. To bring the elements of real causality within his cognition,

"the scientist must develop faculties which are absolutely dormant-save in a few rare and exceptional cases-in the constitution of the offshoots of our present Fifth Root-Race in Europe and America. He can in no other conceivable manner collect the facts on which to bear his operations. Is this not apparent on the principles of Inductive Logic and Metaphysics alike?"[5]

Science, however, asserts that we can predicate nothing of the nature of the metaphysical realm, unless and until our instruments bring its data within our sensuous purview. Occultists answer: earlier beings evolved on this or other planets have already developed the powers through which these metaphysical realities are brought under observation. Occultism adds that these claims are not based on imagination, but on the experience of those who have taken the trouble by right methods of discipline to prove for themselves the existence and reach of the powers in dispute. They are simply latent capacities of the human soul, as all our other capacities were once latent, and time and training will convince any one of their presence in the organism as an integral part of the endowment of man. The occultist rests his case at last, not on fantasy, but on a fancy empiricism. He ends by flaunting in the face of science its own present- day admissions that the door to further scientific knowledge of the world is barred by the limitations of its instruments and methods, not by the limitations of human experience.

Madame Blavatsky, fifty-odd years ago, prophesied the arrival of the present scientific predicament, and were she alive today she would doubtless register the "I-told-you-so" expression. She would tell the modern world that it is at the end of its survey of the mechanical activities of matter and that the search has left it uninstructed and unenlightened; it has but driven the mystery from the realm of the actual into that of the occult.

The development of Madame Blavatsky's treatise on the relation of the Old Science to the up-start modern pretender proceeds with the presentation of many angles, sides, or facets of the theories above propounded and the introduction of much evidence in support of the position. She begins by showing that science admits knowing nothing in reality of Matter, the Atom, Ether, Force. The atom is

a fanciful construction, and variously constituted to suit the needs of each separate department of science, be it physics or chemistry. It is not known what Light is, whether corpuscular or not. First it was an undulation of matter, waves in the ether; then it was the passage of particles. Now it is discovered or believed to be both waves and particles, or wavicles.[6] "The atom is the most metaphysical object in creation," she says. "It is an entified abstraction."

Matter, in its true inner essence, can not be fathomed by physical science, for the actual components of it lie several degrees (of rarefaction) further back on the inner planes. It is ether, and the soul of that, in its turn, is the elemental primordial substance, the Akasha. "It is matter on quite another plane of perception and being," and only the occult science can apprehend it. Newton is quoted[7] as saying that "there is some subtle spirit by the force and action of which all movements of matter are determined." He adds that it is inconceivable that inanimate brute matter should act upon other matter in the billiard-ball fashion, without the mediation of something else which is not material. Occultism sees the universe run by the Noumenon, "which is a distinct and intelligent individuality on the other side of the manifested mechanical universe." Matter is not the agent; it is rather the condition, the necessary vehicle, or sine qua non, for the exhibition of these subtler forces on the material plane.

We have noted Madame Blavatsky's references in Isis to the idea that gravitation was the wrong concept for the attractive power exerted by all bodies, and that magnetism was the better description. The same idea is emphasized in The Secret Doctrine repeatedly. She says that Kepler came to this "curious hypothesis" nearly three hundred years ago. It was what Empedocles meant by his Love and Hate, symbols of the intelligent forces of nature.

"That such magnetism exists in Nature is as certain as that gravitation does not; not at any rate in the way in which it is taught by science."[8]

Matter, to the occultist, has many more forms of existence than the one that science knows, and these more refined ones are the most important. Theosophy is largely built up on the supposed gradations of matter from the gross to the ultimately fine. It is the existence of the rarer ethereal grades which supply to thought the data essential for the construction of a metaphysical science.
The true or essential nature of the higher potencies can never be inferred from their remote existential manifestations; and this is why science can never hope to come upon more fundamental knowledge while misled by the merely phenomenal phalanx of outward effects. Matter in its outer veil of solid substantiality is illusive, for it is the dead appearance of a living thing.

"It is on the doctrine of the illusive nature of matter and the infinite divisibility of the atom that the whole science of Occultism is built."[9]

This, she says, opens limitless horizons to states of substance of unimaginable tenuity, but all informed by the Divine Breath. Nature is as unlimited in her possibilities of fineness as she is in those of gross size, in the interior direction as in outward spatial extent.

Occult philosophy describes the Sun as a living glowing magnet. The photosphere is the reservoir of solar vital energy, "the vital electricity that feeds the whole system." The real living Sun, its Spirit, is continually "self-generating its vital fluid, and ever receiving as much as it gives out."10 There is thus a regular circulation-analogous to that in the human body-of vital fluid throughout our solar system during its Manvantaric or life period. The sun

contracts rhythmically at every return of it, as does the heart. Only it takes the "solar blood" eleven years to pass through its auricles and ventricles before it washes the lungs and passes thence to the great veins and arteries of the system.

Madame Blavatsky notes modern science's statements about the eleven-year periodicity in the increase and diminution of sunspot activity as corroboration of her circulatory theory. The universe breathes as men do, and as our globe breathes every twenty-four hours, she asserts.

Madame Blavatsky has to reconcile the two seemingly contradictory statements of occultism "that matter is eternal" and that "the atom is periodical and not eternal." The trick is done by resorting to the distinction that matter, while eternal in its undifferentiated basic form, assumes periodically the atomic structure during each stage of manifestation. Sir William Crookes' "meta- elements" are referred to and his statement that atoms of certain elements showed "sensitive character" in effecting certain combinations. Sir William's assertion that the atoms share with all other creatures the attributes of decay and death is also noted. There will be a dissolution of the universe at the end of the Manvantara; but not a destruction, in the terms of physical science. That is, the energy will not be lost.

Sound is said to be--

"a stupendous force, of which the electricity generated by a million of Niagaras could never counteract the smallest potentiality, when directed with occult knowledge."11

In the chapter on the "Elements and Atoms" chemistry is affirmed to be the science that will lead to the discovery of occult truth. Crookes, she says, is near to the lair of the "protyle." Scientists have often sought for an element of sub-zero atomic weight, hydrogen equalling 1. "A substance of negative weight is not inconceivable," says Helmholtz. Such a substance would approach the nature of the occult protyle, or sub-atomic spirit-matter. In other spheres and in interstellar regions there are infinite variations of material composition, of life formations, of semi- and super-intelligent beings.

Yet the life forces of these higher and lower existences are interblended with our own objective world; they are around us, and, what is more, in us; and they vitally affect our life. All forms of life are linked together in one immense chain. Some of these existent worlds may be as formless as Breathe, like the tail of a comet, which would sweep over our globe unknown to us, yet not without influence upon us.

Chemistry, she announces, once the unit protyle is hypothetically accepted, as ether was, will perish, to be reincarnated as the New Alchemy, or Metachemistry. "The discoverer of radiant matter will have vindicated in time the archaic Aryan works on Occultism and even the Vedas and Puranas."12

Madame Blavatsky formulates a law of occult dynamics that a given amount of energy expended on the spiritual or astral plane is productive of far greater results than the same amount expended on the physical objective plane of existence. This law becomes fundamental in the Theosophic system of ethics.

On page 612 of Book I, Madame Blavatsky makes a prophecy which was remarkably fulfilled, that "between this time (1886) and 1897 there will be a large rent made in the veil of nature and materialistic science will receive a death-blow."

All science is familiar with the rapid incidence of new discoveries and revelations that fell within that period, crowned with the enunciation of the electrical nature of matter and the facts of radiant energy.

Madame Blavatsky's position with regard to modern scientific discovery and theory has been provocative of much discussion since her day. The same general situation obtains in her case as with Paracelsus, Boehme, Swedenborg, and other mystical prophets of science, who spoke with a show of authority of the hypotheses which science has in recent years taken up. They have repeatedly anticipated the propositions of our most advanced learning. Madame Blavatsky's achievement in this line is notable; and it is the common assertion of Theosophists that science in the past five decades has done little but verify their Founder's scientific pronouncements. Dr. A. Marques' book, Scientific Corroborations of Theosophy and William Kingsland's The Physics of the Secret Doctrine have set forth the many basic confirmations of H.P.B.'s work by our evolving physical science.13 It must be remembered in this connection that the scientific theories put forth by Madame Blavatsky can not be credited to her as spiritual intuitions or guesses, a certain proportion of which chanced to be well grounded. She did not arrive at these constructions in her own mentality; she gave them out as elaborations of an ancient science, of which she was merely the reinterpreter. Furthermore the various theories are put forward, not as isolated items of knowledge, but as integral parts of a comprehensive system which in its reach and inclusiveness has hardly elsewhere been matched. While science is obviously not proving the correctness of that large portion of her ideas which pass beyond its domain, in those matters touching its special province, into which she so boldly ventured now and again, it has frequently substantiated her "re-discoveries," though not all of them.

It is significant that Madame Blavatsky's occult philosophy aims to restore to scientific method the deductive procedure. It is her insistent claim that materialistic science, with its inductive method-an attempt to work from the rind back into the kernel, from effects back to causes-could never learn anything deep or true of the real universe. The world can only be explained in the light of great archaic principles; and these the modern world foolishly contemns, not knowing they were taught to disciplined students of old. They postulated that all things had their origin in spirit and thence they reasoned outward and downward; until they saw facts as items in a vast deductive plan. If man persists in rejecting such deduction, he will naturally never find the key to the great mystery; for by mulling around amongst the shadows of earthly existence, he merely learns to know the interplay of shadows. To understand the shadows he must start with the light.

CHAPTER XI THEOSOPHY IN ETHICAL PRACTICE

The Secret Doctrine set forth the basic conceptions of Theosophy; there remained for Madame Blavatsky one more task of large proportions-to make an application of the principles she had expounded to the problem of practical living. This was done to a large extent in a work which occupied her during a portion of the three or four years of life left her after the completion of her major effort.

The Key to Theosophy was put out by her in response to much questioning as to how the vast body of knowledge outlined in her works could be related more closely to common understanding. It is done in the form of a dialogue between a questioner and a Theosophist, Madame Blavatsky herself. The work shows as much of the author's dynamic mind as do her other publications, but there is no attempt to make a further display of scholarship. It was an endeavor to bring out the intent and meaning of the doctrines, to ease difficulties, and to clarify and reënforce some earlier presentations. It was intended to serve as a manual, but it is far from elementary in parts. In it are two now notable items; her warning against Spiritualism in the early section, and near the end her seemingly prophetic statement that there would later develop an irresistible trend among her successors, in spite of her clarion warnings, to make a church out of her Society.

Reflection, her own experience, and her observations of the behavior of many Theosophists, who were figuratively staggering about under the intoxicating spell of so strong a stimulant, deeply impressed her with the necessity of placing a far greater emphasis upon the relation of occult philosophy and ethics and spirituality. Her own performances of extraordinary psychic feats, she saw, had helped to create the peril that lay in an overemphasis on the desirability of unfolding the latent powers of the soul. Madame Blavatsky was thus made keenly aware of her responsibility in giving out freely what supposedly had been wisely guarded.

Her solicitude was particularly aroused by the rush of many new devotees into the cultivation of the psychic senses, a feature implicit in the esoteric teachings. The persistent presupposition that psychic abilities were the infallible badge of lofty spirituality, soon showed its presence. Then, too, the subtle temptation to regard one's predisposition to Theosophy and one's connection with it as evidence that one has been singled out by the great Masters as uniquely worthy, or that one is far on in the line of evolution, was certain to come to the surface. Madame Blavatsky could be charitable to ordinary human frailties in these directions, but shallow spiritual pretension bought forth her lash.

We are prepared, then, to understand the vehemence with which she uttered her first official statement on this subject through the editorial pages of her new magazine, Lucifer, May 15, 1888. The article had the suggestive title: "Occultism versus the Occult Arts." It is prefaced with a triad from Milton:

"I have oft heard, but ne'er believed till now, There are who can by potent magic spells Bend to their crooked purpose Nature's laws." She minces no words.

"Will these candidates to wisdom and power feel very indignant if told the plain truth? It is not only useful, but it has now become necessary to disabuse most of them and before it is too late. The truth may be said in a few words: There are not in the West half a dozen among the fervent hundreds who call themselves 'Occultists' who have even an approximately correct idea of the nature of the science they seek to master. With a few exceptions they are all on the highway to Sorcery. Let them restore some order in the chaos that reigns in their minds, before they protest against this statement. Let them first learn the true relation in which the occult sciences stand to occultism, and the difference between the two, and then feel wrathful if they still think themselves right.

Meanwhile let them learn that Occultism differs from magic and other secret sciences as the glorious sun does from the rushlight, . . . as the immortal Spirit of Man . . . differs from the mortal clay . . . the human body."

She then enumerates four kinds of Esoteric Knowledge or Sciences:

1. Yajna-Vidya:1 Occult powers awakened by ceremonies and rites.

2. Mahavidya:2 The Great Knowledge, the magic of the Kabalists and the Tantrika worship, often sorcery of the worst description.

3. Guhya-Vidya:3 Knowledge of the mystic powers residing in sound; mantras and hymns, rhythm and melody; also knowledge of the forces of nature and their correlation.

4. Atma-Vidya:4 Knowledge of the Soul, called true wisdom by the Orientalists, but means much more.

It is the last of these that constitutes the only real Occultism that a genuine Theosophist ought to seek after. "All the rest are based on things pertaining to the realm of material Nature, however invisible that essence may be, and however much it has hitherto eluded the grasp of science."

The article continues:

"Let him aspire to no higher than he feels able to accomplish. Let him not take a burden on himself too heavy for him to carry.

Without ever becoming a Mahatma, a Buddha, or a Great Saint, let him study the philosophy and the science of the Soul, and he can become one of the modest benefactors of humanity, without any superhuman 'powers.' Siddhis (or the Arhat powers) are only for those who are able to 'lead the life,' to comply with the terrible sacrifices required for such a training, and . . . to the very letter.

Let them know at once and remember always that true Occultism, or Theosophy, is the 'Great Renunciation of Self,' unconditionally and absolutely, in thought as in action. It is Altruism, and it throws him who practices it out of calculation of the ranks of the living altogether. 'Not for himself but for the world he lives,' as soon as he has pledged himself to the work. Much is forgiven during the first years of probation. But no sooner is he accepted than his personality must disappear, and he has to become a mere beneficent force in Nature. There are two poles for him after that, two paths, and no midward place of rest. He has either to ascend laboriously step by step, often through numerous incarnations and no Devachanic break, the golden ladder leading to Mahatmaship, or-he will let himself slide down the ladder at the first false step and roll down into Dugaship."

In another Lucifer article near the same time entitled "Practical Occultism," she defines a Theosophist as follows:

"Any person of average intellectual capacities and a leaning towards the metaphysical; of pure unselfish life, who finds more joy in helping his neighbor than in receiving help himself; one who is ever ready to sacrifice his own pleasures for the sake of other people; and who loves Truth, Goodness and Wisdom for their own sake, not for the benefit they may confer-is a Theosophist.

"It is impossible to employ spiritual forces if there is the slightest tinge of selfishness remaining in the operator. For unless the intuition is entirely unalloyed, the spiritual will transform itself into the psychic, act on the astral plane, and dire results may be produced by it. The powers and forces of animal nature can equally be used by the selfish and revengeful, as by the unselfish and the all-forgiving; the powers and forces of spirit lend themselves only to the perfectly pure in heart-and this is Divine Magic."

The article proceeds to set forth a list of conditions requisite for the practice of the soul science. The necessary conditions are eleven, taken from a list of seventy-three which she says are prescribed for Eastern neophytes. They are: suitable magnetic conditions of the spot selected (for meditation); membership in a company of harmonized students; a mind at peace and purified; a sense of unity with all that lives; renunciation of all vanities; obliteration of a sense of separateness or superiority; avoidance of impurely magnetized contacts; the blunting of the mind to terrestrial distractions; abstention from all animal foods, spirits, opium; expression of good will in thought, speech, and act; and oblivion of self. These precepts form much of the basis of Theosophic cult practice.

The result of such decisive utterances from the leader was to give pause to the fast-growing Society membership in its haste to enter upon the Occult Path.
Enthusiasm was chilled. As the nature of the Master Science was revealed and its hardships and scant earthly rewards envisioned, the high qualities demanded and the perils depicted frightened many from the deliberate attempt to enroll as spiritual candidates. Yet there were aspirants both sincere and resolute. The needs of these had to be met, at the same time that the folly of the rash had to be rebuked.

To serve both purposes Madame Blavatsky issued many articles through the pages of Lucifer in London, from 1888 onward. And along with them came a booklet of one hundred and ten small pages which has since taken its place as one of the most beautiful expressions of Oriental spirituality now extant. This was The Voice of the Silence. The Preface states that it is a translation of a portion of the slokas or verses from The Book of the Golden Precepts, one of the works

put into the hands of students in the East.[5] She had learned many of these Precepts by heart, a fact which made translation a relatively easy task for her. The Book of the Golden Precepts formed part of the same series as that from which the "Stanzas of Dzyan" were taken, on which The Secret Doctrine is based. The Voice of the Silence may be said to be the ethical corollary of the cosmic and anthropological teachings of The Secret Doctrine. Its maxims form part of the basic system of the Yogacharya school of Mahayana Buddhism. Of the ninety distinct little treatises which The Book of the Golden Precepts contains, Madame Blavatsky states that she had learned thirty-nine by heart years before. The remainder is omitted.

"To translate the rest," says the Preface, "I should have to resort to notes scattered among a too large number of papers and memoranda collected for the last twenty years and never put in order, to make it by any means an easy task. Nor could they be all translated and given to a world too selfish and too much attached to objects of sense to be in any way prepared to receive such exalted ethics in the right spirit. . . . Therefore it has been thought better to make a judicious selection only from those treatises which will best suit the few real mystics in this country and which are sure to answer their needs."

The opening sentence says:

"These instructions are for those ignorant of the dangers of the lower Iddhi," or psychic faculties.

The second page holds two short sentences which have ever since rung in the ears of occult students:

"The Mind is the great slayer of the Real. Let the disciple slay the Slayer."

We must still the restless outgoing mind before we can hope to see into the depths of the reality within. We must strive with our unclean thoughts and overpower them, or they will dominate us. Our deepest sympathies must be linked with all that lives and breathes, we must lend our ears to every cry of mortal pain, or we can not hope to merge our consciousness into the Universal Soul. It is better to trust the heart than the head, for "even ignorance is better than head-learning with no Soul-wisdom to illuminate and guide it." Asceticism is a Via Dolorosa; it is not by self-torture that the lower self can be lifted to union with the higher. Homiletic morality breathes in the following: "Sow kindly acts and thou shalt reap their fruition." But stinging rebuke to negative righteousness echoes in the next sentence, one that has assumed large proportions in Theosophic ethics: "Inaction in a deed of mercy becomes an action in a deadly sin." The basis of much Theosophic morality, as of equanimity and serenity, is found in this text as well as in its corollary, which assures us that no efforts-not the smallest-whether in right or wrong direction, can vanish from the world of causes. "If sun thou canst not be, then be the humble planet" is our admonition to stay modestly within the sphere of our capabilities, and not strain after things unmeet for us. We should humble ourselves before those greater than ourselves in wisdom, seek earnestly their counsel and strive to tread the high path they have traversed. At the same time we must not withhold the blessing of what knowledge we have acquired from the circle of lesser evolved souls who may come within our influence. We must be humble if we would learn; we will be humbler still when knowledge has begun to dawn. Reward for patient striving is held out to all devotees. The holy germs that took root in the disciple's soul will expand and send out shoots under the influence of steady spiritual zeal; the stalks will wax stronger at each new trial, they may bend like reeds, but will never break; and when the time of harvest comes, they

blossom forth. When the persevering soul has crossed the seventh path "all nature thrills with joyous awe." But does the victorious pilgrim then enter selfishly into the enjoyment of his hard-won guerdon of bliss, forgetful of his fellows who have toiled less successfully than he? Is selfishness justified in nature? The verses ask, "Can there be bliss when all that lives must suffer?
Shalt though be saved and hear the whole world cry?" The answer is the key to all Theosophic ethic: the Nirmanakaya (literally, the "possessor of a transformation-body"), even he, facing his natural right to enter upon a higher state of being in the upper cycle where he will be free from limitation, turns back to aid the "great orphan humanity." He takes his place in that high Brotherhood whose members form a "Guardian Wall" about mankind. He joins the Society of the Masters of Compassion who by spiritual masonry build the wall "raised by their tortures, by their blood cemented, protecting him (man) from further and far greater misery and sorrow." This is the Great Renunciation of Self, the mighty sacrifice, itself typical of the cosmic sacrifice of Deity in its self-limitation under the cross of matter, and again typified by every symbolic sacrificial rite of the religions. But the universal life can not restrain a thrill of gladness as the prodigal's long exile in the worlds of matter is ended, and he returns to the Father's house. For "Hark . . . from the deep unfathomable vortex of that golden light in which the Victor bathes, all Nature's wordless voice in thousand tones ariseth to proclaim: A New Arhan is Born."

Such is The Voice of the Silence. Its verses ripple on in a rhythmic cadence aptly suited to assist the feeling of mystical devotion. Like other of the Oriental books it consists of ethico-spiritual maxims, which hardly so much attempt to give a systematic exposition of moral principles, as to reduce the spiritual essence of these principles to a mantric form capable of exerting a magical potency when used ritually. But it is not difficult to discover in the book the mainspring of much of that distrust of the purely psychic which marks Theosophy so distinctively among the modern cults. To carry a heart "heavy with a whole world's woe" is accounted a far more substantial merit than to bend some of the etheric and electric forces of nature to one's will.

What The Voice of the Silence aims to do is to strike the spiritual keynote of the ancient science of mystic union or Yoga as essentially a spiritual technique and not a system of magical practices. It is not at all a text-book of the great Yoga philosophy and its art, although it may be said that it in no way clashes with the general Oriental teachings on the subject of Yoga. Madame Blavatsky did not find it needful to formulate a distinctive technique of her own for the cultivation of the great science.

The Theosophical science of Yoga will be found delineated in three or four books which, along with The Voice of the Silence, are: the Bhagavad Gita, Light on the Path (a small collection of precepts alleged to have been dictated mystically by a Master to Mabel Collins in London about 1885), and the several commentaries on the Yoga Aphorisms (or Sutras) of Patanjali, written, according to Vyasa, perhaps 10,000 B.C., according to scholars, a few centuries B.C. Portions of the New Testament, when given esoteric interpretation, are accepted as descriptive of Yoga development. Light on the Path is highly mystico-spiritual in tone, a companion work to The Voice of the Silence. It is couched in allegorical and figurative language, depicting forms of nature as symbolical of spiritual truth. The Bhagavad Gita, or Lord's Lay, is a portion of the Mahabharata, and is by now so widely disseminated among Western students as to need no description or comment in this connection. It enjoys perhaps the place of foremost popularity among all the Oriental religious dissertations. But the Yoga Sutras of Patanjali come perhaps nearest to being a definite text-book of Theosophic devotional

discipline. It is therefore important to look carefully at the features of the physical, moral, intellectual, and spiritual regimen prescribed in this ancient text for the cultivation of the highest Theosophic virtue.

It is a handbook for the practice of the Science of Yoga. Yoga, in brief, means union,6 having specific reference to the eventual merging of the individual Soul or Monad into the Universal or World Soul, and in a larger view the absorption of all finite souls into the Absolute. Its rules and injunctions are the natural outgrowth of a philosophy which holds that man is an ensemble of several separate entities or principles, whose harmonious evolution postulates a cultus demanding the unification under one central control of the different individualities which, till that harmonization is effected, live together at odds and cross purposes within the same organism. To mollify that discordance it is requisite first of all that man should rise above the delusion that he is essentially his body, or his feelings, or even his mind. He must first learn through an inner realization that he, in his true Self, is none of these, but that he, the real inner man, uses these as his servants. He must recognize himself as the divine imperishable Ego, the Jivatma,7 and in so doing he will cease to commit the error of identifying himself with those temporary and transient aspects of himself which he so long mistook for his real being. This orientation of himself from his lower manifestations into his true plane of Selfhood will release him from all the pain and distress that attends his illusion that he is the impermanent lower self.

This in brief is the general aim of Eastern occult practices; but its complete rationale involves an understanding of the details of a labyrinthine science of soul unfoldment that in its intricacy staggers the psychological neophyte in the West. It is necessary in some degree to go into this psychological technology for a better comprehension of the theme.

Its adept devotees in the East tell us that Yoga is no mere cult, but an exact and complex science, with precise rules, very definite stages, and a quite scientific methodology.

There are several types or forms of Yoga practice, which must first be differentiated. The most definite forms are: (1), Karma Yoga; (2), Bhakti Yoga; and (3), Raja Yoga. Karma Yoga is the path of active exertion (Karma meaning "action"), by which the man at an early stage of evolution learns to acquire control of his physical organism and his sense apparatus for the purposes of an energetic bodily career in the world. It has been subdivided into two types, called Hatha Yoga and Laya Yoga. The first, or "forceful," gives control over the physical mechanism of the body; the second, or "inactive," governs the emotional or etheric component of man. In this process there are gradually brought into active operation the four force centers, wheels or chakras, which lie below the diaphragm. Karma Yoga is supposed to have been employed by the Lemurian or Third Race people, to enable them to perform their appropriate functions in the line of earthly racial evolution. It is not to be practiced by us.

Bhakti ("Love") Yoga, the second type, awakens the heart and throat centers in the etheric body, which latter is achieved by the exercise of devotion and affectional qualities. Love, affection, loyalty, attachment to personality, are the powerful stimuli that rouse the centers above the diaphragm to active functioning. It is the path of feeling and emotion, using the astral body. Its use was credited to the Atlanteans, or Fourth Race folk, as their most appropriate type of evolutionary expression, and is no longer our task.

Raja ("King") Yoga, type three, is the specific discipline for our Fifth Race, the Aryan. It is designed to awaken the centers in the head (the pineal gland and the pituitary body) crowning the work of the two earlier Yogas in the development of the functions of the etheric body. It is consequently the path of mentality, which is the Fifth principle in man; and hence it becomes the appointed task of the Fifth or Aryan Race to unfold it. As the work of Yoga is to unify the various principles in man into harmonious accord, it will be seen that, as Karma Yoga arouses the four lower centers, and Bhakti Yoga unites them with the two middle centers (the heart and throat), so it is the purpose of Raja Yoga to link the ascending forces with the centers in the head (the brain and the two glands mentioned above), and to use this uppermost station as the controlling and distributing center for all the energies of the unified personality.8 There are many stages in the long process of Yoga development.

First the physical must be brought under control. Then the etheric centers must be quickened and linked with the head centers. Then the mind must be linked with the true soul, and eventually the latter with the common Soul of all things.

According to Mrs. Bailey, Raja Yoga is a system giving the rules and means whereby,

1. Conscious contact can be made with the soul, the second aspect of the Christ within.
2. Knowledge of the Self can be achieved and its control over the Not-Self maintained.
3. The power of the Ego or Soul can be felt in daily life, and the soul powers manifested.
4. The lower psychic nature can be subdued and the higher psychic faculties developed.
5. The brain can be brought en rapport with the soul and the messages from the latter received.
6. The "light in the head" can be increased so that a man becomes a living Flame.
7. The Path can be found, and man himself becomes that Path.

The initial work of Raja Yoga is the recognition of the true nature of the Self as distinct from the illusory character of man's life in the three lower worlds- the difference between the Man himself and his lower vestures. This is achieved by a long course of meditation, with thought turned inward, until one empirically learns that he is not either his body, or his feelings, or his sensations, or even his thoughts; that all these belong to the world of evanescent things, and that he himself is the entity, the point of conscious being, which abides in unaffected permanence at the center of this changing world of experience. This is his first task-to learn to distinguish that which comes into being and goes out from that which abides. And the work involves more than a merely mental grasp of the fact; it requires that one should act, feel, and think, and at the same time learn to stand aside from the act, the feeling, the thought, and remain unaffected by them. For ages during his preceding evolution, before the scales of illusion were torn from his eyes, the man was under the delusion that he was the lower objective self, as reported by his senses. This identification of himself with what is in reality but his outer clothing, is the cause of all the pain that besets his path. For this thinking himself to be the vestures which he wears subjects him to the vicissitudes which they themselves must undergo. He thus prescribes physical and sensuous limits to his destiny. He puts himself at the mercy of the fate which befalls his outward life. Before serenity can be achieved he must learn to detach himself from his vehicles, so that he can sit unaffected in the midst of changing fortunes. Ere long he must realize himself as part of the whole of being, yet as detached from it, free from the dominance of the world of form and the impressions of the senses. He must learn to use them, and no longer let them use him. His dominance over matter is achieved by a mastery of the subtle forces resident in the atom. This is done by developing a conscious control over what are called the Gunas, the three qualities of matter, which are Sattva, Rajas, and Tamas; or rhythm, action or mobility, and inertia. In Indian philosophy, however, these three terms mean, rather, "goodness, passion, and darkness," or "virtue, foulness, and ignorance." Therefore it is necessary to understand the theosophic interpretation of Gunas. Eventually the disciple must be able to command the wind and the waves by instituting the proper balance between the rhythmic and the inert qualities of matter. Thus he learns to know of a surety that he is not those forms but a dynamic entity immeasurably greater than them. The acquirement of this knowledge is a part of the process necessary to the realization of his true character as a living spirit, and to the gradual withdrawing of himself from his entanglement in the world of matter. The five elements, earth, water, fire, air, and ether, and the five senses, as well as the distinctive forms of mental action, are the specific results of the interplay of the three Gunas in the world of material forces. But back of these external manifestations there are the "unspecific" or subjective forms of ethereal force; and eventually the disciple has to touch these unseen elements and control them.

To help detach himself from the influence of visible forms, the seeker must aim to actualize the unseen force which operates behind every form, and thus look through and beyond the form, which is but the effect of some cause, to that cause itself. The crucial operation in every Yoga practice is to work back from effects, which are material and secondary, to causes, which are spiritual and primary; from the material periphery of life in to its spiritual core. This he believes possible by virtue of the theory that "the whole world of forms is the result of the thought activity of some life; the whole universe of matter is the field for the experience of some existence."9

All objective forms are frozen thoughts of some mind, which gives its own coloring to both the objective and the subjective worlds presented to it. Hence, one of the first things the Ego has to do in seeking Yoga is to take the mind in charge and render it a perfect instrument for the Soul's higher vision. The central aim of the great discipline of meditation is summed up in the phrase "to still the modifications of the thinking principle." The mind's proper function, in the Yoga system, is to serve as a sublimated sixth sense, transcending yet supplementing all the others. Through persistent practice it is to be rendered into a finely poised spiritual sense, to become the organ of the Soul's acquisition of the higher knowledge. This is the use for which it is destined in the unfolding economy of nature; but it has hitherto failed to reveal this purpose because it has not been subjected-in the West-to the necessary discipline. In preceding aeons of evolution it subserved nature's intent by growing facile and mobile. It displayed the Rajas Guna, or mobility, to an advanced degree. But when spirit begins the long process of retirement from the thraldom of the form, this quality of the mind becomes more and more a hindrance. Its incessant activity must be poised. It must be brought under the sway of the Sattva Guna,--rhythm.

Hitherto the mind has been the slave of every lower sense. This was its proper service at the Lemurian or Karma Yoga stage. It is so no longer. It must be made

blind and deaf to the insistent cry of the outer world, so that it may become prepared to picture forth, like a clear lens, the realities of an inner world, whose impressions it was never focused to reflect heretofore.

As it turns away from the clamorous din of sense contacts, it finds itself in a realm, first, where only emotions are left to be dwelt upon. The material world shut out, there is nothing but astral or feeling impulses to absorb its attention. Next all passional content must be rejected, leaving only intellectual material to deal with. At last even abstract thought must be stilled, until the mind is utterly emptied of content. It dwells in pure abstraction, in a state void of anything concrete. Or it may take an object, concrete and substantial, and by a supreme effort, successful after long trial, lose sight of its materiality and finally see it as a thing of pure spiritual construction. The actual substance of things disappears and only the noumenal concept of it is seen. The mind approaches nearer and nearer to sheer vacuity. Is Yoga thus to end in a blank of empty abstraction, with all concreteness gone from experience?

For a time it may seem so. But suddenly when the persevering devotee has at last succeeded in holding the mind calm and still as the placid surface of a lake, there ensues an experience of the light that never was on land or sea. With the increasing glow of the light there pours down into consciousness knowledge, mystic vision, and clear illumination, as the vibratory energies of the Augoeides, or Spiritual Soul, flood down into the brain. The mind now serves as the luminous pathway between the inner realm of spiritual light and the physical brain, and over that bridge the individual human soul may advance into a direct knowledge of the interior heart of nature.

"When a man can detach his eyes from all that concerns the physical, emotional and mental, and will raise his eye and direct them away from himself, he will become aware of 'the overshadowing cloud of spiritual knowledge,' or the 'raincloud of knowable things.'"

The human soul empties itself of earthly content, in order that it may be filled with heavenly light and wisdom.

The perfecting of the mind as a sublimated sense instrument thus enables the Seer to do three important things:

1. To see the world of spiritual causation, as the eye sees the physical world.
2. To interpret that causal world in terms of the intellect.
3. To transmit this high knowledge to the physical brain.

The advance to this superior consciousness is made through the gateway of a number of Initiations, or specific stages in the expansion of conscious capacity. The training requisite to unify the soul with its organism constitutes the first stage called the Probationary Path. Stage two brings one to the Third Initiation, when the union of the mind with the Ego on his own plane is completed. The third stage accomplishes the union of the whole lower personality with the Monad, and covers the final steps on the Path of Initiation.

These stages of the Path are further symbolized in the literature of occultism by three halls through which man passes as he ascends: the Hall of Ignorance; the Hall of Learning; and the Hall of Wisdom. While he is in the realm of purely human life and identified with the phenomenal world, he is said to be in the

Hall of Ignorance. The termination of his residence there brings him to the entrance to the Probationary Path. He then enters the Hall of Learning, wherein he follows the path of discipleship and instruction. This is the Mystic Life. At its end he passes by another initiation into the Occult Life and dwells within the Hall of Wisdom. Here he attains realization, undergoes heightened expansion of his consciousness, and identifies himself with the spiritual essence of his being.

The central features of occult discipline from the standpoint of the novitiate is the oft-mentioned "stilling of the senses and the mind." In the Bhagavad Gita Arjuna, the disciple, remonstrates with Krishna, the Lord, that he can not accept the Yoga teaching as to the steadfastness of the controlled mind. It is hard to tame he says, as the prancing horse or the fitful wind. Krishna answers:

"Well sayest thou, O Prince, that the mind is restless and as difficult to restrain as the winds. Yet by constant practice, discipline and care may it be mastered. . . . The Soul, when it has recognized the master-touch of the real Self, may attain unto true Yoga by care and patience, coupled with firm resolution and determination."

A little later he adds:

"Close tightly those gates of the body which men call the avenues of the senses. Concentrate thy mind upon thine inner self. Let thine 'I' dwell in full strength within its abode, not seeking to move outward. . . . He who thinketh constantly and fixedly on Me, O Prince, letting not his mind ever stray toward another object, will be able to find Me without overmuch trouble,--yea, he will find Me, will that devoted one."

There is a law of esotericism which governs the operation of all these psychic forces in mind and body. It is likewise the guarantee of the Soul's ultimate hegemony among the principles making up man's life. It is the occult law that "energy follows thought." It was this law which brought the universe into existence out of the Unmanifest; it is this law by which man has himself fashioned the instruments for his objective expression on the outer planes in the lower worlds. He, like the macrocosmic Logos before him, sent forth thought- waves, which, vibrating and impacting upon cosmic matter, moulded it to forms commensurate with the type of their activity. Thus he has built his own universe, which, however, binds him while it gives him expression. Now the same law must, in reverse motion, so to say, be utilized to release him from the trammels of flesh and sense, of feeling and mind-wandering. With energy flowing in the grooves marked by thought, he must cease to send thought outward to the periphery of life, the material world. Essentially a psychic being, he must concern himself not with things but with psychic states. He must withdraw his attention from sense contacts, whether pleasurable or painful, and end his subjection to the pairs of opposites, joy and sorrow, delight and anguish. He must cease to set his affections on things of desire; he must restrain wayward streams of thought. Refusing to direct further energies outward to these spheres, he invokes the law to terminate his further creations of form that will bind him to the world of the Not-Self.

The mind-stuff is susceptible to vibrations both from the lower bodies and from the Soul above. Man's destiny is in his own hands; it is daily decreed by the direction in which he turns his mind. As a man changes the nature and direction of his desires he changes himself.

Mind-control is acquired through two lines of endeavor: tireless effort and non- attachment. The first requirement explains why the Yoga student must be virtually a religious devotee. From no other source than religious devotion to the Way of Attainment can the necessary persistence spring to carry the candidate through to eventual success. The second prerequisite, non-attachment, is often spoken of as "renunciation of the fruits of action." It signifies that attitude toward things and toward the life of the personality which enables the Soul or Ego to regard the events that touch these with a sense of equanimity or nonchalance. It is the sublimation of Stoic ataraxia, and is called vairagya in Sanskrit. Our term indifference does not convey the correct significance of the concept. It connotes a combination of positive and negative attitudes practically unknown to the West. Krishna explains to Arjuna the seeming paradox in his injunction to service through action, which is coupled with a similar abjuration to ignore the fruits of action. The devotee is enjoined to perform right action for the sake of dharma, or duty, as the West has it, but at the same time to renounce the fruits of the action. In our vernacular this would mean to act with the zeal born of an interesting objective, but to leave the results with God. If one binds himself to the fruits of his actions, he creates ever new Karma for future expiation. He must act, and act resolutely; yet without thought of reward. Says the Bhagavad Gita:

"The wise man, setting himself free, mentally, from actions and their results, dwelleth in the Temple of the Spirit, even that which men call the body, resting calmly therein, at peace, and neither desiring to act nor causing to act, and yet always willing to play well his part in action, when Duty calleth him."10

Krishna clarifies the contradictory demands of duty and renunciation in the following:

". . . he who performeth honorably and to the best of his ability, such Action as may appear to him to be plain and righteous Duty, remembering always that he has nought to do with the reward or fruits of the Action, is both a Renouncer of Action, and also a Performer of the Service of Right Action. More truly is he an Ascetic and Renouncer than he who merely refuses to perform Actions; for the one hath the spirit of the doctrine, while the other hath grasped merely the empty shell of form and letter. Know thou such Intelligent Right Action as Renunciation; and also that the best of Right Action without Intelligent understanding of the renunciation of results is not Right Action at all."11

On the road to Seership, the aspirant advances by two stages. First there is the long Path of Probation; later the Path of Discipleship. He passes over many steps, commencing with the aspiration, entering upon Discipline, leading to Purification, followed by Initiation, Realization, and final union with the

Over-soul. There are said to be seven major modifications of the thinking principle, or seven states of consciousness, as follows: desire for knowledge; desire for freedom; desire for happiness; desire to perform duty; sorrow; fear; and doubt. These seven basic yearnings severally reach their fulfillment as illumination ensues upon strenuous effort. These are called the seven stages of bliss, or the seven stations on the Way of the Cross.

The practice of Yoga involves the employment of what are known as the Eight Means. These are:

1. Yama: self-control, restraint; it relates to the disciple's contacts with others and with the outside world.

2. Nyana: right observances; the keeping of the Five Commandments and the Five Rules.

The Five Commandments are:

(a) Harmlessness: the aspirant must use the physical forces in the spirit of beneficence to all that lives. He hurts no thing.

(b) Truth: precise and straightforward speech, expressing inward truth. The voice must have lost the power to injure.

(c) Abstention from theft: rendering each his due; not using more than one's share; making one's maintenance cost no more than is right; not taking what others need.

(d) Abstention from incontinence: control of the relation between the sexes; unloosing of the Soul from too strong attachment to any physical or sense expression.

(e) Abstention from avarice: covetousness is theft on the mental plane.

The Five Rules enjoin:

(a) Magnetic purity: internal and external purity of the three bodies; unhindered flow of Prana through the system.

(b) Contentment: mind at rest; not a state of inertia, but one of poise and balance of energies.

(c) Fiery aspiration: a sine qua non before a disciple is accepted. Zeal to win through is a primary qualification.

(d) Spiritual reading: power to discern things in their spiritual, not physical, aspects; inner vision.

(e) Devotion to Ishvara: consecration of the lower man to the service of the higher. Devotion to God, or the Divine Spark within us.

3. Asana: right poise; correct physical, emotional and mental attitudes. It coördinates the three principles of the lower man into a perfect instrument.

4. Pranayama: breath control; control of the subtle energies of the inner sheaths; leads to organization of the etheric or vital body.

5. Pratyahara: abstraction; withdrawal of the Soul from the interests of the outer life.

6. Dharana: concentration; fixation of the mind; leads to coordination of the mind as the sixth sense of the Soul.

7. Dhyana: meditation; development of the capability of the Soul to transmit to the brain its higher ideas.

8. Samadhi: contemplation; dwelling consciously upon the "things of God"; leads to full illumination. It is the final stage of mystic vision, when the individual Ego looks upon the full splendor of the spiritual universe.

As the purification of the three lower vehicles proceeds, certain physical changes are said to occur within the head, following the awakening of the "lotus centers" below. "The vital airs" are organized to flow in regular currents up and down the two channels in the spinal cord; they rise to the head, circulate around the temples and pass inward to touch and arouse to active functioning the pineal gland and the pituitary body, located close to each other near the center of the cranium. This is the Kundalini or Serpent Fire, typified in may symbolisms of the ancients. Its play of force fills the whole body with light.

It is so high-powered a current of etheric energy that its stirring to activity is attended with much danger, and, Theosophists say, should only be undertaken with the help of a Master.

No bizarre style of ascetic living is demanded of a Yogi. "Celibacy is not enjoined. Self-control is." If we may use Mrs. Bailey's words once more,

"The right use of the sex principle, along with entire conformity to the law of the land, is characteristic of every true aspirant."12

The basic principle of personal conduct is subsumed under the one rule: "Let every man attend to his own Dharma." The meddler, the reformer, the uplifter is looked upon askance in the Orient. The individual's kingdom to conquer is within. When he becomes master there he will be given larger worlds to subdue to law and harmony.

An interesting development at a later stage is the Yogi's increasing power to create on the mental plane by the use of the word or of sounds. He becomes a magician-a white one if his motive is pure and selfless. This power is achieved through continence, pure living, and clean thinking, and not through any perversions of the occult, such as sex magic, as emphasized by some so-called schools of occultism. The latter are on the black path, which does not lead to the portals of initiation.

There are four types of purity to be achieved, one for each vehicle: external (for the physical body); magnetic (of the etheric body); psychic (of the astral body); and mental (of the mental body). All kinds require refinement of the matter of which each body is composed. The law of synchronous and asynchronous vibrations attends to this, pure thoughts sifting out coarser particles from the bodies and building in finer ones. This is what is meant by burning out the dross.

Mrs. Bailey tells us that

"in this cycle the interest of the hierarchy is being largely centered on the question of psychic purity, and this is the reason for the trend of the occult teaching at present developing. It is away from what is commonly understood as psychic development, lays no emphasis on the lower psychic powers and seeks to train the aspirant in the laws of the spiritual life."13

"The pure heart shall see God,"-who is the higher inner principle which suddenly manifests itself to the open-visioned seeker.

It is most necessary-Mrs. Bailey agrees with Madame Blavatsky-that students should follow the means of Yoga in the order laid down by Patanjali, and should thence see to it that the purificatory process, the discipline of the inner and the outer life, and one-pointedness of mind, should be undertaken prior to attempting the regulation of the etheric principle through breathing. The premature awakening of the centers is attended with positive danger, as before

noted. The natural barriers between this world and the astral may be broken down before the pupil is ready to deal with the forces thus released. The untimely development of the lower psychism is regarded as the cause of insanity in many cases.

One must be a mystic before he becomes an occultist. The mystic rises to God through the path of feeling; the occultist through the path of knowledge. Each person must become both, but more fittingly the mystic first.

The eight final siddhis or powers are given as:

1. Minuteness: the ability to enter the infinitely small, the atom.
2. Magnitude: ability to expand the vision to embrace the cosmos.
3. Gravity: the ability to use the law of gravity.
4. Lightness: power to counteract gravity, and cause levitation.
5. Attainment of one's objective: the ability to gain one's purpose.
6. Irresistible will: sovereignty over the forces of nature.
7. Creative power: art of combining and recombining the elements.
8. Power to command: power of the word to organize matter into form.

At this stage we are at last dowered with some of the powers of gods. For "God meditated, visualized, spoke, and the worlds were made," and when our Christ principle is awakened to full functioning we become joint heirs of his power. At the final stage knowledge becomes possible even without the use of the senses, though these have themselves been refined to ethereal sensitivity and continue to serve the Ego in various capacities.

In the end spirit is victor over matter, because the long struggle eventuates in three attainments, described as:

1. The inability of matter and form to hold the Yogi confined.
2. The powerlessness of substance to prevent the Yogi cognizing any aspect of life he desires.
3. The helplessness of matter to withstand the will of the Yogi.

Freedom from the limitations of matter forms the basis of all white magic. Through his transcendent powers the Yogi now transforms the very vehicles into instruments of more expanded efficiency. The Soul and its vehicles now form a unit, and the Son of God can function unrestrictedly on earth, on any plane. The human Ego has become what he was all along, but had not demonstrated till now,-- a God. His life is now hid with the Christos in the bosom of God, and for him humanity is transcended, and he needs no further rebirth as a mortal. The Spirit has then transcended space and time. Matter can no longer imprison him. He dwells consciously in the timeless Now.

A beautiful passage in the Bhagavad Gita may fittingly summarize this entire regimen of Yoga, which is the ideal of the Theosophist:14

"Having purified his mind and cleared his understanding; having mastered his personal self by firm resolution and having forsaken the objects of sense; having delivered himself from desire, dislike and passion; worshipping with intelligent discretion and understanding; eating with moderation and temperance; with controlled speech, body and mind; being well practiced in meditation and concentration; being dispassionate; having freed himself from ostentation, egotism, tyranny, vain-glory, lust, anger, avarice, covetousness and

selfishness-possessing calmness and peace amidst the feverish unrest of the world around him-such a man is fitted to enter into the consciousness of the Universal Life."

How naturally unfitted Occidentals are to undertake the rigid discipline is evidenced by Madame Blavatsky's statement that hardly half a dozen of her followers faced any fair prospects of success in mastering the difficulties of the thorny path. Her own warming words disillusioned those whose hopeful and enthusiastic efforts had not already reaped for them a harvest of barren result. Leading the occult life was seen not to be at all the sensational and spectacular road to a magical victory. On the contrary it presented rather a drab and dreary prospect.

Thus while the life of a Yogi is the ultimate Theosophic ideal, the accepted code of morality and devotion, like many another body of ideal teaching, is seldom actualized in performance. It is too intense for the average sincere person in the West. And perhaps, too, its practice and exemplification would mark the practitioner as eccentric.

The outcome of this disparity between goal and achievement is that the cult practice of Theosophy has become a sort of compromise; and the "life Theosophic" may be said to have been reduced for the rank and file of the membership to one or other, or all, of the following lines of endeavor: (1), the performance of one's dharma; (2), living the life of brotherhood; (3), practicing meditation; (4) dietary regulation; (5), a general effort to progress by reading, study, and service, to grow by enlarging the knowledge of life.

This menu is interesting as affording concrete demonstration of just how far the cult of Oriental subjectivism can be carried out in real life by a large segment of sincere and intelligent persons in our Western milieu.

Many Theosophic students at one time or another have seriously contemplated attacking the whole problem of spiritual attainment with all its obligations. But for the greater part they have elected the winding, if longer, road up the mountain, rather than challenge the rigors and the perils of the straight steep path. The latter course entails the "challenging of one's entire block of past evil Karma"; one undertakes to climb to the Mount of Transfiguration carrying the whole bundle of one's former wrongdoing. It is the testimony of hundreds of Theosophic idealists that their first virginal enthusiasm for a trial of the higher life of renunciation has in reality operated upon them in this way, so that they have been disposed by the severity of their experience to relinquish the harder method and be content with more gradual progress.

Yet in truth the compromise is regarded more as the consequence of want of resolute purpose than as a necessity occasioned by untoward circumstances. The claim is made that quiet and leisure are by no means indispensable conditions of success; that one can as well cultivate the fruits of the spirit amid the noise of modern life as in sequestered solitudes. The voice of the silence can be detected and heeded above the roar of traffic. The asceticisms which the Buddha decried are in no wise essential to the conquest of the inner nature. It is not

outward circumstance but inner resolution that determines achievement or failure.

The five specified forms of leading the life of Theosophic culture may now be touched upon. The first one is the performance of one's dharma, one of the several translations of which is our "duty." For many Theosophists this covers their entire practice of occultism. Dharma is not quite the same thing as Karma, but it is taken to mean the obligations and duties incumbent upon one by virtue of one's karmic situation. It is equivalent to the Right Action spoken of by Krishna in the Bhagavad Gita. It is the performance of our duty in that particular place, time, and circumstance in which our lot is cast.

It has often been objected against Theosophic belief in reincarnation that its influence would be to narcotize earthly ambition and effort. On the presupposition that many more lives are to come, endeavor will be less strenuous, it is argued. But no Theosophist would concede the validity of this reasoning. He will contend that the effect of his philosophy is to energize his activities. A definite amount of work has to be done, and the sooner the better. Further, evolution couples its own peculiar penalties to wasted opportunity.

Therefore the Theosophist will strive to be diligent in business and fervent in spirit, he will not be thrown off his balance by the urge to feverish haste which the one-life theory may engender. From his vastly extended perspective he may derive that calmness which comes from living in the spirit of eternity instead of in that of the temporal flux. An event which perturbs the mind of another as being absolute good or ill, is accepted by him in an equable mood, as it is seen to be but temporary and relative.

Contributing to his attitude of mental poise also is the doctrine that each fling of adverse fortune is the final rendering of some particular account, the last payment on some old claim, which, if borne with some patience, will soon be scratched off his slate. Physical ills are regarded as the eventual outcropping of spiritual faults on the material plane; they are therefore on their way out. Each stroke of ill is thought of as one more debt paid off. The debtor rejoices that he is thus one step nearer freedom.

To keep striving in the line of regular duty under every stress and strain is therefore a primary virtue. It makes Theosophists good, loyal, and dependable citizens of the state. Their native membership in any particular society is looked upon as entailing certain obligations laid upon them by the hand of Karma.

Along with racial, national, and professional dharma there is that other, especially sacred to the Theosophist, the family dharma. The relation of helpfulness in the family weighs with considerable impressiveness upon Theosophists. This function may be assumed from necessity, from the bare force of the idea of dharma, or from the belief that it may pay exceptional rewards for meritorious service to humanity.

The tenets of Theosophy likewise dispose their practitioners to the happy procedure of minding their own business, in the main. The Bhagavad Gita is insistent that one's dharma, insignificant as it may seem, is energy productively expended, while the effort to perform that dharma of another is a fruitless waste. Theosophy believes that charity begins at home, and "know thyself" is the main call to duty. To render oneself whole and lovely is the finest-ultimately the only-service one can do for the world. The world can ask no more from you than this, and to it you should devote yourself chiefly, using

social contacts as in part the means of growth. "One's own dharma is good; the dharma of another is bad"-for you.

But humanity forms a brotherhood and the relation entails upon the Theosophist- who proclaims it as his central theme and only creedal requirement-a distinctive course of behavior toward his fellowmen. As Theosophy is an effort at scientific altruism, the conduct of members must involve no element that either positively harms, or, negatively, withholds good from a fellow mortal. "Do not hurt to any creature,"-this to insure peace and safety and good will as the basic condition of fraternity among mankind. Harmlessness is one of the Five Commandments, as we have seen. Abstinence from theft is another; and this is a further-reaching prohibition than it may seem at first sight. It means that one should not take from the common store more than one needs, lest another suffer privation. This places a ban on all ostentation, luxury, extravagance, which is living at the expense of others' labor.15

And herein is seen a most important aspect of Theosophic morality, one that sets a sharp contrast between the cult and others that have fed on its fundamental occult principles. There is in Theosophy an absence of that preachment concerning the "demonstration of prosperity," success, material well-being, which has been the bait held out by so many cults especially in America.

Theosophists are taught that service to one's fellows, and not demonstrations of superiority over them, or ability to tax their labors, is the truest demonstration of godly power and the most direct way to put one's shoulder to evolution's wheel. To demonstrate prosperity is but to demonstrate selfishness, unless prosperity is rigidly made utilitarian to brotherhood. The cults in question regard Theosophy as partaking too strongly of Oriental non- aggressiveness in these respects, and they have attempted to supply to Eastern occultism the desirable quality of Yankee thrift, which the originators of the science were so thoughtless as to leave out. But Theosophy, with Ruskin, affirms that true spirituality demands neither your prosperity nor your poverty, is not signalized by either, but may utilize either or both for its ends. On the whole the possession of spirituality has been marked throughout history by demonstrations of poverty rather than by a parade of material wealth. Though there is no necessary relation of cause and effect between the two, poverty has probably engendered more spirituality than has success. Prosperity is no criterion of success, and may be the road to spiritual ruin. A man may gain the world and lose his soul. So Theosophy is no party to the "how to get what you want" ballyhoo, and is so loyal to the true spiritual ideal of service that it does not hesitate to characterize New Thought, Christian Science, Unity, Applied Psychology, and the others as forms of sorcery, and gray, if not quite black, magic.

Much the same considerations restrain occultists from rushing into the healing cults, which have added therapy to the lure of "prosperity." Theosophy has paused long enough to reflect that there may be ethical factors in the matter of healing. It is inclined to feel that there is a breach of both natural and moral law in the use of spiritual energies to heal bodily diseases. If one is ill as the result of intemperance in living, eating, or as a consequence of wrong thinking, the disturbance is to be remedied by a rectification of ill-advised habits, not by resort to spiritual affirmation. Human welfare is to be achieved and promoted by obedience to the laws of life on all planes, not by jugglery of so-called spiritual forces. To use spiritual power as a means of escaping the penalties of violated physical laws is a perversion of high energies to base ends. Furthermore, it is a deduction from the technology of life on the several planes that a physical ill is the working out on the physical level of causes engendered on the inner planes, and that if ceremonial, or theurgical, or psychological powers are invoked to prevent its full deploying into the realm of the body on its way out to a final dispersion of its energies, it will be driven back into the inner bodies, only to emerge at some favorable time in the future with more pain than now. Mental healing but drowns the symptoms, which are the effects, and does not cause or prevent its discovery. Theosophists tell us that there are infinitely deeper laws governing the processes of healing than either materia medica or cult therapy dreams of, and it is foolish for uninstructed zealots to rush into this field. The program of Theosophy in the face of the blatant cry for healing directed at every sect and cult, is to learn the basic laws of life, on all planes. Obedience to them will obviate the necessity for the special intervention of exceptional forces. Moreover, disease is needed by nature as a means to apprise us of our errors, and hence to enlighten our ignorance. Were it not for pain we could not grow in knowledge. It is more important that the laws of life be mastered than that some pains be removed.

Likewise not even happiness is made the criterion of Theosophical ethical idealism. Mankind has the right to happiness, to be sure, since Ananda (bliss) is the ultimate nature of the All. In the end, the abundant life, with happiness as its concomitant, will be the fruit of effort, and one of the marks of attainment. But in the present status of evolution, happiness is for the most part only tentative, or epiphenomenal, as transient as pain. Then, too, pain if often likely to be a more certain guide to progress than is joy. The primary task is to master the laws of life; and the processes of learning may not be the happiest experience. Dharma overshadows mere happiness.

Those Theosophists, then, who lay stress upon the dharmic aspect of ethical teaching may be said to live their faith through the practice of a sort of Karma Yoga. They follow neither the path of mysticism nor those of occultism and devotion in their purely psychological phases. They seek to build character through right action and to reach the inner kingdom through "meritorious deeds." They live Theosophy in conduct rather than in thinking.

A second type of occult practice is that which grows out of the emphasis laid upon the principle of Brotherhood.

One of the first and most striking forms in which this spirit emerges into practical conduct is the control of speech in the avoidance of gossip. New students of Theosophy have often been surprised at the emphasis laid in the ethical literature of the cult on the primary importance of this item of behavior. It is therein regarded as one of the most direct forms of sin against the law of love, the law of brotherhood, since the victim is not present to defend himself. It is the subterfuge of weakness and baseness. It foments discord and strife.

It is but the simplest sort of homiletic wisdom to realize that the exercise of brotherhood demands the obliteration of such harsh and gross emotions as anger, hatred, envy, jealousy, greed, avarice, brutality. They all spring from "the heresy of separateness" and feed on the sense of self as isolated from the common weal.

But perhaps the highest virtue in the way of human solidarity in the occultist's catalogue is that of tolerance. Theosophists are asked to exemplify tolerance because it is a prima facie fundamentum of any scheme of social friendliness whatever.

Esoterically the Theosophical Society was organized to form a nucleus of Universal Brotherhood, to bring under a common stimulus a group of men and women who should endeavor to manifest perfect unity on the basis of that one principle, who should constitute a node of spiritual force giving vitality to the evolution of the unified racial consciousness. Tolerance was the indispensable element in this enterprise.

The third road to Yoga followed by many in the movement is that of meditation. The degree of its actual employment by members of the Society is a variable quantity. Meditation was a requirement of the discipline in the Esoteric Section to the minimum extent of fifteen minutes a day. But outside that section few students held themselves to any set schedule. Its practice is intermittent and irregular, when undertaken at all. Avid beginners often bind themselves to a course of daily meditation, with fair results. But the task seems in most cases to prove irksome or to be attended with unsatisfactory consequences of one kind or another. It many cases it is eventually given up. The influences militating against its fruitful continuance are not entirely clear. Whether the pressure of the actual in our Western life is too heavy for steady progress in the art, or whether our nervous systems are not sufficiently receptive of the forces which would take us deeper into the core of consciousness, we are unable to determine.

This systematic character of spiritual exercise under a technique that has the sanction of hoary antiquity is one of the features of Theosophy that commends it to earnest folk in contrast with the loose indefinite procedure of most Christian practice. The occult system provides a regimen of definite discipline, with the promise of growth in the conscious spiritualization of life. It does not leave one in the atmosphere of a vague idealism, but furnishes the formula of an exact science. Certain definite results are promised, in the event of sustained effort.

Most Theosophic meditation consists in concentrating upon a certain virtue of a lofty nature that the student desires to embody in his character. Working upon the theory that "a man becomes that upon which he thinks," he labors to implant new elements into his personality by the steady contemplation of desirable qualities. The keynote of the whole process is concentration. To focus consciousness in a steady stream upon one item of knowledge or one phase of virtue is tremendously to enhance the mental product. The effort of mind and will is supplemented here by the law of automatism, brought into operation by repetition. It is a variant of the old law of habit formation, and is regarded by the occultists as the only direct method of soul-culture that can be consciously applied, with safety, by the individual.

The objects of contemplation may vary from those which are concrete to those which are personal, or intellectual, or abstract. One may think of virtue as impersonal or as personally embodied. It is an aid in the earlier stages to visualize virtue, beauty, nobility, wisdom, truth as exemplified in some strong character. But eventually the aim is to absorb the spirit of those qualities in their pure or impersonal form. As Adeptship is reached and some of the loftier ranges of spirituality are attained, meditation tends to empty the mind of all content, whether intellectual or rhapsodic, and to bring into consciousness the cognition of sheer pure Being itself.

The fourth avenue of occult progress leads through a régime of bodily purification by means of diet. It grows out of the recognition of the relation between body and spirit, between the indwelling life and its various sheaths. Hence progress in the occult life is held to be materially conditioned by the dietary régime one follows.

The occultist is concerned with his food, then, with reference to its purity and its magnetic qualities, in addition to its general agency in sustaining life. It is a question of kind and quality first, and secondly of quantity. Theosophists long ago talked of the magnetic properties of foods. Certain ones tended to make one sluggish, as they contained heavier earthy elements. Others built coarse and sensuous fibre into the tissue and blood. Others heightened nervous instability. Some coarsened, others refined, the body. As the bodies of animals were attached to undeveloped intelligences, and were in the first place organized by the far slower vibrations of the soul of the beast, their edible flesh was indubitably permeated with the elemental constituents of sensuality and bestiality. To partake of it would be to introduce an inherent disposition to animal coarseness into the human vehicle, which would thus give freer course to the sensual impulses. The elemental qualities of the animal cells would stimulate the lower energies of the astral body. Meat would be a force retarding evolution, holding the man closer to the animal characteristics, which it is his task now to transcend. Hence it became catalogued as a definite enemy of the higher life, and was taboo.

Very many Theosophists have discarded it utterly from their diet for periods ranging from months to a score of years. Many have abandoned its use in their homes, but indulge when eating with others who use it. Thousands partake of it only in the most sparing degree. There are few who have not cut into their consumption of it drastically. Its total abandonment was once an obligatory requirement in certain degrees of the Esoteric Section. But members are under no compulsion in the matter. If the student eats no meat it is his own voluntary action, though it may have been determined by the suggestion of some one regarded as a leader. Some of these utterances have gone so far as to declare that spiritual progress beyond a certain point was impossible if one ate meat. Mr. C. W. Leadbeater listed eggs as hardly less detrimental.

Vegetable foods, fruits, nuts, plants, are regarded as best adapted for human use, as being most Sattvic in quality. But it is a mistake to classify Theosophists generally as vegetarians. Few in fact are. Most of them have eliminated meat in all forms, but such animal product foods as milk, cheese, eggs, butter, lard, still figure in the diet. With large numbers of Theosophists strict adherence to a non-meat régime is tempered by the countervailing influence of that other precept of good occult behavior, which says that any conduct becomes discordant with the brotherhood platform if it makes of one a spectacle of eccentricity. To render oneself "queer" in the eyes of others is largely to defeat one's usefulness in the rôle of a promoter of human solidarity. So it is often regarded as better to eat meat than to bring occultism into disrepute as an oddity.

It is quite well to reiterate, before dismissing this topic, that there is no prescribed regimen of life for Theosophists, and that many of the peculiarities of dietary habit observed here and there-and hardly more patently among Theosophists than among members of other sects-are to be assigned largely to individual whims.

There remains the last of our subdivisions of cult activity,--the constant effort to progress in the line of occult knowledge and wisdom. It is perhaps too broad an aim to be thus particularized, but it embraces the main currents in the drift of the average Theosophic life. Chiefly it consists in the steady endeavor to learn more of the occult version of life by continuous reading and study. It is primarily an intellectual enterprise. Its instrumentalities are study classes, addresses, magazines, and books, with the recent addition of

correspondence courses. Originally captivated by the large cosmic graph which the system outlines, the disciple sets himself sedulously to the great task of mastering the complexities of the vast science. A few years will not complete it. It is the intellectual attempt to square oneself with the universe and with life by means of the rationale which the elaborate scheme of Theosophic ideology unfolds. This entails for the earnest student ever more reading, more study, more reflection. Then as the outlines are grasped and the basic doctrines assimilated into the thinking, there follows the serious problem of making a readjustment of both theoretical and practical attitudes toward a world that is now differently rationalized. The first practical outcome of the study of so large a cosmic picture is a certain relaxation of life strain, with the acquisition of poise, steadiness, patience, and eventually tolerance, all framed against a background of non-attachment. The long vista of an infinite evolution to higher states, replaced the hurry and flurry of a one-life conception, tends to ground the life firmly in complacency. There is a decided approach to philosophic calm. From the assurance of the general beneficence of the evolutionary plan there arises a broader charity, a pervading kindliness and deep psychic sympathy, all of which dispose to equanimity.

There is a brief statement of the general aim and spirit of Theosophy that has been used for years by Lodges of the Society printed on leaflets for the benefit of inquirers. It might well have served as the text for this analysis.

"The Theosophical Society is composed of students, belonging to any religion in the world or to none, who are united in their approval of the three objects (brotherhood, psychism and eclecticism) by their wish to remove religious antagonisms and to draw together men of good will whatsoever their religious opinions, and by their desire to study religious truths and to share the results of their studies with others. Their bond of union is not the profession of a common belief, but a common search and aspiration for truth. They hold that any truth should be sought by study, by reflection, by purity of life, by devotion to high ideals, and they regard truth as a prize to be striven for, not as a dogma to be imposed by authority. They consider that belief should be the result of individual study or intuition, and not its antecedent, and should rest on knowledge, not on assertion. They extend tolerance to all, even to the intolerant, not as a privilege they bestow, but as a duty they perform, and they seek to remove ignorance, not to punish it. They see every religion as an expression of the Divine Wisdom, and prefer its study to its condemnation, and its practice to its proselytism. Peace is their watchword as truth is their aim."

Perhaps no one has translated the ethics of this philosophy into its practical expressions better than has Madame Blavatsky herself. Her digest of Theosophic morality, highly treasured by her followers, is given in the little work of hers entitled Practical Occultism:

"A clean life, an open mind, a pure heart, an eager intellect, an unveiled spiritual perception, a brotherliness for all, a readiness to give and receive advice and instruction, a courageous endurance of personal injustice, a brave declaration of principles, a valiant defence of those who are unjustly attacked, a constant eye to the ideal of human progression and perfection which the sacred science depicts-these are the golden stairs up the steps of which the learner must climb to the Temple of Divine Wisdom."

CHAPTER XII LATER THEOSOPHICAL HISTORY

While Madame Blavatsky in Europe was explaining the cosmos and acquainting mankind with its own origin, nature, and destiny, Theosophic affairs in America were moving forward under the steady guidance of Mr. Judge; but there was also a series of disturbances which culminated in the "Sun Libel Suit" in 1890.1 This latter event had its remote beginnings in a situation arising out of the question of the inspired authorship of Light on the Path, The Idyll of the White Lotus, The Blossom and the Fruit, and Through the Gates of Gold, four small volumes given out by Miss Mabel Collins in England after 1884. Miss Collins had herself declared them dictated to her by a mysterious Master, though later she said that she had merely "written them down" from their astral inscription on a wall in the mystical "Hall of Learning" described in one of the four books.

Aspiring eagerly for leadership in the Theosophical Society in America at the time was Prof. Elliott F. Coues, a man of talent and ability, somewhat versed in the field of science and anthropology, who had been led through his interest in psychic phenomena to affiliate with the Theosophical Society. He seems to have resented Mr. Judge's preferment over him in the esoteric counsels and leadership and urged himself upon Madame Blavatsky as the logical choice for the supreme office in the United States. Rebuffed by H.P.B., he became embittered. In the Religio-Philosophical Journal, of Chicago, he published his correspondence with Miss Collins relative to the mooted authorship of the brochures. This magazine, an organ of spiritistic-psychic interests, had given an airing to Mr. W. Emmette Coleman's attacks upon the authenticity of Madame Blavatsky's classical scholarship in Isis. Prof. Coues now used its columns to discredit Madame Blavatsky's theories of Mahatmaship by presenting some of Miss Collins' statements which virtually cast the charge of intellectual dishonesty at H.P.B.'s door. Miss Collins had stated to Prof. Coues in the first of her letters to him that she had made her declaration as to the Mahatma-inspired authorship of her Idyll of the White Lotus only because Madame Blavatsky had "implored and begged her to do so." This was as much as to say that she had lied about the inspirational nature of the writings because Madame Blavatsky urged her to do so.2 When H.P.B. came to London in 1887 she associated Miss Collins with herself as a sub-editor of her magazine Lucifer. This relation subsisted for two years, when Miss Collins' name was dropped from the editorial staff and her connection with the publication ended. No reason for the breach was given out publicly, but a letter of Madame Blavatsky's later charged that her protégé had proved unreliable and untrustworthy in her occult pledges.

Prof. Coues became more openly hostile to the Blavatsky-Judge hegemony in America and finally, upon preferment of formal charges of untheosophical conduct lodged against him by Mr. Arthur B. Griggs, of Boston, he was expelled from the Theosophical Society in June, 1889. Now fighting in the open, Prof. Coues, early

in the next year, 1890, gave interviews to a correspondent of the New York Sun in Washington D.C., and painted his former cult-associates with the black hue of out-and-out imposture. In its Sunday issue, June 1, 1890, the Sun gave a half- column to a general statement of Theosophic and Blavatskian charlatanry. Tasting blood, Prof. Coues gave to the Sun representative an extended article detailing the whole alleged career of Madame Blavatsky and her dupes. It made a seven- column finely printed article in the Sun of Sunday, July 20. It included open declarations that Madame Blavatsky had in several instances been a member of the demi-monde in Paris and the mistress of two Russians mentioned by name, by one of whom she had given birth to a deformed child that died at Kieff in 1868. Every untoward incident in the life of his subject was revamped and given a plausible rôle in a vast scheme of deceptive posing, with the Russian spy motive once more doing service. This was considered going too far, and Mr. Judge at once filed suit in New York against the Sun for libel. The case was delayed by congestion in the courts, and before it ever came to trial Madame Blavatsky passed from the stormy scene. Her death left the newspaper free from further legal responsibility. But its efforts to procure material evidence to defend its position revealed that Prof. Coues had overreached himself and that the allegations were for the greater part, if not entirely, unjust to the deceased leader. Finally, in its issue of Sept. 26, 1892, the Sun voluntarily retracted its offensive articles of 1891, repudiated the Coues interview, and gave Mr.
Judge space to write a devoted tribute to his late co-worker.

"We were misled," the Sun observes, "into admitting into the Sun's columns an article by Dr. E. F. Coues, of Washington, in which allegations were made against Madame Blavatsky's character, and also against her followers, which appear to have been without solid foundation . . . we desire to say that his allegations respecting the Theosophical Society and Mr. Judge personally are not sustained by evidence, and should not have been printed."

The failure of so well-equipped an agency as the New York Sun to secure incriminating evidence on any of the many charges lodged by Prof. Coues against Madame Blavatsky is pointed to by Theosophists as a complete vindication of her name.

Charges too much the same general effect were launched in a renewed attack on the good faith of H.P.B. by V. S. Solovyoff in his volume, A Modern Priestess of Isis, after her death. Solovyoff, a Russian of good family, had met Madame Blavatsky in Paris in 1884, had been fascinated by her personality and her intriguing philosophy and occult powers and had joined her Society. He manifested every desire to be admitted to the inner mysteries of occultism, and it is the opinion of impartial students of the data of this controversy that Madame Blavatsky's knowledge of his spiritual unpreparedness for acceptance as a chela under her Master and her refusal to have him admitted to this exalted relationship turned his worship of her into feelings of another kind.[3] His own letters during the years of his acquaintance with Madame Blavatsky and her sister Madame Jelihowsky discloses his enthusiastic interest in the esoteric program, and his own description of a number of psychic experiences which occurred to him in person through the agency of his compatriot and her Adept aides is noteworthy. He recounts the personal appearance to him one night of the Master Morya himself, and gives the gist of the conversation he had with the exalted personage who stood before him in his astral (materialized) form. M. Solovyoff's testimony was considerably weakened later when he repudiated the reality of this phenomenon and endeavored to explain it away with the statement that he was at the time suffering from overwrought nerves. The current of his entire narrative in the Modern Priestess thinly disguises a general inconsistency between the attitude his letters show at the time of his close

association with H.P.B. (and her sister) and that which he assumed when he came to write his books after her death. Madame Jelihowsky's letters to him and her rebuttal of many of his specific charges, which are appended to his book as a supplement, indicate that the foundation of his accusations is erected on very shifty sands. M. Solovyoff shows the capabilities of a good novelist, and Theosophists are persuaded, after painstaking analysis of the entire situation, that he drew largely for the material of his book upon the romantic inventiveness of his literary genius. In any case, his book is added testimony to H.P.B.'s powerful personality, whatever inferences one draws from it regarding her methods.

In 1888 the General Convention in India adopted the policy of reorganizing the Theosophical Society on the plan of autonomous sections. The Society was thus changed from a quasi-autocracy to a constitutional federation, each part independent as to its internal and local affairs, but responsible to every other part for its loyal support of the movement, and to the headship which bound the sections together.

As Col. Olcott and his partner were driving each in his own direction-the one for an exoteric goal and the other toward an esoteric one-the history of the Society in the years antedating Madame Blavatsky's death reflects a struggle between the aims and interests of the two. Col. Olcott was cool to the establishment of the Esoteric Section. He frequently resented H.P.B.'s arbitrary overriding of his authority. It was in miniature the clash between church and state, the spiritual and the temporal power, all over again. While the priestess lived she left no doubts as to which had supremacy. And hardly less than in her day, the later developments of Theosophic history can be understood only in the light of the reverence given the Masters. A word dropped from their lips is the highest law in the Theosophic kingdom. Material interest or temporal expediency must bend before its authority.

Curiously also the attitudes taken toward their common enterprise by the two Founders reflect the views of two opposing schools of thought. Col. Olcott looked upon the growth of the movement as a development, not a teleological unfoldment. It had no determinate purpose in the beginning, no definite lines of direction, but was largely the product of unintended and unexpected events. Even its declared objects were a "development." His views on these matters were reflected in an article, "The Theosophical Society," signed by "F.T.S." (thought to have been Mr. Richard Harte, one of the Colonel's lieutenants at Adyar), published in Theosophist for Jan, 1889. But at least one gesture of assent to the contrary view is made in the article when it says:

"This variation in the declared objects of the Society must not be taken as indicating any real change in the intentions of the Founders. There is abundant evidence in their writings and speeches that from the first their purposes were to stimulate the spiritual development of the individual and to awaken in the race the sentiment of Brotherhood."

Nevertheless, the Theosophist, during 1889, and thereafter, kept printing articles from Mr. Harte's pen, emphasizing the need of the Society's standing before the world divested of secret and mystical connection with, or at any rate vital dependence upon, the mysterious wire-pullers behind the scenes, the Mahatmas. Olcott's party, including Mr. Sinnett, Mr. Hume, and other prominent members, desired to avoid the inevitable storm of worldly contumely which adherence to the legend of the Masters provoked. They claimed that the organization rested on high scientific, philosophical, and ethical principles that stood on their own merits without adventitious supernatural aid. They

wished it thus to take on the colors of anthroposophism and humanism. They desired first of all that the Theosophical Society should appear eminently respectable in the sight of intelligent people and not expose the questionable Masters to public view. To the Masters, on the other hand, H.P.B. and Mr. Judge were irretrievably committed. From the standpoint of these two the danger to be guarded against was that the exoteric leaders might make of the Society a worldly success, at the risk of occult failure. They feared that Theosophy might gain the whole world but lose its own soul. This division of aims explains most of the internal troubles which have arisen on board the ship of Theosophy.

In one of the Harte articles mention was made of Madame Blavatsky's "loyalty to Adyar," i.e., to Col. Olcott's outer headship and authority. She replied by saying that:

"H.P.B. is loyal to death to the Theosophic Cause, and those great Teachers whose philosophy alone can bind the whole of humanity into one Brotherhood."
She would be loyal to Olcott and the Theosophic officialdom only so long as they held true to the Masters and their Cause. Her loyalty to the Colonel was based on his tireless labors for that Cause. If he deserted it her nexus of loyalty to him was broken.

Events moved on from year to year, with "crises" and storms every few years, yet with rapid increase in membership. In 1886 there were 8 Lodges in the United States; in 1887, 12; in 1888, 19; in 1889, 26; in 1890, 45; in 1891, 57; and in 1892, 69. The American Section worked for the ethical ideals of Theosophy. In Europe and India the interests of Fellows were largely centered upon the second and third objects, comparative religion and psychism.

In 1889 the Esoteric Section was changed to the "Eastern School of Theosophy," and about the same time the European branches and unattached Fellows were incorporated in a separate autonomous organization known as the Theosophical Society in Europe, of which Madame Blavatsky was constituted President.

In 1888 a most notable event in the life of Theosophy occurred in England, soon to be followed by momentous consequences for the movement everywhere. This was the accession to the ranks of Mrs. Annie Besant, the noted and eloquent radical leader in England. Her life is now so well known4 that it is needless here to recount the events of her long and notable public career in her native country. A child of deep religious feeling and almost Catholic devotion, she passed through the stages of doubt and unbelief to atheism; threw herself ardently into such movements as the Fabian Society, Socialism, and the Secular Society; worked for birth control and slum amelioration and education; and finally found her destiny and her spiritual refuge when in 1888 she was asked by Mr. W. T. Stead to write for his magazine a review of the new publication-The Secret Doctrine.
She testifies that here, in the great scheme of cosmogony and wedded science and faith, she saw the

light that she had so earnestly been seeking. She instantly adopted the new teaching, met H.P.B., and threw her great abilities for service at her feet. She was accepted, and soon became the very right hand of the aging messenger. One of the most eloquent orators of her sex in history, she brought the message of Theosophy to crowded halls in most convincing terms. Her advocacy gave to Theosophy a vigorous stimulus. She had attended the American General Convention in 1890, and her second visit to this country was made in 1891. Her name and standing made her lecture tour in that year a great success.

Mrs. Besant again visited America in 1892, her speaking tour of leading cities lasting from her arrival in November of that year until February of 1893. The largest halls were packed, and a new wave of public interest surged forward.

She and Mr. Judge had been made the two heads of the Esoteric Section, to carry on the functions of that body after Madame Blavatsky should have passed from earth. H.P.B. had in writing (1888) constituted Mr. Judge as her "only representative for said Section in America"; and she had appointed Mrs. Besant as "Chief Secretary of the Inner Group and Recorder of the Teachings" given in the organization. After Judge's death (Saturday, March 21, 1896) she was left as the sole guardian of the inner society, and through it she wielded for the years to come a potent sway over the destinies of the whole Theosophic body.

On May 8, 1891, not quite sixty years of age, Madame Blavatsky ceased her earthy labors for Theosophy. There was for a brief time a feeling of disorganization and helpless bewilderment when her leadership and strong guardian hand were withdrawn; but her death at the same time served to unite Theosophists everywhere, at least temporarily, in a glow of fraternal good will and renewed loyalty to her message. The leader gone, the message became the thing of paramount importance. She had held no office save that of Recording Secretary, which was declared unique and abolished with her death. So she could properly have no successor. But innumerable mystics, mediums, and psychics the world over sprang forth with assertions that they had had commissions from her spirit to step into her earthly place. Probably most prominent among these was Mr. Henry B. Foulke, of Philadelphia, who declared that H.P.B.'s spirit had appeared to him, reproduced her portrait to identify herself, and given him her mantle of leadership. His claims were officially repudiated by Mr. Judge.

In 1892 Col. Olcott presented his resignation as President of the whole Society, alleging ill-health as the reason. He was requested by the American Section to withdraw his action and later in the year did so, after a vacation in the Nilgiri Hills. The American Section had gone so far, however, as to vote for the election of Mr. Judge as his successor in office, and this choice was endorsed by similar action on the part of the European Section a little later. Mr. Judge was Vice-President of the Theosophical Society as well as head of the General Council in America.

In March, 1892, Col. Olcott began the serial publication of Old Diary Leaves, with the sub-title, "The True History of the Theosophical Society," in his magazine The Theosophist. He represented Madame Blavatsky as a very human person, with great weaknesses and foibles. He apparently wished to combat a natural disposition on the part of members to erect a "worship" of H.P.B., and to accept her writings as Theosophic "dogma." The Diary ran on for many years, and its effect was to weaken her prestige to an extent hardly less than the open attack of the Society for Psychical Research had done in 1885. There is reason to believe that the Colonel's representation of her in this narrative is an uncritical account. His estimate of her does not accord with several other statements he had at times made as to her greatness. Even to those who had associated most closely with her she remained an enigma, an insoluble mystery.

One of Koot Hoomi's letters had intimated that she was a great soul (Mahatma) in her own right, a far greater Adept in the spiritual hierarchy than her outward personality seemed to indicate. This, at any rate, is the Blavatsky legend in some quarters of the movement. But the Colonel reduced the emphasis on this note in his reminiscences. He had always felt that the Theosophical Society could succeed, even without her and her invisible Sages.

In 1895 occurred the next momentous episode in American Theosophical history-the "Judge Case." It is a long story. It arose out of the elements of the situation already noted, viz., the emphasis of Col. Olcott and his party on the exoteric work of the Society, and the opposing attitude of Mr. Judge, consistently supported at first by Mrs. Besant, who emphasized Madame Blavatsky's esoteric teachings. The actual bone of contention was found in the articles put forth by Mr. T. Subba Row (Rao), eminent Hindu Theosophist and high chela, as far back at 1886, questioning Mr. Sinnett's transcriptions of the Master's teachings regarding the sevenfold constitution of man in Esoteric Buddhism, and the debate involving the status of Mars and Mercury in the solar chain. Madame Blavatsky's The Secret Doctrine had reversed the earlier cosmological teaching of K.H. as given out through Sinnett. The situation, of course, threw doubt on the trustworthy character of Mahatmic instruction and, by inference, on Madame Blavatsky's rôle as the agent of higher Sages. From this point discussion was carried further into the domain of Mahatmic messages in general, and the spurious or genuine nature of their reception by individuals. This question was thrown into more violent agitation about 1892 when Mr. Judge, together with his editorial assistant on The Path, Julia Campbell-Ver Planck (the "Jasper Niemand" of editorial prominence), and Mrs. Annie Besant, the latter most startlingly in her farewell address to her former Secularist associates, all publicly declared that they had had bona fide messages from the living Mahatmas. The significance of these declarations-H.P.B., the accused agent of all Mahatmic communication while she lived, being now not on the scene-was hardly to be exaggerated. But in the eyes of the Olcott-Sinnett faction they tended to lengthen the shadow of H.P.B., where its shortening was to be desired in furtherance of their partisan interests. They fell in opposition, too, to the hosts of psychic and mediumistic messages received by numerous members of the Society at séances and circles. Mr. Judge stood out for the authenticity of these messages, some of which he stated came to him, though he refused to submit, in corroboration of their genuineness, the "seal," handwriting or the other usual outward marks of the Master's letters. His opponents began more and more to allege forgery or invention on his part. The leading articles in the Theosophist, Lucifer, and The Path at this epoch dealt with phases of this debate. The insistent charges emanating from the exoteric party were that Judge and Mrs. Besant were trying to erect, in the matter of Mahatmic messages, a Theosophic dogmatism or orthodoxy. They reasserted the right of every Theosophist to accept or reject messages, and reiterated the cardinal principle of Theosophic free-thought. In fine, it was Judge's firm adherence to the fundamental thesis of Blavatskian hierarchical deputyship that made him more and more a thorn in the flesh of the other group. As long as Mrs. Besant stood with him it was difficult to weaken his position. The "anti-Blavatsky conspirators" then sought to wean her away from his support, and this was accomplished in 1893 through a series of circumstances.

In the fall of that year the notable Congress of Religions was held at Chicago in connection with the Columbian Exposition, and Mrs. Besant was the representative of Theosophy. Through Theosophical influence and financial assistance, the delegate chosen to represent Brahmanism in the Congress was one Prof. Gyanendra Nath Chakravarti, instructor in India and a member of the Theosophical Society. He and Mrs. Besant became almost the leading sensations of the convention, she through her eloquence and power, he through his dignity, suavity, and show of erudition. Interesting as they proved to be to outsiders, they shortly became far more so to each other. It was the delight of Chakravarti to keep watch and ward over the brilliant Western champion of his country's traditions, and on Mrs. Besant's part his reputed possession of great psychic abilities was a lure which, with her mental and spiritual leanings, became well nigh irresistible. It is said that Chakravarti slept outside her room door at the hotel to guard her from intrusion.5 A close association began between the

two which lasted for some ten or twelve years, when Chakravarti's place of foremost psychic interest in her regard was usurped by Mr. C. W. Leadbeater. It appears beyond question that the Brahmin's influence upon the mind of Mrs.

Besant was profound, and in directions which the future course of Theosophical history readily reveals.

In the late fall of 1893 Mrs. Besant went for the first time to India, her tours there veritably "trailing clouds of glory" for herself and the cause of Theosophy. At the annual General Convention, always held near Christmas, Col.

Olcott announced in his presidential address that a complete accord had been reached between his office and the renowned leader, and that the latter would shortly measure up to the spiritual status of H.P.B. herself. This accord indicated, among other things, that Mrs. Besant had admitted into her mind some of the animus against the purely esoteric view of Theosophy, as upheld by H.P.B. and Judge. She had begun to look upon the latter with suspicion. Chakravarti's influence in her "conversion" brought into view the conflicting ethics of Brahmanism and Buddhism. Madame Blavatsky's Theosophy adhered to the Tibetan Buddhistic, or Mahayana, theory of the sacrifice by the Nirmanakayas of their Nirvanic bliss for a service in behalf of humanity. The Brahmanical philosophy, on the other hand, held before its followers the acceptance, rather than the renunciation, of the higher blessedness. The latter taught individual salvation, the former the "Great Renunciation." Madame Blavatsky's principle of Brotherhood rather than mystical isolation and exaltation, would be undermined by the Brahmanical hypothesis. Hence Chakravarti's influence tended to reduce the high status of H.P.B. in the eyes of Mrs. Besant, and to increase her animus toward Judge.

The specific charges brought by Mrs. Besant (founded on "complaints" of members, so it was stated) against Judge were "alleged misuse of the Mahatmas' names and handwriting." Mrs. Besant became the mouthpiece of the "demand for an investigation." Mr. Judge denied the charges as absolutely false, and demurred to the trial as illegal under the Constitution of the Theosophical Society because it would involve a decision by the President of the Society as to the existence or non-existence of the Mahatmas, which would of itself establish at least one dogma of Theosophy, a thing forbidden. The Society must remain neutral on this as on all other questions of belief, save Brotherhood.

"Letters from Mahatmas," he says in his answer, "prove nothing at all except to the recipient, and then only when in his inner nature is the standard of proof and the power of judgment. Precipitation does not prove Mahatmas. . . . By one's soul alone can this matter be judged. . . . By following the course prescribed in all ages the inner faculties may be awakened so as to furnish the true confirmatory evidence."6

He reasserted that he had received letters from Masters, both during and since the life of Madame Blavatsky.

Before the charges had even been formulated or his accuser named to him, Mr. Judge received an ultimatum from Col. Olcott, giving him the choice of resigning or of being investigated. Judge, instead of accepting either alternative, denied his guilt. At the ensuing Convention of the Theosophical Society in America, the Section unanimously upheld Judge, and urged that if he could be tried for allegations of having received Mahatmic letters, so, in fairness, could Mr.
Sinnett, Col. Olcott, Mrs. Besant, and the others who had stated publicly that they had been favored with such letters.

The Secretaries of both the European and the Indian Sections issued letters to the membership condemning the President's unconstitutional methods of attacking Mr. Judge. Col. Olcott, thus thrown unexpectedly on the defensive, was aided by a new National Section, the Australian, which Mrs. Besant founded at that time and which voted on his side; and on the advice of Chakravarti and other lawyers at Adyar he appointed a Judicial Committee, to meet in London on June 27, 1894, to try the charges against the accused. He himself, contrary to his earlier intentions, found it imperative to attend the "trial" in person. The General Council did not meet in London until July 7. Its first act was to pass the motion that Mr. Judge could not be tried as an official of the Society, his guilt, if any, being that of an individual and hence not litigable.

The Special Judicial Committee met on July 10. Col. Olcott's party was in control. Mr. Judge was represented by his friends, Mr. Oliver Firth and Mr. E.
T. Hargrove. Some of the eleven members of the Committee were convinced of the guilt of Judge beforehand; three or four were impartial, rather feeling he could not be tried; four others were convinced of his innocence. Probably half of them felt that the whole proceeding was a stupid business. Under the circumstances it was not surprising that the accusers saw the shabby nature of their accusation, and, with what grace they could muster, practically backed out of the transaction. Mr. Judge's dignity, frankness, and discretion turned the tables against his accusers. He denied the truth of the charges, protested that he could not be officially tried for his acts as an individual, but averred his readiness to produce actual proofs of his intercourse with Mahatmas. The opposition was forced to admit the legality of his position, and was naturally inclined to refrain from letting him produce his evidence on the last point. The Judicial Committee of July 10 adjourned after arriving at the de-

cision that it had no jurisdiction to inquire into the charges. Col. Olcott reinstated Mr. Judge in his office of Vice-President of the Society.

Two days thereafter Mrs. Besant, stung by the failure of the procedure against Judge, read a full statement of her side of the case before the British-European Sections' Convention (the "trial" having been set to antedate the annual meeting by a few days). She said in one place, after telling how messages may be received in a variety of ways from invisible Intelligences,

"Any good medium may be used for precipitating messages by any of the varied entities in the occult world; and the outcome of these proceedings will be, I hope, to put an end to the craze for receiving letters and messages, which are more likely to be sublunary or human in their origin than superhuman, and to throw people back on the evolution of their own spiritual nature, by which alone they can be safely guided through the mazes of the superphysical world."

Nowhere, perhaps, is she truer to the cause of Blavatskian Spiritualism, or the true occult and sacred science of the Ancient Wisdom, than in this utterance; and nowhere are the contrasting aims of Theosophy and Spiritism so clearly delineated. She ended by asking Judge's pardon for any pain she may have given him in trying to do her duty.

A plan had been agreed upon that both accuser and accused should issue statements elucidating their positions. Mr. Judge gave his review of the case. He repeated his denial of having forged the names or writing of the Masters; he readmitted having received what he regarded as genuine letters from them; he declared himself to be an agent of the said Masters, but repudiated the claim that he was their only channel-that communication with them was "open to any human being who, by endeavoring to serve mankind, affords the necessary conditions." He agreed that there were diverse methods of receiving messages

from higher intelligences, but that the genuineness of such communications must be tested by the inner subjective evidences in each case. He ended by admitting his human fallibility and forgiving "anyone who may be thought to have injured or tried to injure me."

The questions raised in the "Judge Case" are of great significance, for they are the key to most of the controversial history of the Theosophical movement. The question of alleged messages from the High Ones has been the opening wedge of most of the schisms of the cult. This should be kept in mind during the remaining sections of the history.

It is of interest to note that in her editorial in Lucifer following the dismissal of the case, Mrs. Besant ends with the statement that the disturbance caused by her bringing the charges against Mr. Judge will have been of value to the Society in having aired and settled the point at issue, that the precipitation of a letter gives it no authoritative character; and she adds that the Society would now be freer from "credulity and superstition, two of the deadliest foes of a true spiritual movement." Her critics have reminded her since that those were precisely the things that H.P.B. and Judge had tried to impress on Theosophic students from time to time. The episode did not clear the air of one persistent obsession for which Madame Blavatsky might, on Theosophic reasoning, be held karmically responsible to some extent. It was now understood, in theory at least, that "occult" phenomena, genuine or false, mediumistic or adept, formed no part of the legitimate pursuit of the Theosophical Society.

Madame Blavatsky had insisted upon this fact, yet the very weight of interest aroused by her own performances in that line exerted its natural gravitational force.

Another outgrowth of the case was the realization "that occult phenomena cannot in the present state of human evolution be proved . . . in the same sense and to the same extent that physical phenomena can be proved."7

They must continue to rest on subjective evidence. The trial threw the whole case for the Mahatmas, their superior teachings, their hierarchical position, back into the locale of faith and inner sanction. Here such ideas had always been kept in antiquity. The West, true to mechanistic instinct, tried to "prove" them empirically.

At any rate, Madame Blavatsky had, in the Preliminary Memorandum sent out at the time of the formation of the Esoteric Section, expressly declared that in the higher section "the student will not be taught how to produce physical phenomena, nor will any magical powers be allowed to develop in him,"-that a mastery of self, ethically and psychologically, was the antecedent condition. If Judge or any other already had phenomenal abilities, their use must be subordinated to the needs of morality and unselfishness. One of the ethical prescriptions of the Esoteric Section itself was that no member should attack another. One was forbidden to bring charges against a fellow member or to hold suspicious or malevolent feelings towards him. Mrs. Besant in opposing Judge was charged with violating these rules though her opposition was not, strictly speaking, personal.

But the storm, temporarily lulled, was to rage again. Some wounded feelings and sullen resentments were not fully allayed. In October, 1894, the London Westminster Gazette commenced a series of articles by Edmund Garrett entitled "Isis Very Much Unveiled: The Story of the Great Mahatmic Hoax." It was an attempt to expose Madame Blavatsky's and Mr. Judge's alleged invention of the whole Mahatmic structure. His material had been furnished him by Mr. W. R. Old,

one of Col. Olcott's sub-editors on the Theosophist, who was nursing a grudge for having been suspended from the Esoteric Section by Mrs. Besant for violation of his pledge of secrecy. With a mass of authentic data in his hand, Mr. Garrett made a vicious assault upon Theosophy and its Society. The attack stimulated the anti-Judge faction into renewed hostility, and they rushed again to the fray. On his part Judge, believing Mrs. Besant had violated her pledges to the Esoteric Section, by virtue of his authority as H.P.B.'s American representative in that organization, summarily deposed Mrs. Besant from her joint-headship with him. In his written notice to that effect, he stated that Mrs. Besant had fallen under the influence of minds hostile to the "tradition clustering around the work of H.P.B.," and named Chakravarti as the chief culprit. Judge in this connection reminded all concerned of the "Prayag Letter" (one sent to Mr. Sinnett in 1881 by Master K.H.) in which the Master himself had warned the Allahabad Lodge (the branch in which Sinnett, Hume, and Chakravarti were leading members), of the false occultism in the Brahmanical teachings. Judge set forth the conflict of two views in the Theosophical Society regarding the movement itself. The first one, implanted by H.P.B. herself, was that Theosophy is a body of eternal knowledge, unchanging, known of old, held in custody by Adept Guardians, of whom H.P.B. was the responsible and accredited agent in the world for her century. The other was that the whole teaching was itself a growth, a development, and as such had taken gradual shape as changing circumstances had led Madame Blavatsky onward to new vistas. He, Judge, was the official upholder of the first view, and would use his proxy from Madame Blavatsky to maintain her tradition. If his mentor could be proven false in one matter, doubt would be thrown upon all her work. Either Theosophy and its promulgator were what she said they were, or the Society might as well close its doors.

Mrs. Besant saw the order dismissing her from the Esoteric Section office, but refused to heed it. Instead of resigning she called upon loyal members to follow her. Her action thus split the Esoteric Section organization. She sent out a circular stating that not only had Madame Blavatsky made her the Chief Secretary of the Inner Group and Recorder of the Teachings, but had named her as her "Successor." She thus stood out against Judge's authority and proceeded to lay plans to drive him out of the Society. She made a journey to Australia and thence to India in the fall of 1894, and at the annual holiday Convention in India she and Olcott managed to swing the whole body of delegates against Judge, on the old charge of sending out forged Mahatma messages. He was vilified openly by a dozen orators, and a resolution was carried upon Col. Olcott to demand his resignation from the Vice-Presidency or his expulsion from the Society. Judge's first response was a statement that he could not reply to the charges because they had never been given to him. He refused to resign from the Vice-Presidency.

In April of 1895 the Convention of the American Section was held at Boston. With practical unanimity it upheld Mr. Judge. It went further. A resolution presented by Mr. C. A. Griscom, Jr., urged that the American Section declare its autonomy and take a new name, The Theosophical Society in America. The resolution was carried by a vote of nine to one and a new organization effected. A fraternal greeting, with a pledge of solidarity in the movement, was drawn up and sent to the Convention of the European Section then meeting. Judge was elected President. This act placed the Movement as paramount in importance to the Society. (A minority faction remained true to the old organization, and this became later the nucleus of the restored American Section of the Theosophical Society, now the largest numerical body.)

In London the overtures of the new American autonomous body were coldly received by the European Convention, dominated by Mrs. Besant. Olcott declared the greeting out of order, but it was read and "laid on the table." It amounted to

an actual rejection of the overtures. The step taken by the American Section was spoken of as "secession."

The new organization in the United States got quietly to work, but Mr. Judge had been broken in health by the long struggle and his death came on March 21, 1896. He had conducted himself, all the while he was the target of the heavy attacks against his integrity, with a dignity, a lack of rancor, and a poise which in the light of later developments stand out in marked contrast to the fury and venom exhibited by his assailants. Whatever the merit or demerit of his position in the Theosophic movement, the fact is that he adhered with firm loyalty to his avowed principles of belief and conduct. He was at least free from that inconstancy to program or to theory which has since been so conspicuous a characteristic of Theosophic leadership. It is of record that Mr. Sinnett later "forgave" him, and that Mrs. Besant and Col. Olcott repented of having persecuted him on personal charges to the detriment of Theosophical practice.

His death plunged Theosophy in America into its darkest days. It precipitated a period marked not so much by attacks from outside as by increasing dissensions and divergences within the ranks. Although Mrs. Katherine Tingley came forward almost immediately as Outer Head and successor to Judge, she did not long command the support and esteem of American Theosophists which he had enjoyed.

One after another, small groups refused to follow her and established themselves as independent organizations, until the ranks were decimated by separate societies, each claiming to be the embodiment of true Theosophy, and each tracing its lineage to Madame Blavatsky. From this condition Theosophy in America has not yet recovered; consequently, it remains for us to describe the origins and aims of these various groups, leaving it to the reason of the reader and to the logic of history to decide the issues involved. The records of the time are none too clear, and the literature highly controversial. Since many of the documents of the Esoteric Section are necessarily secret, and since many of the issues are centered in personalities, it is impossible to get a clear picture of the events without an intimate acquaintance with the temperaments, the incidental circumstances, and the petty details which gave color and direction to the theoretical issues debated on paper and platform.

Immediately upon Judge's death a group of leading Theosophists in New York City, with Mr. E. T. Hargrove as an active spirit, called meetings as early as March 29 to consider a course of action. Mr. Hargrove read a statement to the effect that Mr. Judge had not left his followers without guidance; that among his private papers directions had been found as to successorship and future leadership; and that the form of assistance which Judge had enjoyed from the Hierarchy would be continued to them. This announcement was signed by E. T. Hargrove, James M. Pryse, Joseph H. Fussell, H. T. Patterson, Claude Falls Wright, Genevieve L. Griscom, C. A. Griscom, Jr., and E. Aug. Neresheimer, all people of character and prominence. Circulars and announcements were repeatedly issued to the membership from this group in New York, intimating that Mr. Judge's wishes concerning his successor were known and would be carried out.8 It was also announced that the Masters had imposed a condition, namely, that the name of the new head must be withheld for a year. Presumably this was to be a trial period during which the new leader was to test his abilities and readiness to assume the heavy responsibilities borne by Judge. Veiled references were made to him under the name of "Promise." It was stated that "a new light had gone out from the Lodge," and that this "Promise" was a person of psychic gifts and the recipient of messages from the Masters. From a speech made by Mrs. Tingley at this time we quote:

"Today the needs of humanity are embodied in one great call: 'Oh God, my God, is there no help for us?' All people should heed the call of the Master and help to belt the world within the compass of the 'cable-tow' of the crusaders, for in their force is the quality of the 'golden promise'-the Light of the Lodge. It will radiate throughout the world, and with the aid of the widow's mite will make perfect the Master's plan."

At the end of April, 1896, the Annual Convention of the Theosophical Society in America met in New York City. Mr. Hargrove was elected President of the organization. The Path was changed to Theosophy. Mrs. Tingley was present and spoke. She announced plans for founding a "School for the Revival of the Lost Mysteries of Antiquity." Money was contributed liberally, and the leaders went ahead with their plans for the expansion of the movement.

Suddenly, on May 17, Mrs. Tingley announced to her associates that she had been informed that the New York press had discovered that she was the person referred to as the new Outer Head, and that they would publish the news the next day. To avoid such a "leak," Mr. Hargrove, as President of the Society, that morning anticipated the newspapers and made a public announcement to the effect that Mrs. Tingley had been designated as Judge's successor. On the following morning, May 18, 1896, a long article appeared in the New York Tribune on the subject.
Thus the safeguard of anonymity, originally prescribed as a condition of Mrs. Tingley's appointment, was abrogated.

Meanwhile the leaders had announced their plans for a "Crusade" to carry the message of Theosophy around the world and more especially to vindicate the strength and authenticity of Judge's American Society before the eyes of Theosophists in Europe and India. Accordingly in June Mrs. Tingley, Mr.
Hargrove, Mr. and Mrs. Claude F. Wright, Mr. Pierce, and two or three others, set sail for a trip around the world. They made numerous addresses at various points en route defending their cause. They also completed plans for the establishment of the School for the Revival of the Lost Mysteries of Antiquity at Point Loma, California, and on the return voyage Mrs. Tingley laid the corner-stone of the school. Returning to New York early in 1897, they began the task of consolidating and organizing "The Universal Brotherhood."
But dissension arose almost immediately after their return from the "Crusade." A group of the leaders became increasingly suspicious that Mrs. Tingley's policies and practices were not in line with those established by Judge. The forces of ambition and jealousy also entered into the scene. Whatever the deeper issues were, the external friction came to a head in the dispute between Mrs. Keightley and Mr. Neresheimer over the control of the publishing business and the editorial policy of the magazine, Theosophy. Mr. Neresheimer was supported by Mrs. Tingley, whereas Mrs. Keightley, Mr. Hargrove, and their friends, took a firm stand against him. As a result of this disagreement, Mr. Hargrove resigned the presidency of the Theosophical Society in America, and Dr. Keightley resigned the presidency of the affiliated Theosophical Society in England. In January, 1898, Mrs. Tingley called representatives of the Theosophical Society from different parts of the United States to her home, and they drew up and adopted the Constitution of The Universal Brotherhood Organization. Meanwhile some of the friends of Mr. Hargrove proposed a rival plan calling for the election of Mr. Hargrove as President and Mrs. Tingley as "Corresponding Secretary" (H.P.B.'s former title). But Mrs. Tingley repudiated this scheme and in return Mr. Hargrove and his friends rejected Mrs. Tingley's leadership.

At the Annual Convention in Chicago, February, 1898, the whole issue was decided. Mrs. Tingley proceeded aggressively with her plans for The Universal

Brotherhood, which she wished to absorb the Theosophic Society in America. Mr. Hargrove and his friends, on the other hand, refused to recognize the legitimacy of the new organization. When the issue was put to a vote, over ninety per cent of the delegates followed Mrs. Tingley.

Thereupon Mr. Hargrove and his associates withdrew with a few dozen delegates to another hall, declared the action of the majority to be illegal, and agreed to maintain the Theosophical Society as a distinct body. A month later they formally announced Mrs. Tingley's removal as Outer Head on the grounds that by slandering fellow members she had violated her vows and conducted her organization on policies unworthy of Theosophy.9 Several E.S.T. pamphlets were issued explaining the causes of their repudiation of Mrs. Tingley and incidentally throwing additional light on the circumstances of Mrs. Tingley's coming into power. This body then published The Theosophical Forum, in which it further defined its stand and claimed to be the legitimate continuation of Judge's work and organization. Legal proceedings were begun to recover the membership lists and archives of the Society from The Universal Brother-

hood, but this move was unsuccessful. During the next few months several hundred Theosophists expressed their adherence to this Society. This group, now known simply as The Theosophical Society, with headquarters in the New York Branch, continues to carry on its work through local branches. It publishes The Theosophic Quarterly, to which Mrs. Charles Johnston has contributed extensively. It naturally has its own Esoteric Section and has made many scholarly contributions to Theosophic research and literature. True to the spirit of Judge, it has emphasized Western rather than Oriental esoteric traditions, emphasizing the mystic elements in Christianity. It venerates the wisdom of the Master, Jesus, and some of the Christian Saints, but it has no ecclesiastical tendencies. It refuses to commit its members to any Theosophic creed, to any official pronouncements on the subject of "phenomena," or in general to any matters which concern personalities and personal beliefs. Its meetings are devoted largely to study, discussion, and meditation upon the writings of H.P.B. and other Theosophic classics. It remains a small but distinguished group.

After the Chicago Convention of 1898, the vast majority of American Theosophists followed Mrs. Tingley in The Universal Brotherhood and Theosophical Society, with headquarters at Point Loma. Its official organ, The Searchlight, conducted a vigorous campaign and under the leadership of Mrs. Tingley, the organization flourished for several years. Through Mr. A. G. Spalding, of baseball fame, Ex- Secretary of the Treasury Lyman J. Gage, and others, sufficient funds were secured to establish permanent headquarters at Point Loma, a beautiful site overlooking the Pacific. The place became a colony, where new ventures in the education of children according to Theosophic ideas were embarked on, with results said to be exceptional. In 1900 the Râja-Yoga School was founded which was later expanded into the Theosophical University. An Aryan Memorial Temple was erected, now known as the Temple of Peace; and a Greek theatre was built, the first in the country, where Greek and Shakespearean dramas have been performed. The Headquarters are now conducted under the direction of Dr.

Gottfried de Purucker and Mr. J. H. Fussell, both of whom were associated with Mrs. Tingley from 1898.

Mrs. Tingley lived until July 11, 1929, when her death was announced from Visingso, Sweden, where she had gone to a Theosophic community to recover from an automobile accident suffered in Germany.10 She had done much work of a humanitarian nature. Besides the School of Antiquity at Point Loma she had founded an International Brotherhood League, a summer home for children at

Spring Valley, New York, and a home for orphan children at Buffalo. She had opened three schools in Cuba.

Another group of Theosophists in 1899 drifted into "The Temple of the People," sponsored by Dr. W. H. Dower and Frances J. Meyers, of Syracuse, New York.
Messages coming through a Mrs. Francia A. La Due, known mediumistically as "Blue Star," were its inspiration until her death in 1923. A remnant of this group is established in a colony at Halcyon, California.

In 1899 another offshoot came to growth in "The Theosophical Society of New York," which is to be distinguished from "The New York Branch of the Theosophical Society" mentioned above. Dr. H. H. Salisbury, long a friend of Mr. Judge, Mr. Donald Nicholson, editor of the New York Tribune, also a friend of Judge and H.P.B., and Mr. Harold W. Percival, headed a group which numbered Dr. Alexander Wilder and Mrs. Laura Langford among its adherents. Mr. Percival for years edited a successful magazine, The Word.

Dr. J. D. Buck, of Cincinnati, an early member of the American Section and devoted supporter of Judge, later threw his strong influence on the side of the claims of a Mr. Richardson-known as "T.K."-and Mrs. Florence Huntley, to represent the Masters. Some of his friends went with him in this allegiance, but the exposure of "T.K." undermined his movement and he died shortly afterward.

Mrs. Alice L. Cleather, one of the inner group of students around Madame Blavatsky during the years preceding her death, formed a "Blavatsky Association," organized to combat the successorship of Mrs. Besant in particular. It was declared that Mr. Judge had fallen under the deception of Mrs. Tingley. Mrs. Cleather wrote three or four books upholding the esoteric character of Madame Blavatsky's mission.

In England Mr. G. R. S. Mead, long co-editor with Mrs. Besant of Lucifer, parted from her after 1907 and founded "The Quest Society," which until recently published The Quest. His Society has a highly respectable membership and devotes its energies to comparative religion and psychical research. Mr. Mead is most active in the scholarly activities of the Society.

In California, home of many cults, Mr. Max Heindel, originally a Theosophist, launched later a Rosicrucian Society, and published a valuable work, Rosicrucian Cosmo-Conception. His association maintains headquarters at Oceanside, California, and following his death his wife has continued the direction of its activities.

Likewise in California Mr. Robert Crosbie established the parent United Lodge of Theosophists at Los Angeles in 1909. Mr. Crosbie adhered to the conviction that Mr. Judge alone worked in the true direction of H.P.B.'s movement, and he gave to his organization the task of perpetuating the original teaching of Blavatskian Theosophy, as promulgated by Judge. He founded the periodical Theosophy, a revival of The Path. He labored to restore the unique status of
H.P.B. and Judge as esoteric teachers, and his society thus became a "drift back to source." As H.P.B. herself had looked after the spiritual side of the movement, regarding that as more important than

its outward organization, so the United Lodge of Theosophists has discounted the value of organization and of personalities in it. The names of the speakers are usually not attached to lecture announcements, nor those of authors to books and articles. The interests of the association are primarily in Theosophy and the movement, not in any Society; in Theosophic truth, not in any individual expression of it. A spirit of accord binds together various Lodges, isolated groups and scattered

associates throughout the United States, and in recent years there has been marked growth, as the disturbances in the larger "Besant" section drove many of its old adherents into the U.L.T. The defection of Mr. P. B. Wadia, eloquent Hindu Theosophist, from the Besant fold and his affiliation with the United Lodge in 1922, furnished no small impetus to the latter's increased power. Mr. John Garrigues, of Los Angeles, has devoted indefatigable energy to the work of this body, and few persons have a wider acquaintance with the facts of Theosophic history than he. Residing in New York until 1930, he exerted a pronounced influence in the councils of the U.L.T. throughout the country.

In Washington, D.C., there has been published for many years by Mr. H. N. Stokes, a leaflet called The Oriental Esoteric Library Critic. Mr. Stokes conducts a circulating library of occult and Theosophic books, but finds time in addition to edit his diminutive sheet, which has been a veritable thorn in the flesh of the Besant leadership for many years. He seizes upon every inconsistency in the statements or policies of the Besant-Leadbeater-Wedgewood hegemony and subjects it to critical analysis. Many Theosophists tolerate his belligerent spirit and strong language for the sake of the facts he adduces, which have usually great pertinence to Theosophic affairs. He is particularly hostile to the developments of Neo-Theosophy under the Besant and Leadbeater régime, and above all to the institution of the Liberal Catholic Church as a Theosophic appanage.

As a result of the great impetus given by the Theosophical movement, scores of organizations with aims mystic, occult, divine, spiritual, Oriental, astrological, fraternal, and inspirational, have sprung up on all sides, to emphasize one or another aspect of the teaching, real or fancied. A reference to Hartmann's Who's Who in Occult, Psychic, and Spiritual Realms will astonish one with the number and diversified character of these bodies. Their existence marks one of the surprising phenomena of our contemporary religious life.

It remains to sketch with the greatest brevity the history since 1896 of the large international body of the Theosophical Society over which Mrs. Annie Besant has presided since 1907.

It will be recalled that when in Boston in 1895 the American Section, out of loyalty to its leader, Judge, "seceded" from the parent organization and became autonomous, a minority dissented from the action of the Convention and remained in adherence to Col. Olcott's Society. Prominent in this party were Dr. Mary Weeks Burnett, Mr. Alexander Fullerton, Dr. La Pierre, and others. This faction became the nucleus around which, as the larger Judge group disintegrated, gradual accretions of strength materialized. This was in part due to the prestige which officialdom and regularity carries with it, and in part to the position and prominence of Col. Olcott and the great influence wielded by Mrs. Besant. In a few years it became numerically far the strongest group, and today includes some ninety per cent of American Theosophical membership.

After Judge passed from the scene, Col. Olcott and Mrs. Besant could devote their undivided energies to Theosophic propaganda, both in the Society at large and in the Esoteric Section, so that the movement expanded rapidly in all parts of the world. Charters were given to National Sections in most of the countries on the map. The Society flourished outwardly and organically. The question as to whether it held true to its original spirit and purpose is of course a debatable one. It was at this time that the beginnings of the drift toward those later presentations of Theosophical teaching which have come to be known as Neo- Theosophy were becoming manifest. Mrs. Besant and Mr. Leadbeater stood out unrivalled as the literary exponents and formulators of Theosophy. Their

statements were hailed with as much respect and authority as those of Madame Blavatsky in the earlier days. Both of them wrote assiduously and lectured with great frequency, and their publications rapidly began to supplant all other works on the Theosophic shelves. With The Ancient Wisdom, A Study in Consciousness, and Esoteric Christianity Mrs. Besant began a literary output which has been rarely matched in volume. Some eighty or more works now stand in her name. Mr. Leadbeater's total may reach twenty, but they are mostly of a more pretentious character than Mrs. Besant's, being accounts of his clairvoyant investigations into the nature and history of the world and man. His works had to do mostly with subjects connected with the Third Object of the Society, the psychic powers latent in man. Mrs. Besant touched alike on all three of the objects, not neglecting the ethical aspects of Theosophy, which she emphasized in such works as The Path of Discipleship and In The Outer Court. Predominantly under the influence of these two leaders the power of Theosophy spread widely in the world.

Mr. Leadbeater was one of the participants with Mr. Sinnett and others in occult investigations carried on in the London Lodge, an autonomous group not fully in sympathy with some phases of Madame Blavatsky's work. He developed, as was reported, great psychic abilities, as the result of which, notwithstanding his frequent disclaiming of occult authority, he exercised great influence over the thought of a large number of members of the Society. His studies and his books reflected the attitude of "scientific common sense." He claims to have brought the phenomena of the super-physical realms of life, of the astral and the mental plane, of the future disembodied life, and of the past and future of this and other spheres, under his direct clairvoyant gaze. He wrote elaborate descriptions of these things in a style of simplicity and clearness. He asserted that such powers enabled one to review any event in the past history of the race, inasmuch as all that ever happened is imprinted indelibly on the substance of the Astral Light or the Akasha, and the psychic faculties of trained occultists permit them to bring these pictures under observation. With the same faculties he asserted his ability to investigate the facts of nature in both her realms of the infinite and the infinitesimal. Hence he explored the nature of the atom, its electrons and its whorls, and in collaboration with Mrs. Besant, who was alleged also to possess high psychic powers, published a work entitled Occult Chemistry. For years he stood as perhaps the world's greatest "seer," and in books dealing with Clairvoyance, Dreams, The Astral Plane, Some Glimpses of Occultism, The Inner Life, The Hidden Side of Things, Man: Whence, How and Whither, he labored to particularize and complement Madame Blavatsky's sweeping outline of cosmic evolution and human character, as given in The Secret Doctrine. Certain schools of his critics assert flatly that he has only succeeded in vitiating her original presentation. Two years ago The Canadian Theosophist, a magazine published under the editorship of Mr. Albert Smythe at Toronto, published a series of articles in which parallel passages from the writings of Madame Blavatsky and the Mahatma Letters on one side, and from the books of Mrs. Besant, Mr. Leadbeater, Mr. C. Jinarajadasa, on the other, give specific evidence bearing on the claims of perversion of the original theories by those whom they call Neo-Theosophists. The articles indicate wide deviations, in some cases complete reversal, made by the later interpreters from the fundamental statements of the Russian Messenger and her Overlords. The differences concern such matters as the personality of God, the historicity of Jesus, his identity as an individual or a principle, the desirability of churches, priestcraft and religious ceremonial, the genuineness of an apostolic succession, and a vicarious atonement, the authority of Sacraments, the nature and nomenclature of the seven planes of man's constitution, the planetary chains, the monad, the course of evolution, and many other important phases of Theosophic doctrine. This exhaustive research has made it apparent that the

later exponents have allowed themselves to depart in many important points from the teachings of H.P.B.11

Whatever may be the causes operating to influence their intellectual developments, they have succeeded in giving Theosophy a somewhat different direction which, on the whole, has emphasized the religious temper and content of its doctrines. It should be added that these criticisms are not representative of the great majority of followers of the movement, who regard the later elaborations from fundamentals as both logical and desirable.

For years Mr. Leadbeater was looked upon as the genuine link between the Society and its Mahatmic Wardens, and his utterances were received as law and authority by members of the organization from the President downward. But at the height of his influence in 1906 came charges of privately teaching to boys under his care sexual practices similar to some of those practiced in certain Hindu temple rites. They cleft through the ranks of the Society like a bolt of lightning.

Mrs. Besant, horrified, asked for his resignation. Mr. Leadbeater admitted the charges, explained his occult and hygienic reasons for his instruction, and resigned. But not many months had passed before Mrs. Besant reversed her position and began a campaign to restore Mr. Leadbeater to fellowship and good repute, she having received from him a promise to discontinue such teaching.

Col. Olcott had conducted an inquiry at London, and the disclosure probably hastened the aging President's death, though the main contributing cause was an accident on board ship. He died early in 1907, and the event caused a conflict over the matter of succession. It was noised about Adyar, Madras, where his death occurred, that there had been a visitation of a number of the Masters at the bedside of the dying President-Founder and that the succession had there been indicated. The extraordinary occurrence was said to have been witnessed by those present in the death chamber, who were Mrs. Besant, Mrs. Marie Russak Hotchener, and two or three others. As the matter is one of considerable moment in the history of the Theosophical Society, I take the liberty to quote several sentences from a personal letter which Mrs. Hotchener wrote me from Los Angeles under date of August 3, 1915, relative to the event:

"I was present when the Masters came to Col. Olcott. There was no possibility of hallucination, for too many things occurred physically which could be proven. I did some writing even, and did two or three things I was told to do, and besides the whole visit of the Masters to Colonel Olcott was to help him and to better the future of the Society. I also saw the Master lift Colonel from the floor where he had prostrated himself as HIS feet, and put him on the bed as though the Colonel were a baby. Master M. (Morya) did it, who is seven feet tall. When the Doctor came a few minutes later (when the Masters had gone) he scolded the nurse and myself for the fact that Colonel had been out of bed-his heart and condition of the body showed it and the terrible excitement. We were told of things which were afterwards proven and which none of us knew at the time; whole sentences were quoted from the Master's letters to H.P.B. which none of us had seen, and objects mentioned the existence of which none of us knew, and many other things. Then, too, the Colonel had seen the Masters with H.P.B. and there was no possibility of his being deceived. Their coming saved the Society from going into an era of the 'letter of the law' dominating completely the spirit, and both Mr. Leadbeater and Mrs. Besant have confirmed their coming and in their physical bodies. There is sufficient proof, but I could not write it all now."

The witnesses affirmed that the Masters had designated Mrs. Besant as the successor of Col. Olcott, as she was already that of H.P.B. This demonstration

of the living interest of the Masters in the affairs of the Society12 vitally enhanced Mrs. Besant's prestige, and as she was already in control of the "throbbing heart of the Theosophical Society," viz., the Esoteric Section, the ensuing world-wide election of a new President, held in 1907, could have but one result. She had practically no opposition, and has been re-elected at intervals since that time. Mr. Leadbeater was restored soon after these events, and the exposition of the major phases of the Neo-Theosophy began in earnest. Many old and loyal members were forced out by the advent of one disagreeable situation or utterance after another, as they saw the old teachings warped or strangely reinterpreted; but the new interest brought in others in larger numbers. Perhaps the most spectacular of all Mrs. Besant's enterprises was inaugurated in 1909-- the formation of The Order of the Star in the East, for spreading the idea, which she and Mr. Leadbeater had promulgated, of the approaching manifestation of the Lord Maitreya as the World Teacher. The basis of her grandiose scheme was Mr. Leadbeater's psychic discovery that the very body which the Lord was to occupy during the years of His coming earthly sojourn was already among them in the person of one Jiddu Krishnamurti, a fine young Brahmin, then in his early 'teens. Mrs. Besant forthwith legally adopted the youth, aided with his education, part of which was gained in England, and successfully resisted a law- suit of the boy's father to regain control of him. She then exploited him before the world as the "vehicle" of the coming World Teacher. An abundance of effective publicity was gained, if nothing more substantial. Several times the lad's body seemed to have been obsessed by an overshadowing presence, and his lips at such times spoke unwonted words of wisdom. The young man was elevated to the headship of the Order of the Star in the East; a neat magazine, The Herald of the Star, was established for propaganda purposes, and the thousands of Theosophists and some outsiders who followed Mrs. Besant in this new field were worked up to a high pitch of hushed expectancy of the dénouement. Krishnamurti's sponsors had originally stated that the spirit of the Great Lord could be expected to use the body of the young Hindu fully in some fifteen or twenty-five years, but on the occasion of the visit of Mrs. Besant and the youth to America in August of 1926, the announcement was made that the consummation of the divine event was certain to be delayed no longer than Christmas of that year. The affable young man bravely carried the mantle of near-divinity during all the intervening years; but finally in the course of the year 1929, speaking at a meeting of the followers of his cult at their European headquarters at Ommen, in Holland, he rather suddenly executed what he had intimated to some of his friends, who had noted his utterances against organizations for spiritual purposes, by dissolving the Order of the Star, by refusing to be regarded as an authority, and retaining for himself only the humble rôle of spiritual teacher. In spite of the exalted position gratuitously foisted upon him, he had evidently grown restive under Mrs. Besant's dominance. His action has been generally interpreted as a courageous assertion of his independence of mind and spirit. By it he has apparently gained rather than lost prestige. His public appearances continue to draw large audiences which express sympathy with his aims and react kindly to the appeal of his personality and spiritual cast of mind. Mrs. Besant was left to find devices of her own to explain the twenty-year-long fiasco. She has explained that Mr. Krishnamurti is a teacher in his own right.

In the early days of the Krishnamurti agitation, probably about 1912, Mr. Leadbeater published in serial form the results of a pretentious clairvoyant investigation, being no less than an account in much detail of the last forty reincarnations of the Indian lad in various nations including the Atlantean countries, with the concurrent lives of some score or more of individuals, nearly all prominent then in the Theosophical Society, who had been keeping in the same group life after life down through the ages. His work was styled The

Lives of Alcyone, the latter appellation having been given to Krishnamurti as his true or cosmic name.13

About 1914 Mrs. Marie Russak was commissioned to introduce a ritualistic order within the Theosophic Society and in the course of the next two or three years she installed some twenty or more chapters of an organization given the name of "The Temple of the Rosy Cross." An elaborate regalia was required and a ceremonial was devised which a member of the Masonic body told the author equalled in beauty and dignity anything he was conversant with in the higher degrees of Masonry. The initiates took a solemn pledge to do nothing contrary to the interests of their Higher Selves and the ceremonies were said to have been attended with elevated types of spiritual experience. Great emphasis was laid on the "magnetic purity" of everything handled by the officiants. Powerful sublimations of spiritual forces were thought to be operative through the instrumentality of the ritual. Mrs. Russak had proved to be an efficient organizer and the "Temple" had apparently done much to spiritualize the appeal of Theosophy. But suddenly after an existence of about three years the organization was declared at an end, for reasons never given out frankly to the membership.

Coincident with the "Alcyone" campaign a movement within the Theosophical Society was launched, again actuated by Mr. Leadbeater's mystic observations, that went in direct contradiction to Madame Blavatsky's warnings and prognostications on the subject of religious sectarianism. This was the establishment of "The Old Catholic Church" (later changed to "The Liberal Catholic Church") as carrying the true apostolic succession from the original non-Roman Catholic Church, the primitive Christian Church. The link of succession brought down from the early Middle Ages was picked up in Holland in the remnants of the Old Catholic Church still lingering there, and the first Bishop consecrated from the old line was Mr. James I. Wedgewood, English Theosophist. He in turn anointed Mr. Leadbeater, who thus received the title of Bishop, by which he is now known. It was declared that the true unction of the original consecration was thus transmitted down to the present and reawakened to new virility in Theosophic hands. Mr. Leadbeater wrote The Science of the Sacraments to give a new and living potency to ritual through occult science, and the new Church was declared to be the felicitous channel of expression for such Theosophists as needed the uplifting virtue of a dynamic ceremonial. The teachings of Theosophy might be intellectually satisfying; the Liberal Catholic Church would round out the Theosophic life by providing for the nourishment of the aesthetic and emotional nature, through means of white-magical potency. Mr. Leadbeater was more Catholic than any Roman in his claims of marvelous efficacy in the performance of the rituals. His pictures of the congregational thought- forms, the aggregate vibrational energies set in motion by devotion, which he says take definite shapes and hover over the edifice during a service, are daring and original.14

Agitation over Mr. Leadbeater's sex ideas cropped out at intervals, and in 1922 there was a renewed stir over this subject when a Mr. Martyn, of Sydney, Australia, a Theosophist of high standing, gave out a letter in which he recounted certain incidents which he alleged took place while Mr. Leadbeater was a guest in his home some time before.

There were charges and denials; and it should in fairness be said that Mr. Leadbeater had confided to personal friends that through his clairvoyant vision he was enabled to discern that much suffering could be saved the boys later on in their lives if some of the pent-up sexual energies could be given vent in the way he prescribed. He asserted that the "bad Karma" of such sex expression would

be confined to the boys themselves and easily lived down, whereas otherwise they would be led to actions which would involve them in the sex Karma of others.

Some Theosophists, including one or two medical men and women, have gone on record as declaring that the principles underlying Mr. Leadbeater's sexual philosophy in this particular might well save the world some of the misery and evil that arises from improper understanding of the issues involved. Mrs. Besant herself may have seen some such saving grace in the situation, which would account for her sudden and definite swing to Mr. Leadbeater's support following her first outraged sensibilities. The issue is not at present a live one.

Certainly Mr. Leadbeater's ideas on sex, though tolerated by some, are to be regarded as generally repudiated by the vast majority of Theosophists.

Later Theosophical leadership in America passed successively through the hands of Dr. Weller Van Hook, of Chicago, Mr. A. P. Warrington, an attorney from Virginia and Mr. L. W. Rogers, a capable business executive, who is now the President of the large American Section. It was in Mr. Warrington's régime that the Theosophical settlement, under the name of Krotona, was located in Hollywood, Los Angeles, California. This settlement was the outcome of a plan conceived by Mr. Warrington quite apart from any Theosophical connection, and it was not until after the leaders of the movement learned of the plan that it was determined to carry it out in the interest of

Theosophists. After an exhaustive search of the South and the West for a suitable site, covering a period of five years or more,15 it was finally decided to locate in California; acreage was secured in the Hollywood hills, some beautiful buildings erected, and the Theosophical Headquarters was transferred from Chicago. The Headquarters has since been transferred to Wheaton, Illinois, a suburb of Chicago, for the advantage of a centralized location; and the Krotona settlement has been removed to a beautiful site in Ojai Valley where it now flourishes and is known as Krotona, as before. Here institute courses in Theosophy and related subjects are given and headquarters are maintained for the E.S. in the Western Hemisphere.16

When Mrs. Besant's "Karma" (as Theosophists phrase it) took her to India, she saw India moving towards the fulfilment of her vision and (as has been recently publicly asserted) the wish of the Himalayan Adepts, in the constituting of India as a Dominion of the British Commonwealth. The Theosophical headquarters at Adyar, in Madras, has long been recognized as a center of educational reform in India, and of propaganda for the modern revival of Hindu painting in the oriental manner.

Dr. Besant, still a prominent figure, is advancing into the eighties, and Mr. Leadbeater, too, is aging. What direction the course of future Theosophic activity will take when these two dominant figures have been withdrawn, is matter for current speculation. Their policies have alienated some of the staunchest early adherents of Madame Blavatsky and Judge. Already certain trends are discernible which indicate the setting in of a back-to-Blavatsky movement within the ranks of the Theosophical Society. There is already in full swing in the West a tendency to turn to a study of oriental spiritual science, and the contributions of Madame Blavatsky to this field are hardly likely to diminish in importance during the coming decades. She herself prophesied that her

Captain Kidd could be discovered-by clairvoyant means-and utilized to finance the undertaking. A rusty key was actually found in the hands of a skeleton discovered where the clairvoyant described it as lying buried, but evidently the treasure chests were not unearthed. This item was given to the author by one of the group meeting with the clairvoyant at the time.

The Secret Doctrine would be accepted as a text-book on modern science in the twentieth century. Whether that prophecy be fulfilled or not, it is of note that the list of students who are dragging it down from dusty shelves is rapidly increasing at the present writing. Through the efforts mainly of the United Lodge of Theosophists reprints of the original plates of the two (First and Second) volumes have been made, and the book made more readily available to the public. Announcement has also been made from Adyar that H. P. Blavatsky's first draft of volume one of The Secret Doctrine will be published in 1931.17

Some statistics as to book circulation are indicative of the spread of this stream of philosophic thought. Officials at the United Lodge of Theosophists, New York City, supplied data on this score. As the U.L.T. is one of the lesser bodies propagating Theosophy, the figures here given would cover but a minor fraction of the actual circulation of Theosophic literature. In recent years the United Lodge organization has sold:

Ocean of Theosophy, W. Q. Judge 50,000
Translation of the Bhagavad Gita, W. Q. Judge 40,000

The Voice of the Silence, H. P. Blavatsky 30,000
Patanjali's Yoga Sutras, W. Q. Judge. 25,000
Key to Theosophy, H. P. Blavatsky (Original Text).   10,000
Conversations on Theosophy: Pamphlet.   150,000

In addition, there are constantly increasing calls for the two ponderous Blavatskian works, Isis and The Secret Doctrine. These figures may be indicative of the strength of the back-to-Blavatsky movement in Theosophic ranks.

Theosophy is now organized in more than forty countries of the world, with an active enrolled membership of more than fifty thousand. There are said to be some ten thousand members in America with over two hundred forty branches or lodges. Many more thousands have come in and gone out of the Society. Various reasons account for these desertions, but in few cases does relinquishment of formal membership indicate a rejection of Theosophical fundamentals of doctrine. "Once a Theosophist always a Theosophist," is approximately true, pointing to the profound influence which the sweeping cosmology and anthropology of the system exercises over a mind that has once absorbed it. It may then be said that there are several millions of people who have assimilated organically the teachings of Theosophy, and who yield a degree of assent to those formulations.

14

CHAPTER XIII SOME FACTS AND FIGURES

The Theosophical Society is therefore not composed of a band of believers in certain creedal items, but a body of students and seekers. They are travelers on a quest, not the settled dwellers in a creed. They seek to keep fluidic the impulses, intuitions, and propensities of the life of spiritual aspiration, in opposition to the tendency to harden them into dogma.

It is quite impossible for any one to trace with precision the influence of the Theosophic ideology, first, upon the psychology and then upon the conduct of devotees. It can be done only within the limits of general outlines. The one consideration that determines for the Theosophist the value of any thought or act is whether it tends to promote that unification of human mass consciousness along the spiritual ideals pictured in the Ancient Wisdom. This demands of the individual Theosophist that he make of himself, through the gradual expansion of his own consciousness, a channel for the increased flow of high cosmic forces that will work like leaven through the corporate body of humanity and dissipate human misery by the power of light and virtue.

Nevertheless it seems possible to attempt to ascertain the type of people who have been attracted to Theosophy and to examine the special traits and environments, if any such were manifest, which have afforded the most fruitful ground for the seed of the Theosophic faith. Likewise it seems desirable to estimate the influence of Theosophy upon the lives of its votaries. Through the cordial coöperation of the Theosophical Headquarters at Wheaton, Illinois, a questionnaire was sent out.1 Answers were received from nearly seventy per cent of the two hundred addresses-an unusually high return-and they have been carefully tabulated. The names submitted for the mailing of the questionnaire were selected by the President of the American Section of the Theosophical Society, and they must therefore presumably be considered to represent, not all Theosophists, but those of the "Besant Society" exclusively.2

The professions and occupations represented an average cross-section of American life. A few admitted membership in no profession. There were included editor, bishop, railroad executive, corporation president, manufacturer, doctor, lawyer, dentist, teacher, musician, artist, writer, nurse, college tutor, house painter, army officer, insurance agent, draughtsman, carpenter, stenographer, merchant, realtor, business manager, engineer, college secretary, hotel consultant, photographer, advertising writer, Post Office inspector, restaurant proprietor, public accountant, social service worker, veterinary, beauty culturist, oil

operator, jeweler, optometrist, Braille worker, and a college teacher of biology. In the list also were a motor car company president, a newspaper publisher, a life insurance superintendent, an educator, a motion picture producer, a city sanitary engineer, a sheet metal contractor, a factory head, and a railroad comptroller. It may be said that these Theosophists are a picked group and hardly to be regarded as truly typical of the rank and file of the personnel. Whether this be true or no, it appears that Theosophists are representative American people, gaining their livelihood in conventional and respectable ways. The mark of their Theosophy would have to be looked for in their avocations, not in how they earn their living. They seem to be of the typical urban middle class, with few farmers or workers.

The ages of those answering the letters ranged from 21 to 86, with an average at about 45. The average length of time the respondents had been actively affiliated with Theosophy was about 15 years. The replies chanced to come from an exactly equal number of men and women. This proportion is hardly to be explained as a result of artificial selection in the mailing list and is significant in view of the fact that in practically all Christian denominations women considerably outnumber men. Indirect evidence of this fact was revealed by the preponderance of women over men among those who came to Theosophy from the various Christian churches; which was offset by the preponderance of men over women among those who had previously been members of no religious organizations.

Geographically the distribution revealed that the strength of the movement lies in the Middle West. Illinois, California, and New York are the headquarters of the Society, and the replies indicated that the most active Theosophists were concentrated in these areas. New England and the South (with the exception of Florida) show only a very slight membership.

As to the matter of the former religious connections, the figures brought out several interesting facts. The complete table follows:

Methodists   32
Greek Catholics   2
Episcopalians   26
Christian (unspecified) . . .   2
Presbyterians   11
Spiritualists   2
Congregationalists   10
Atheists   2
Lutherans   9
Reformed   1
Roman Catholics   8
Masonic   1
Baptists   6
Freethinkers   1
Unitarians   6
Agnostic   1
Jewish   3
Non-Church   27

Aligning these into significant groups we get: Evangelicals   69
Episcopalians   26

Catholics   10
Non-Church   31
Scattering   14

As might be expected, those who had been Episcopalians were most numerous in the East and South. The Evangelical denominations were, of course, most strongly represented in the Middle West, and they prove to be the most fertile soil for the inroads of Theosophy. The reasons for this fact are suggested below. About eighteen per cent of the respondents explicitly spoke of themselves as still Christians. About ten per cent came to Theosophy through an interest in psychic phenomena, healing or magic, of whom about fifty per cent came from Evangelical churches and none from the Catholic churches. The number of those who came to Theosophy from non-church environments is seen to be a fairly large proportion of the total. As to this element Illinois showed the heaviest rating, with California next, though the group was on the whole fairly evenly distributed over the country. Those from the non-church group supplied a disproportionately large percentage of the most active workers and leaders. The Liberal Catholic members seemed to come almost exclusively from the Episcopalian and the Evangelical groups, and those who had been Catholics were practically negligible. The reasons given for the abandonment of their former faiths to embrace Theosophy are of interest. Theosophy came in the main to people who had already experienced a pronounced distaste for the creeds of the churches.

However suddenly the transfer of loyalty and faith may have come, the way thereto had apparently been long in preparation. There is in the letters either a tacit inference or a direct statement that the espousal of Theosophy was largely attributable to the failure of the churches in meeting their intellectual needs. The increasing inadequacy of the church doctrines made Theosophy seem richer, or, to put the same fact positively, the largeness of the Theosophical system made Christian theology seem impoverished. The percentage of those explicitly noting their dissatisfaction with the churches was 47, while almost all the remainder emphasized the positive intellectual stimulation given them by Theosophy. However, such vague personal testimony must be received with a measure of caution until we estimate what particular elements were most effective.

While the specific motives for shifting from religious regularity, or from no institutional or creedal anchorage over to a new and exotic cult, have been quite variously set forth by the respondents, almost all of them used the general formula: Theosophy rendered life more intelligible than any other system. All the more detailed statements as to the reason for faith in Theosophy are but amplifications of this one theme. It is the only cult, we are told, that furnishes to the seeker after light and understanding an adequate rational support for the assumption of Law, Order, Love, Wisdom, Purpose, and Intelligence in the Course of Things. A closer examination into the meaning of these phrases soon reveals that certain specific issues were uppermost.

Theosophy appeared to reconcile science (especially evolutionary science) with religion; it enlarged the moral drama to the vast proportions of cosmic epochs demanded by evolution. It gave a teleological explanation of evolution which was nevertheless not narrowly anthropocentric, and an explanation of the origin of evil which was not arbitrary or cruel. Then, too, as many replies definitely stated, the doctrine of reincarnation was regarded as an improvement over the orthodox doctrine of resurrection, day of judgment, heaven and hell, as well as over the vague liberal doctrine of immortality. And the law of Karma was felt to be more rational than salvation by forgiveness, vicarious atonement, or "faith" or "grace." Some of the writers found a higher form of theism in Theosophy, but the majority said little about God, and were quite content to substitute meditation and study for praying to a personal God. Here are a few typical statements:

"Theosophy answered the great problems. It made life intelligible on the basis of Love, Law, Intelligence."

"Orthodoxy nowhere furnished a satisfactory solution to the riddles of life."

"Theosophy presented a logical and reasonable theory of life,which in turn served as an inspiration to self-discipline and right living. It provides the only sure 'ground for morals.'"

"The general narrowness and inconsistency of religions and particularly their inability to explain wrong and suffering turned me away from the churches.
Theosophy brought satisfaction, peace and happiness."

"Theosophy reconciled science and religion with each other, and both with philosophy, and me with all of them in one great synthesis."

"Theosophy gave me a satisfying philosophy of life and religion and restored me to Christianity after the church had lost me."

"I never knew there existed so rational and complete a theory of life until I met with Theosophy."

"Theosophy alone answered the questions that must be raised by any reflective mind."

"Theosophy appealed to me by its vast comprehensibility. It leaves no fact of life unexplained in a system into which the single facts fit with amazing aptness."

"Theosophy came to me through the death of my husband, when I stood face to face with a disenchanted universe and sought to break through to a rational understanding of the meaning of things."

"I felt the need for some way out such as that provided by reincarnation. I found Theosophy a complete philosophy answering my mental demands to the full."

"Christianity could not stand the test of thinking; Theosophy gave me the larger truths which could bear the brunt of logical questioning."

"Theosophy presented the only rational scheme of life that I had ever heard of."

"The laws of reincarnation and Karma for the first time enabled me to see life as under the reign of Order and Love."

"Theosophy was the first system I ever met with that reconciled me with the universe. I was a rebel before."

"I was happy to find in Theosophy an acceptable explanation of the soul-harrying problems connected with the apparent cruelty of life."

"Not only did Theosophy solve for me the riddles of the universe but it opened up new vistas of meaning in the service, rituals and traditions of the church itself."

"Theosophy quieted my feeling of uneasiness over the fact that so many religions must be wrong, by revealing the synthesis of truth back of all religions alike."

"My special studies in the lines of Social and Criminal Psychology made reincarnation a necessity for my thinking, and no longer a speculative luxury."

"While the church evades the main issues, Theosophy courageously attacks the vital problems at their root and succeeds in solving their meaning by revealing the hidden side of truth."

"I revolted at the fear which the churches, through some of their repellent doctrines, instil into the minds of children. Theosophy dispelled all this dark shadow and let in the light."

"I felt the hypocrisies of the religious leaders. I went from Applied Psychology to Christian Science, to Spiritualism and found rest only in Theosophy at last."

"The shallowness of church teaching drove me to agnosticism, from which happily Theosophy rescued me."

"From Christian Science I went to occultism, and I was once more happy to be shown that life could be understood after all."

"I found in Theosophy an unshakable foundation on which to base my logic."

"Theosophy came to me in the crisis of a nervous breakdown, and by giving me a flashing clear understanding of life and its problems, brought me safely through the ordeal. It revealed that I was part of the plan and gave me a new zest for living."

"Perhaps nothing within the scope of mind can solve the Mystery of Life, but Theosophy rendered it no longer a mystification."

"There were the sneers of skeptics and unbelievers on one side and horrified piety of believers on the other. Neither had any rational scheme of life to offer. Theosophy was a joyous refuge from this dilemma."

"There was something clearly wanting and illogical in the doctrine of salvation through the vicarious sacrifice and atonement; now all is clear."

"I found here a body of ideas systematized and unified, which, furthermore, rang true when tested out against the hard facts of life itself."

"I was a freethinker by nature, but after all one must think systematically, not loosely, and Theosophy presented to me a marvelous compact and well-knit structure."

"Work in the slums brought a sense of the breakdown of orthodox faith in the face of social disaster. I saw religion as a drug and curse to the lowly. I wanted Truth rather than religion. I found it in Theosophy."

"Theosophy gave me light after I had long been immersed in the grossness of materialism."

"Exactly where the church fell down Theosophy held its ground."

"A Sunday School teacher, what I taught choked me. Theosophy was like a cup of water to one dying of thirst."3

Some sixty-five per cent of the replies indicated that the philosophical and scientific aspects of Theosophy were the primary interests, leaving about thirty-five per cent attracted chiefly to the religious or devotional phases.

Forty-two per cent gave definite time to daily meditation. Thirty- six per cent explicitly avowed a non-meat diet, though the proportion of abstainers from animal food is undoubtedly must larger.

A few ladies testified to having forsworn the wearing of furs on humanitarian grounds. Alcohol and tobacco were taboo along with flesh foods in the case of several.

Whereas almost all the respondents spontaneously emphasized the intellectual aspects of Theosophy, comparatively few were explicit on the element which is supposed to be central in their faith, viz., the practice of universal brotherhood. Only about twenty per cent emphasized such interests (brotherhood, social service, etc.) as in Theosophic terminology would belong to the practice of Karma Yoga; and of these an unusually large percentage were women. They came mostly from Evangelical churches or no-church; few were Episcopalians. This group, emphasizing Karma Yoga, proved to be fairly distinct from the group which emphasized meditation, though both groups were recruited largely from former Evangelical Protestants. The practice of meditation seemed to have little measurable effect one way or the other on the amount of time and energy devoted to work for the Theosophical Society. About fifty per cent said they gave a definite amount of time to specific Theosophic activities, and of these about thirteen per cent gave at least one-half of their time to the cause. Many gave from a half hour to three, four, five hours per day; some "three evenings a week, with home study"; others "one-fourth to one-half of all time." Many devoted "all spare time" to it. But a significant element that crept into quite a large percentage of the answers was the statement that the pursuit of Theosophy "permeates all my activity"; "enters into my whole life as an undercurrent"; "colors all my behavior, modifies my attitude toward all I do"; is "a subconscious influence directing my entire life"; is "the background of my life, polarizing all I do to the one central principle of brotherhood"; forms "the pervasive spirit of all I do;" is "the motivating agent in all my efforts to work and to serve"; and the like expressions. In other words there is the persuasion with these people that one is a Theosophist all the time, whatever be one's momentary mode of activity. "The specific time I give to it is impossible to estimate," says one; and "it absorbs my thought and is the determining motive in every act of my life," avers another. The percentage so declaring themselves ran as high as seventy-four.

The query desiring to ascertain which leaders and which Theosophic organizations commanded higher allegiance brought answers which were a foregone conclusion from the fact that all the respondents were attached to the "Besant" organization. The favored leaders were naturally Mr. C. Jinarajadasa, Mr. A. P. Sinnett, Mr. G. S. Arundale, Mr. L. W. Rogers, Mr. Max Wardall, Bishop Irving Cooper, and others. Although the name of the Society's great Founder, Madame Blavatsky, was brought in apparantly in most cases incidentally or as an after- thought, she or her writings were mentioned by one out of every three. Only two failed to name Mrs. Besant or Mr. Leadbeater at all. As to favored writings, those of Mrs. Besant and her colleague again led the list, with J. Krishnamurti's books a good third. As to choice of organization the International Theosophical Society, of which Mrs. Besant is the presiding genius, found a unanimous approval in this selected group. Only two declared they were impartial or indifferent to all organization.

As a secondary interest (all Theosophists are urged to devote some energy to at least one outside humanitarian movement) many expressed allegiance to the Order of the Star in the East, Mrs. Besant's vehicle to prepare the way for the reception of the announced Avatar (since renounced by Krishnamurti himself and disbanded by him), the Order of Service, the League of Brotherhood, the Karma and Reincarnation Legion, the Liberal Catholic Church, the Co-Masonic Order,

Anti-Vivisection Societies, the League for Prison Work, the Order of the Round Table (for children), and other subsidiary forms of extra-Theosophic activity.

15

FOOTNOTES

CHAPTER I THEOSOPHY

1 The same idea is voiced by William James (Pragmatism, p. 299): "I thoroughly disbelieve, myself, that our human experience is the highest form of experience extant in the universe. I believe rather that we stand in much the same relation to the whole of the universe as our canine and feline pets do to the whole of human life. They inhabit our drawing rooms and libraries. They take part in scenes of whose significance they have no inkling. They are merely tangent to curves of history, the beginnings and ends and forms of which pass wholly beyond their ken. So we are tangent to the wider life of things."

2 See in particular such works as From Religion to Philosophy, by F. M. Cornford (London, 1912), and From Orpheus to Paul, by Prof. Vittorio D. Macchioro (New York, Henry Holt & Co., 1930).

3 "The work of philosophy thus appears as an elucidation and clarifying of religious material. It does not create its new conceptual tools; it rather discovers them by ever subtler analysis and closer definition of the elements confused in the original datum."-From Religion to Philosophy, by F. M. Cornford,

p. 126.

4 Ibid., pp. 94 ff.

5 "Physis was not an object, but a metaphysical substance. It differs from modern ether in being thought actual. It is important to notice that Greek speculation was not based on observation of external nature. It is more easily understood as an echo from the Orphic teachings."-Ibid., pp. 136 ff.

6 "The fate of man was sympathetically related to the circling lights of heaven."-Ibid., p. 171.

7 Ibid., pp. 176 ff

8 The universal soul substance.

9 Quoted by F. M. Cornford, From Religion to Philosophy, p. 185.

10 For the Orphic origin of Heraclitus' philosophy consult From Orpheus to Paul, by Prof. Vittorio D. Macchioro, pp. 169 ff.

11 "The most primitive of these (cardinal doctrines of mysticism) is Reincarnation (palingenesis). This life, which is perpetually renewed, is reborn out of that opposite state called 'death,' into which, at the other end of its arc, it passes again. In this idea of Reincarnation . . . we have the first conception of a cycle of existence, a Wheel of Life, divided into two hemicycles of light and darkness, through which the one life, or soul, continuously revolves."-From Religion to Philosophy, p. 160.

12   "Caught in the wheel of birth, the soul passes through the forms of man and beast and plant."-From Religion to Philosophy, p. 178.

13   From Religion to Philosophy, p. 197. Also From Orpheus to Paul, Chapter VIII.

14   John Burnet, Early Greek Philosophy (London, 1920), p. 138.

15   Ibid., p. 156.

16   "That the doctrine (exile of the soul from God) . . . was not invented by Empedocles is certain from the fact that the essential features of it are found in Pindar's second Olympian, written for Theron of Acragas, where Empedocles was born, at a date when Empedocles was a boy. Throughout the course of that majestic Ode revolves the Wheel of Time, Destiny and Judgment. The doctrine can be classed unhesitatingly as 'Orphic.' The soul is conceived as falling from the region of light down into the 'roofed-in cave,' the 'dark meadow of Ate.' (Frag. 119, 120, 121.) This fall is a penalty for sin, flesh-eating or oath-breaking. Caught in the Wheel of Time, the soul, preserving its individual identity, passes through all shapes of life. This implies that man's soul is not 'human'; human life is only one of the shapes it passes through. Its substance is divine and immutable, and it is the same substance as all other soul in the world. In this sense the unity of all life is maintained; but, on the other hand, each soul is an atomic individual, which persists throughout its ten thousand years' cycle of reincarnations. The soul travels the round of the four elements: 'For I have been ere now, a body, and a girl, a bush (earth), a bird (air) and a dumb fish in the sea.' (Frag. 117.) These four elements compose the bodies which it successively inhabits.

"The soul is further called 'an exile from God' and a wanderer, and its offence, which entailed this exile, is described as 'following Strife,' 'putting trust in Strife.' At the end of the cycle of births, men may hope to 'appear among mortals as prophets, song-writers, physicians and princes; and thence they rise up, as gods exalted in honor, sharing the hearth of the other immortals and the same table, free from human woes, delivered from destiny and harm.' (Frags. 146, 147.) Thus the course of the soul begins with separation from God, and ends in reunion with him, after passing through all the moirai of the elements."-From Religion to Philosophy, p. 228.

17   By comparison with the passage expounding Empedocles' theory of rebirth (supra), the following assumes significance: "From these (Golden Verses of Pythagoras) we learn that it had some striking resemblance to the beliefs prevalent in India about the same time, though it is really impossible to assume any Indian influence on Greece at this date. In any case the main purpose of the Orphic observances and rites was to release the soul from the 'wheel of birth,' that is, from reincarnation in animal or vegetable forms. The soul so released became once more a god enjoying everlasting bliss."-John Burnet, Early Greek Philosophy, p. 82.

18   From Religion to Philosophy, p. 247.

19   R. D. Hicks: Introduction to Aristotle's De Anima, (Cambridge, 1907).

20   Ibid. "It is now generally agreed that we may distinguish a group of early dialogues commonly called 'Socratic' from a larger group in which the doctrines characteristic of Orphism and Pythagoreanism for the first time make their appearance"-From Religion to Philosophy, p. 242.

"Thus, the Megarian and Eleatic doctrines, though they had not satisfied him, had impelled Plato to look for a point of union of the One and the Many; but he was enabled to find it only by a more thorough acquaintance with the Pythagoreans. It is only after his return from Italy that his doctrine appears

fully established and rounded off into a complete system."-Johann Edward Erdmann: History of Philosophy (London, 1891), Vol. I, p. 231.

21   "Constantly perfecting himself in perfect Mysteries, a man in them alone becomes truly perfect, says he in the Phaedrus."-Isaac Preston Cory: Ancient Fragments: Plato; Phaedrus, I, p. 328.

22   This passage, from Cory's Ancient Fragments, is in a translation somewhat different from that of Jowett and other editors, though Jowett (Plato's Works, Vol. I, Phaedrus, p. 450) gives the following: ". . . and he who has part in this gift, and is truly possessed and duly out of his mind, is by the use of purifications and mysteries made whole and exempt from evil. . . ." The term "pure light" appears to be a reference to the Astral Light, or Akasha, of the Theosophists. For this term, Astral Light, Madame Blavatsky gives in the Theosophical Glossary the following definition: "A subtle essence visible only to the clairvoyant eye, and the lowest but one (viz., the earth) of the Seven Akashic or Kosmic principles." She further says that it corresponds to the astral body in man.

28 See argument in Dr. Annie Besant's Esoteric Christianity (London, 1895).

29 See Samuel Angus: The Mystery Religions and Christianity; and H. A. A. Kennedy: St. Paul and the Mystery Religions (London, New York, Bombay, Madras, Calcutta; Hodder and Stoughton, 1913).

30 As in 2 Corinthians, XII, 1-5.

31 "Plotinus, read in a Latin translation, was the schoolmaster who brought Augustine to Christ. There is therefore nothing startling in the considered opinion of Rudolph Eucken that Plotinus has influenced Christian theology more than any other thinker."-Dean R. W. Inge: The Philosophy of Plotinus (New York, London, 1918), Vol. I.

23   I. P. Cory: Ancient Fragments, Plato, Ep. II, p. 312.

24   Porphyry: Life of Plotinus, in the Introduction to Vol. I, of the Works of Plotinus, edited by Dr. Kenneth S. Guthrie.

25   "Proclus maintained that the philosophical doctrines (chiefly Platonism) are of the same content as the mystic revelations, that philosophy in fact borrowed from the Mysteries, from Orphism, through Pythagoras, from whom Plato borrowed."-Samuel Angus: The Mystery Religions and Christianity (London, J. Murray, 1925), p. 267.

26   Quoted by Madame Blavatsky in Isis Unveiled (New York, J. W. Bouton, 1877), Vol. I, p. 432. Proclus' familiarity with the Mysteries is revealed in the following, also quoted by Madame Blavatsky in Isis Unveiled, Vol. II, p. 113: "In all the Initiations and Mysteries the gods exhibit many forms of themselves, and appear in a variety of shapes, and sometimes indeed a formless light of themselves is held forth to view; sometimes this light is according to a human form and sometimes it proceeds into a different shape."

27   "For over a thousand years the ancient Mediterranean world was familiar with a type of religion known as Mystery-Religions, which changed the religious outlook of the Western world and which are operative in European philosophy and in the Christian Church to this day. Dean Inge, in his Christian Mysticism, p. 354, says that Catholicism owes to the Mysteries . . . the notions of

secrecy,

of symbolism, of mystical brotherhood, of sacramental grace, and above all, of the three stages of the spiritual life; ascetic purification, illumination and epopteia as the crown."-Samuel Angus: The Mystery Religions and Christianity: Foreword.

32 C. W. Leadbeater: The Christian Creed (London, 1897); Dr. Annie Besant: Esoteric Christianity.

CHAPTER II THE AMERICAN BACKGROUND

1 Paul Morphy, a chess "wizard" of startling capabilities, excited wonder at the time, like the eight-year-old Polish lad of more recent times.

2 Encyclopedia Britannica: Article, "Swedenborgianism."

3 William Howitt: History of the Supernatural (J. B. Lippincott & Co., Philadelphia, 1863), Vol. II, p. 213.

4 Ibid. 5 Ibid., p. 214.

6 Ibid.

7 As early as 1824 Unitarians in America took a lively interest in the Hindu leader Rammohun Roy, who had "adopted Unitarianism," and also in the work of the Rev. William Adam, a Baptist missionary, who had become converted to Unitarianism in India. A British-Indian Unitarian Association was formed, and the Rev. Chas. H. A. Dall was sent to Calcutta, where he effected the alliance with the Brahmo-Somaj.

8 Article: Emerson's Debt to the Orient, by Arthur E. Christy, in The Monist, January, 1928.

9 Ibid.

10 The Journal shows that as early as 1822 he had looked into Zoroaster. In 1823 he refers to two articles in Hindu mathematics and mythology in Vol. 29 of the Edinburgh Review. By 1832 he had dipped into Pythagoras. In 1836 he quotes Confucius, Empedocles, and Xenophanes. By 1838 he had read the Institutes of Menu, and again quoted Zoroaster, Buddha, and Confucius. The first reference to the Vedas is made in 1839. In 1841 he had seen the Vishnu Sarna (a corrupt spelling of Vishnu Sharman), together with Hermes Trismegistus and the Neo- Platonists, Iamblichus, and Proclus. The She-King and the Chinese Classics are noted in 1843, and the first reference to the Bhagavad Gita in 1845. In 1847 comes the Vishnu Purana, and in 1849 the Desatir, a supposedly Persian work, and in 1855 the Rig Veda Sanhita.

11 This passage is found in Letters of Emerson to a Friend, edited by Charles Eliot Norton.

12 Emerson's Journal for 1845, p. 130.

13 Emerson's Journals, Vol. V, p. 334.

14 Emerson's Journals, Vol. VII, p. 241.

15 Biblioteca Indica, Vol. XV, translated by E. Roer, Calcutta, 1853.

16 Emerson's Works (Centenary Edition), Vol. II, p. 270.

17 Emerson's Journals, Vol. X, p. 162.

18 Article: "Emerson's Debt to the Orient," Arthur E. Christy, The Monist, January, 1928.

19   In 1854 a most significant fact was recorded in New England history. A young Englishman, Thomas Cholmondeley, friend of Arthur Hugh Clough, and nephew of Bishop Heber, came to Concord with letters of introduction to Emerson. The latter sent him to board at Mrs. John Thoreau's. A short time after Cholmondeley's return to England, Henry Thoreau received forty-four volumes of Hindu literature as a gift from the young nobleman. Of these, twenty-three were bequeathed to Emerson at Thoreau's death. The list contained the names of such eminent translators as H. H. Milman, H. H. Wilson, M. E. Burnouff and Sir William Jones. The books were the texts from the Vedas, the Vishnu Purana, the Mahabarhata, with the Bhagavad Gita. Tradition has it that Emerson died with a copy of the Bhagavad Gita (said to have been one of three copies in the country at the time) in his faltering grasp. It is known that he read, besides, numerous volumes of Persian poetry, translations of Confucius and other Chinese philosophers, by James Ligge, Marshman and David Collier, and books on Hindu mathematics and mythology. The poem "Brahma" first appeared in the Journal of July, 1856, and in the Atlantic Monthly, for November, 1867. He did not receive Thoreau's bequest until 1852, but it requires no stretch of imagination to presume that the two friends had access to each other's libraries in the interval between 1854 and 1862.

20   This difference between the two cults may perhaps be best depicted by quoting the words used in the author's presence by a woman of intelligence who had founded two Christian Science churches and had been notably successful as a healing practitioner, but who later united with the Theosophical Society. She said: "Christian Science had rather well satisfied my spiritual needs, but had totally starved my intellect." Her experience is doubtless typical of that of many others, in whom, after the first burst of sensational interest in healing has receded, the yearning for a satisfactory philosophy of life and the cosmos surged uppermost again.

21   It has been conservatively estimated that in 1852 there were three hundred mediumistic circles in Philadelphia. The number of mediums in the United States in 1853 was thirty thousand. In 1855 there were two and a half million Spiritualists in the land, with an increase of three hundred each year. The rate of increase far outran those of the Lutheran and Methodist denominations. An interesting feature of this rapid spread of the movement was its political significance and results. Not inherently concerned with politics, its devotees mostly adopted strong anti-slavery tenets. Judge Edmonds, an eminent jurist, converted to Spiritualism by his (at first skeptical) investigations of it, asserted that the Spiritualist vote came near to carrying the election of 1856, and actually did carry that of 1860 for the North against the Democratic party. Another most interesting side-light is the fact that the sweep of Spiritualistic excitement redeemed thousands of atheists to an acceptance of religious verities. (For these and other interesting data see Howitt's History of the Supernatural, Vol. II.)

22   Spiritualists say that Lincoln was eventually moved to emancipate the slaves by his reception of a spirit message through Hattie Colburn, a medium who came to see him about a furlough for her son. Horace Greeley was favorably impressed

by the evidence presented. And a later President, McKinley, maintained a deep concern in the phenomena, along with his powerful political manager, Senator Mark Hanna, who seldom undertook a move of any consequence without first consulting a medium, Mrs. Gutekunst, to whom, for purposes of ready availability, he had given a residence in his home. Senators and Cabinet members were by no means immune.

23   Others prominent in the movement at the time were Governor N. P. Tallmadge, of Wisconsin, Rev. Adin Ballou, J. P. Davis and Benjamin Coleman; and Profs. Bush, Mapes, Gray, and Channing from leading universities. Mr. Epes Sargeant, of Boston, added prestige to the cult. A Dr. Gardner, of Boston, and the Unitarian Theodore Parker gave testimony as to the beneficent influence exerted by the Spiritualistic faith.

24   By strange and fortuitous circumstances he became the guest of the Emperor of the French, of the King of Holland, of the Czar of Russia, and of many lesser princes. His demonstrations before these grandees were extensions of the phenomena occurring in his youth. See Howitt's History of the Supernatural, Vol. II, pp. 222 ff.

25   Howitt's History of the Supernatural, Vol. II, p. 225.

26   He published his The Great Harmonia (Boston 1850); The Philosophy of Spiritual Intercourse (New York, 1851); The Penetralia (Boston, 1856); The Present Age and Inner Life (New York, 1853); and The Magic Staff (Boston, 1858). He edited a periodical, The Herald of Progress.

27   Howitt's The History of the Supernatural, Vol. II, p. 228.

28   That there was much very real theosophy among the early German Pietists who settled north and west of Philadelphia in the Pennsylvania colony is indicated by the following extract from The German Sectarians of Pennsylvania, by Julius Friedrich Sachse (Vol. I, pp. 457 ff.). He says: "Thus far but little attention has been given by writers on Pennsylvania history to the influences exercised by the various mystical, theosophical and cabbalistic societies and fraternities of Europe in the evangelization of this Province and in reclaiming the German settlers from the rationalism with which they were threatened by their contact with the English Quakers.

"Labadie's teachings; Boehme's visions; the true Rosicrucianism of the original Kelpius party; the Philadelphian Society, whose chief apostle was Jane Leade; the fraternity which taught the restitution of all things; the mystical fraternity led by Dr. Julian Wilhelm Petersen and his wife Eleanor von Merlau- both members of the Frankfort community-all found a foothold upon the soil of Penn's colony and exercised a much larger share in the development of this country than is accorded to them. It has even been claimed by some superficial writers and historians of the day that there was no strain of mysticism whatever in the Ephrata Community, or, in fact, connected with any of the early German movements in Pennsylvania. Such a view is refuted by the writings of Kelpius, Beissel, Miller, and many others who then lived, sought the Celestial Bridegroom and awaited the millennium which they earnestly believed to be near.

"With the advent of the Moravian Brethren in Pennsylvania the number of these mystical orders was increased by the introduction of two others, viz., The Order of the Passion of Jesus (Der Orden des Leidens Jesu), of which Count Zinzendorf was Grand Commander, and the Order of the Mustard Seed (Der Senfkorn Orden)."

CHAPTER III HELENA P. BLAVATSKY: HER LIFE AND PSYCHIC CAREER

1   Incidents in the Life of Madame Blavatsky, by A. P. Sinnett (Theosophical Publishing Society, London, 1913), p. 35. See also footnote at bottom of page 155, in Letters of H. P. Blavatsky to A. P.

Sinnett (New York, Frederick A. Stokes Co.,

2   Incidents in the Life of Madame Blavatsky, by A. P. Sinnett, pp. 39-40.

3   Vol. II, p. 599.

4   Her recital of marvels seen in Tibet corresponds in the main with similar narratives related by the Abbé Huc in the first edition of his Recollections of Travel in Tartary, Tibet and China. Mr. Sinnett makes the statement, without giving his evidence, that the "miracles" related by the Abbé in his first edition were expurgated by Catholic authority in the later editions of the work.

5   Madame Blavatsky later verified the long distance phenomenon by receiving in writing, in response to an inquiry by mail, a letter from the Rumanian friend stating that at the identical time of the Shaman's concentration she had swooned, but dreamed she saw Madame Blavatsky in a tent in a wild country among menacing tribes, and that she had communicated with her. Madame Blavatsky states that the friend's astral form was visible in the tent.

6   In 1873 while at the Eddy farmhouse with her new friend Col. Olcott, she revealed to him this chapter in her life, proving it by showing him where her left arm had been broken in two places by a saber stroke, and having him feel a musket ball in her right shoulder and another in her leg, revealing also a scar just below the heart where she had been stabbed by a stiletto.

7   It must have been about this time that Madame did some traveling in an altogether different capacity than occult research. She is known by her family to have made tours in Italy and Russia under a pseudonym, giving piano concerts. She had been a pupil of Moscheles, and when with her father in London as a young girl she had played at a charity concert with Madame Clara Schumann and Madame Arabella Goddard in a piece for three pianos.

8   Incidents in the Life of Madame Blavatsky, by A. P. Sinnett, p. 125.

9   An incident highly characteristic of her nature marked her coming to this country, and her followers would hardly pardon our omitting it. Having purchased her steamer ticket, she was about to board the vessel when her attention was attracted to a peasant woman weeping bitterly on the wharf. Her quick sympathies touched, Madame Blavatsky approached her and inquired the trouble. She soon gathered that a "sharp" had sold the woman a worthless ticket, and that she was stranded without funds. Madame Blavatsky's finances had barely sufficed to procure her own passage, she having sent a dispatch to Russia instructing her father to forward her additional money in New York. In the emergency she did not hesitate. Going to the office of the Company, she arranged to exchange her cabin ticket for two steerage ones, and packed the grateful emigrant on board along with her.-See Old Diary Leaves, by Col. H. S. Olcott (New York and London, G. P. Putnam's Sons, 1895), pp. 28-29.

10   Old Diary Leaves, by Col. H. S. Olcott, Vol. I, p. 440.

11   Col. Olcott (Old Diary Leaves, Vol. I, p. 440) states that during this period of her own need she held in custody the sum of about 23,000 francs, which she later told him her "guardians" had charged her to deliver a person in the United States whose definite location would be given her after her arrival here. The

order came after a time, and she went to Buffalo, was given a name and street number, where she delivered the money without question to a man who was on the point of committing suicide. It was understood that she had been made the agent of rectifying a great wrong done him.

12   Mr. O'Sullivan rallied her about her possession of so easy a road to wealth. "No, indeed," she answered, "'tis but a psychological trick. We who have the power of doing this, dare not use it for our own or any other's interests, any more than you would dare commit the forgery by methods of the counterfeiters. It would be stealing from the government in either case."-Old Diary Leaves, Vol. I, p. 435.

13   Old Diary Leaves, Vol. I., p. 106.

14   Mr. W. Q. Judge as her counsel and the decree was granted on May 25, 1878. Col. Olcott had retained the original papers in the case.

15   Old Diary Letters, Vol. I, p. 417.

16   Ibid., p. 4.

17   Published by The Constables, London, 1910.

18   The Arena, April, 1895.

19   Quoted in Old Diary Leaves, Vol. I, p. 4 (footnote), from a letter written by her entitled "The Knout" to the R. P. Journal of March 16, 1878.

20   Mr. Sinnett (Incidents in the Life of Madame Blavatsky, Chapter VI) emphasizes the fact that she was about this time in a transition state from passive mediumship to active control over her phenomena. He doubtless wishes to make this matter clear in view of its important bearing upon the divergence between Spiritualism and Theosophy which was accentuated when the latter put forth claims somewhat at variance with the usual theses presented by the former.

21   Incidents in the Life of Madame Blavatsky, p. 61.

22   Ibid., p. 72.

23   In Russian, "little hare."

24   Incidents in the Life of Madame Blavatsky, p. 116.

25   Ibid., p. 120

26   Ibid., p. 120

27   Ibid., p. 128

28   Ibid., p. 127

29   Old Diary Leaves, Vol. I, p. 36. In this work Col. Olcott undertakes to classify the various types of phenomena produced by Madame Blavatsky.

30   Ibid., Vol. I, Chapter III, pp. 40 ff.

31   Theosophists are so much in the habit of referring to their leader by her three initials that we may be pardoned for falling into the same convenient usage at times.

32   Old Diary Leaves, Vol. I, p. 380.

33   Mr. Sinnett devotes some pages of his little volume, The Occult World, to a critical examination of every conceivable possibility of this incident's being other than it ostensibly was, and he is unable to find a loophole for the admission of any theory of deception. All the witnesses to the event made affidavit to the effect of its evident genuineness. The reader is referred to his analysis of the

case, to be found on pages 64-71 in the work just mentioned. For close scrutiny of the other events of the same period the same volume should be consulted.

34   Vlesevold Solovyoff, who afterwards sought to discredit Madame Blavatsky's genuine status, himself witnessed this scene. In fact he wrote out his own statement of the occurrence and sent it for publication to the St. Petersburg Rebus, which printed it on July 1, 1884, over his signature. He closes that account with the following paragraph: "The circumstances under which the phenomenon occurred in its smallest details, carefully checked by myself, do not leave in me the smallest doubt as to its genuineness and reality. Deception or fraud in this particular case are really out of the question."

CHAPTER IV FROM SPIRITUALISM TO THEOSOPHY

1   It seems that she had been in Peru and Brazil in 1857, according to her later statement to A. P. Sinnett as found on page 154 of the Letters of H. P. Blavatsky to A. P. Sinnett. A sentence in Vol. I, of Isis Unveiled makes mention of her personal knowledge of great underground labyrinths in Peru.

2   Not assuredly of the séance-room type. She is obviously using the term here in the wider sense that it came to have in her larger Theosophic system, as expounded in this chapter.

3   Old Diary Leaves, Vol. I, p. 12.

4   Ibid., p. 13.

5   Ibid., p. 68.

6   Mrs. Emma Hardinge Britten, herself a medium and among the foremost Spiritualists of her day-also a charter member of the Theosophical Society-made

a statement to the same effect to Col. Olcott in 1875. See Old Diary Leaves, Vol. I, p. 83.

7   Quoted in William Kingsland's The Real H. P. Blavatsky (J. M. Watkins, London, 1928), p. 123.

8   Mahatma Letters to A. P. Sinnett (New York, Frederick A. Stokes Co., 1924), p. 289.

9   The Theosophist, Vol. I, 1879.

10   Isis Unveiled, Vol. I, p. 13.

11   Ibid., p. 53.

12   Ibid., p. 489.

13   Ibid., Vol. II, p. 586.

14   Old Diary Leaves, Vol. I, p. 110.

15   Page 27.

16   That H. P. B. was by no means alone in predicating the existence of other than human spirits denizening the astral world is shown by Col. Olcott, who (Old Diary Leaves, Vol. I, p. 438), cites Mrs. Britten's statement printed in an article in The Banner of Light, as follows: "I know of the existence of other than human spirits and have seen apparitions of spiritual or elementary existences evoked by cabalistic words and practices."

17   Isis Unveiled, Vol. II, p. 636. 18 Ibid., Vol. I, p. 67

19   Collected Fruits of Occult Teaching (London, T. F. Unwin, Ltd., 1919).

20   Mahatma Letters to A. P. Sinnett, p. 101.

21   Old Diary Leaves, Vol. I, p. 119. From notes taken at the meeting by Mrs. Emma Hardinge Britten, and published a day or two later in a New York daily.

22   Ibid., Vol. I, p. 119.

23   He was in active command of the Army of the Potomac at the Battle of Gettysburg, following the death of General Reynolds on the 1st of July until the arrival of General Meade.

24   He devised the modern game of baseball.

25   Old Diary Leaves, Vol. I, p. 399.

26   Ibid., Vol. I., p. 400.

CHAPTER V ISIS UNVEILED

1   Old Diary Leaves, Vol. I, p. 203.

2   Ibid., Vol. I, p. 33.

3   The term Chaldean in these titles is thought by modern scholars to veil an actual Greek origin of the texts in question. The existence of Chaldea and Chaldeans appears to be regarded as highly uncertain. Of the Chaldeans Madame Blavatsky says in The Theosophical Glossary: "Chaldeans, or Kasdim. At first a tribe, then a caste of learned Kabbalists. They were the savants, the magians of Babylonia, astrologers and diviners." Of the Chaldean Book of Numbers she says: "A work which contains all that is found in the Zohar of Simeon Ben-Jochai and much more. . . . It contains all the fundamental principles taught in the Jewish Kabbalistic works, but none of their blinds. It is very rare indeed, there being perhaps only two or three copies extant and these in private hands."

4   Scholars have thrown doubt on the Persian authorship of this book. Madame Blavatsky in the Glossary describes it as "a very ancient Persian work called the Book of Shet. It speaks of the thirteen Zoroasters and is very mystical."

5   It is clear that Madame Blavatsky was not a literary person before the epoch of the writing of Isis. She herself, in the last article for Lucifer that she wrote before her death in 1891, entitled My Books, wrote:

1.   When I came to America in 1873 I had not spoken English-which I had learned in my childhood colloquially-for over thirty years. I could understand when I read it, but could hardly speak the language.

2 I had never been at any college, and what I knew I had taught myself; I had never pretended to any scholarship in the sense of modern research; I had then hardly read any scientific European works, knew little of Western philosophy and sciences. The little which I had studied and learned of these disgusted me with its materialism, its limitations, narrow cut-and-dried spirit of dogmatism and air of superiority over the philosophies and sciences of antiquity.

3.   Until 1874 I had never written one word in English, nor had I published any work in any language. Therefore:--

4.   I had not the least idea of literary rules. The art of writing books, of preparing them for print and publication, reading and correcting proofs, were so many closed secrets to me.

5.   When I started to write that which later developed into Isis Unveiled, I had no more idea than the man in the moon what would come of it. I had no plan; . . . I knew that I had to write it, that was all.-Old Diary Leaves, Vol. I, p. 223.

6   Old Diary Leaves, Vol. I, p. 208.

7   Ibid., p. 208.

8   Ibid., p. 211. The Countess Wachtmeister testified to similar productions of pages of manuscript in connection with the writing of The Secret Doctrine ten years later.

9   Old Diary Leaves, Vol. I. p. 239.

10 Ibid., p. 240.

11. Ibid., p. 210.

12   Published in The Path, Vol. IX, p. 300.

13   The Path, Vol. IX, p. 266

14   Letter quoted in Mr. Sinnett's Incidents in the Life of Madame Blavatsky, p. 205.

15   It is of some interest to see how it was received in 1877. The Boston Transcript says: "It must be acknowledged that she is a remarkable woman, who has read more, seen more and thought more than most wise men. Her work abounds in quotations from a dozen different languages, not for the purpose of vain display of erudition, but to substantiate her peculiar views. Her pages are garnished with footnotes, establishing as her authorities some of the profoundest writers of the past. To a large class of readers this remarkable work will prove of absorbing interest . . . it demands the earnest attention of thinkers and merits an analytic reading."

From the New York Independent came the following: "The appearance of erudition is stupendous. References to and quotations from the most unknown and obscure writers in all languages abound; interspersed with allusions to writers of the highest repute, which have evidently been more than skimmed through."

This from the New York World: "An extremely readable and exhaustive essay upon the paramount importance of reëstablishing the Hermetic philosophy in a world which blindly believes that it has outgrown it."

Olcott's own paper, The New York Daily Graphic, said: "A marvelous book, both in matter and manner of treatment. Some idea may be formed of the rarity and extent of its contents when the index alone comprises 50 pages, and we venture nothing in saying that such an index of subjects was never before compiled by any human being."

The New York Tribune confined itself to saying: "The present work is the fruit of her remarkable course of education and amply confirms her claims to the character of an adept in secret science, and even to the rank of an hierophant in the exposition of its mystic lore."

And the New York Herald: "It is easy to forecast the reception of this book. With its striking peculiarities, its audacity, its versatility and the prodigious variety of subjects which it notices and handles, it is one of the remarkable productions of the century."

16 Appendix to V. S. Solovyoff's A Modern Priestess of Isis (London, 1895), p. 354.

17 Isis Unveiled, Vol. I, p. 165.

18 Ibid., Vol. I, p. xiv.

19 Ibid., Vol. I, p. xlii.

20 Ibid., Vol. I, p. xiv.

21 Ibid., Vol. I, Preface, p. 1.

22 Perhaps the following excerpt states the intent of Isis more specifically:

"What we desire to prove is that underlying every ancient popular religion was the same ancient wisdom-doctrine, one and identical, professed and practiced by the initiates of every country, who alone were aware of its existence and importance. To ascertain its origin and precise age in which it was matured, is now beyond human possibility. A single glance, however, is enough to assure one that it could not have attained the marvelous perfection in which we find it

pictured to us in the relics of the various esoteric systems, except after a succession of ages. A philosophy so profound, a moral code so ennobling, and practical results so conclusive and so uniformly demonstrable, is not the growth of a generation. . . . Myriads of the brightest human intellects must have reflected upon the laws of nature before this ancient doctrine had taken concrete shape. The proofs of this identity of fundamental doctrine in the old religions are found in the prevalence of a system of initiation; in the secret sacerdotal castes, who had the guardianship of mystical words of power, and a public display of a phenomenal control over natural forces, indicating association with preter-human beings. Every approach to the Mysteries of all these nations was guarded with the same jealous care, and in all, the penalty of death was inflicted upon initiates of any degree who divulged secrets entrusted to them."

23 Isis Unveiled, Vol. I, p. 281.

24 Ibid., Vol. I, p. 36.

25 Ibid., Vol. I, p. 14.

26 Ibid., Vol. I, p. 243.

27 Ibid., Vol. I, p. 62.

28 Ibid., Vol. I, p. 184. Theosophists appear to be in the habit of using the terms Akasha and Astral Light more or less synonymously. In the Glossary Madame Blavatsky defines Akasha (Akasa, Akaz) as "the subtle supersensuous spiritual essence which pervades all spaces; the primordial substance erroneously identified with Ether. But it is to Ether what Spirit is to Matter, or Atma to Kamarupa. It is in fact the Universal Space in which lies inherent the eternal Ideation of the Universe in its ever-changing aspects on the plane of matter and objectivity. This power is the . . . same anima mundi on the higher plane as the astral light is on the lower."

29 Isis Unveiled, Vol. I, p . 271 ff.

30 Ibid., Vol. I, p. 210.

31 Ibid., Vol. I, p. 218.

32 Ibid., Vol. I, p. 216.

33   Ibid., Vol. I, p. 218.

34   Ibid., Vol. II, p. 493.

35   Ibid., Vol. II, p. 406.

36   Ibid., Vol. II, p. 431.

37   Ibid., Vol. II, p. 337.

38   Quoted in Old Diary Leaves, Vol. I, p. 106.

39   Isis Unveiled, Vol. II, p. 98.

40   Ibid., Vol. II, p. 32.

41   Ibid., Vol. II, p. 34.

42   Ibid., Vol. II, p. 121

43   Ibid., Vol. II, p. 139.

44   A wealth of curious citations is drawn up behind these positions. The whole Passion Week story is stated to be the reproduction of the drama of initiation into the Mysteries, and not to have taken place in historical fact. And practically every other chapter of Christ's life story is paralleled in the lives of the twenty or more "World Saviors," including Thoth, Orpheus, Vyasa, Buddha, Krishna, Dionysus, Osiris, Zoroaster, Zagreus, Apollonius, and others.

45   Isis Unveiled, Vol. II, p. 406.

46   Ibid., Vol. II, p. 38.

47   Ibid., Vol. II, p. 227.

48   Ibid., Vol. II, p. 639.

49   Dr. Annie Besant: Esoteric Christianity, p. 8.

50   E.g., cf. C. W. Leadbeater: The Christian Creed.

51   Isis Unveiled, Vol. II, p. 535.

CHAPTER VI THE MAHATMAS AND THEIR LETTERS

1   Old Diary Leaves, Vol. I, of June, 1893.

2   A. P. Sinnett: The Occult World, p. 1.

3   Ibid., p. 14. More detailed requirements in the way of preparation for Adeptship will be set forth when we undertake the general critique of the occult life, in Chapter XI.

4   In 1883 he published the general outlines of the cosmology involved in their communications in a work called Esoteric Buddhism.

5   Mahatma Letters to A. P. Sinnett, p. 24.

6   Ibid., p. 57.

7   Ibid., p. 52.

8   Ibid., p. 56.

9   Ibid., p. 141.

10 Ibid., p. 142.

11   Ibid.

12   Ibid.

13   Ibid., p. 71.

14   Ibid., p. 137.

15   Ibid., p. 167. "En passant to show you that not only were not the 'Races' invented by us, but that they are a cardinal dogma with the Lama Buddhists, and with all who study our esoteric doctrines, I send you an explanation on a page or two of Rhys Davids' Buddhism,--otherwise incomprehensible, meaningless and absurd. It is written with the special permission of the Chohan (my Master) and- for your benefit. No Orientalist has ever suspected the truths contained in it, and-you are the first Western man (outside Tibet) to whom it is now explained."- The Mahatma Letters, p. 158.

16   Mahatma Letters to A. P. Sinnett, p. 158.

17   Ibid., p. 52.

18   Devachanna would be equivalent to the Sanskrit devachhanna, hidden (abode) of the gods. On page 373 of the Mahatma Letters the Master K.H. writes: "The meaning of the terms 'Devachan' and 'Deva-Loka,' is identical; 'chan' and 'loka'

equally signifying place or abode. Deva is a word too indiscriminately used in Eastern writings, and is at times merely a blind." Deva may be roughly translated as "the shining one" or god. Devachan written alternatively Deva- Chan) is thus used to signify "the abode of the gods." Theosophists interchange it with our term "heaven-world."

19   Mahatma Letters to A. P. Sinnett, p. 179.

20   Ibid., p. 197.

21   Ibid., p. 187.

22   Ibid., p. 187.

23   Ibid., p. 183.

24   Ibid., p. 194.

25   Ibid., p. 241

26   Ibid., p. 255.

27   Maya, a word frequent in several schools of Indian Philosophy, commonly used to denote the illusory or merely phenomenal character of man's experience which he gains through his sense equipment. It is often identified with avidya or ajnana and contrasted with Brahmavidya or knowledge of truth and reality, in their unconditioned form.

28   Mahatma Letters to A. P. Sinnett, p. 274.

29   Ibid., p. 276.

30   Ibid., p. 281.

31   Ibid., p. 305.

32   Ibid., p. 322.

33   Ibid., p. 337

34   The terms Purusha and Prakriti are employed in the Sankhya school of Indian philosophy to designate spirit and matter as the two opposing phases of the one life when in active manifestation.

35   Mahatma Letters to A. P. Sinnett, p. 348.

36   Of the Dhyan Chohans Madame Blavatsky speaks in the Glossary as follows: "The Lords of Light," the highest gods, answering to the Roman Catholic Archangels, the divine intelligences charged with the supervision of Kosmos. Dhyan is a Sanskrit term signifying "wisdom" or "illumination," but the name Chohans seems to be more obscure in origin, and is probably Tibetan, used in the general sense of "Lords" of "Masters."

CHAPTER VII STORM, WRECK, AND REBUILDING

1   The official reports of the S.P.R. are to be found in Vol. III, pages 201 to 400 of the Proceedings of the S.P.R. A very adequate review of the entire affair is made by William Kingsland in the text and appendix of his recent work, The Real H. P. Blavatsky (M. Watkins, London, 1928). Partial accounts are found in many other works, as for instance, The Theosophical Movement.

2   It was from some three hundred native students of this same Christian College that Madame Blavatsky received a welcoming ovation on her return from Paris to India, and was given a testimonial of their assured faith in her lofty motives.

3   In The Proceedings of the S.P.R., Vol. III, pp. 201 to 400.

4   Further distrust of the Coulomb's charges against H.P.B. is justifiable in view of the statement given on June 5, 1879 by Madame Coulomb to the Ceylon Times, of which she sent the subject of her remarks a copy. She wrote: "I have known this lady for the last eight years and I must say the truth that there is nothing against her character. We lived in the same town, and on the contrary she was considered one of the cleverest ladies of the age. Madame Blavatsky is a musician, a painter, a linguist, an author, and I may say that very few ladies and indeed few gentlemen, have a knowledge of things as general as Madame Blavatsky."

5   It is in this article that Madame Blavatsky gives out that important declaration of hers, that as soon as the sincere aspirant steps upon the Path

leading to the higher initiations, his accumulated Karma is thrown upon him, in condensed form. The determination to pursue the occult life is therefore often spoken of as involving the "challenging of one's Karma."

6   He was the instigator of the "Sun Libel Case," which will be outlined in Chapter XII.

7   The Theosophical Movement, p. 132.

8   Old Diary Leaves, Vol. IV.

9   Found in the Appendix to The Mahatma Letters to A. P. Sinnett, pp. 480-481.

10   Letters of H. P. Blavatsky to A. P. Sinnett (New York: Frederick A. Stokes Co.), p. 194.

11   The Path, Vol. IX, p. 300.

12   Ibid., p. 266.

13   The Countess Wachtmeister herself went to the pains of verifying a quotation already written out by Madame Blavatsky, which the latter said would be found in a volume in the Bodleian Library. She found the excerpt to be correct as to wording, page, chapter, and title of the book quoted. She adds that Miss Emily Kislingbury, a devoted member of the Society, verified a quotation from Cardinal Weisman's Lectures on Science and Religion.

14   Reminiscences of H. P. Blavatsky and The Secret Doctrine, Appendix, p. 105 ff.

15   Ibid., Appendix, p. 89 ff.

16   The experience of Mr. C. Carter Blake, a scientist is pertinent on this point. He asserts that her learning was extraordinary, in consideration of her lack of early education and her want of books. He testifies that she knew more than he did on his own lines of anthropology, specifying her abstruse knowledge on the subject of the Naulette jaw. He says: "Page 744 in the Second Volume of the Secret Doctrine refers to facts which she could not easily have gathered from any published book." She had declared that the raised beaches of Tarija were pliocene, when Blake argued that they were pleistocene. She was afterwards proved correct. On page 755 of Vol. II, she mentions the fossil footprints at Carson, Indiana. Says Blake: "When Madame Blavatsky spoke to me of the footprints I did not know of their existence, and Mr. G. W. Bloxam, Assistant Secretary of the Anthropological Institute, afterwards told me that a pamphlet on the subject in the library had never been out. Madame Blavatsky certainly had sources of information (I don't say what) transcending the knowledge of experts on their own lines."-Reminiscences of H. P. Blavatsky and The Secret Doctrine, Appendix, pp. 117 ff.

17   Reminiscences of H. P. Blavatsky and The Secret Doctrine, Appendix, pp. 96 ff.

CHAPTER VIII THE SECRET DOCTRINE

1   The word Dzyan presents some etymological difficulties. Madame Blavatsky in the Glossary states that Dzyan (also written Dzyn and Dzen) is a corruption of the Sanskrit Dhyana, meaning meditation. In Tibetan, learning is called Dzin.

2   This document (spelled variously Koumboum, Kumbum, Kounboum, etc.) was a Buddhist text connected with the Koumboum monastery, in Tibet. On the monastery grounds grew the sacred Tree of Tibet, the 'tree of the ten thousand images,' as Huc describes it. . . . "Tradition has it that it grew out of the hair of
Tsonka-pa, who was buried on that spot. . . . In the words of the Abbé Huc, who lived several months with another missionary, named Gabet, near this phenomenal tree: 'Each of its leaves in opening, bears either a letter or a religious sentence, written in sacred characters, and these letters are, of their kind, of such a perfection that the type-foundries of Didot contain nothing to excel them. Open the leaves, which vegetation is about to unroll, and you will there discover, on the point of appearing, the letters or the distinct words which are the marvel of this unique tree. Turn your attention from the plant to the bark of its branches, and new characters will meet your eyes! Do not allow your interest to flag; raise the layers of this bark and still other characters will show themselves

below those whose beauty has surprised you. For, do not fancy that these superposed layers repeat the same printing. No, quite the contrary; for each lamina you lift presents to view its distinct type. How, then, can we suspect jugglery? I have done my best in that direction to discover the slightest trace of human trick, and my baffled mind could not retain the slightest suspicion.' Yet promptly the kind French Abbé suspects-the Devil."- Quoted from Madame Blavatsky, article Kounboum in The Theosophical Glossary.

3   The Dzungarians were a section of the Mongolian Empire at its height, whose name now remains only as the name of a mountain range. They have disappeared geographically.

4   Page vii.

5   The Secret Doctrine, Introductory, p. xxxvii.

6   Ibid., p. xxxviii.

7   Pralaya, as given in Sanskrit dictionaries, means "dissolution, reabsorption, destruction, annihilation, death"; especially the destruction of the whole world at the end of a Kalpa; also "fainting, loss of sense of consciousness; sleep." It apparently is derived from the Sanskrit stem li, one of whose meanings is to disappear or vanish. Madame Blavatsky describes Pralaya in the Glossary as "a period of obscuration or repose-planetary, cosmic or universal-the opposite of Manvantara."

8   Manvantara (Manu plus antara, between) is described as the period or age of a Manu. It comprised a period of 4,320,000 human years, supposedly the period intervening between two Manus.

9   The Secret Doctrine, Vol. I, p. 75.

10   Ibid., Vol. I, p. 83.

11   The word Pitris commonly means "fathers, ancestors, progenitors." Madame Blavatsky, however, on the authority of her Mahatmic instructors, employs the term in a wider sense. She uses it in a racial sense. In the Glossary she speaks of the Pitris as "the ancestors or creators of mankind. They are of the seven

classes, three of which are incorporeal. In popular theology they are said to be created from Brahma's side. . . . The Pitris are not the ancestors of the present living men, but those of the human kind or Adamic races; the spirits of the human races, which on the great scale of descending evolution preceded our races of men, and they were physically, as well as spiritually, far superior to our modern pigmies. In Manava Dharma Shastra they are called the Lunar Ancestors."

12   The Secret Doctrine, Vol. II, p. 235.

13   Ibid., Vol. I, p. 198.

14   The term Atma-Buddhi-Manas is the Theosophical manner of designating the "higher triplicity" in man, the union of the three higher principles which constitutes him an individual Ego. If one were to say, man is composed of mind, soul and spirit in his higher nature, it would roughly approximate the Theosophic description. Sanskrit dictionaries give Atma as meaning, "breath, life, soul"; Buddhi as meaning "intelligence, reason, intellect, mind, discernment, judgment, the power of forming and retaining conceptions and general notions; perception, apprehension, understanding"; and Manas as "the principle of mind or spirit."

15   The Secret Doctrine, Vol. I, p. 103.

16   Ibid., p. 246.

17   "The fourth dimension of space" enters the discussion at this point. The phrase should be, says the writer, "the fourth dimension of matter in space," since obviously space has no dimensions. The dimensions, or characteristics of matter are those determinations which the five senses of man give to it. Matter has extension, color, motion (molecular), taste, and smell; and it is the development of the next sense in man-normal clairvoyance-that will give matter its sixth characteristic, which she calls permeability. Extension-which covers all concepts of dimension in our world-is limited to three directions. Only when man's perceptive faculties unfold will there be a real fourth dimension.

18   The Secret Doctrine, Vol. I, p. 277.

19   Quoted in The Secret Doctrine, Vol. I, p. 295.

20   Ibid., Vol. I, p. 311. Quoted from H. Grattan Guinness, F. R. G. S.: The Approaching End of the Age.

21   The races of "intelligent" animals and semi-human apes will then be advanced to our present station.

22.   Ignatius Donnelley endeavored to substantiate the claims for its existence in an elaborate work, Atlantis: The Antediluvian World, some sixty or seventy years ago. By tracing numberless similarities in the languages, customs, and ideas of Old World civilizations with those of Central America he adduced a formidable body of evidence pointing to the former existence of a linking area. Madame Blavatsky counts more heavily than science has done upon this authority. Soundings have revealed the presence of a great raised plateau on the ocean floor at about one-third the depth of the general main, extending from Northern Brazil toward Ireland.

23   She assigns a tentative date of 78,000 years ago for the erection of the great pyramid of Cheops, reaching this conclusion from reasoning and

calculations based on the Dendera Zodiac, which indicates that three sidereal years (25,686 years each) had passed since the pole star was in a position suggested by the various features of the great pile's construction.

25   The sexless (First) race was Adam solus. Then came the Second Race; Adam-Eve, or Jah-Heva, inactive androgynes; and finally the Third, or the "separating hermaphrodite," Cain and Abel, who produced the Fourth, Seth-Enos, etc.-The Secret Doctrine, Vol. II, p. 134.

26   Kriyasakti means "capacity to act, a sakti or supernatural power as appearing in actions." By Madame Blavatsky the term is taken as meaning creative power or capability of doing work.

27   The Secret Doctrine, Vol. II, p. 517.

28   Ibid., Vol. II, p. 328.

29   Ibid., p. 330.

CHAPTER IX EVOLUTION, REBIRTH AND KARMA

1   "Growth is regarded as having an end instead of being and end.   In reality there is nothing to which growth is relative save more growth."-John Dewey: Democracy and Education.

2   Sir Edwin Arnold, The Light of Asia.

3   See Ogden and Richards, The Meaning of Meaning.

4   Article in The Atlantic Monthly, May, 1926.

5   The instantaneous (from our point of view) retrospect of our whole past life in elaborate detail recounted by thousands of persons who had drowned or suffocated or fallen or been struck a blow, and lived to tell the tale, are, say Theosophists, instances of the vision falling this side of death. Nor is the phenomenon wanting with persons who pass out peacefully on their beds. The rapturous prevision of heaven usually includes elements of a life review.

6   Persons who have slept but ten seconds of clock time have told of the richness and vividness of this type of consciousness, in which the events of a lifetime are reviewed, weighed, and morally judged in a moment.

7   On page 646 of Vol. I, our seeress makes what looks like a prophecy of the World War of 1914: "Europe in general is threatened with, or rather is on the eve of, a cataclysm which her own cycle of racial Karma has led her to."

CHAPTER X ESOTERIC WISOM AND PHYSICAL SCIENCE

1   The Secret Doctrine, Vol. II, p. 650.

2   Ibid., Vol. II, p. 654.

3   Ibid., Vol. II, p. 170.

4   Ibid., Vol. II, p. 262.

5   Ibid., Vol. I, p. 478.

6   A. S. Eddington: The Nature of the Physical World (Cambridge, 1928). Madame Blavatsky had long ago hypothecated this dual nature of light. See The Secret Doctrine, passim.

7   Section XI of the Introduction to the Principia.

8   The Secret Doctrine, Vol. I, p. 517.

9   Ibid., Vol. I, p. 520.

10   Ibid., Vol. I, p. 541. Prof. Millikan's recent conclusions as to the constant refueling of the spheres by the influx of atomic structures "fixated" out of the ether of space may perhaps be regarded as in some sense corroborative of Madame Blavatsky's statement on this subject.

11   The Secret Doctrine, Vol. I, p. 547.

12   Ibid., Vol. I, p. 631.13 The magazine Theosophy, published monthly by The United Lodge of Theosophists, runs a "Lookout Section" in which for fifteen or more years comment has been made upon the argument of current scientific discovery with Madame Blavatsky's systemology.

CHAPTER XI THEOSOPHY IN ETHICAL PRACTICE

1   Yajnavidya in Sanskrit means "knowledge of (or through) sacrifice;" but in the Vedanta and the Upanishads it ranks low in the scheme of wisdom. Madame Blavatsky in the Glossary gives Yajna as meaning "sacrifice" and describes it as "one of the forms of Akasa within which the mystic Word (or its underlying 'sound') calls it into existence. Pronounced by the Priest-Initiate or Yogi this word receives creative powers and is communicated as an impulse on the terrestrial plane through a trained Will-Power."

2   In Sanskrit mahavidya means "great or exalted knowledge;" it ranks high in the scheme of wisdom. Madame Blavatsky calls it the great esoteric science and says that the highest Initiates alone are in possession of it. It embraces almost universal knowledge.

3   In Sanskrit this term means "knowledge to be hidden, esoteric knowledge," especially of the use of incantations and spells. Madame Blavatsky so describes it in the Glossary.

4   Atma (Sanskrit "breath, soul") and Vidya. The term connotes knowledge of the Soul or Supreme Spirit in man. This is in agreement with Madame Blavatsky's use of the term.

5   "The knowledge of them is obligatory in that School the teachings of which are accepted by many Theosophists."-From the Preface.

6   The term Yoga is commonly taken to mean union and its root is the same as that of our word yoke. However, Sanskrit dictionaries give other meanings of the word, several of which have relevance to its use to denote a system of spiritual practice. So far as the use of the word in Indian philosophy goes, it is a

matter of dispute whether yoga is union of the individual soul with Brahma or the subjection of the human senses and emotions. Madame Blavatsky characterizes it as the practice of meditation as leading to spiritual liberation.

7   In Sanskrit jivatman means "the living or personal or individual soul" as distinguished from paramatma, the universal soul. By Theosophists, too, it is applied only to the individual.

8   Raja Yoga is thus characterized in The Light of the Soul, a commentary on the Yoga Sutras of Pantanjali, by Alice A. Bailey: "Raja Yoga stands by itself and is the king science of them all; it is the summation of all the others, it is the climax of the work of development in the human kingdom. It is the science of the mind and the purposeful will, and brings the higher of man's sheaths under the subjection of the inner Ruler. This science coördinates the entire lower threefold man, forcing him into a position where he is nothing but the vehicle for the soul, or the God within. It includes the other Yogas and profits by their achievements. It synthesizes the work of evolution and crowns man as king."

9   Alice A. Bailey, The Light of the Soul, p. 164.

10   Page 65.

11   Ibid., p. 60.

12   The Light of the Soul, p. 234.

13   Ibid., p. 241.

14   Bhagavad Gita, p. 177.

15   John Ruskin, English art critic and economist, labored to impress this theory on modern attention.

CHAPTER XII LATER THEOSOPHICAL HISTORY

1   The material of this chapter has been drawn largely from the anonymous work, The Theosophical Movement, the statements in which are fortified throughout with an abundance of documen-

tary data, and from the Theosophic periodical literature of the years covered by the narrative, as well as in a number of instances from the author's first-hand acquaintance with the events narrated.

2   Evidence arrived at by comparison of dates and known facts as to Madame Blavatsky's slight acquaintance with Miss Collins before 1887, and the testimony of prefatory remarks in each of the four books in question, leads to the definite conclusion that Miss Collins did herself ascribe the source of her books to Mahatmic or other high dictation, and that she had taken this position without any influence whatever from H.P.B. The whole matter is set forth in elaborate detail in The Theosophical Movement, pp. 195-210.

3   See statement of A. Trevor Barker, in his Introduction to Letters of H.P. Blavatsky to A. P. Sinnett, p. vii, as follows: "Much fresh light is thrown on .
. . her relation with the notorious Solovyoff, who in his rage and resentment at
being refused the privilege of chelaship, did so much to injure her reputation."

4   See her Autobiography, and a recent work by Jeoffrey West, The Life of Annie Besant (Gerald Howe, Limited, London, 1929).

5   See statement made in The Theosophical Movement, p. 453. The author has been informed by several veteran Theosophists that this is not likely, that perhaps Chakravarti deputed others to guard her in this way. She regarded him at this time as actually her Master, and he could not with dignity have assumed a rôle of such condescension.

6   The Theosophical Movement, p. 479.7 Ibid., p. 559.

8   Mr. Judge's papers concerning Theosophy were turned over to the Theosophical Society in the presence of Mrs. Judge and are now in the possession of the International Headquarters at Point Loma, California. As most of them pertained to the Esoteric Section, their contents have naturally been kept secret. Consequently the evidence on which the claims that Mr. Judge had made his wishes known are based is still unavailable.

9   See signed statement by E. T. Hargrove in the New York Sun of March 13, 1898.

10   The career of the Theosophic leader was beset with at least three law-suits instituted against her by relatives of wealthy followers contesting the disposition of funds allotted to her under the terms of wills. Both the Thurston and the Spalding suits were settled with compromise agreements. In still another sensational case Mrs. Tingley was sued by Irene M. Mohn for damages in the amount of $200,000 for alienation of the affections of her husband, George F. Mohn, a follower of Theosophy. Mrs. Mohn was awarded $100,000 by a California jury, but Mrs. Tingley won a reversal of the judgment before the California Supreme Court.

11   The work of an independent Theosophist, Mr. Roy Mitchell, lecturing in New York and Toronto, has also emphasized the extent of these variations. He lays particular emphasis on the Blavatskian doctrine of the descent of angelic hosts into the Adamic races of humanity to perform the work of redeeming them from a fallen estate, by means of the gift of Promethean fire or wisdom.

12   The occurrence came to be known among the Theosophists as "the Adyar Manifestations."

13   Persons who have lived at the Theosophical headquarters at Adyar at the period of the publication of The Lives of Alcyone, have intimated to the author that certain residents of the colony who were not "put in" the early "Lives" went to Mr. Leadbeater and requested that he look into their

past and if possible bring them into the story, with the result that he did as requested in certain instances. About 1925 also there was published in England, by Mr. W. Loftus Hare, in The Occult Review, an exposé of the whole "Alcyone" proceeding, the alleged sources of Mr. Leadbeater's material being divulged in the shape of some articles in old encyclopedias.

14   Brief mention should here be made of an incident arising out of the general situation occasioned by the founding of this Church, in view of the principles involved. Dr. William L. Robins, of Washington, D.C., long an honored member of the Theosophical Society, looked with disfavor upon the establishment of an ecclesiastical order in connection with Theosophy, and went so far as to adduce considerable evidence to show that the Liberal Catholic Church was not free from subserviency to the Roman Catholic Church. He resented the movement as an attempt to saddle religionism upon Theosophy, and endeavored to show the hand of Roman machination in the whole business. His statements and letters, coming to

the notice of Mrs. Besant, were taken as an open attack upon the religion of members of the Theosophical Society, and as such constituted a breach of Theosophic conduct. Mrs. Besant straightway asked Dr. Robins to resign from the Esoteric Section, with a statement to the effect that no member ought to attack the religious affiliations of any member of the Theosophical Society.

15   It was his intention first to locate the colony somewhere in the James River region in Virginia, and it was thought for a time that some of the pirate gold of

16   In 1929 an order was issued from Adyar by Dr. Besant suspending the Esoteric Section. A later order revived it in 1930.

17   Although Dr. Besant and her friends deny any substantial significance in the claims made, yet the two Keightleys, who typed the manuscript of H.P.B.'s The Secret Doctrine for the press, stated that Madame Blavatsky had completed not only a third volume which dealt with the lives of outstanding occultists down the ages, but practically a fourth volume, also; and Mrs. Alice L. Cleather has been quoted as saying that she herself saw literally hundreds of changes made in Madame Blavatsky's manuscripts in the handwriting of Mrs. Besant and Mr. Mead. As to these changes, Mr. C. Jinarajadasa, when Vice-President of the Theosophical Society, made a statement which will be found on page 110 of The Golden Book of The Theosophical Society:

"The facts are that H.P.B. always recognized that her English was often defective. . . . When The Secret Doctrine was published, she realized that there were many emendations necessary in a subsequent edition. . . . This very heavy task of checking and revising was largely the work of G. R. S. Mead, who devoted a great deal of his time to carrying out H.P.B.'s wishes in the matter. . . .

"After H.P.B.'s death, all her remaining manuscript material was published as a third volume of The Secret Doctrine. She was under the impression that the material she had slowly collected during many years would make five volumes in all of The Secret Doctrine. But steadily as she wrote the first two volumes of The Secret Doctrine more and more of her material was incorporated into the first two volumes, and the remaining manuscript material made only one more volume."

The Keightleys insisted, however, that they had carefully revised the language of the first edition, working with H.P.B. through the various stages of proof, and that the extensive revisions in the second edition were uncalled for. They also stated that they had seen the manuscript of the third volume "ready to be given to the printers," and Alice Cleather pointed out that H.P.B. had made several direct references to it in the first edition which were deleted in the second. Because so little of the data has been made public, the issue is still too much beclouded for judgment.

CHAPTER XIII SOME FACTS AND FIGURES

1   An official of the United Lodge of Theosophists declined to aid in sending letters to persons in that branch, stating that a questionnaire was irrelevant to the interests of true Theosophy.

2   The questions asked covered the points of age, sex, profession, and length of time connected with Theosophy; previous church affiliations, if any, and reason for abandoning them for Theosophy; the phase of Theosophy appealing most strongly to the individual, whether its philosophical, its religious and

devotional side, or its scientific aspect; meditational practice and adherence to non-meat diet; favorite Theosophic authors and literature; and lastly the amount of time devoted to the Theosophic cause in one form or another.

3   But one person adds: "I heard a Theosophic lecturer who had something in his face no other man had ever had save Bishop Brent."

16

BIBLIOGRAPHY

BIOGRAPHICAL SKETCHES OF MADAME HELENA P. BLAVATSKY
A Trevor Barker: Letters of H. P. Blavatsky to A. P. Sinnett,Edited by A. Trevor Barker. London; Theosophical Publishing House, 1924. 381 pp.

G. Baseden Butt: Life of Madame Blavatsky. Philadelphia; David McKay Co., 1927. 268 pp.

Alice L. Cleather: H. P. Blavatsky; Her Life and Work for Humanity. Calcutta; Thatcher, Spink & Co., 1922. 124 pp.

-------- H. P. Blavatsky, As I Knew Her; with an addendum by Basil Crump. Calcutta; Thatcher, Spink & Co., 1923.76 pp.

-------- H. P. Blavatsky: A Great Betrayal. Calcutta; Thatcher,Spink & Co., 1922. 96 pp.

Mme. E. Coulomb: Some Accounts of My Intercourse with Madame Blavatsky from 1872 to 1884. London, 1885.

John N. Farquhar: Modern Religious Movements in India. Chapter, "Theosophy." London, 1915.

Franz Hartmann: Observations during a Nine Months' Stay at the Headquarters of the Theosophical Society. Madras, 1884.

Richard Hodgson: Report on the Theosophic psychic phenomena,published in the Proceedings of the British Society for Psychic Research, Vol. III, 1885.

William Kingsland: The Real H. P. Blavatsky. London; John M.Watkins, 1928. 278 pp.

Arthur Lillie: Madame Blavatsky and Her Theosophy. London, 1895.Col. H. S. Olcott: Old Diary Leaves. Madras; Theosophical Publishing Society, 1910, Four Vols. 1927 pp.

A. P. Sinnett: Early Days of Theosophy in Europe. London; Theosophical Publishing House, 1922. 118 pp.

-------- Incidents in the Life of Madame Blavatsky; based largely on a narrative in Russian by her sister, Madame Vera Jelihowsky. London; Theosophical Publishing Society, 1913. 256 pp.

Vsevolod S. Solovyoff: A Modern Priestess of Isis; Abridged and translated on behalf of the Society for Psychic Research from the Russian of V. S. Solovyoff by Walter Leaf, Litt.D., with appendices. London and New York; Longmans,Green and Co., 1895. xix and 366 pp.

Zinaida Vengerova: Sketch in Russian in the Kritico-biograficheskii slovar russkikh pisatelsi i uchenikh. St. Petersburg,1889-1904, Vol. III. (On this are mostly based the sketches in other Russian Encyclopedias.)Princess Helene von Racowitza: Autobiography; Translated from the German by Cecil Marr and published by the Constables, London, 1910.

Countess Constance Wachtmeister: Reminiscences of H. P. Blavatsky and the Secret Doctrine. London; Theosophical Publishing Society, 1893. 138 pp.

Herbert Whyte: H. P. Blavatsky; An Outline of Her Life. London; The Lotus Journal, 1909. 60 pp.

LITERATURE ON THE GENERAL SUBJECT OF THEOSOPHY

NOTE: Literature bearing more or less directly upon the general theme of Theosophy is so enormous that several thousand titles would not exhaust the body of works touching upon the subject. Books written by modern students of Theosophy alone run into the hundreds. Mr. Roy Mitchell, Theosophic lecturer, of New York City, has estimated some two hundred to three hundred early Theosophic books that are now out of print. It is difficult to determine a specifically Theosophic book from those that deal with phases of mysticism, esotericism and occultism in general. Books of the sort are all more or less amenable to classification as Theosophic. The list of several hundred here given is highly representative of the books to be found in a good library of a Theosophical Society. There are hundreds of ancient and mediæval theosophic works that have never been translated into modern tongues. The Moorish literature of Spain is particularly a rich mine of theosophic treatises.

A. Square (Edwin Abbott): Flatland: A Romance of Many Dimensions; with Introduction by William Garnett, M. A., D.C.L. Boston; Little, Brown & Co., 1928. 151 pp.

Swami Abhedananda: Reincarnation; (three lectures). Published by the Vedanta Society, New York. 57 pp.

-------- Spiritual Unfoldment; (three lectures). New York; The Vedanta Society, 1901.

Sri Ananda Acharya: Brahmadarsanam; being an introduction to the study of Hindu Philosophy. New York; The Macmillan Co., 1917. 210 pp.

W. R. C. Coode Adams: A Primer of Occult Physics. London; The Theosophical Publishing House, Ltd., 1927. 65 pp.

W. Marsham Adams: The Book of The Master; or, The Egyptian Doctrine of Light Born of the Virgin Mother. London; John Murray; New York; G. P. Putnam's Sons, 1898.204 pp.

-------- The House of the Hidden Places; A Clue to the Creed of Early Egypt; from Egyptian Sources. London; John Murray, 1893. 249 pp.

Helen R. Albee: The Gleam. New York, Henry Holt & Co., 1911. 312 pp.

Jerome A. Anderson; M. D., F.T.S.: Septenary Man; or, The Microcosm. A Study of the Human Soul. San Francisco; The Lotus Publishing Co., 1895. 122 pp.

Anonymous: Christ in You. New York; Dodd, Mead & Co., 1918. 184 pp.

-------- The Theosophical Movement: 1875-1925. A History and a Survey. New York; E. P. Dutton & Co., 1925. 705 pp.

-------- Man: Fragments of Forgotten History. (By two chelas of the Theosophical Society.) London, 1874.

Sir Edwin Arnold: The Light of Asia; The life and teachings of Gautama Buddha, in verse. Philadelphia, Henry Altemus. 239 pp.

-------- The Light of the World; or, The Great Consummation. New York, Funk and Wagnalls, 1891. 286 pp.

G. S. Arundale: Thoughts on 'At the Feet of the Master.' Madras, Theosophical Publishing House, 1919. 315 pp.

-------- Thoughts of the Great. Madras, Theosophical Publishing House, 1925. 222 pp.

-------- Nirvana. Chicago; The Theosophical Press, 1926. 192 pp. Adolph D'Assier: Posthumous Humanity; A Study of Phantoms; Translated and annotated by Henry S. Olcott. London; George Redway, 1887. 360 pp.

"Brother Atisha": Exposition of the Doctrine of Karma. London; Theosophical Publishing Society, 1920. 120 pp.

May Anne Atwood: A Suggestive Inquiry Into the Hermetic Mystery, with a dissertation on the more celebrated of the Alchemical Philosophers. Being an attempt toward the recovery of the ancient Experiment of Nature. Belfast; William Tait; London; J. M. Watkins, 1920. 64, xxv, 597 pp.

E. D. Babbitt, M. D., LL.D.: The Principles of Light and Color. The Harmonic Laws of the Universe; the Etherio-Atomic Philosophy of Force, Chromo-Chemistry, Chromo-Therapeutics, and the General Philosophy of the Finer Forces, etc.) Pub. by the author, at the College of Finer Forces, E. Orange, N. J., 1896. 560 pp.

-------- Religion: As Revealed by the Material and Spiritual Universe. New York; Babbitt & Co., 1881. 358 pp.

Benjamin Wisner Bacon: The Fourth Gospel in Research and Debate; A series of lessons on problems concerning the origin and value of the anonymous writings attributed to the Apostle John. New York; Moffat Yard & Co., 1910. 544 pp.

Alice A. Bailey: The Consciousness of the Atom. New York; Lucifer Publishing Co., 1922. 104 pp.

-------- Initiation: Human and Solar. New York; Lucifer Publishing Co., 1922. 255 pp.

-------- Letters on Occult Meditation. New York; Lucifer Publishing Co., 1922. 357 pp.

James L. M. Bain: Corpus meum. London; Percy Lund, Humphries & Co., Ltd., 1911. 104 pp.

-------- The Christ of the Holy Grail; or, The Great Christ of the Cosmos and the Little Christ of the Soul. London; Theosophical Publishing Society, 1909. 116 pp.

The Right Honorable J. W. Balfour: The Ear of Dionysius. New York; Henry Holt & Co., 1920. 127 pp.

Mrs. L. Dow Balliett: The Philosophy of Numbers. Published by the author, Atlantic City, N. J., 1908. 161 pp.

-------- Nature's Symphony; or, Lessons in Number Vibration. Published by the author, Atlantic City, N. J., 1911. 132 pp.

A. Trevor Barker: Mahatma Letters To A. P. Sinnett from the Mahatmas M. and K. H. Transcribed, compiled and with an Introduction by A. Trevor Barker. New York; Frederick A. Stokes Co., 1924. 492 pp.

Harriet Tuttle Bartlett: An Esoteric Reading of Biblical Symbolism. Krotona, Hollywood, Los Angeles, Cal.; Theosophical Publishing Co., 1920. 218 pp.

L. Adams Beck (E. Barrington): The Story of Oriental Philosophy. New York; Cosmopolitan Book Corporation, 1928. 429 pp.

Dr. Annie Besant: Ancient Ideals in Modern Life. Four lectures delivered at Benares, December 1900. London and Benares; Theosophical Publishing Society, 1901. 145 pp.

-------- The Ancient Wisdom; An Outline of Theosophical Teachings. Adyar, Madras, India; Theosophical Publishing House, 1897. 328 pp.

-------- Annie Besant; An Autobiography. London; T. Fisher Unwin, 1908. 368 pp.

-------- Australian Lectures; delivered in 1908. Sydney; George Robertson & Co., Ltd., 1908. 163 pp.

-------- Avatars; Four lectures delivered at Adyar, Madras, India, 1900. Theosophical Publishing Society, London, 1900. 124 pp.

-------- H. P. Blavatsky and the Masters of the Wisdom. Krotona,Hollywood, California; Theosophical Publishing House,1918. 109 pp.

-------- Britain's Place in the Great Plan: Four lectures delivered in London, 1921. London; Theosophical Publishing House, 1921. 104 pp.

-------- Buddhist Popular Lectures; Delivered in Ceylon, 1907.Madras, India; The Theosophist Office, 1908. 129 pp.

-------- The Building of the Cosmos, and other lectures. Delivered at Adyar, Madras, India, 1893. London: Theosophical Publishing House, 1894. 157 pp.

-------- The Changing World, and Lectures to Theosophical Students. Lectures delivered in London, 1909. Chicago; Theosophical Book Concern, 1910. 333 pp.

-------- Civilization's Deadlock, and the Keys. Five lectures delivered in London, 1924. London; Theosophical Publishing House, Ltd., 1924. 142 pp.

-------- Death-And After? London; Theosophical Publishing Society, 1894. 94 pp.

-------- Karma; Three lectures delivered at Benares, 1898. Benares; Theosophical Publishing Society, 1899. 70 pp.

-------- Sanatana Dharma; an elementary textbook on Hindu religion and morals. Benares; the Board of Trustees, Central Hindu College, 1902. 229 pp.

-------- Esoteric Christianity; or, The Lesser Mysteries. New York; John Lane; The Bodley Head, 1904. 384 pp.

-------- The Evolution of Life and Form. London; Theosophical Publishing Society, 1900. 161 pp.

-------- Evolution and Man's Destiny. London; Theosophical Publishing Society in England, 1924. 226 pp.

-------- Evolution and Occultism. London; Theosophical Publishing Society, 1913.

295 pp.

------- For India's Uplift. A collection of speeches and writings on Indian Questions. Madras; G. A. Natesan & Co. 283 pp.

------- Four Great Religions; Four lectures delivered at Adyar. London,
Theosophical Publishing Society, 1897. 183 pp.

------- The Great Plan. Four lectures delivered at Adyar, 1920. Madras; Theosophical Publishing House, 1921. 109 pp.

------- How a World Teacher Comes; as seen by ancient and modern psychology. Four lectures delivered in London, 1926.
London, Theosophical Publishing House, Ltd., 1926. 90 pp.

------- The Ideals of Theosophy. Four lectures delivered at Ben- ares, 1911. Adyar, Madras; The Theosophist Office, 1912. 130 pp.

------- The Immediate Future. Lectures delivered in London,
1912. The Rajput Press, 1911. 176 pp.

------- In Defense of Hinduism. Benares and London; Theosophical Publishing Society. 72 pp.

------- Initiation: The Perfecting of Man. Chicago; The Theosophical Press, 1923. 149 pp.

------- In The Outer Court. Adyar; Theosophical Publishing House, 1914. 176 pp.

------- An Introduction to the Science of Peace. Adyar; The Theosophist Office, 1912. 86 pp.

------- An Introduction to Yoga. Four lectures delivered at Ben- ares, 1907. Adyar; Theosophical Publishing House, 1913. 159 pp.

------- Karma. London; Theosophical Publishing Society, 1895. 83 pp.

------- A Study in Karma. Krotona, Hollywood, Los Angeles, Calif.; Theosophical Publishing House, 1918. 114 pp.

------- London Lectures of 1907. London and Benares; Theosophical Publishing Society, 1907. 198 pp.

------- Man and His Bodies. Krotona, Hollywood, Los Angeles, Calif.; Theosophical Publishing House, 1918. 111 pp.

------- Man's Life In This and Other Worlds. Adyar, Madras,India; Theosophical Publishing House, 1913. 101 pp.

------- The Masters. Adyar, Madras; The Theosophist Office, 1912. 66 pp.

------- Mysticism. London; Theosophical Publishing Society, 1914,
143 pp.

------- The Path of Discipleship. Four lectures delivered at Adyar. 1895. London; Theosophical Publishing Society; Reprint,1917. 150 pp.

------- The Pedigree of Man. Four lectures delivered at Adyar, 1903. Benares and London; Theosophical Publishing Society, 1908. 151 pp.

------- Reincarnation. Krotona, Hollywood, Los Angeles, Calif.;Theosophical Publishing House, 1919. 73 pp.

------- Psychology. Krotona, California; Theosophical Publishing House, 1919.
311 pp.

------- The Riddle of Life; And How Theosophy Explains It. London; Theosophical Publishing Society, 1911. 58 pp.

------- The Self and Its Sheaths. Four lectures delivered at Adyar, 1894. London; Theosophical Publishing Society, 1903.
120 pp.

------- The Seven Principles of Man. London; Theosophical Publishing Society.
90 pp.

------- Shri Rama Chandra; The Ideal King. Some Lessons from the Ramayana, for the use of Hindu students in the schools of India. Benares and London; Theosophical Publishing Society, 1905. 188 pp.

------- Some Problems of Life. London; Theosophical Publishing Society, 1920.
139 pp.

------- The Spiritual Life. London; Theosophical Publishing Society, 1912. 296 pp.

------- The Story of the Great War. Some Lessons from the Mahabharata. For the use of Hindu students in the schools of India. Benares and London; Theosophical Publishing Society, 1899. 271 pp.

------- A Study in Consciousness; A Contribution to the Science of Psychology. Krotona, California; Theosophical Publishing House, 1918. 273 pp.

------- Superhuman Men, in History and in Religion. London; Theosophical Publishing Society, 1913. 133 pp.

------- Theosophy and Human Life. Four lectures delivered at
Benares 1904. London and Benares; Theosophical Publishing Society, 1905. 123 pp.

------- Theosophy and the New Psychology. Krotona, California; Theosophical Publishing House, 1918. 124 pp.

------- The Theosophical Society and the Occult Hierarchy. London; Theosophical Publishing House, Ltd., 1925. 62 pp.

------- Theosophy and the Theosophical Society. Four lectures delivered at Adyar, 1912. Adyar; Theosophical Publishing House, 1913. 112 pp.

------- Theosophy and World Problems. Four letters delivered at Benares, 1921, by Annie Besant, C. Jinarajadasa, J. Krishnamurti, and G. S. Arundale. Adyar; Theosophical Publishing House, 1922. 104 pp.

------- Thought Power: Its Culture and Control. Krotona: Theosophical Publishing House, 1918. 133 pp.

------- The Three Paths and Dharma. London; Theosophical Publishing Society, 1922. 157 pp.

------- The Universal Text Book of Religion and Morals. Edited by Annie Besant. Adyar; Theosophical Publishing House. 157 pp.

------- The War and Its Lessons. Four lectures delivered at London, 1919. London; Theosophical Publishing House, 1920. 87 pp.

------- The Wisdom of the Upanishads. Four lectures delivered at Adyar, 1906. Benares and London; Theosophical Publishing Society, 1907. 103 pp.

------- World Problems of Today. London; Theosophical Publishing House, Ltd., 1925. 144 pp.

C. H. A. Bjerregaard: The Great Mother; A Gospel of the Eternal Feminine. Occult and scientific studies and experiences in the sacred and secret life. New York; The Inner Life Publishing Co., 1913. 325 pp.

Algernon Blackwood: Karma-A Reincarnation Play. By Algernon Blackwood and Violet Pearn. New York; E. P. Dutton & Co., 1918. 207 pp.

Helena P. Blavatsky: Alchemy and the Secret Doctrine; Compiled and Edited by Alexander Horne. Wheaton, Ill.; The Theosophical Press, 1927. 205 pp.

-------- First Steps in Occultism; Reprint from Lucifer. San Francisco; Mercury Publishing Co., 1898. 135 pp.

-------- From the Caves and Jungles of Hindustan. Translated from the Russian of H. P. Blavatsky. London; Theosophical Publishing Society, 1892. 318 pp.

-------- The Key to Theosophy; being a clear exposition in the form of question and answer, of the Ethics, Science and Philosophy for the study of which the Theosophical Society has been founded. Los Angeles; The United Lodge of Theoso- phists, 1920. 243 pp.

-------- A Modern Panarion; A Collection of Fugitive Fragments. London; Theosophical Publishing Society, 1895. 504 pp.

-------- Isis Unveiled; A Master Key to the Mysteries of Ancient and Modern Science and Theology. Two Vols. New York; J. W. Bouton, 1877. 705 and 691 pp.

-------- Nightmare Tales. London; Theosophical Publishing House. 133 pp.

-------- The Secret Doctrine; The Synthesis of Science, Religion, and Philosophy. London; Theosophical Publishing House, 1893. Several reprints, 3 Vols.

-------- The Voice of the Silence, and other chosen fragments from the Book of the Golden Precepts, for the daily use of Lanoos. New York; Theosophical Publishing House of New York, 1919. 107 pp.

-------- The Theosophical Glossary. Krotona; Theosophical Publishing House, 1918. 360 pp.

Jacob Boehme: The Way to Christ. London; J. M. Watkins, 1911. 301 pp.

-------- The Signature of All Things. London and Toronto; J. M. Dent; New York; E. P. Dutton & Co., 1912. 295 pp.

-------- Six Theosophic Points, and other writings; Newly translated into English by John Rolleston Earle, M. A. London; Constable & Co., Ltd., 1919. 208 pp.

-------- The Threefold Life of Man; According to the three principles. London; J. M. Watkins, 1909. 547 pp.

Columbus Bradford, A. M.: Birth: A New Chance. Chicago; A. C. McClurg & Co., 1901. 362 pp.

Claude Bragdon: The Beautiful Necessity; Seven Essays on Theosophy and Architecture. New York; Alfred A. Knopf, 1922. 171 pp.

-------- Four-Dimensional Vistas. New York; Alfred A. Knopf, 1916. 134 pp.

-------- Old Lamps for New; The Ancient Wisdom in the Modern World. New York; Alfred A. Knopf, 1925. 206 pp.

-------- A Primer of Higher Space. New York; Alfred A. Knopf,1923. 81 pp. Robert T. Browne: The Mystery of Space; A Study of the Hyperspace Movement in the Light of the Evolution of New Psychic Faculties; and, An Inquiry into the Genesis and Essential Nature of Space. New York; E. P.

Dutton & Co., 1919. 358 pp.

Joseph Rodes Buchanan: Psychometry: The Dawn of a New Civilization. Boston; Published by the Author, 1883. 288 pp.

J. D. Buck, M. D.: A Study of Man. Cincinnati: Robert Clarke & Co., 1889. 302 pp.

Dr. Rickard Maurice Bucke: Cosmic Consciousness. Philadelphia; Jones & Jones, 1905. 318 pp.

Marie, Countess of Caithness, Duchess of Pomar: The Mystery of the Ages, Contained in the Secret Doctrine of All Religions. London; C. L. H. Wallace, 1887. 541 pp.

Edward Carpenter: The Art of Creation; Essays on the Self and its Powers. London; George Allen and Unwin, Ltd., 1904. 234 pp. and Appendix.

-------- Pagan and Christian Creeds; Their Origin and Meaning. New York; Harcourt, Brace & Co., 1920. 308 pp.

Paul Carus: The Gospel of Buddha. Chicago; The Open Court Publishing Co., 1909. 260 pp.

Clara M. Codd: Theosophy as the Masters See It. Adyar; Theosophical Publishing House, 1926. 369 pp.

-------- Masters and Disciples. London; Theosophical Publishing Co., Ltd., 1928. 94 pp.

Mabel Collins (Mrs. K. Cook): A Cry From Afar. London; Theosophical Publishing Society, 1905. 54 pp.

-------- As the Flower Grows: Some Visions and an Interpretation. London; Theosophical Publishing Society, 1915. 112 pp.

-------- The Awakening. London; Theosophical Publishing Society, 1906. 102 pp.

-------- The Blossom and the Fruit: A True Story of a Black Magician. New York; Theosophical Publishing Society. 332 pp.

-------- The Transparent Jewel: London; Wm. Rider and Son, Ltd., 1912. 142 pp.

-------- The Idyll of the White Lotus. Adyar; Theosophical Publishing House, 1919. 168 pp.

-------- Fragments of Thought and Life. London; Theosophical Publishing Society, 1908. 121 pp.

-------- The Crucible. London; Theosophical Publishing Society, 1914. 125 pp.

-------- The Builders. London; Theosophical Publishing Society, 1920. 70 pp.

-------- Illusions. London; Theosophical Publishing Society, 1905. 71 pp.

-------- Light on the Path. Boston; Occult Publishing Co. 89 pp.

-------- Our Glorious Future. Edinburgh; Theosophical Book Shop, 1917. 113 pp.

-------- Through the Gates of Gold. London; J. M. Watkins, 1901. 138 pp.

-------- When the Sun Moves Northward. London; Theosophical Publishing House, Ltd., 1923. 183 pp.

Irving S. Cooper: Methods of Psychic Development. Chicago; The Theosophical Press, 1926. 113 pp.

-------- Reincarnation: The Hope of the World. Chicago; The Theosophical Press, 1927. 121 pp.

James H. Cousins: The Basis of Theosophy. Adyar; Theosophical Publishing House, 1913, 64 pp.

Bhagavan Das: The Science of the Emotions. Adyar; Theosophical Publishing House,

1924. 524 pp.

-------- The Science of Peace. London; Theosophical Publishing Society, 1904.
332 pp.

-------- The Science of Social Organization; or, The Laws of Manu in the Light of Theosophy. London and Benares; Theosophical Publishing Society, 1910. 358 pp.

-------- The Science of the Sacred Word: Being a summarized translation of The Pranava-Vada of Gargyayana, by Bhagavan Das. Adyar; The Theosophist Office, 1910. 374 pp.

Surendranath Dasgupta: Yoga: As Philosophy and Religion. London; Kegan Paul, Trench, Trubner & Co., Ltd., 1924. 187 pp.

Rev. John Bathurst Deane, M. A.: The Worship of the Serpent;
Attesting the Temptation and Fall of Man. London; J. G. and F. Rivington, 1883.
475 pp.

Leon Denis (Leon Denizarth Hippolyte Rivail): Here and Hereafter. London; Wm. Rider and Son, Ltd., 1910. 352 pp.

-------- Jeanne D'Arc, Medium; ses voix, ses visions, ses prémonitions, ses vues actuelles exprimées en ses propres messages. Paris; Libraire des Sciences Psychiques, 1910. 450 pp.

-------- Life and Destiny; Translated into English by Ella Wheeler Wilcox. London; Gay and Hancock, Ltd., 1919. 313 pp.

-------- The Mystery of Joan of Arc. Translated by Arthur Conan Doyle. London:
J. Murray, 1924. 233 pp.

Ignatius Donnelly: Atlantis; The Antediluvian World. New York and London; Harper and Brother, 1882. 480 pp.

J. W. Dunne: An Experiment with Time. New York; The Macmillan Co., 1927. 208 pp.

A. E. (George Russell): The Candle of Vision. London; The Macmillan Co., Ltd., 1920. 175 pp.

Lillian Edger, M. A.: The Elements of Theosophy. London; Theosophical Publishing House, 1903.
202 pp.

W. Scott-Elliot: The Lost Lemuria. London; Theosophical Publishing Society, 1904. 44 pp.

-------- Man's Place in the Universe. London and Benares; Theosophical Publishing Society, 1902.
132 pp.

-------- The Story of Atlantis. London; Theosophical Publishing Society, 1914.
87 pp.

Edward C. Farnsworth: Special Teachings From the Arcane Science. Portland: Smith & Sale, Printers. 1918. 189 pp.

Benedictus Figulus: A Golden and Blessed Casket of Nature's Marvels, concerning the blessed mystery of the Philosopher's Stone, containing the Revelation of the most illuminated Egyptian King and Philosopher, Hermes Trismegistus. Published by Benedictus Figulus of Utenhofen. 357 pp.

Adolph Francke: The Kabbalah; or, The Religious Philosophy of the Hebrews. New York; The Kabbalah Publishing Co.,1926. 311 pp.

Will L. Garver: Brother of the Third Degree. Chicago; Purdy Publishing Co., 1894. 377 pp.

Elias Gewurz: The Hidden Treasures of the Ancient Qabalah. Vol. I. (The

Transmutation of Passion Into Power.) Krotona; The Theosophical Publishing House, 1915. 133 pp.

L. Hayden Guest: Theosophy and Social Reconstruction. London; Theosophical Publishing Society, 1912. 138 pp.

H. Fielding Hall: The Soul of a People. London; The Macmillan Co., Ltd., 1905. 314 pp.

Franz Hartmann, M. D.: Among the Gnomes. An Occult Tale of Adventure in the Untersburg. London; T. Fisher Unwin,1895. 272 pp.

-------- The Life and Doctrines of Jacob Boehme, the God-Taught Philosopher. New York; Macoy Publishing Co., 1929. 336 pp.

-------- The Life of Jehoshua, The Prophet of Nazareth. An Occult Study and the Key to the Bible. Boston; Occult Publishing Co., 1889. 208 pp.

-------- The Life of Philippus Theophrastus Bombast of Hohenheim-known by the name of Paracelsus, and the substance of his teachings. London; Kegan Paul, Trench, Trubner & Co., Ltd., 1896. 304 pp.

-------- Occult Science in Medicine. New York; Theosophical Publishing Society. 1890, 100 pp.

-------- The Talking Image of Urur. New York; John W. Lovell Co., 1890. 306 pp.

-------- In the Pronaos of the Temple; Concerning the History of the True and the False Rosicrucians. London; Theosophical Publishing Society, 1890. 134 pp.

-------- Magic, White and Black; or, The Science of Finite and Infinite Life. London; George Redway, 1886. 228 pp.

-------- With the Adepts; An Adventure Among the Rosicrucians. New York; Theosophical Publishing Co., 1910. 180 pp.

William C. Hartmann, Ph. D.: Who's Who in Occult, Psychic, and Spiritual Realms. Jamaica, New York; The Occult Press, 1925. 196 pp.

Max Heindel: The Rosicrucian Cosmo-Conception. Seattle, Wash.; Rosicrucian Fellowship, 1910. 542 pp.

C. H. Hinton, M. A.: The Fourth Dimension. London; Swan, Sonnenschein & Co., Ltd., 1914. 247 pp.

-------- A New Era of Thought. London; Swan, Sonnenschein & Co., Ltd., 1900. 210 pp.

-------- Scientific Romances. London; Geo. Allen & Unwin, Ltd., 1882. 229 pp. Geoffrey Hodson: The Kingdom of Faerie. London; Theosophical Publishing House, Ltd., 1927. 112 pp.

-------- The Fairies at Work and at Play. London; Theosophical Publishing House, Ltd., 1925. 126 pp.

-------- An Occult View of Health and Disease. London; Theosophical Publishing House, Ltd., 1925. 52 pp.

-------- The Science of Seership. London; Wm. Rider & Co., 1925, 220 pp. Alexander Horne: Theosophy and the Fourth Dimension. London; Theosophical Publishing House, Ltd., 1928. 108 pp.

Powis Hoult: A Dictionary of Theosophical Terms. London; Theosophical Publishing Society, 1910. 161 pp.

Olive Stevenson Howell: Heredity and Reincarnation. London; Theosophical Publishing House, Ltd., 1926. 68 pp.

Thomas Inman: Ancient Pagan and Modern Christian Symbolism. New York; J. W. Bouton, 1876. 175 pp.

-------- Ancient Faiths and Modern. New York; J. W. Bouton, 1876. 498 pp. Hargrave Jennings: The Rosicrucians; Their Rites and Mysteries. London; George Routledge & Sons, Ltd. 464 pp.

C. Jinarajadasa: The Law of Christ. Adyar; Theosophical Publishing House, 1924. 292 pp.

-------- The Early Teachings of the Masters. Chicago; The Theosophical Press, 1923. 245 pp.

-------- The Golden Book of the Theosophical Society, edited by C. Jinarajadasa. A Brief History of the Society's Growth from 1875 to 1925. Adyar; Theosophical Publishing House, 1925. 421 pp.

-------- How We Remember Our Past Lives. Chicago; Theosophical Press, 1923. 110 pp.

-------- Letters From the Masters of the Wisdom. Chicago; The Theosophical Press, 1926. 220 pp.

-------- The Message of the Future. Glasgow; Star Publishing Trust. 157 pp.

-------- Theosophy and Modern Thought. Adyar; Theosophical Publishing House, 1915. 171 pp.

Charles Johnston: Karma: Works and Wisdom. New York; The Metaphysical Publishing Co., 1900. 56 pp.

-------- The Yoga Sutras of Patanjali. New York; Charles Johnston, 1912. 119 pp.

-------- The Memory of Past Births. New York; The Metaphysical Publishing Co., 1909. 55 pp.

William Q. Judge: Echoes From the Orient. New York; The Path, 1890. 68 pp.

-------- Letters That Have Helped Me. Compiled by W. Q. Judge. New York; The Path. 90 pp.

-------- The Ocean of Theosophy. Los Angeles; The United Lodge of Theosophists, 1915. 154 pp.

-------- The Yoga Aphorisms of Patanjali; An Interpretation. New York; The Path, 1889. 64 pp.

Anna B. Kingsford: Clothed with the Sun. Birmingham; The Ruskin Press, 1906. 340 pp.

-------- The Perfect Way; or, The Finding of Christ. London; J. M. Watkins, 1909. 357 pp.

-------- The Virgin of the World; or, Hermes Mercurius Trismegistus. Madras; Spiritualistic Book Depot, 1895.

William Kingsland: The Esoteric Basis of Christianity. London; Theosophical Publishing Society, 1895. 195 pp.

-------- The Mystic Quest; A Tale of Two Incarnations. London; George Allen & Unwin, 1891. 215 pp.

-------- Our Infinite Life. New York; Moffat, Yard & Co., 1923. 200 pp.

-------- The Physics of the Secret Doctrine. London; Theosophical Publishing Society. 1910. 152 pp.

J. Krishnamurti: At the Feet of the Master. Adyar; Theosophical Publishing House, 1913. 71 pp.

-------- Education as Service. Chicago; The Rajput Press, 1912. 160 pp.

-------- The Kingdom of Happiness. New York; Boni & Liveright, 1927. 112 pp.

-------- Life in Freedom. New York; Horace Liveright, 1928. 96 pp.

-------- The Pool of Wisdom, and Poems. Eerde, Ommen, Holland; The Star Publishing Trust, 1928.

99 pp.

-------- Self-Preparation. Eerde, Ommen, Holland; Star Publishing Trust, 1926. 94 pp.

-------- Towards Discipleship. Chicago; The Theosophical Press, 1926. 106 pp. Charles W. Leadbeater: The Astral Plane; Its Scenery, Inhabitants and Phenomena. Krotona, California; Theosophical Publishing House, 1918. 127 pp.

-------- The Devachanic Plane; or, The Heaven World. Krotona; Theosophical Publishing House, 1919. 120 pp.

-------- Dreams-What They Are and How They Are Caused. London; Theosophical Publishing Society, 1903. 69 pp.

-------- Clairvoyance. Krotona; Theosophical Publishing House, 1918. 161 pp.

-------- The Christian Creed: Its Origin and Signification. London; Theosophical Publishing House, 1904. 172 pp.

-------- Glimpses of Masonic History. Adyar; Theosophical Publishing House, 1926. 380 pp.

-------- The Hidden Life in Freemasonry. Adyar; Theosophical Publishing House, 1926. 352 pp.

-------- The Hidden Side of Things. Adyar; Theosophical Publishing House, 1918. 482 pp.

-------- The Hidden Side of Christian Festivals. London and Sydney; The St. Alban Press, 1920. 499 pp.

-------- The Inner Life. Adyar; Theosophical Publishing House,1911. 2 Vols. 324 and 318 pp.

-------- Man, Visible and Invisible. London; Theosophical Publishing House, 1920. (Reprint.) 149 pp.

-------- Invisible Helpers. Chicago; Theosophical Book Concern, 1915. 133 pp.

-------- The Life After Death-And How Theosophy Unveils It.London; Theosophical Publishing Society, 1912. 58 pp.

-------- The Lives of Alcyone. Adyar; Theosophical Publishing House, 1924. 351 and 383 pp. (2 Vols.)

-------- The Masters and the Path. Chicago; The Theosophical Press, 1925. 328 pp.

-------- The Monad; And Other Essays Upon the Higher Consciousness. Adyar; Theosophical Publishing House, 1920. 133 pp.

-------- The Other Side of Death; Scientifically Examined and Carefully Described. Adyar; Theosophical Publishing House, 1928. 826 pp.

-------- An Outline of Theosophy. Chicago; Theosophical Book Concern, 1916. 99 pp.

-------- The Perfume of Egypt, and Other Weird Stories. Adyar; The Theosophist Office, 1912. 306 pp.

-------- The Science of the Sacraments. London and Sydney; St. Alban Press, 920. 550 pp.

-------- Some Glimpses of Occultism, Ancient and Modern. Chicago; Theosophical Book Concern, 1903. 391 pp.

-------- Talks on 'At the Feet of the Master.' Chicago; The Theosophical Press,

923. 514 pp.

-------- A Textbook of Theosophy. Krotona; Theosophical Publishing House, 1918. 148 pp.

Annie Besant and C. W. Leadbeater (in collaboration): Thought Forms. (With 58 illustrations.) London and Benares; Theosophical Publishing Society, 1905. 84 pp.

-------- Talks on the Path of Occultism. Adyar; Theosophical Publishing House, 1926. 925 pp.

-------- Man: Whence, How, and Whither? A Record of Clairvoyant Investigation. Chicago; The Theosophical Press,1922. 483 pp.

-------- Occult Chemistry. Clairvoyant Observations on the Chemical Elements. London; Theosophical Publishing House, 1919. 108 pp.

Eliphas Levi (Baron Alphonse Louis Constant): The Aquarian Gospel of Jesus the Christ. London; C. F. Cazenove, 1909. 260 pp.

-------- The History of Magic; Including a Clear and Precise Exposition of Its Procedure, Its Rites, and Its Mysteries.(Translated by A. E. Waite.) London; Wm. Rider & Son, 1913. 525 pp.

Sir Oliver Lodge: Science and Immortality. New York; Moffat, Yard & Co., 1909. 294 pp.

-------- The Survival of Man; A Study in Unrecognized Human Faculty. New York; Moffat, Yard & Co., 1916. 357 pp.

Sir Edward Bulwer-Lytton: The Coming Race. London; George Routledge & Son, 1874. 248 pp.

-------- A Strange Story. London; George Routledge & Sons, 1876. 531 pp.

-------- Zanoni. Boston; Little, Brown & Co., 1927. 540 pp. Dr. A. Marques: Scientific Corporations of Theosophy. London;Theosophical Publishing Society, 1908. 152 pp.

Gerald Massey: A Book of Beginnings; Containing an attempt to recover and reconstitute the lost origins of the myths and mysteries, types and symbols, religion and language,with Egypt for the mouthpiece and Africa as the birthplace. London; Williams and Norgate, 1881. 503 pp.

S. L. MacGregor Mathers: The Kabbalah Unveiled. London; Theosophical Publishing Society, 1905. 341 pp.

George R. S. Mead: Echoes from the Gnosis: The Gnosis of the Mind. London and Benares; Theosophical Publishing Society, 1906. 69 pp.

-------- The Hymns of Hermes. London and Benares; Theosophical Publishing Society, 1907. 84 pp.

-------- The Hymn of Jesus. London and Benares; Theosophical Publishing Society, 1907. 83 pp.

-------- The Mysteries of Mithra. London and Benares; Theosophical Publishing Society, 1907. 90 pp.

-------- The Vision of Aridæus. London and Benares; Theosophical Publishing Society, 1907. 74 pp.

-------- Did Jesus Live 100 B. C.? An inquiry into the Talmud Jesus stories, the Toldoth Jeschu, and other curious statements of Epiphanius, being a contribution to the study of Christian origins. London and Benares; Theosophical Publishing Society, 1903. 436 pp.

-------- Fragments of a Faith Forgotten. Some short sketches among the Gnostics, mainly of the First and Second centuries, based on the most recently recovered material. London and Benares; Theosophical Publishing Society, 1900.607 pp.

-------- Simon Magus: An Essay. London and Benares; Theosophical Publishing Society, 1902. 92 pp.

-------- The World Mystery. London and Benares; Theosophical Publishing Society, 1907. 185 pp.

-------- The Theosophy of the Vedas. London and Benares; Theosophical Publishing Society, 1905. 2 Vols.

-------- The Pistis Sophia; A Gnostic Gospel. London and Benares; Theosophical Publishing Society, 1898. 394 pp.

-------- The Gnostic John the Baptizer. Selections from the Mandæan John-Book. Together with studies on John and Christian origins; the Slavonic Josephus' account of John and Jesus, and John and the Fourth Gospel Proem.
London; J. M. Watkins, 1924. 137 pp.

-------- The Gospels and the Gospel. A study in the most recent results of the lower and the higher criticism. London and Benares; Theosophical Publishing Society, 1902. 214 pp.

-------- Orpheus: The Theosophy of the Greeks. London and Benares; Theosophical Publishing Society, 1896. 320 pp.

-------- Plotinus. London; Theosophical Publishing Society, 1895. 48 pp.

-------- Quests Old and New. London; G. Bell and Sons, Ltd., 1913.328 pp.

-------- Some Mystical Adventures. London; J. M. Watkins, 1910.303 pp.

-------- Thrice Greatest Hermes. Studies in Hellenistic Theosophy and Gnosis. London and Benares; Theosophical Publishing Society, 1906. 3 Vols. 481, 403, and 330 pp.

Roy F. Mitchell: The Creative Theater. New York, John Day Co.,1930. 256 pp. Frederic W. H. Myers: Human Personality and Its Survival of Bodily Death. New York; Longmans, Green & Co., 1904.2 Vols. 700 and 627 pp.

Robert W. Norwood: The Heresy of Antioch. Garden City, New York; Doubleday, Doran & Co., 1928. 303 pp.

Isabel Cooper-Oakley: The Comte De St. Germain, The Secret Emissary of Kings. London; Theosophical Publishing House, Ltd., 1912. 247 pp.

-------- Mystical Traditions. Milan, Italy; Libreria Editrice del Dr. G. Sulli- Rao, 1909. 296 pp.

-------- Traces of a Hidden Tradition in Masonry and Mediæval Mysticism. London; Theosophical Publishing Society, 1900. 192 pp.

Col. Henry S. Olcott: People of the Other World. Hartford, Conn.;American Publishing Co., 1875. 492 pp.

-------- Old Diary Leaves. Madras; Theosophical Publishing Society, 1910. Four Vols. 491, 476, 446, and 514 pp.

-------- Theosophy, Religion, and Occult Science. London; John Redway, 1885. 385 pp.

Walter Gorn Old: The Shu King. London and Benares; Theosophical Publishing Society, 1904. 306 pp.

-------- What is Theosophy? London; Hay, Nisbet & Co., 1892. 128 pp.

P. D. Ouspensky: Tertium Organum: The Third Canon of Thought; A Key to the Enigmas of the World. New York; Alfred A. Knopf, 1929. 336 pp.

Dr. Th. Pascal: Reincarnation: A Study in Human Evolution. London; Theosophical Publishing Society, 1910. 303 pp.

P. Pavri: Theosophy Explained in Questions and Answers. Adyar; Theosophical Publishing House, 1921. 276 pp.

A. J. Penny: Studies in Jacob Boehme. London; J. M. Watkins,1912. 473 pp. James Morgan Pryse: Reincarnation in the New Testament. New York; Elliott B. Page & Co., 1900. 92 pp.

-------- The Apocalypse Unsealed; being an esoteric interpretation of the initiation of Ioannes. New York; J. M. Pryse, 1910. 222 pp.

-------- The Magical Message According to Ioannes. New York; Theosophical Publishing Co. of New York, 1909. 230 pp.

-------- The Restored New Testament. The Jewish Fragments, freed from the Pseudo-Jewish Interpolations. New York; J. M. Pryse; London; John M. Watkins, 1914. 817 pp.

W. Winwood Reade: The Veil of Isis: or, Mysteries of the Druids. New York; Peter Eckler Publishing Co., 1917. 250 pp.

H. Stanley Redgrove: Alchemy Ancient and Modern. London; William Rider & Son, Ltd., 1911. 141 pp.

L. W. Rogers: Dreams and Premonitions. Los Angeles; Theosophic Book Concern, 916. 121 pp.

-------- Elementary Theosophy. Chicago; Theosophical Book Concern, 1923. 260 pp.

-------- Gods in the Making; and other lectures. Chicago; Theosophical Book Concern, 1925. 133 pp.

-------- The Ghosts in Shakespeare. Chicago; Thesophical Book Concern, 1925. 185 pp.

-------- The Hidden Side of Evolution. Chicago; Theosophical Book Concern, 1926. 195 pp.

-------- The Purpose of Life, and other lectures. Chicago; Theosophical Book Concern, 1925. 140 pp.

-------- Reincarnation, and other lectures. Chicago; TheosophicalBook Concern, 1925. 138 pp.

G. Krishna Sastri: The Tattvasarayana, The Occult Philosophy Taught by the Great Sage Sri Vasishtha. (Translated by Sri Rama Gita.) Madras; Published by the translator,1902. 135 pp.

Edouard Schure: The Great Initiates. Sketch of the Secret History of Religions. Philadelphia; David McKay Co. 3 Vols. 362, 394, and 394 pp.

-------- Hermes and Plato. London; William Rider & Son, Ltd. 117 pp.

-------- Jesus, the Last Great Initiate. Chicago; Yogi Publishing Society, 125 pp.

-------- Krishna and Orpheus; The Great Initiates of the East and West. Chicago; Yogi Publishing Society, 1908.121 pp.

-------- The Priestess of Isis. London; William Rider & Son, Ltd.,1910. 318 pp.

-------- Rama and Moses. New York; Theosophical Publishing Co., 1910. 147 pp. Sir Walter Scott: Letters on Demonology and Witchcraft. With an Introduction by Henry Morley. London; George Routledge and Sons, 1887. 320 pp.

William Simpson: The Buddhist Praying Wheel. London; The Macmillan & Co., Ltd., 1896. 294 pp.

A. P. Sinnett: Esoteric Buddhism. Boston and New York; Houghton, Mifflin & Co., 1884. 330 pp.

-------- The Early Days of Theosophy in Europe. London; Theosophical Publishing House, Ltd., 1922. 118 pp.

-------- Collected Fruits of Occult Teaching. Philadelphia; J. B.Lippincott Co., 1920. 307 pp.

-------- The Growth of the Soul. London and Benares; Theosophical Publishing Society, 1905. 483 pp.

-------- In the Next World. Actual Narratives of Personal Experiences by Some Who have Passed On. London; Theosophical Publishing Society, 1914. 102 pp.

-------- Karma. A novel. Chicago; Rand, McNally & Co., 1887.
285 pp.

-------- Nature's Mysteries. London and Benares; Theosophical Publishing Society, 1901. 184 pp.

-------- Occult Essays. London; Theosophical Publishing Society, 1905. 226 pp.

-------- The Occult World. London; Theosophical Publishing Society, 1884. 194 pp.

-------- The Rationale of Mesmerism. Boston and New York; Houghton, Mifflin & Co., 1892. 228 pp.

-------- Tennyson an Occultist; As His Writings Prove. London; Theosophical Publishing House, 1920. 89 pp.

Lewis Spence: Atlantis in America. New York; Brentano's, 1925. 232 pp.

-------- The Problem of Atlantis. New York; Brentano's, 1928. 205 pp. Rudolf Steiner: Atlantis and Lemuria. Their History and Civili- zation. Chicago; The Rajput Press, 1911. 231 pp.

-------- Initiation and Its Results. New York; Macoy Publishing and Masonic Supply Co., 1909. 134 pp.

-------- Mystics of the Renaissance. New York and London; G. P. Putnam's Sons, 1911. 278 pp.

-------- The Philosophy of Freedom. New York and London; G. P. Putnam's Sons, 1916. 301 pp.

-------- A Road to Self-Knowledge. London and New York; G. P. Putnam's Sons, 1918. 124 pp.

-------- Theosophy. Chicago and New York; Rand, McNally & Co.,1910. 230 pp.

-------- Three Essays on Haeckel and Karma. London; Theosophical Publishing Society, 1914. 223 pp.

-------- The Way of Initiation. Chicago; The Occult Publishing Co., 1908. 210 pp.

J. C. Street: The Hidden Way Across the Threshold. Boston; Lee and Shepard, 1887. 587 pp.

Arthur Edward Waite: Lives of the Alchemistical Philosophers.London; George Redway, 1888. 275 pp.

-------- The Turba Philosophorum; or, Assembly of the Sages. London; George Redway, 1896. 207 pp.

-------- The Way of Divine Union. London; William Rider & Son, 1915. 327 pp.

E. D. Walker: Reincarnation: A study of Forgotten Truth. New York; Theosophical Publishing Co., 1916. 325 pp.

W. Wynn Westcott: Numbers, Their Occult Power and Mystical Virtues. London and Benares; Theosophical Publishing Society, 1902. 116 pp.

Charles J. Whitby: The Wisdom of Plotinus. A Metaphysical Study. London; William Rider & Son,

1909. 130 pp.

F. Milton Willis: Recurring Earth Lives; How and Why? New York; E. P. Dutton & Co., 1921. 92 pp.

-------- The Return of the World Teacher; Purifying Christianity.The Common Voice of Religion. New York; E. P. Dutton & Co., 1924. 121 pp.

-------- The Spiritual Life; How to Attain It and Prepare Children for It. New York; E. P. Dutton & Co., 1922. 99 pp.

-------- The Truth About Christ and the Atonement. New York; E. P. Dutton & Co., 1922. 96 pp.

Ernest Wood: Character Building. Chicago; The Theosophical Press, 1924. 129 pp.

-------- Concentration; A Practical Course. Chicago; The Theosophical Press, 1923. 172 pp.

-------- Memory Training. Chicago; The Theosophical Press, 1925. 158 pp.

-------- The Seven Rays. Chicago; The Theosophical Press, 1925. 185 pp.

Transactions of the London Lodge of the Theosophical Society. 20 Vols. Transactions of the First Annual Congress of the Federation of European Sections of the Theosophical Society held in Amsterdam, June, 1904. Edited by Johan Van Manen,Amsterdam, 1906. 398 pp.

Transactions of the Second and Third Annual Congresses in London and Paris, 1907. 444 and 366 pp.

PERIODICALS

In Bound Volumes

The Theosophic Review (formerly Lucifer). The Theosophist.

The Path.

The Word.

The Herald of the Star.

Extracts from the Vahan. The Theosophical Messenger. The Canadian Theosophist.

Theosophy.

The Theosophical Quarterly. The American Theosophist.

The Quest.

The Occult Review.